CORPORATIONS LAW
CONCEPTS, CASES AND CULTURE

ANDREW CLARKE

OXFORD
UNIVERSITY PRESS
AUSTRALIA & NEW ZEALAND

Oxford University Press is a department of the University of Oxford.
It furthers the University's objective of excellence in research,
scholarship, and education by publishing worldwide. Oxford is a registered
trademark of Oxford University Press in the UK and in certain other
countries.

Published in Australia by
Oxford University Press
Level 8, 737 Bourke Street, Docklands, Victoria 3008, Australia.

© Andrew Clarke 2021

The moral rights of the author have been asserted

First published 2021

All rights reserved. No part of this publication may be reproduced, stored in a retrieval system, or transmitted, in any form or by any means, without the prior permission in writing of Oxford University Press, or as expressly permitted by law, by licence, or under terms agreed with the reprographics rights organisation. Enquiries concerning reproduction outside the scope of the above should be sent to the Rights Department, Oxford University Press, at the address above.

You must not circulate this work in any other form and you must impose this same condition on any acquirer.

 A catalogue record for this book is available from the National Library of Australia

ISBN 9780190322984

Reproduction and communication for educational purposes
The Australian *Copyright Act 1968* (the Act) allows educational institutions that are covered by remuneration arrangements with Copyright Agency to reproduce and communicate certain material for educational purposes. For more information, see copyright.com.au.

Edited by Natasha Broadstock
Typeset by Integra Software Services Pvt. Ltd.
Proofread by Naomi Saligari
Indexed by Karen Gillen
Printed in Singapore by Markono Print Media Pte Ltd

Links to third party websites are provided by Oxford in good faith and for information only.
Oxford disclaims any responsibility for the materials contained in any third party website referenced in this work.

TABLE OF CONTENTS

Chapter 1 (Week 1) The Corporation: Introduction and Overview — 2
1.1 Studying corporate law — 4
1.2 The corporation: an overview — 9
1.3 A brief history of companies — 12
1.4 Constitutional foundations of Australian corporate law — 16
1.5 The context and culture of the corporation — 22
    Chapter 1 revision activities — 30

Chapter 2 (Week 1) Business and Business Entities — 38
2.1 The basic elements of conducting business — 40
2.2 The choice of business entities — 43
2.3 The company as a business entity — 45
2.4 Partnerships — 51
2.5 'Not-for-profit' and 'for-purpose' entities — 60
2.6 The role and rationale of business — 66
    Chapter 2 revision activities — 70

Chapter 3 (Week 2) Establishing the Corporation—Practicalities of Registration — 78
3.1 Registration of the company — 80
3.2 The company as a separate legal entity — 82
3.3 The 'corporate veil': maintaining it; piercing it — 83
3.4 Company record keeping and reporting — 86
3.5 The types of corporations — 87
3.6 Specialist corporations — 90
    Chapter 3 revision activities — 95

CONTENTS

Chapter 4 (Week 2) The Rules of the Corporation and the Role of Statute 102

4.1	The relationship between statute and internal rules	104
4.2	The corporate constitution	106
4.3	The replaceable rules	112
4.4	Statutory interpretation regarding companies	115
	Chapter 4 revision activities	124

Chapter 5 (Week 3) The Corporation's Dealings with Third Parties and Potential Liability Issues 132

5.1	Third parties dealing with the company	134
5.2	Corporate contracts	137
5.3	Pre- and post-incorporation contracts and liabilities	139
5.4	Company liability in tort	142
5.5	Company criminal responsibility	144
	Chapter 5 revision activities	148
	Foundational case studies	155

Chapter 6 (Week 4) Stakeholders of the Corporation 160

6.1	The stakeholders of the corporation	162
6.2	The regulation of companies	169
6.3	The role and function of ASIC	174
6.4	The Banking Royal Commission and its aftermath	178
	Chapter 6 revision activities	180

Chapter 7 (Week 5) Company Leadership and the Board of Directors 188

7.1	Directors, officers and managers	190
7.2	The board and its strategic role	192
7.3	Corporate governance	194
7.4	The chair	199
7.5	The CEO	200
	Chapter 7 revision activities	205

Chapter 8 (Week 6) Directors as Agents of the Corporation— Roles and Responsibilities 212

8.1	Laws and rules relevant to directors	214
8.2	The roles undertaken by directors	216
8.3	Directors as agents and fiduciaries of the company	217
8.4	Duties owed by the directors	222
8.5	Issues of skill, competence and negligence relevant to directors	228
8.6	Issues of disclosure, honesty and good faith relevant to directors	228
	Chapter 8 revision activities	233

Chapter 9 (Week 7) Shares and Shareholding: Property, Ownership and Investment 242

9.1	The nature of shares	244
9.2	The ownership of shares: shareholders	245
9.3	Different types of shares	248
9.4	Potential financial returns for shareholders	250
9.5	Shareholding as a risk investment	252
	Chapter 9 revision activities	255

Chapter 10 (Week 7) Membership: Meetings, Rights, Responsibilities 262

10.1	Company membership and its contractual nature	264
10.2	Membership rights and liabilities	265
10.3	Members' meetings	269
10.4	Potential remedies for members	273
10.5	Majority rule vs minority rights	275
	Chapter 10 revision activities	279

Chapter 11 (Week 8) Share Capital: Transactions and Control 286

11.1	Share capital and its maintenance	288
11.2	Share capital transactions: reductions and buy-backs	290

11.3	Transactions affecting control of voting shares: takeovers	295
11.4	Schemes of arrangement: an alternative to takeovers	297
11.5	Groups of companies and control issues	297
	Chapter 11 revision activities	300

Chapter 12 (Week 8) Corporate Finance I: Raising Share Capital — 308

12.1	Corporate finance: the two options	310
12.2	Sources of share capital	312
12.3	Raising share capital from the public	314
12.4	Emerging methods of raising share capital	317
12.5	Hybrid share capital/loan capital arrangements	320
	Chapter 12 revision activities	322

Chapter 13 (Week 9) Corporate Finance II: Loan Capital — 328

13.1	Loan capital: basic principles	330
13.2	Debentures and risk issues for lenders	332
13.3	Securing personal property and the *Personal Property and Securities Act 2009* (Cth)	336
13.4	Hybrid forms of loan capital/share capital: convertible debentures	341
13.5	Comparing loan with share capital	342
	Chapter 13 revision activities	346

Chapter 14 (Week 10) External Administration — 352

14.1	An overview of external administration	354
14.2	Solvency, external administration and directors' duties	356
14.3	Receivership	360
14.4	Voluntary administration	363
14.5	Deeds of company arrangement	365
14.6	Court-ordered schemes of arrangement	366
	Chapter 14 revision activities	368

Chapter 15 (Week 11)   Winding Up the Corporation   376

15.1   Overview of winding-up   378
15.2   Compulsory winding-up   384
15.3   Voluntary winding-up   385
15.4   The role of the liquidator   389
15.5   The role and responsibilities of the directors of a company in liquidation   390
          Chapter 15 revision activities   391

Chapter 16 (Week 12)   Corporations and the Cultural Context   396

16.1   A case study in corporate culture   398
16.2   Corporate law theory   400
16.3   Corporate social responsibility in the 21st century   402
16.4   A brief review of the unit of study: Company Law   405
          Follow-up case studies   414

Chapter 17 Legal Skills and Law in the 21st Century   420

17.1   An overview of legal skills   422
17.2   Developing a toolkit for legal analysis   426
17.3   Law, career planning and life-long learning   427
17.4   Law in the 21st century   429

Chapter 18 Revision Activity Answers   432

CHAPTER 1

THE CORPORATION: INTRODUCTION AND OVERVIEW

Chapter synopsis and links to Textbook Chapter 1

This Workbook Chapter deals with five topics:

- 1.1 Studying corporate law
- 1.2 The corporation: an overview
- 1.3 A brief history of companies
- 1.4 Constitutional foundations of Australian corporate law
- 1.5 The context and culture of the corporation.

Each of these topics is constructively aligned with, and linked to, the same topics in Chapter 1 of the Textbook.

Chapter executive summary

This Chapter, and *Corporations Law: Concepts, Cases and Culture* generally, examines the unit Company Law in several capacities:

- as a compulsory unit of study in law
- by reference to legal history generally and corporate history in particular
- as regards the constitutional law-making basis of the Commonwealth of Australia
- in terms of the dynamic nature of corporate law within the federal system of government, and
- in the context of the corporation in the 21st century as both a wealth-making and society-engaged entity.

CHAPTER DIAGRAMMATIC OVERVIEW

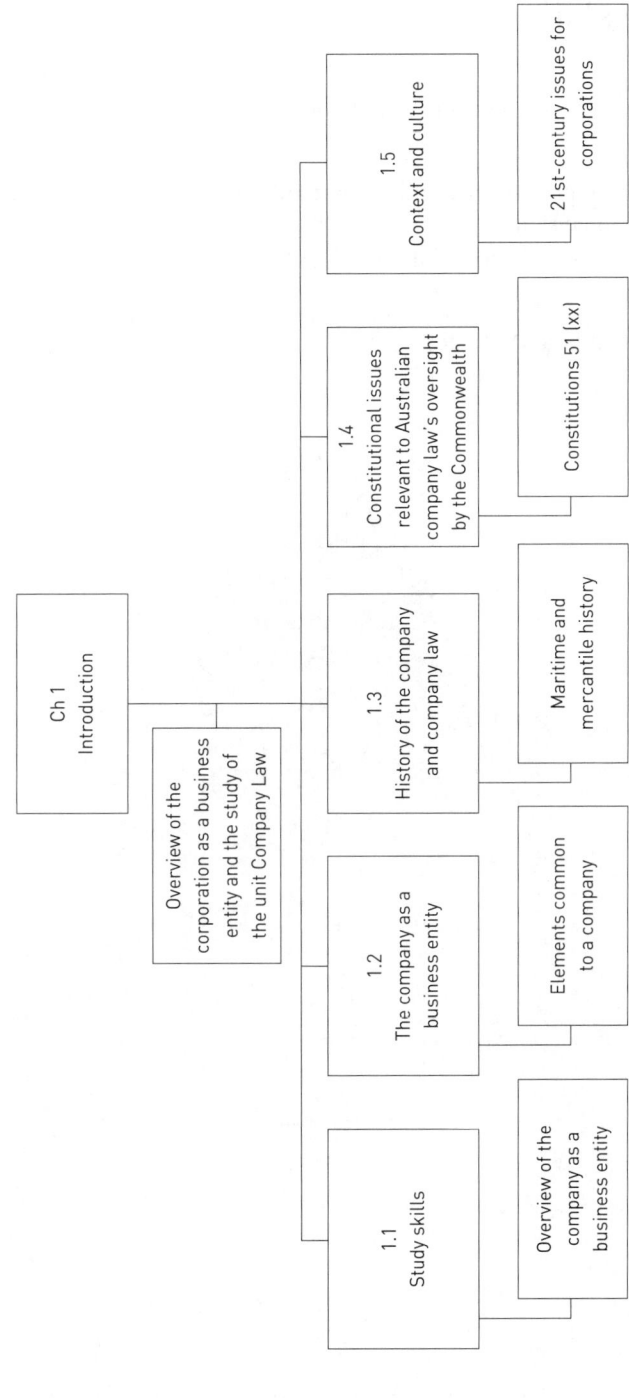

FIGURE 1.1 An overview of Chapter 1

1.1 STUDYING CORPORATE LAW

Developing legal skills

Legal skills include:
- written skills—these are the focus of this Workbook
- oral skills.

Both are more broadly part of professional skills, so obtaining a law degree is very useful in informing a wide range of applicable professional skills.

With legal reading at the base of the pyramid in Fig 1.2, we can construct a hierarchy of written skills in increasing complexity.

FIGURE 1.2 The hierarchy of legal skills

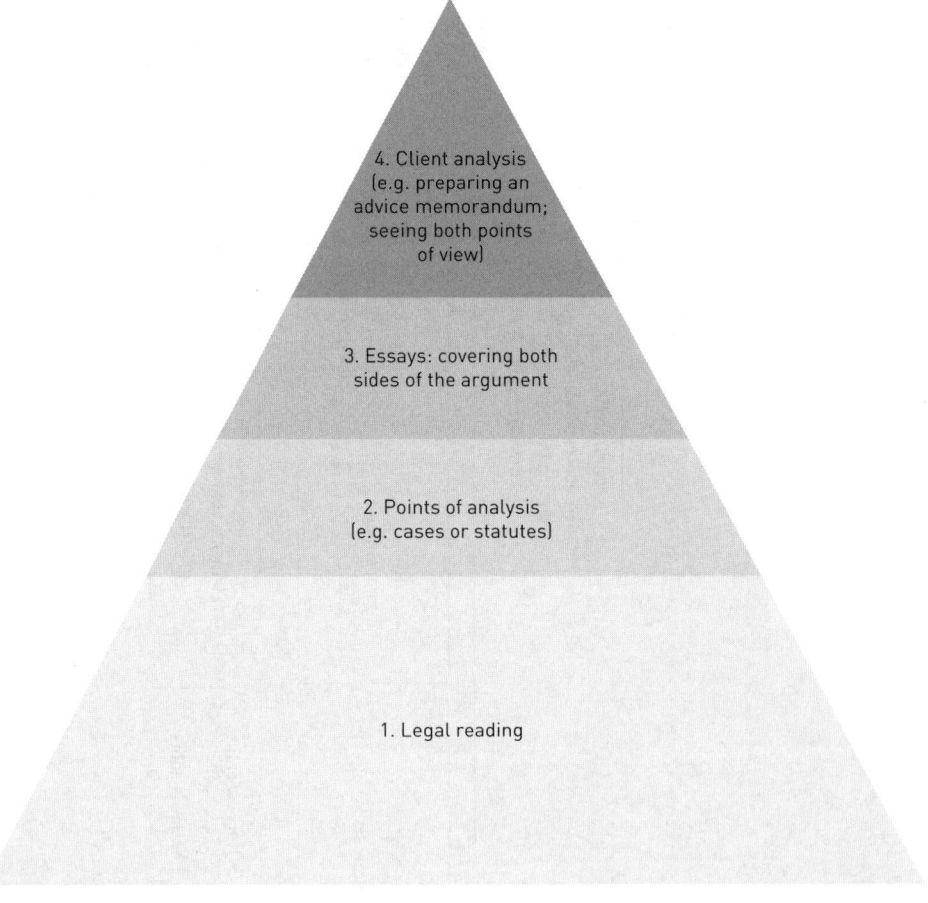

Legal analysis

Law is a system of taxonomy and classification in the way it is both studied and practised.

FIGURE 1.3 The classification of areas of study in a law degree

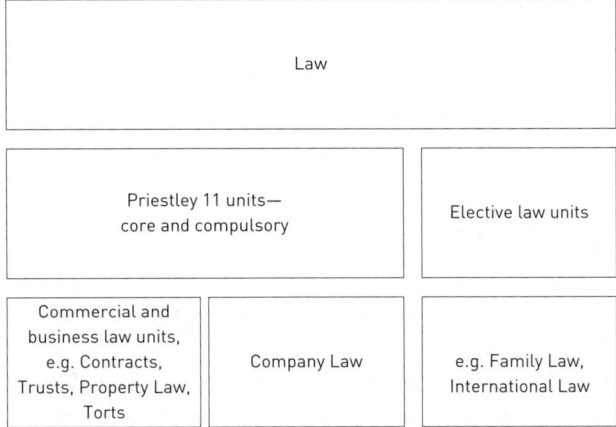

Problem solving and legal analysis

Problem solving and legal analysis involve a taxonomic and classifying approach, as set out in Fig 1.4. This shows the context of corporate law, moving from the general to the particular context, and the importance of primary and secondary sources of law.

FIGURE 1.4 The context of corporate law

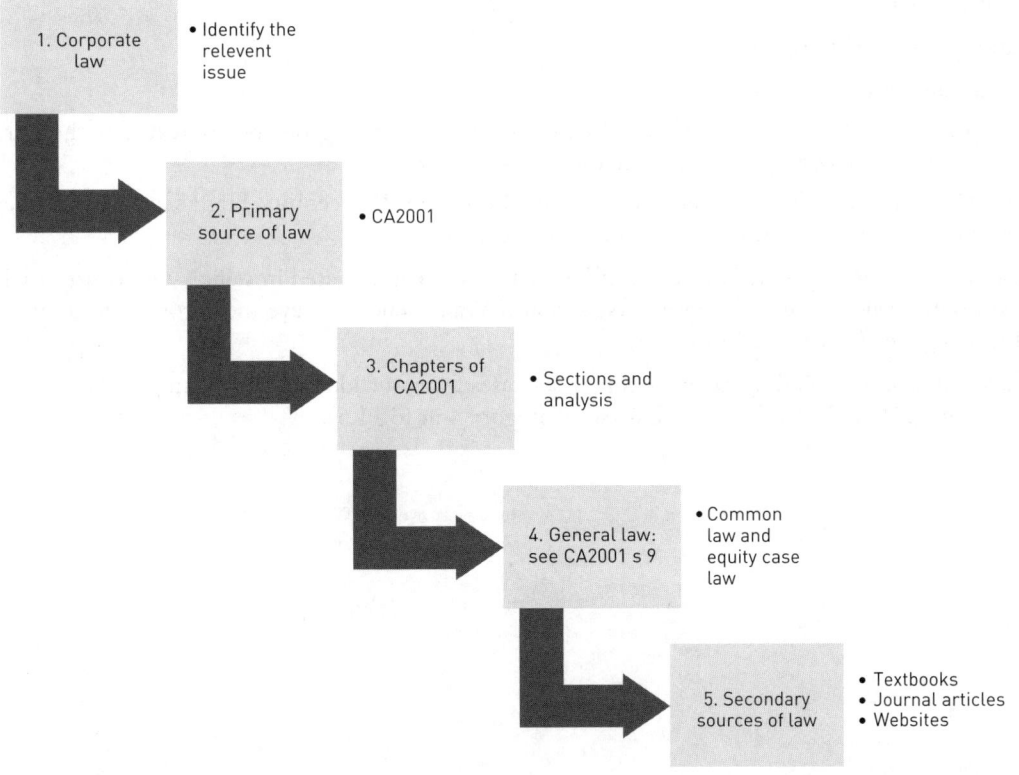

This approach can also be seen as broadly replicating the problem-solving methodologies provided in legal education, and often referred to; for example, the so-called 'IRAC' method:

- **issue** identification
- relevant **research**
- **arguments** for and against on the main issues
- interim **conclusions** based on the facts to date, and available information.

The corpus of corporate law

Corporate law includes a potentially wide array of sources. Primarily, these are statute and general law. They may also include another layer of guidance or rules, such as the Listing Rules provided by the Australian Securities Exchange (ASX).

The first point of contemporary reference is the *Corporations Act 2001* (Cth) (CA2001), which refers to the 'general law'. The general law is found in cases, and includes common law and equitable principles. Hence the case law is important in determining the relevant principles pertinent to a contemporary corporate law problem.

The categories of case law

When studying Priestley 11 substantive subjects, such as Company Law, it is useful to review foundation principles regarding matters such as:

- sources of law
- problem solving
- statutory interpretation, and
- case law analysis.

As to the last of these, the categories of case law vary, depending on the context. For the purpose of Australian corporate law, we can discern the following:

- Key cases: these may be pre-1986 UK cases or 20th- and 21st-century High Court cases; they cover important principles (see Categories 1 and 2 in Fig 1.5).
- Cases on relevant corporate law points of law that have been litigated in senior state courts, such as the New South Wales Court of Appeal—New South Wales tends to have more corporate litigation than other states (see Category 3 in Fig 1.5).
- The fourth and non-binding category comprises cases from outside the Australian jurisdiction, including Hong Kong, New Zealand and the UK (see Category 4 in Fig 1.5).

FIGURE 1.5 The basic categories of case law relevant to corporate law

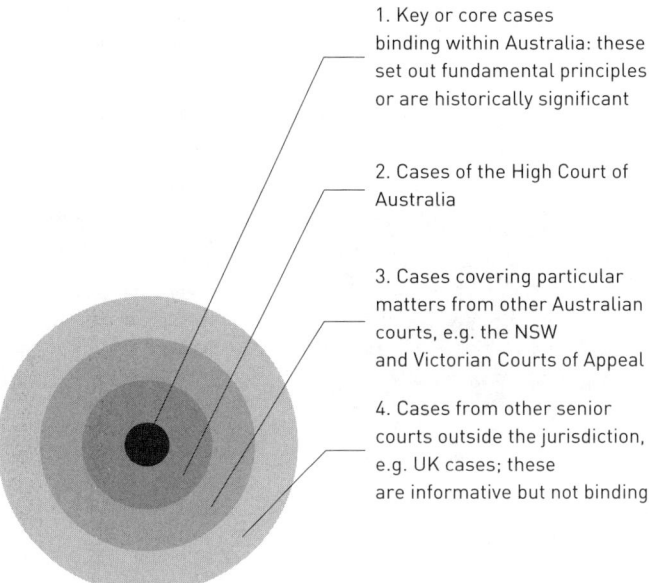

1. Key or core cases binding within Australia: these set out fundamental principles or are historically significant

2. Cases of the High Court of Australia

3. Cases covering particular matters from other Australian courts, e.g. the NSW and Victorian Courts of Appeal

4. Cases from other senior courts outside the jurisdiction, e.g. UK cases; these are informative but not binding

The elements of a case and the development of case law

For a particular case, the foundation principles apply in relation to discerning the two basic elements; that is:
- *ratio decidendi*, and
- *obiter dicta*.

These are encapsulated by Elements 1 and 2 respectively in Fig 1.6.

There are other elements to consider. These include:
- an apex court provides majority and dissenting judgments, and the dissenting judgments may not win the argument in the current case
- the dissenting judgments may, however, theoretically become orthodoxy at some later point, and
- the apex court has the power, at least in theory, of overruling its own prior decision.

These latter points are encapsulated by Elements 3 and 4 respectively in Fig 1.6.

FIGURE 1.6 Elements of case law and the development of the general law by apex courts

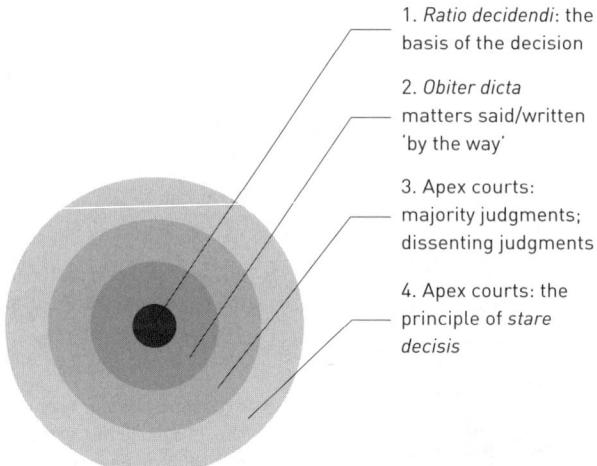

1. *Ratio decidendi*: the basis of the decision
2. *Obiter dicta* matters said/written 'by the way'
3. Apex courts: majority judgments; dissenting judgments
4. Apex courts: the principle of *stare decisis*

Why study company law?

The short answer is that company law is a Priestley 11 compulsory subject in every law program for those students seeking admission to the legal profession.

We can see a law degree as providing different types of units that reflect different student interests and areas of professional practice. These could be broadly divided as follows:

- transactional or non-litigious work, based on advice and effecting legal processes, such as purchase and sales, and contractual drafting; these are strongly focused on traditional elements of a market-based economy
- litigious techniques and the traditional court-based determination of disputes
- public law—involving a government or public entity
- units related to the profession of law and the public officer concept
- other units—those not fitting neatly in the previous categories and occupying the elective category.

There may be other ways to categorise these units, and there may be overlaps in any event, but the traditional, commercial, property-based nature of the project of Australian law as taught by law schools is clear, as shown in the first column of Table 1.1.

TABLE 1.1 The law units in a typical Australian law degree

Transactional commercial law units	Litigious units	Public law units	Legal professional standing—public officer capstone unit	Other (elective) units
Company law Contract law Property law Torts Trusts	Criminal law Criminal procedure Civil procedure	Constitutional law Administrative law	Ethics	Introduction to law Statutory interpretation Family law International law and human rights ADR, negotiation, mediation and arbitration Environmental law

1.2 THE CORPORATION: AN OVERVIEW

The corporation is a flexible, adaptable and, thereby, useful invention of commerce and the law. In the study of this subject, the 17 chapters of *Corporations Law: Concepts, Cases and Culture* divide into eight themes or modules. These are not tightly proscribed, but emerge as a result of the content and aims of the particular bracket or grouping of chapters. They may also conveniently provide for cross-referencing within the modules, or between the modules. Further, they provide an alternative means of viewing the book's content and themes, variously as either:

- breaking down and analysing, or
- 'grossing up' and providing a set of thematic composites.

The eight modules can be represented as shown in Fig 1.7.

FIGURE 1.7 An overview of *Corporations Law: Concepts, Cases and Culture* by reference to eight informal modules

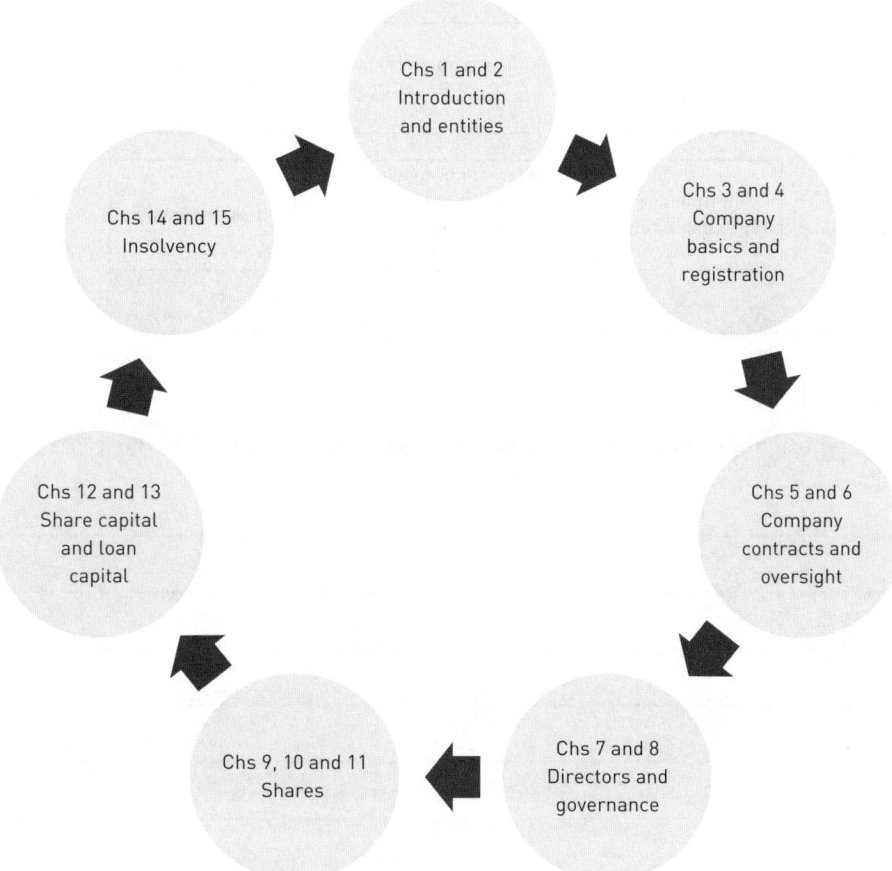

Figure 1.8 gives an overview of topics typical to corporations law.

FIGURE 1.8 The typical elements of the unit of study Company Law

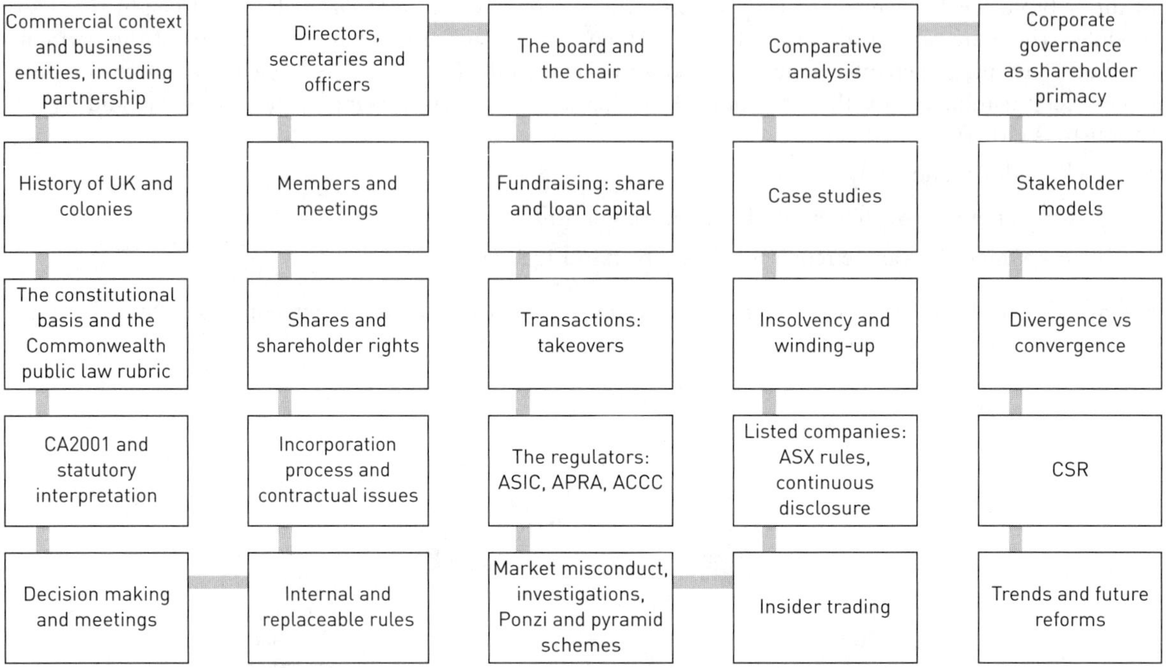

Commercial context and business entities, including partnership	Directors, secretaries and officers	The board and the chair	Comparative analysis	Corporate governance as shareholder primacy
History of UK and colonies	Members and meetings	Fundraising: share and loan capital	Case studies	Stakeholder models
The constitutional basis and the Commonwealth public law rubric	Shares and shareholder rights	Transactions: takeovers	Insolvency and winding-up	Divergence vs convergence
CA2001 and statutory interpretation	Incorporation process and contractual issues	The regulators: ASIC, APRA, ACCC	Listed companies: ASX rules, continuous disclosure	CSR
Decision making and meetings	Internal and replaceable rules	Market misconduct, investigations, Ponzi and pyramid schemes	Insider trading	Trends and future reforms

Activity 1.1

Review the typical topic headings in books on corporate law. Identify the types of patterns that emerge.

_____
_____
_____
_____
_____
_____

Key concepts in corporate law

The term 'business entity' is broader than 'corporation'. It includes a corporation. We look at the other potential business entities or structures in Chapter 2. For the moment, however, we can posit the choice of a corporation as per the client's instructions, based on their optimal needs. This is a basic legal service: to present the options to the client. The legal choice, however, is ultimately up to the client.

FIGURE 1.9 The choice of the company as a business entity

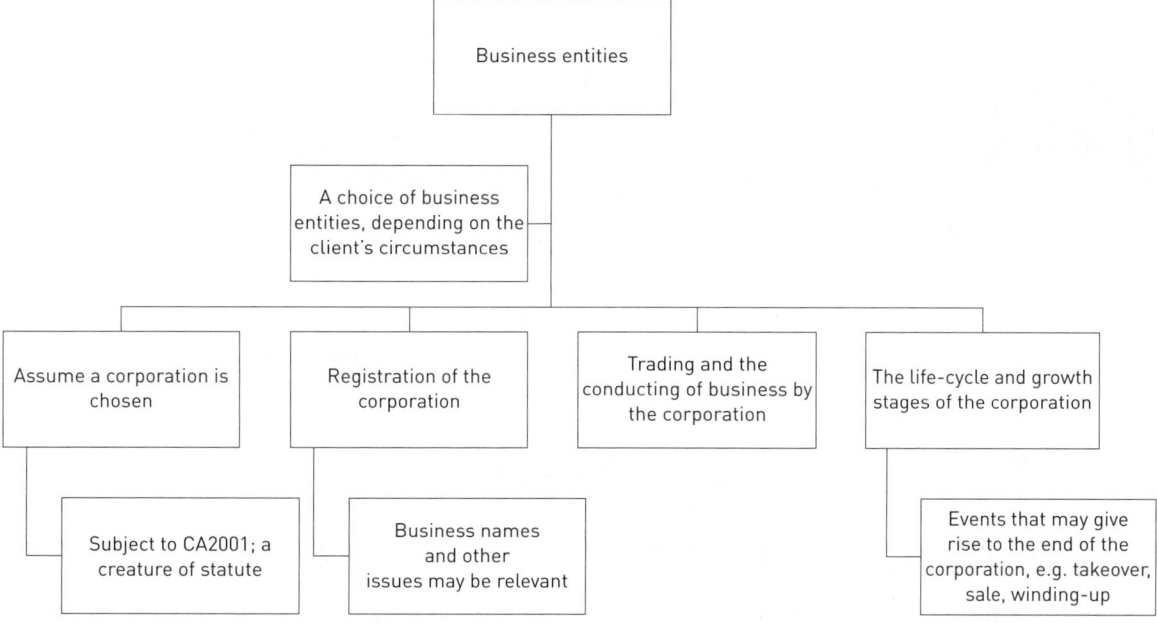

An overview of this book

Corporations Law: Concepts, Cases and Culture, like other books on corporate law, examines the main elements that make up the corporation. These include the roles taken up by various people, including owners/shareholders and directors. It also includes the narrative elements of the corporation from inception, or incorporation, through to (potentially, at least) deregistration. Figure 1.10 reflects these two overlapping elements of relevant parties/actors and potential events/transactions, and how these matters are mapped to Chapters 1–15.

FIGURE 1.10 The chapter topics of the *Corporations Law: Concepts, Cases and Culture* Textbook and Workbook

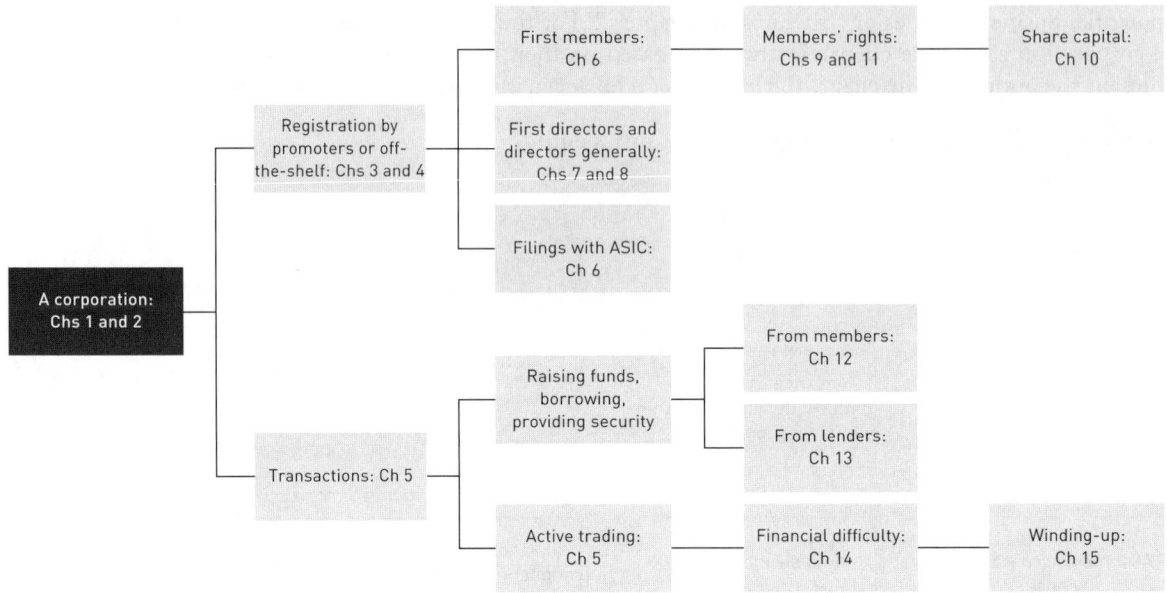

1.3 A BRIEF HISTORY OF COMPANIES

Company or corporate law history

Company law history is a major topic in its own right. In *Corporations Law: Concepts, Cases and Culture*, we examine some of the main trends and developments. History informs the growth and development of the common law. It is an iterative process punctuated by legislative (often seismic) shifts. Figure 1.11 depicts a timeline of the main precursors to modern Australian corporate law.

FIGURE 1.11 The historical advent of companies

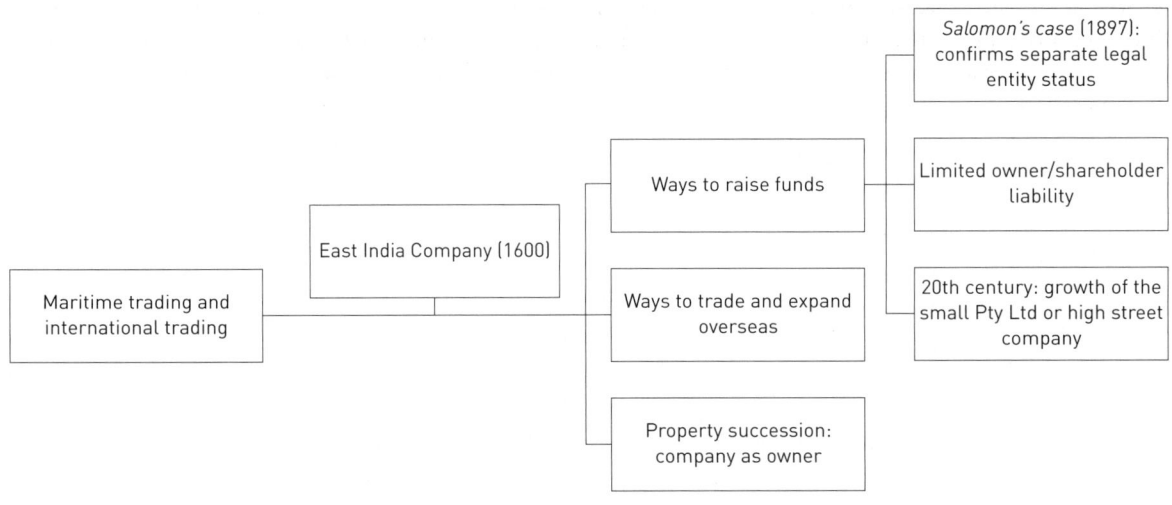

Context and history of company law

The historical development of the limited liability company is illustrated in Fig 1.12. The third 'step' is the critical one, or keystone —the House of Lords case of *Salomon v A Salomon & Co Ltd* [1897] AC 22.

FIGURE 1.12   The various historical phases of development of corporate law and key developments

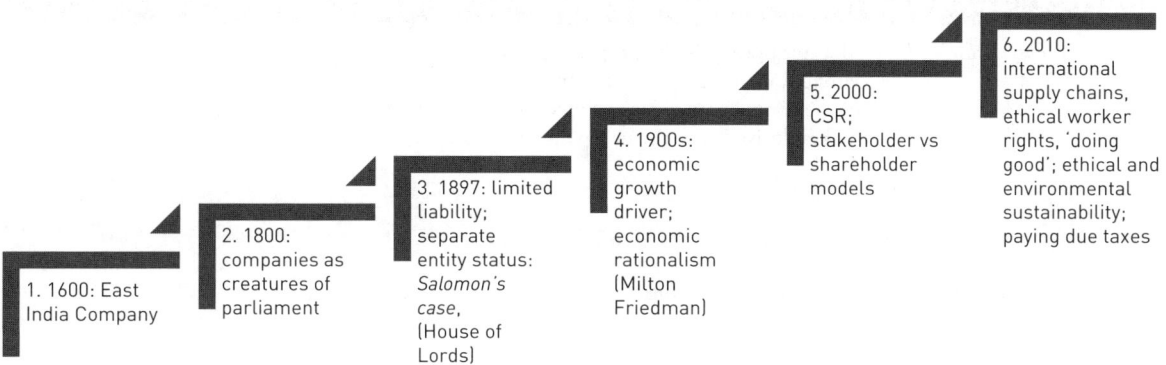

Tables of developments, timelines and milestones

Law's history and development can be presented in multiple ways; for example, via:

- a long history—a 'meta' approach as in a large, expansive narrative, or
- micro-histories, e.g. based on particular cases and developments (the French term for this type of approach is *petit recits*).

Table 1.2 takes the meta-historical approach; while Table 1.3 adopts the micro-histories approach.

TABLE 1.2   The history of the company and key developments over 2,000 years: a meta-history of key common law principles

Date	Developments
Justinian I Roman Empire 527–565CE	The Roman Empire encompassed Europe and Britain, and Roman law, with its codes and *institutiones* (Latin for 'textbook'), was central in asserting power and maintaining control. The *corpus juris* was a complete body or code of law. The most famous code was that ordered by Emperor Justinian: the Justinian Code, or *Corpus Juris Civilis*.
1400–1600	Italian Renaissance
1600s	Joint stock companies, England
1725	Overreach and investment bubbles
1600–1850	East India Company—rise and fall
1800s	Royal Charter companies
1860s	English corporate legislation
1897	*Salomon v A Salomon & Co Ltd*

The cases in Table 1.3 are famous and enduring cases from 19-century UK corporate jurisprudence. Their ongoing relevance is indicated by the fact that they are still discussed in books dealing with the principles and coverage of modern Australian corporate law.

TABLE 1.3 Key 19th-century UK cases in corporate law

Date	Case	Relevant principle of corporations law	Ongoing relevance to the CA2001
1843	*Foss v Harbottle*	The corporation is the proper plaintiff in a wrong done to the company; the majority of the company in a general meeting makes decisions on the company's behalf	
1878	*Erlanger v New Sombrero Phosphate Company*	Corporate opportunities are for the company to decide on	
1887	*Trevor v Whitworth*	The company cannot reduce share capital if it is prejudicial to the interests of the creditors	
1897	*Salomon's case*	The corporation is a separate entity; it is distinct from its shareholders and its directors	
1902	*Percival v Wright*	Directors must act in the best interests of the company—the shareholders as a whole	

Case: *Salomon's case*

The key facts and issues regarding *Salomon's case* are presented in Figs 1.13 and 1.14.

FIGURE 1.13 The key chronology of events in *Salomon's case*

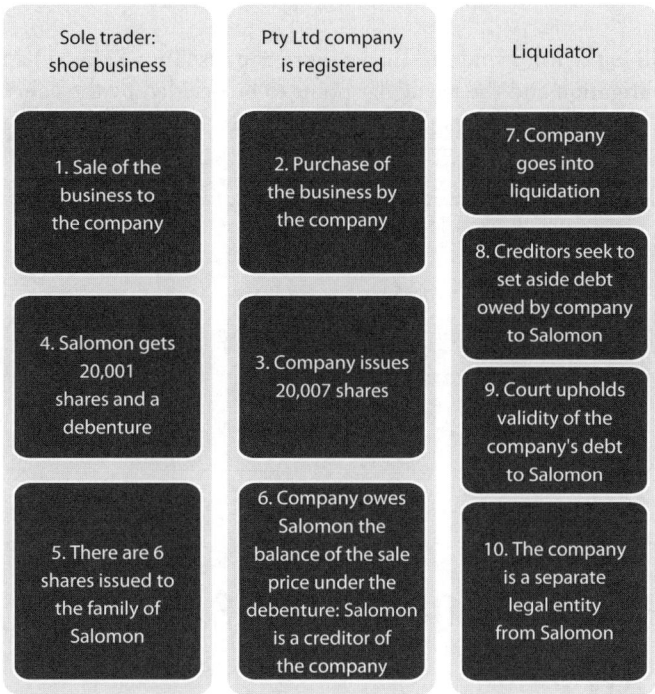

FIGURE 1.14 An overview of the main issues in *Salomon's case*

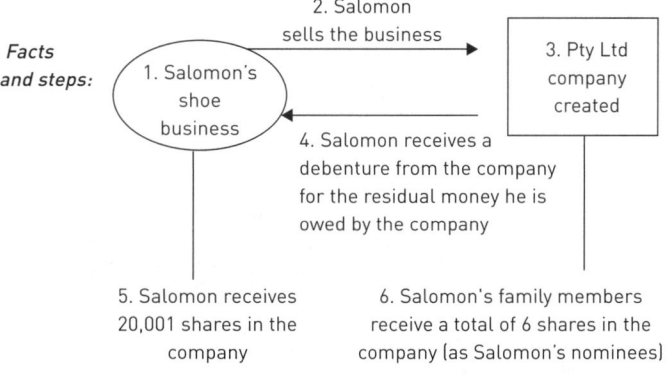

Activity 1.2

Look at Table 1.3. Fill in the third column. Then choose one case (not *Salomon*) and set out the various steps that led to the litigation and the particular point to be decided by the court.

_____
_____
_____
_____
_____
_____
_____

1.4 CONSTITUTIONAL FOUNDATIONS OF AUSTRALIAN CORPORATE LAW

An overview of the CA2001 is set out in Fig 1.15.

FIGURE 1.15 The main areas of the CA2001 relevant to the unit Company Law

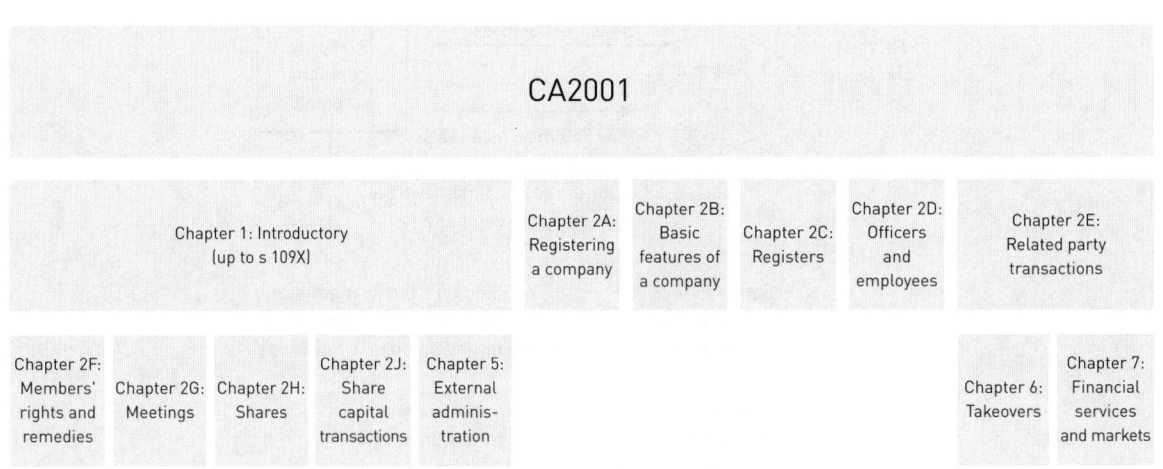

Corporate law legislative foundation in Australia

Just as we have seen corporate law history from several perspectives, we can take an approximately 120-year snapshot of Australian corporate law history. This could be represented as shown in Fig 1.16.

FIGURE 1.16   An overview of the development of corporations law in Australia since Federation

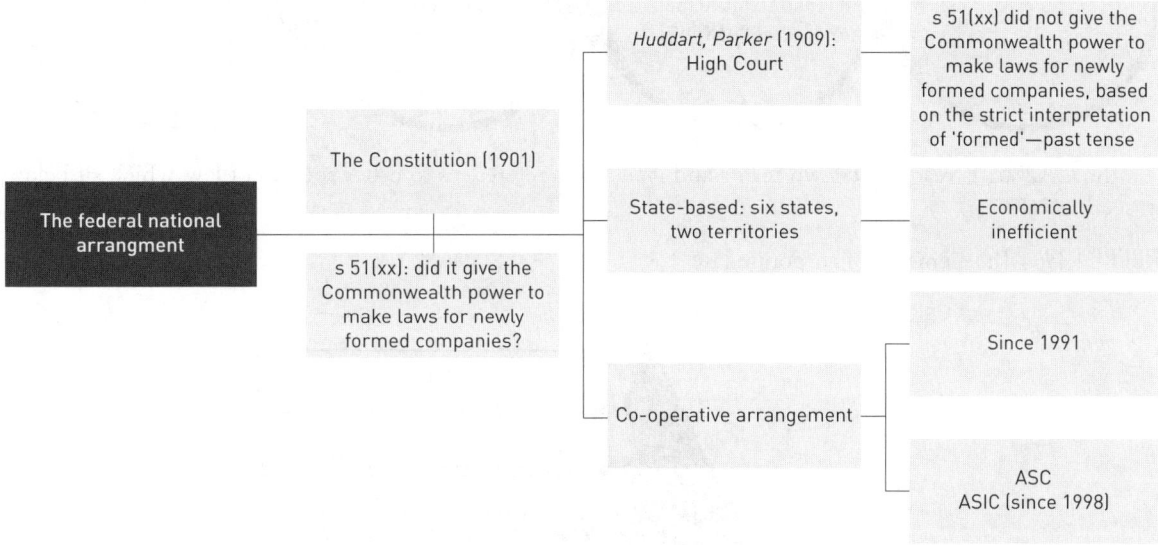

Corporate law in Australia has, in effect, two legislative bases: the Australian Constitution, and the CA2001. Consideration begins with the Constitution. The absence of a Commonwealth power in s 51(xx) is the starting position. The solution to this absence is in the gift of the states: see Figs 1.17 and 1.18.

FIGURE 1.17   The 'double legislative' issues underpinning corporate law provision in Australia

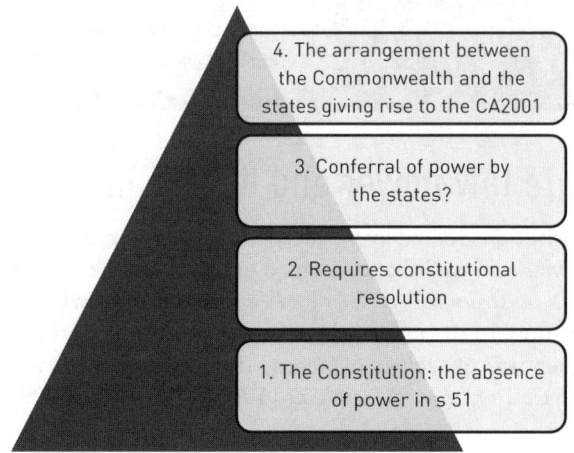

FIGURE 1.18   The interplay between state and Commonwealth power

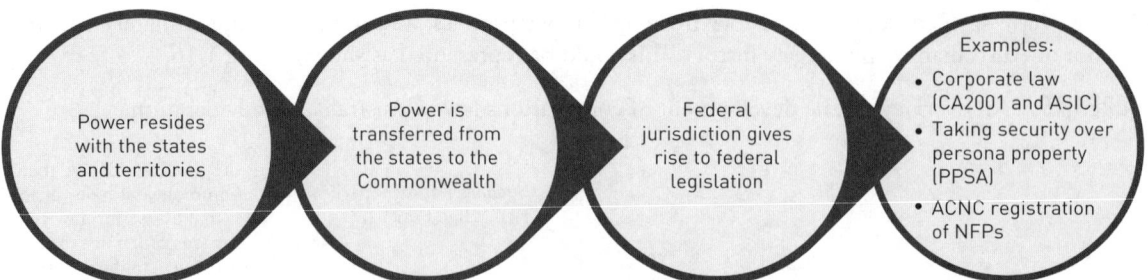

The CA2001 is read on its own terms and it includes references to other sources of law, which sit below it: see Fig 1.19.

FIGURE 1.19   The elements of corporate law

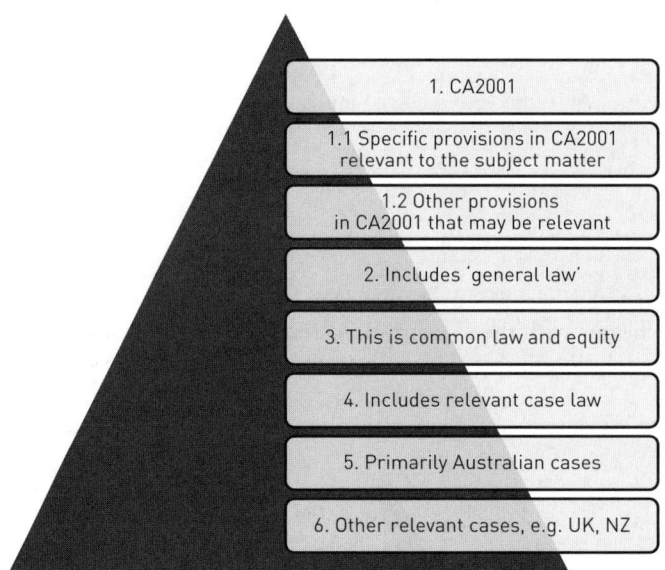

Sources of corporate law power and debate in Australia

The original gap in the Constitution created by s 51(xx) meant there were several steps and missteps before a nationally integrated system was achieved that combined unified law (the CA2001), common administration and oversight (ASIC and the *Australian Securities and Investments Commission Act 2001* (Cth) (ASIC Act 2001)), and resolution of disputes. In the century between 1901 and 2001, there were key developments and attempts, the purpose of which was to seek to overcome the constitutional issues first litigated in the High Court in *Huddart, Parker & Co Pty Ltd v Moorehead* [1909] HCA 36; (1909) 8 CLR 330, referred to in Table 1.4.

CHAPTER 1 THE CORPORATION: INTRODUCTION AND OVERVIEW

TABLE 1.4 Key events in the evolution of Australian corporate law, including the resolution of constitutional law issues

Date	Event	Issue
1897	*Salomon's case*	The confirmation of the separate legal status of the company in *Salomon's case*, decided in the House of Lords just four years prior to the Constitution, is an interesting contextual point. There are now approximately 2 million companies in Australia.
1901	Australian Constitution s 51(xx)	Provides reference to corporations *formed* in Australia—note the use of the past tense; it is not prospective
1909	*Huddart, Parker v Moorehead* (High Court of Australia)	Confirms there is no Commonwealth power in s 51(xx) to oversee companies. The Commonwealth is a creature of statute; it does not have inherent or reserve powers. *The power component is therefore confirmed as absent: Failure No 1.*
1913	Constitutional referendum to amend s 51(xx)	The referendum fails (referenda require a majority of states and a national majority).
1920	*Engineers' case*	Confirms a literal approach to dealing with statute.
1910–60s	States oversaw the establishment and regulation of companies	
1958	Uniform Companies Act	
1960s	Uniform legislation emerges	
1974	Corporate Affairs Commissions established in NSW, Victoria, Qld and WA	The states seek to impose some basic uniformity to the regulation and administration of companies. They drift, however, from this approach over time.
1979	The co-operative scheme	

OXFORD UNIVERSITY PRESS

TABLE 1.4 Key events in the evolution of Australian corporate law, including the resolution of constitutional law issues (continued)

Date	Event	Issue
1989	Corporations Act (Cth) Australian Securities Commission (ASC)	
1990	*Incorporation case*	The High Court invalidates the 1989 Act setting up the ASC. *The administrative component relevant to corporations law is defeated: Failure No 2.*
1991	The Corporations Law scheme	
1998	ASIC established; cross-vesting for courts	This seeks to provide that state courts can hear Commonwealth matters and vice versa.
1999	*Re Wakim*	The High Court rules that the cross-vesting scheme is invalid. *The courts component of the scheme is defeated: Failure No 3.*
1999	Corporate Law Economic Reform Program (CLERP)	
2000	Alice Springs Agreement	State and Commonwealth laws are passed to give the Commonwealth consolidated power over corporations.
2001	*R v Hughes*	*The High Court rejects the argument that offences against WA law could be converted into breaches of Commonwealth law: Failure No 4.*
2001	CA2001 and ASIC Act 2001	The CA2001 is 'locked in' by sunset renewal clauses every five years and by state control; the CA2001 and the ASIC Act 2001 are in effect a scheme in the gift of the states.

An overview of the foundations of Australian corporate law includes examining several components of law:
- legal history
- constitutional law and statutory interpretation
- the CA2001 and general law comprising the relevant legal provision of contemporary corporate law.

FIGURE. 1.20   The overlapping elements relevant to contemporary Australian corporate law

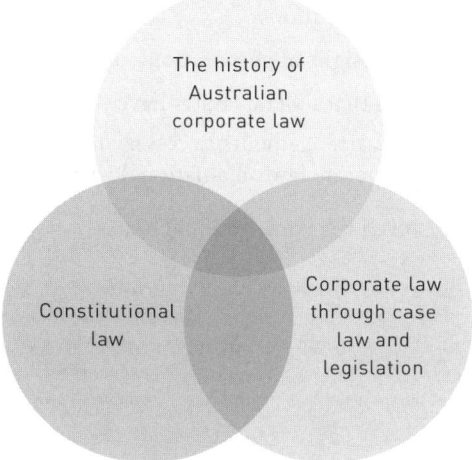

> ## Activity 1.3
> Look at Table 1.4 and fill in the gaps.

Figure 1.21 illustrates the four phases, or chapters of development, in the Commonwealth resolution of the constitutional impasse to Australia's corporate law.

FIGURE 1.21   The phases that gave rise to the CA2001

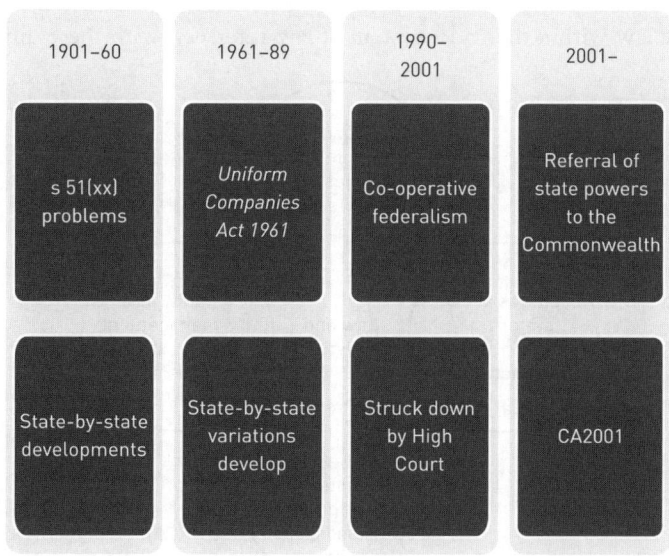

The current scheme is effectively the creation of a Commonwealth-based solution to integrate three extant issues concerning:

- the source of legal power as regards corporations
- the administration, regulation and oversight of corporations, and
- the settlement of disputes, being such that federal courts have powers over Commonwealth law.

The CA2001 made the constitutional arrangements necessary to underpin the power to set up, regulate, administer and adjudicate Australian corporate law on a national basis, as shown in Fig 1.22.

FIGURE 1.22   The CA2001 finally resolved the constitutional issues

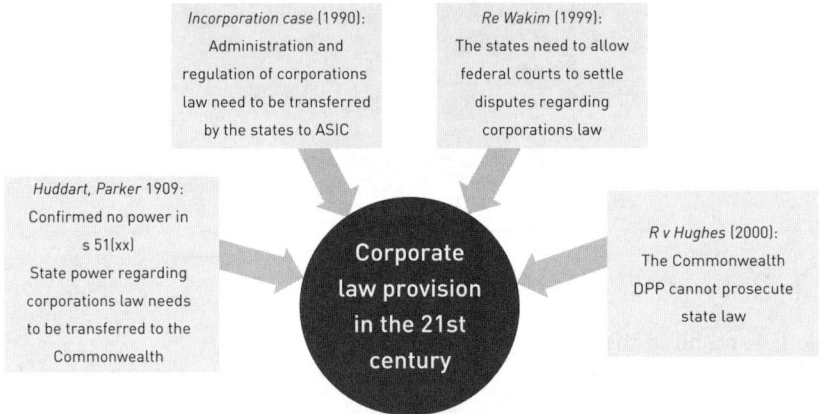

1.5 THE CONTEXT AND CULTURE OF THE CORPORATION

Law as a multi-faceted system can be represented as shown in Figs 1.23 and 1.24.

FIGURE 1.23   Corporate law, within the wider system of law, intersects with these dimensions

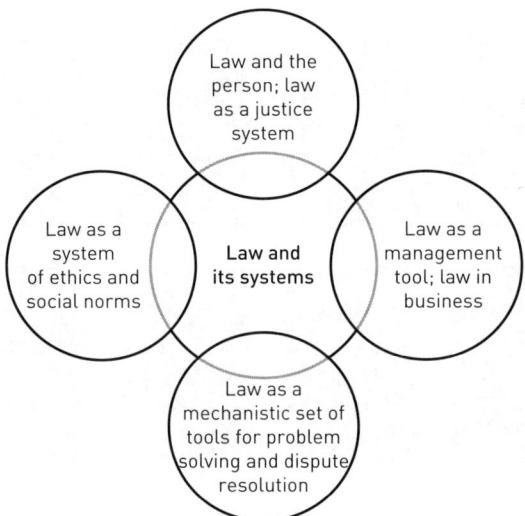

FIGURE 1.24   The aims of corporate law can be bifurcated

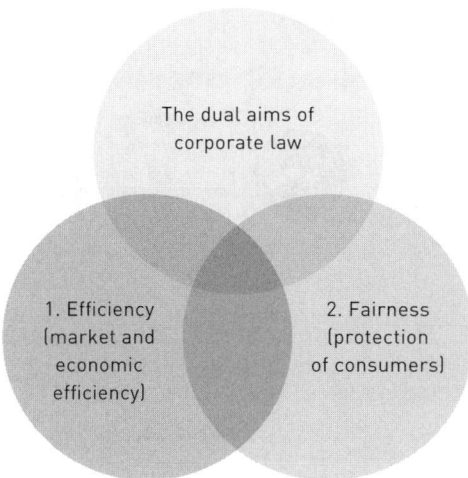

A corporation's stakeholders

A corporation's stakeholders are literally those groups with a 'stake' in, commitment to, or interest in the company: see Table 1.5. Stakeholders are discussed in Chapter 6.

TABLE 1.5   The stakeholders of the company

Internal stakeholders	External stakeholders
• Employees • Shareholders • The board • The senior managers • The CEO	• Customers • Suppliers • Creditors • Regulators? • Competitors? Other intangible/emerging stakeholders: • The environment? • The future? • The community? • The competitive context?

Legal practice—its evolution over the past 40 years

A 40-year snapshot of the practice of law shows how much it has changed. The profession has transformed from a slow-moving group of generalist lawyers, to a highly specialised market characterised by segmentation and niche offerings. Figure 1.25 illustrates the rapidly evolving nature of legal practice, and the intersection between the legal profession and emerging technology.

FIGURE 1.25 The rapidly evolving nature of legal practice

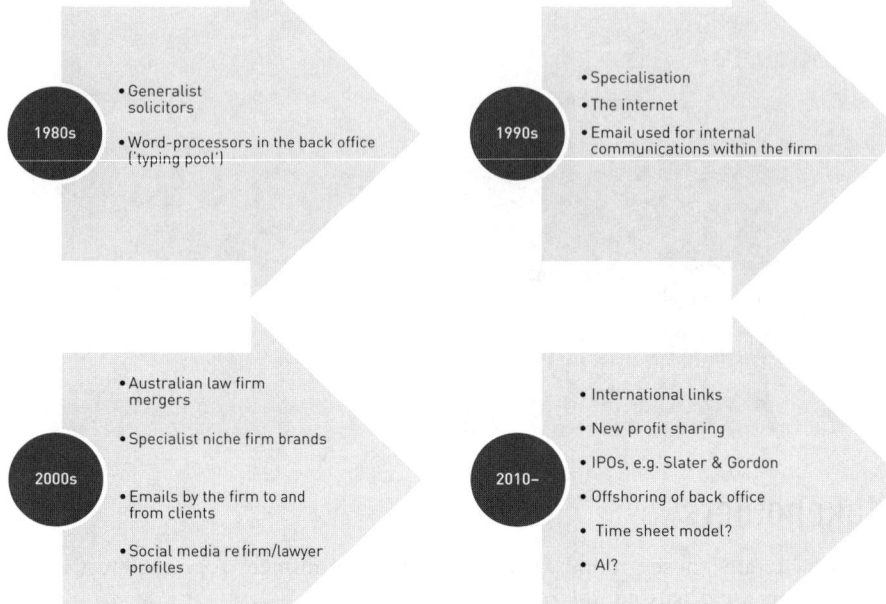

Activity 1.4

Review the timeline in Figure 1.25. Based on a prognosis of the next decade, what are likely to be the big issues affecting legal practice generally, and corporate law in particular?

_____
_____
_____
_____
_____
_____

Law as reactive to commercial/social innovation

Another way of considering law and examining its effects is to see it in its contextual setting. There are various academic areas of discipline, including law and economics, law and literature, and law and culture. There is usually a delay between developments in technology and innovation on the one hand, and law on the other hand: see Fig 1.26.

FIGURE 1.26 The law develops in relation to wider contexts

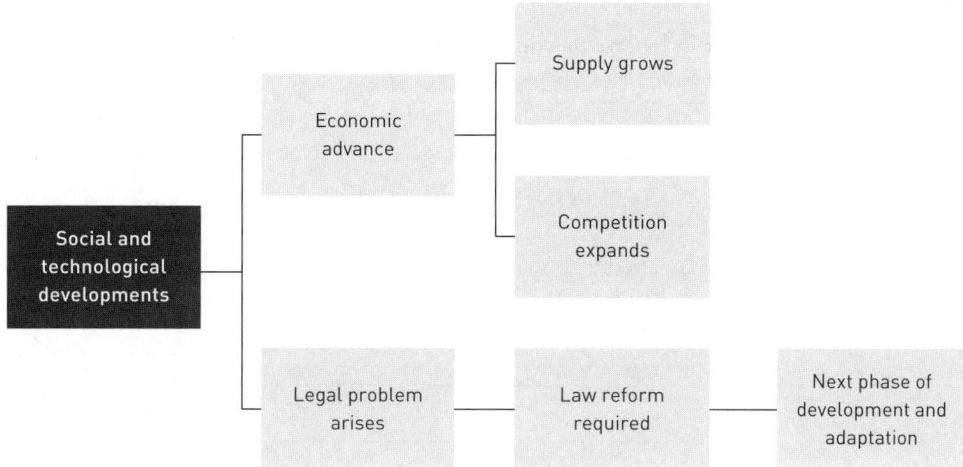

Corporate examples of technology being ahead of law include:
- Facebook, online rules and the protocols of content posting
- the 'sharing economy', with business models such as Uber and Airbnb, and
- privacy issues for users (e.g. Facebook, Google, Amazon).

Activity 1.5

Read the following and then answer the questions below.

IN THE NEWS: CORPORATE CULTURE

The corporation: Virgin Australia, an airline business, February 2019[1]

The context: A new CEO, Mr Paul Scurrah, was appointed by the board, and was announced by the Chair of the Board, Elizabeth Bryan. The corporate headquarters is located in Brisbane. Ms Bryan noted:

> I'm delighted to say that the most outstanding candidate ended up being an Australian, an Australian with impeccable leadership credentials who lives in Brisbane. Who would've thought we could be so lucky?

Mr Scurrah noted:

> I've been transporting people and cargo for a very long time—28 years in fact. At Queensland Rail we carried around 60 million passengers a year; at Aurizon we moved 190 million tonnes of coal; and at DP World we moved two million containers around the country every year. One thing I will be quite obsessed about is having a culture where people thrive and can achieve great things. That translates into happy customers and importantly, I'll be focused on the bottom line for our shareholders.

---

1 Robyn Ironside, 'Virgin boss has long past as prime mover', *The Australian*, 7 February 2019, 2.

QUESTIONS

1. What is corporate culture? What are its constituent elements? How could it be measured?

2. Should a corporation maximise shareholder returns as its Number 1 priority? Explain your answer.

3. Can a corporation simultaneously have satisfied customers and satisfied shareholders? Explain your answer.

4. How has the outlook for airline businesses changed in recent times?

_____
_____
_____
_____
_____
_____

IN THE NEWS: CUSTOMERS VS SUPPLIERS

The corporation: Coles, a publicly listed ASX company[2]

The context:

> The federal Agriculture Minister has taken aim at Coles and Aldi for keeping their cut-price milk lines and urging customers to boycott them. David Littleproud has accused Coles of 'pretending' to be a decent corporate citizen and Aldi of 'hiding under the stairs' after they failed to follow Woolworths and help dairy farmers by no longer selling milk at $1 a litre. He said dairy farmers struggling with drought needed an end to the '$1 milk disaster,' a price war that began eight years ago and has been blamed for sending some farmers to the wall.

> Steven Cain, CEO of Coles, said:

> We are one of the main supporters of farmers ... but it is important we don't disadvantage Coles's customers. All milk brands should be covered and all retailers should participate in lifting prices. If that happens, we'd be very happy to participate in that scheme.

> Oliver Bongardt, Managing Director of Aldi (an unlisted company), said:

> Aldi can best support the long-term sustainability of the dairy industry by accepting price increases from milk processors that reflect difficult market conditions, thereby facilitating its milk processors to pay sustainable prices to dairy farmers.

> It was noted that: 'Aldi said low prices were a core promise to its customers and gave no indication that its pricing policy would change.'

Issues:

Note the various strategies deployed by Coles and Aldi, namely:

- Coles' approach of provisional support based on everyone across the industry doing the same thing. This seeks an industry-wide approach, where there is no 'first mover' or no moral imperative to provide leadership on the issue.
- Aldi's approach focuses on the supply chain. It seeks to suggest that the critical link in the milk price supply chain is from the farmer to the processor. The other links between the wholesaler to the retailer (Aldi) are by this argument removed from and not related to farm gate price. That is, the critical price point is lower down the supply chain between the farmer and the processor.

---

2   Richard Ferguson, 'Woolies' rivals creamed on $1 milk', *The Australian*, 20 February 2019, 21.

QUESTIONS

5. How reasonable are these types of responses to the predicament faced by dairy farmers?

6. How can suppliers, such as dairy farmers, be heard above the central and dominant interests of shareholders and customers?

WORKBOOK CHAPTER 1 REVIEW

An illustrative summary of the key points

Figure 1.27 contextualises the study of corporate law within law school, and the pathway to legal admission, while Fig 1.28 provides a link between the topics covered, and their relationship to each other—hence, they form the basis of foundation issues providing an overview of corporate law.

FIGURE 1.27 Corporate law contextualised

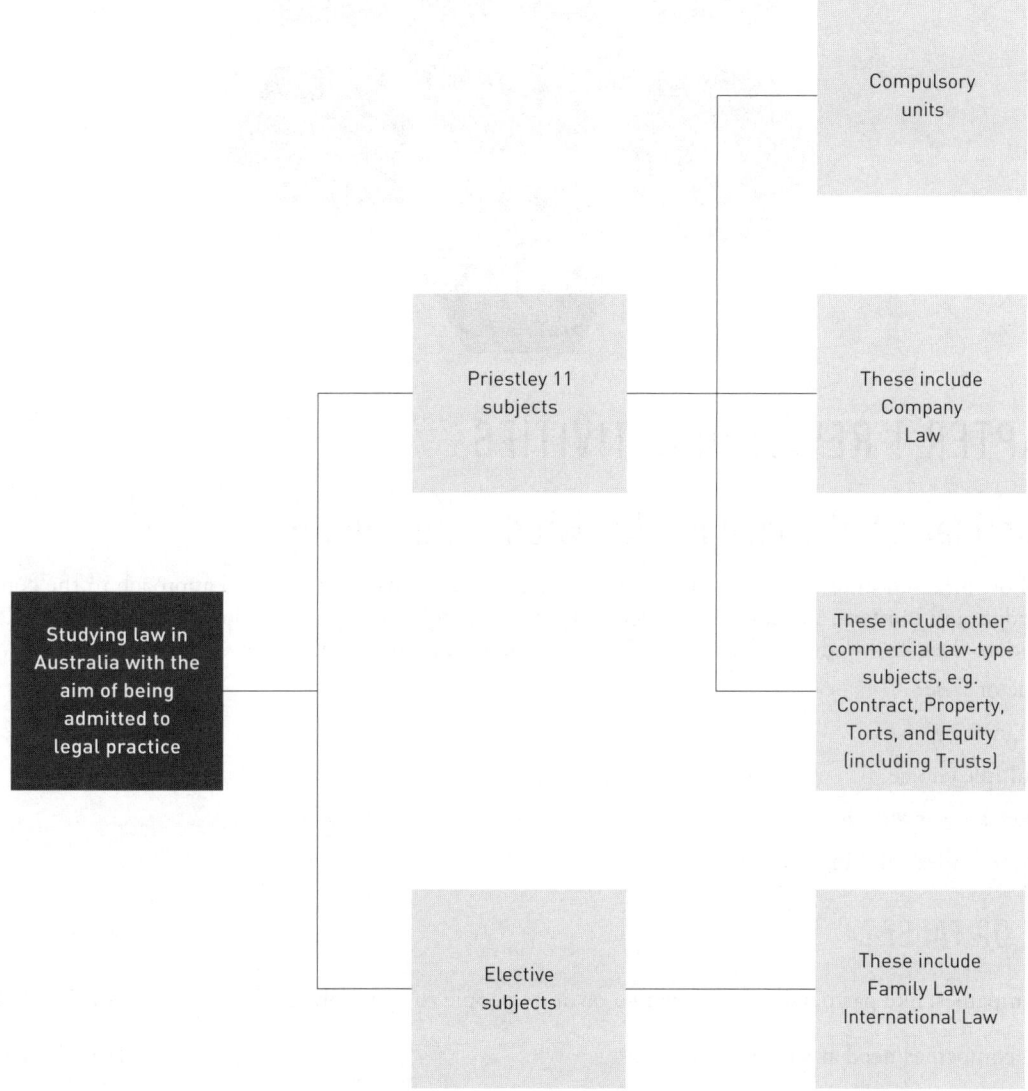

FIGURE 1.28 The topics covered, and their relationship to each other

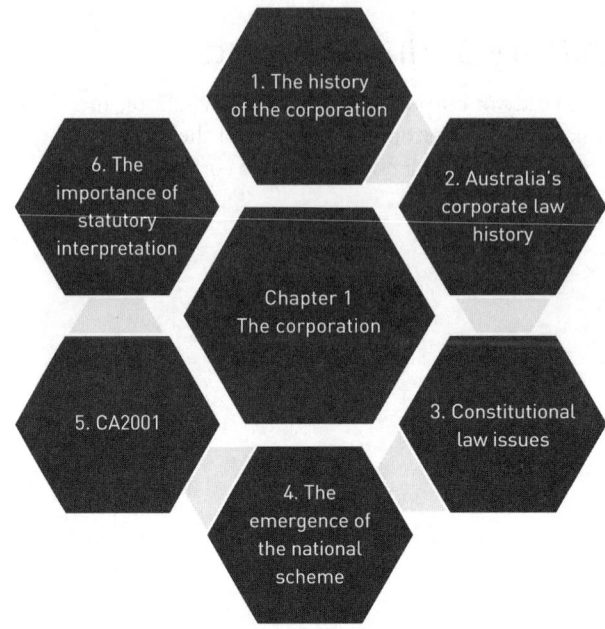

CHAPTER 1 REVISION ACTIVITIES

Consolidation of concepts, knowledge and content

The following revision resources are aimed at providing students with a scaffolded approach to the concepts, knowledge and content. Assessing knowledge by this scaffolded approach allows students to build and consolidate their knowledge. It focuses, in each chapter, on several discrete tasks:

- True or false?
- Fill in the gaps
- Multiple choice
- Short answer questions
- Higher order thinking activities.

TRUE OR FALSE?

1. Companies, like partnerships, require two or more people to be involved.   True ☐ False ☐
2. All companies need at least two directors.   True ☐ False ☐
3. The Constitution contains a power giving the Commonwealth oversight of corporations.   True ☐ False ☐
4. The states and territories could, in theory, end the CA2001.   True ☐ False ☐

5. The CA2001 is a code doing away with the need for general or common law as regards corporations. True ☐ False ☐

FILL IN THE GAPS

1. The relevant provision of the Australian Constitution dealing with the putative power of the Commonwealth regarding corporations is _____

2. The first case in the High Court testing the power of the Commonwealth to regulate companies was in _____

3. The case was called _____

4. The *Engineers' case* (1920) established the _____ type of interpretation as relevant to the Constitution.

5. The Mason High Court (1987–95) is known for adopting the _____ _____ approach to interpreting the Constitution.

6. The first Uniform Companies Legislation in Australia was adopted in _____

MULTIPLE CHOICE

1. ASIC stands for:
   A. Australian Shares, Investors and Corporations
   B. Association of Shareholders, Investors and Corporates
   C. Australian Securities and Investments Commission
   D. Australian Securities and Insurance Corporation

2. The cross-vesting scheme prior to 1990 failed because:
   A. The Commonwealth could not confer jurisdiction on state courts
   B. The states could not confer state jurisdiction on Commonwealth courts
   C. The Commonwealth did not have jurisdiction over corporations
   D. The states did not have immunity from Commonwealth law

3. The High Court in the *Incorporation case* (1990) held:
   A. The individual states could not incorporate corporations
   B. The Commonwealth did not have the power to provide for the incorporation of companies
   C. Only the territories could incorporate corporations
   D. Only the Commonwealth could incorporate corporations

4. The solution to the *Incorporation case* was:
   A. For the Commonwealth to 'go it alone'
   B. For the states to appeal to the Privy Council
   C. For the Australian Constitution to be amended to give the Commonwealth power
   D. For the Commonwealth to seek the cooperation of the states and to establish the Corporations Law scheme
5. COAG stands for:
   A. Corporations, Organisations and Government
   B. Commonwealth Organisation of Australian Government
   C. Council of Australian Governments
   D. Corporate Organisations Advisory Group

SHORT ANSWER QUESTIONS

1. What is the difference between a company and a corporation?

2. What does s 51 of the Australian Constitution provide for?

3. What does s 51(xx) specifically address?

4. What effect did the High Court's narrow interpretation of s 51(xx) have on the powers of the Commonwealth in relation to making laws in respect of corporations?

5. What effect did the *Uniform Companies Act 1961* (Cth) have?

6. What was the High Court's position as regards the corporations law power in the Australian Constitution as enunciated in *New South Wales v Commonwealth* ('*Incorporation case*') (1990)?

7. What important decision/agreement occurred in the year 2000 between the states and Northern Territory regarding corporations law in Australia?

Higher order thinking activities

EXPLANATORY NOTES TO HIGHER ORDER QUESTION

These types of essays reflect different types of student interests. Some students will be guided by process and substantive law. Other students may wish to explore historical, contextual or critical approaches to the law generally, and corporate law particularly. These questions should be useful exploration points, particularly as regards the latter type of approach.

ANALYTICAL OR ESSAY-TYPE QUESTIONS

Consider the following questions and provide detailed discussion and analysis.

TOPIC A

The history of Australian corporations law has been largely focused on issues of constitutional power. Discuss.

QUESTIONS

TOPIC B

Does corporations law necessarily have to choose between the interests of shareholders, customers and employees? Discuss.

CHAPTER 2

BUSINESS AND BUSINESS ENTITIES

Chapter synopsis and links to Textbook Chapter 2

This Workbook Chapter deals with six topics:

- 2.1 The basic elements of conducting business
- 2.2 The choice of business entities
- 2.3 The company as a business entity
- 2.4 Partnerships
- 2.5 'Not-for-profit' and 'for-purpose' entities
- 2.6 The role and rationale of business.

Each of these topics is constructively aligned with, and linked to, the same topics in Chapter 2 of the Textbook.

Chapter executive summary

This Chapter, and *Corporations Law: Concepts, Cases and Culture* generally, looks at the corporation in several different capacities:

- as one of the choices people can make in establishing a business; companies are one of several potential business organisations, entities or 'vehicles', along with partnerships and sole traders
- as a 'creature of statute', in particular by reference to the main legislation relevant to all Australian corporations: the CA2001
- in its practical operating context, subject to the relevant law being the CA2001 and the general or case law, and
- as a for-profit business, as opposed to a not-for-profit or a for-purpose organisation.

CHAPTER DIAGRAMMATIC OVERVIEW

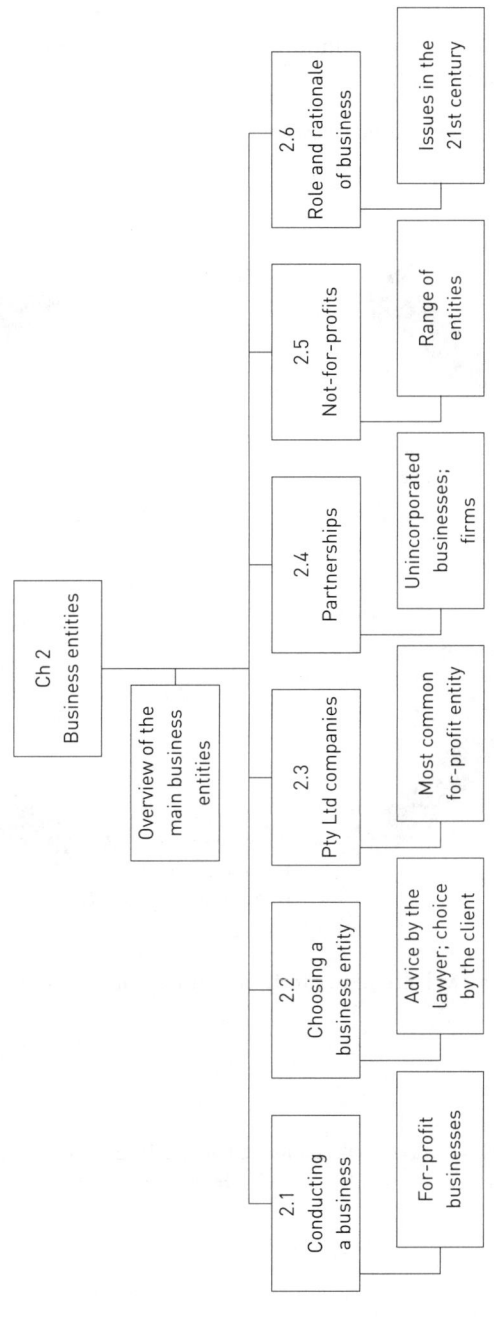

FIGURE 2.1 An overview of Chapter 2

2.1 THE BASIC ELEMENTS OF CONDUCTING BUSINESS

The elements of a business

There are several connected elements to running any type of business (whether for-profit or not). These include the elements set out in Fig 2.2.

FIGURE 2.2   The essential elements of a business

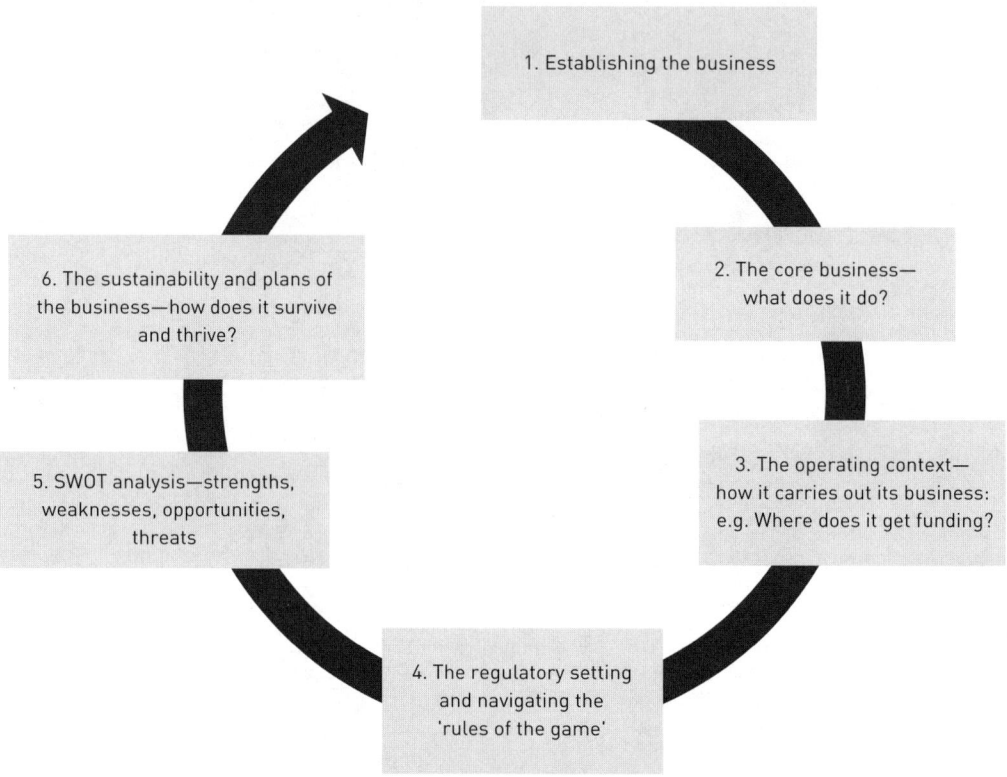

The Australian Government website refers to four primary business for-profit entities:[1]

- sole trader
- partnership
- company
- trust. This requires a trustee who controls an asset for the benefit of others (the beneficiaries). 'Trust' also refers to self-managed superannuation funds, which require a trustee.

---

1   https://register.business.gov.au/helpmedecide/businessstructure/.

The life-cycle of a business

Figure 2.3 illustrates the life-cycle of a business.

FIGURE 2.3   The four phases of the life-cycle of a corporation

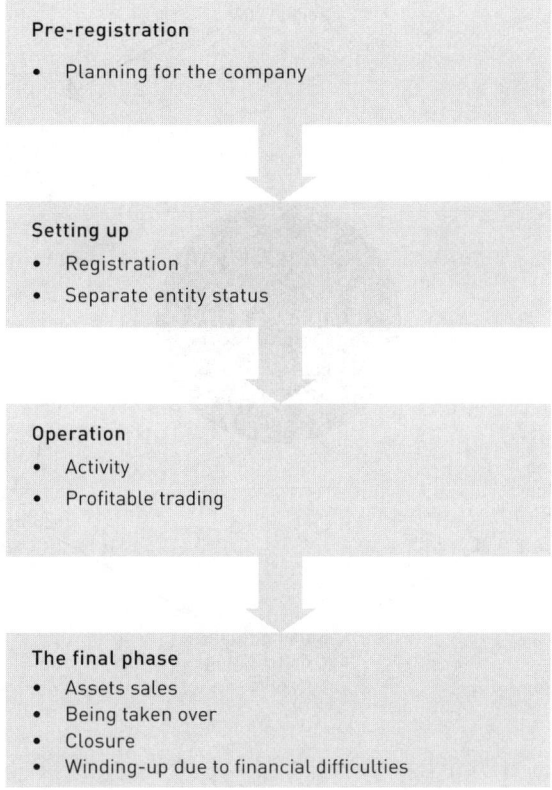

Business entities: the six main sets of issues

There are a cluster of issues common to business entities, irrespective of the business's aim, form, purpose or intent, as illustrated in Fig 2.4.

FIGURE 2.4 The six common areas of the work of businesses

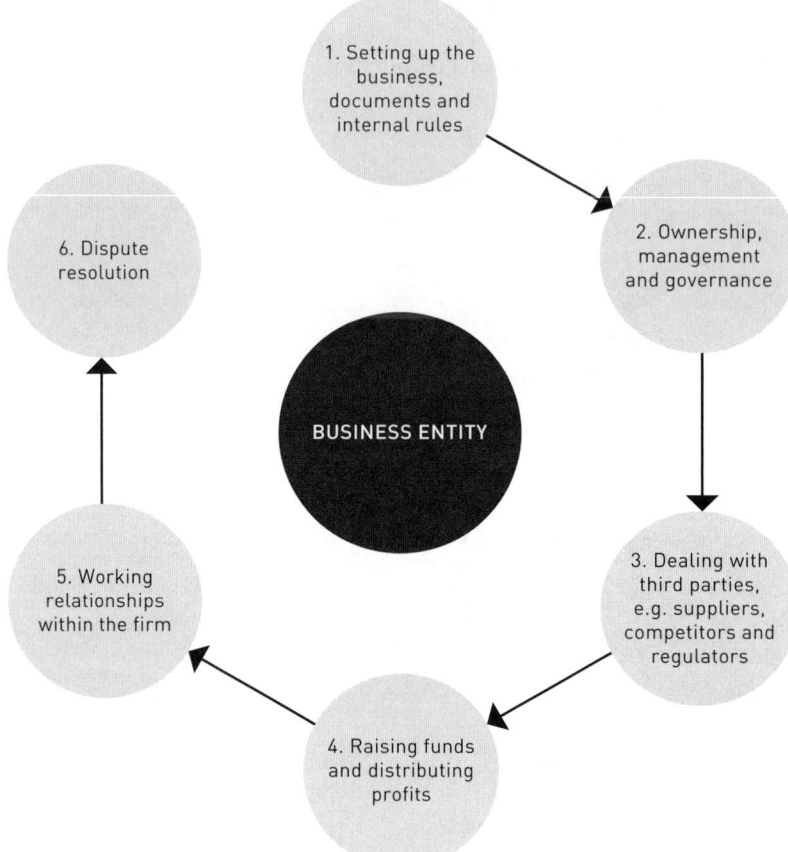

Business support: state and territory governments

Each of the six states and two territories provides government-based assistance for new business through specialised websites: see Table 2.1.

TABLE 2.1 The business support resources provided by state and territory governments

State or territory	Website name	Website address
ACT	Innovate, Industry and Investment	https://www.business.act.gov.au/
NSW	Small business	https://www.nsw.gov.au/working-and-business
NT	Start, Run and Grow a Business	https://nt.gov.au/industry/start-run-and-grow-a-business
Qld	Business Queensland	https://www.business.qld.gov.au/
SA	Business SA	https://www.business-sa.com/
Tas	Business Tasmania	https://www.business.tas.gov.au/

State or territory	Website name	Website address
Vic	Business Victoria	https://www.business.vic.gov.au/
WA	Business Support	https://www.wa.gov.au/service/business-support

> **Activity 2.1**
> Go online to look at the government business website relevant to your state or territory.

2.2 THE CHOICE OF BUSINESS ENTITIES

The array of business entities appears at first impression to be complex and potentially confusing. The first categorisation is to work out whether the business in question has profit in mind, or whether it is (for example) a community-minded venture, which lends itself to a not-for-profit (NFP) entity.

The range of business entities

While *Corporations Law: Concepts, Cases and Culture* focuses on the corporate entity and the company as a way of conducting business, the wider context is that there are a range of potential business entities to choose from. Entities can also be referred to as 'organisations', 'vehicles', 'structures', and the like. The range of business entities can be illustrated as shown in Fig 2.5.

FIGURE 2.5 The range of business entities divides between the corporate form and the non-corporate form

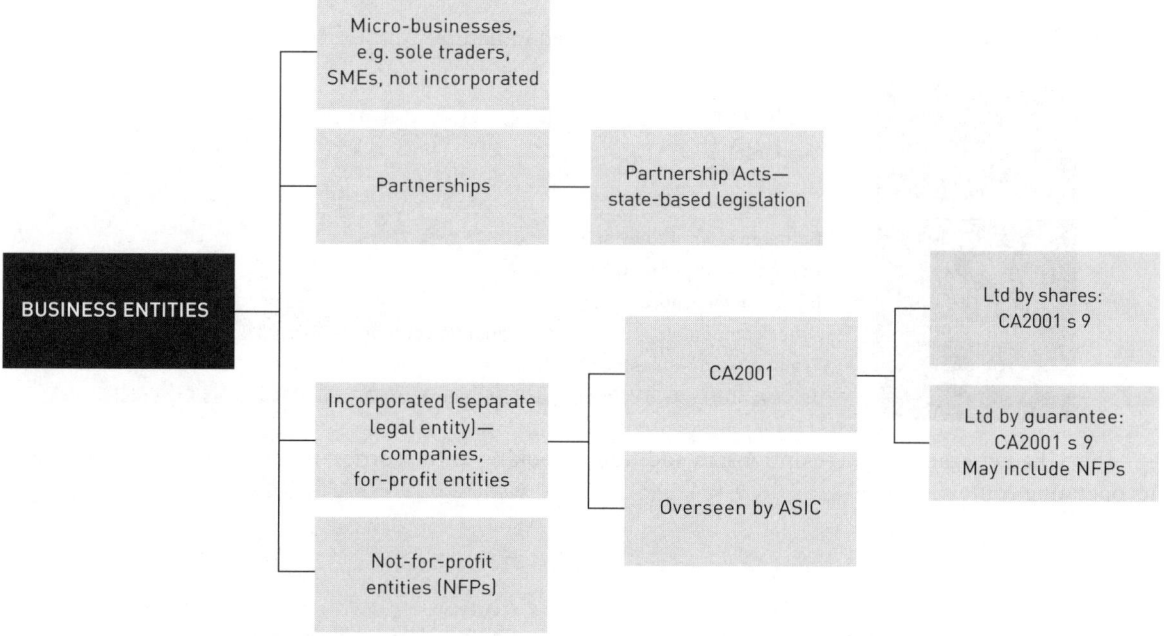

For-profit and NFP entities

As noted, there are two basic delineations for businesses. The first involves the basic aim or foundational idea. Are they designed to make a profit that is returned to owners, or are they designed as NFP entities that reinvest funds into the cause or enterprise? (NFPs are discussed in Section 2.5 below.)

FIGURE 2.6   Business entities are either for-profit or NFP

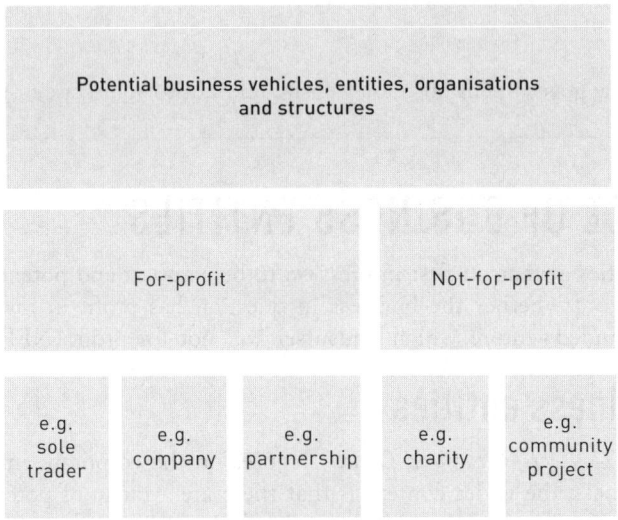

Incorporated and unincorporated entities

The second basic categorisation for a business is whether it is incorporated or not.

FIGURE 2.7   Businesses as incorporated or unincorporated in nature

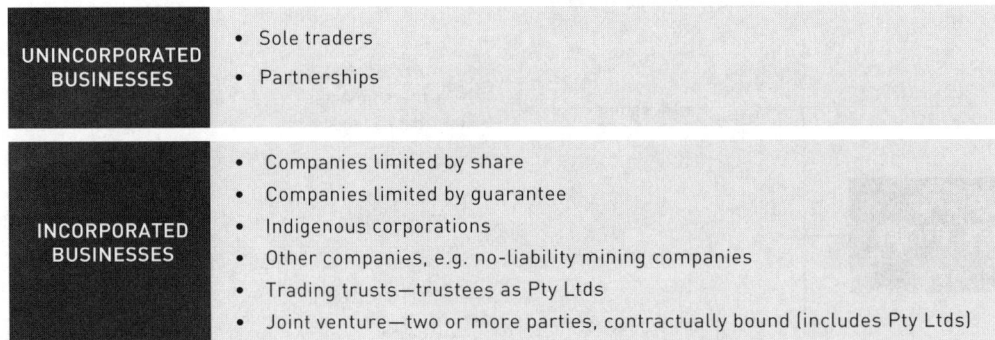

This Chapter examines these options, in addition to looking at the corporation as a creature of statute in its operating context.

> **Activity 2.2**
>
> Identify the range of business entities, whether for-profit, NFP or for-purpose.
>
> _____
> _____
> _____
> _____
> _____
> _____
> _____

2.3 THE COMPANY AS A BUSINESS ENTITY

As we saw in Chapter 1, the narrative of Australian corporate law (historical and ongoing) has several intersecting elements. The four main elements are shown in Fig 2.8.

FIGURE 2.8 The main elements informing the development of Australian corporate law

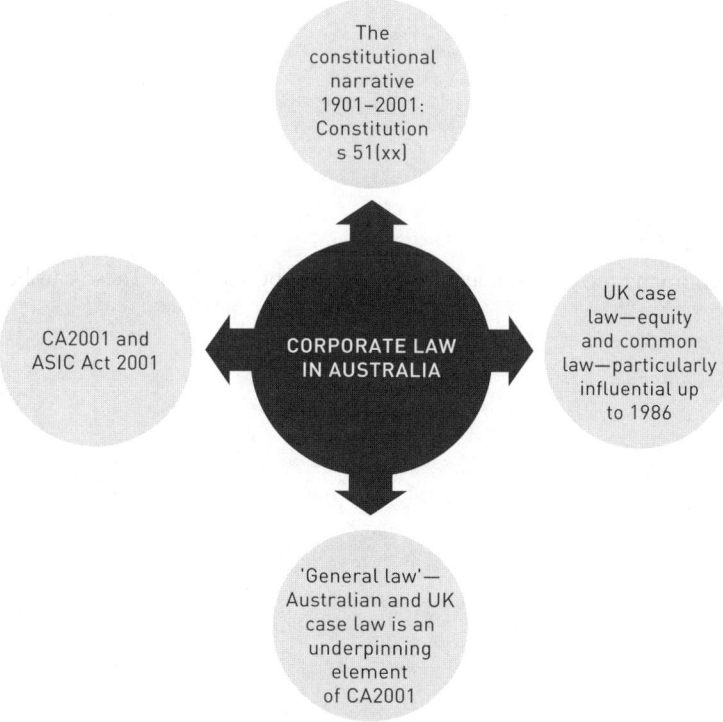

Companies—by size and development

Any 'business' in the generic sense—whether incorporated or not, or for-profit or not—shares common timelines, regarding planning, setting up, trading and ending: see Fig 2.3 above.

Another narrative element is that a company may go through several growth and development phases, from a very small start. Figure 2.9 illustrates the possible steps, but each corporation will have its own circumstances and influences on its growth trajectory.

FIGURE 2.9 Growth and development phases

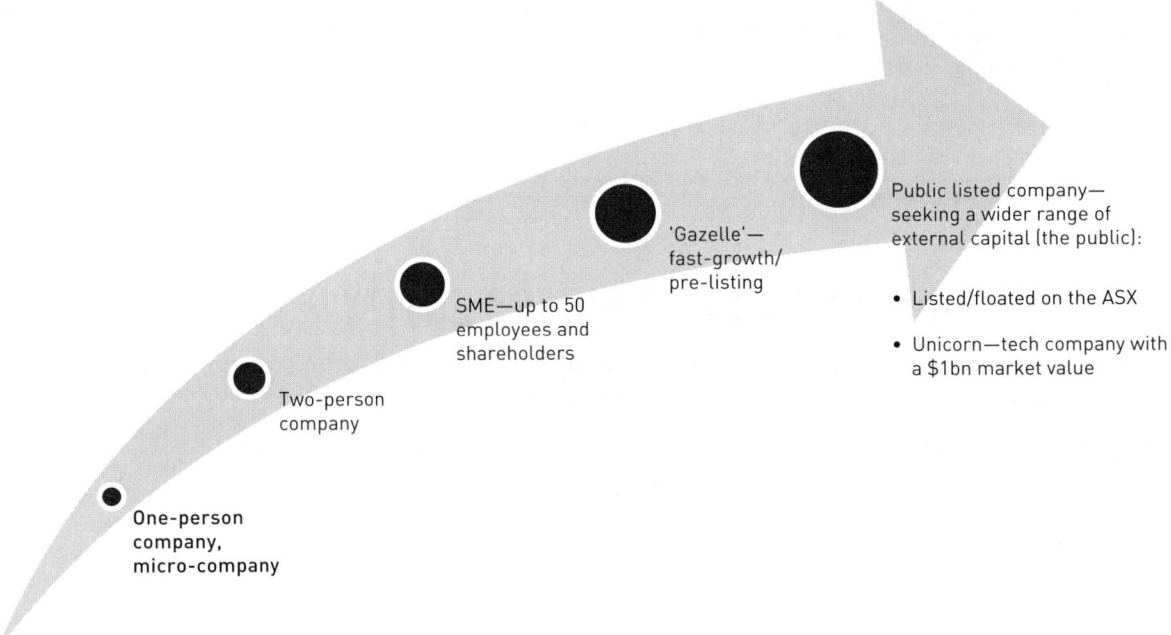

Companies by type

The various types of company in Australia are referred to in the CA2001. These can be set out as shown in Fig 2.10.

FIGURE 2.10   The basic classification of companies under the CA2001

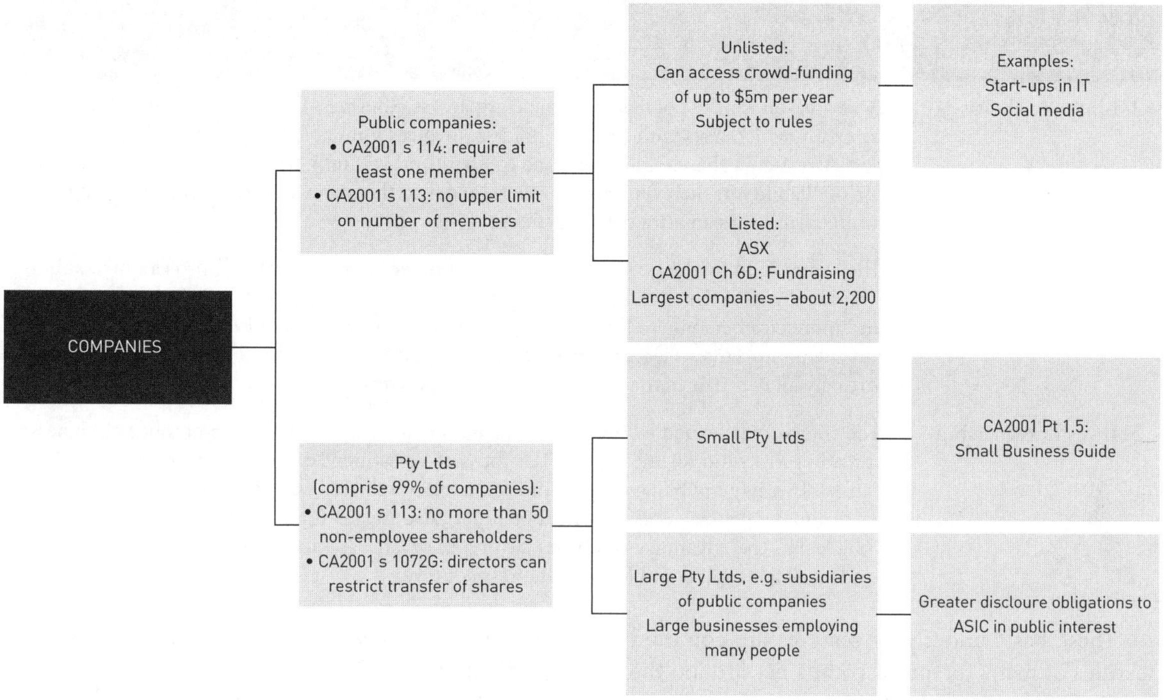

```
COMPANIES
├── Public companies:
│   • CA2001 s 114: require at least one member
│   • CA2001 s 113: no upper limit on number of members
│   ├── Unlisted:
│   │   Can access crowd-funding of up to $5m per year
│   │   Subject to rules
│   │   └── Examples: Start-ups in IT, Social media
│   └── Listed:
│       ASX
│       CA2001 Ch 6D: Fundraising
│       Largest companies—about 2,200
└── Pty Ltds (comprise 99% of companies):
    • CA2001 s 113: no more than 50 non-employee shareholders
    • CA2001 s 1072G: directors can restrict transfer of shares
    ├── Small Pty Ltds
    │   └── CA2001 Pt 1.5: Small Business Guide
    └── Large Pty Ltds, e.g. subsidiaries of public companies
        Large businesses employing many people
        └── Greater disclosure obligations to ASIC in public interest
```

The basic elements of the corporation

Corporations are very common across the world, especially in legally advanced and highly regulated economies such as Australia, the UK, New Zealand and the USA. Corporations have been studied at both national and international level. At an international level, five particular characteristics or elements have been found to be present across many jurisdictions adopting corporate laws.[2]

TABLE 2.2   The five irreducible elements of a corporation

The relevant element of the corporation	Explanatory notes
1. Legal personality	The company is a legal entity in its own right with powers equivalent to an adult person. As such, the company has the power to enter contracts, to be bound by promises, and to assume liability. This breadth of legal agency gives the company the ability to grow as a business entity. The corporation is a legal construct (and a 'creature of statute') or vehicle that acts through and by its directors—hence Point 2 below.
2. Delegated management under a board structure	As noted above at Point 1, the company as an artificial legal entity needs to be activated by people. Key to this is the board of directors. The board has responsibility for the legal and ethical acts of the company.

---

2   Reinier R Kraakman, Paul Davies, Henry Hansmann, Gerard Hertig, Klaus J Hopt, Hideki Kanda and Edward B Rock, *The Anatomy of Corporate Law: A Comparative and Functional Approach*, OUP, 2005.

TABLE 2.2 The five irreducible elements of a corporation (continued)

The relevant element of the corporation	Explanatory notes
3. Limited liability	A key reason for the popularity of the company as a business entity is that ownership of the company, which rests with the shareholders, involves limited liability on their individual part. That is, if a shareholder owns one $1 share and it is fully paid, the shareholder has no further liability in their capacity as a shareholder to the company. Ownership coupled with limited liability is an attractive investment option for the would-be investor.
4. Transferable shares	The shares held by the owner/member/shareholder are transferable. This is a quick and simple process if the shares are publicly tradable on the stock exchange. It may be slower and more cumbersome to find a buyer and agree a price in a small Pty Ltd company, but the point remains—it is a theoretical possibility and a practical feature common to virtually all companies that the shares can be transferred.
5. Investor ownership	The company is owned by investors. This is a device for increasing the number of owners, spreading risk, and raising a particular form of investment capital—in this case, share capital. In a large public company, many shareholders may want to invest. This affords a great many people access to membership. It also means the company, as a business vehicle, has the advantage of raising two types of capital—from shareholders, and from lenders; share capital and loan capital respectively.

These basic underlying features are common to Australian companies and are a common set of basic features of many for-profit companies around the world, particularly in G20 economies.

These links between the five elements can be illustrated as shown in Fig 2.11.

FIGURE 2.11 The core elements of corporations around the world

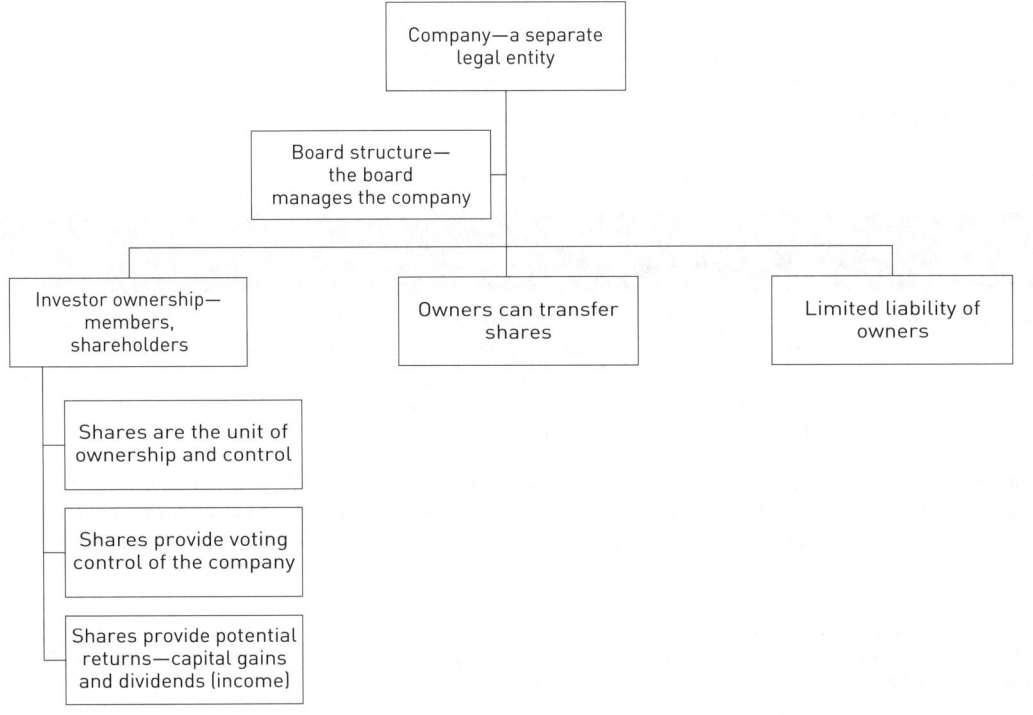

Figure 2.12 compares the sole trader and the small company.

FIGURE 2.12   Comparing sole traders with small Pty Ltd companies

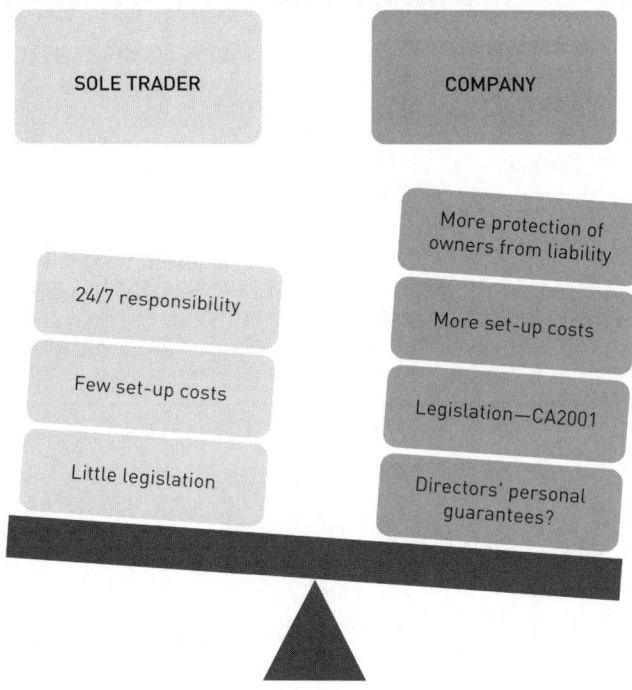

THE COMPANY AS A SEPARATE ENTITY: RELEVANT CASE LAW

While we regard the principle of the company as a separate legal entity from *Salomon's case* as established, there were cases following it that clarified its reach and scope.

TABLE 2.3   Case law dealing with the separate entity status of the company

Year	Case	Principle
1897	*Salomon's case* (House of Lords)	Mr Salomon was a dominant shareholder, having sold his business to the newly formed company. He was held by the Court to be separate from the company. The Court affirmed his status as a creditor of the company. As a secured creditor, the liquidator was required to pay him ahead of unsecured creditors.
1961	*Lee v Lee's Air Farming Ltd* (UK Privy Council, on appeal from New Zealand)	

TABLE 2.3 Case law dealing with the separate entity status of the company (continued)

Year	Case	Principle

Activity 2.3

Fill in the gap in Table 2.3.

What other cases would you add? List these below, together with a summary of the principles in each.

_____
_____
_____
_____
_____
_____
_____
_____
_____
_____
_____
_____
_____
_____
_____
_____

2.4 PARTNERSHIPS

The state and territory Partnership Acts are all based, in many of their essential terms, on the originary UK *Partnership Act 1890*.

TABLE 2.4 The state and territory Partnership Acts

State or territory	Relevant Partnership Act
ACT	*Partnership Act 1963*
NSW	*Partnership Act 1892*
NT	*Partnership Act 1997*
Qld	*Partnership Act 1891*
SA	*Partnership Act 1891*
Tas	*Partnership Act 1891*
Vic	*Partnership Act 1958*
WA	*Partnership Act 1995*

Partnership size and scale in Australia

A key limitation on partnerships is scale—they can only grow so far and so fast. The number of partners is limited. In contrast, a big corporation like the Commonwealth Bank of Australia (CBA) has in excess of 800,000 shareholders.

The two basic types of partnerships are shown in Fig 2.13.

FIGURE 2.13 The contrast between the potential size and scale of 'general' as opposed to 'professional' partnerships

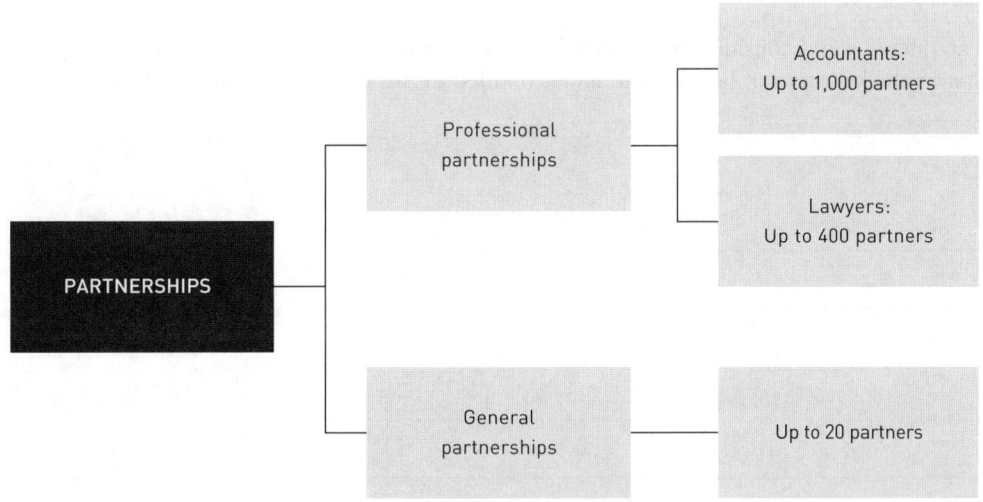

A partnership becoming a company

Entities can change their basic structure if there is sufficient agreement to do so. This depends on the entity's internal rules and any regulatory oversight relevant to the entity. In the case of a partnership, it is a fiduciary relationship; converting it to a company may have an impact on later rights, liabilities, and the resolution of disputes. This will depend on the particular facts, circumstances and context. The previous structure of the partnership may be relevant to settling disputes.

FIGURE 2.14   A partnership converting to a company structure

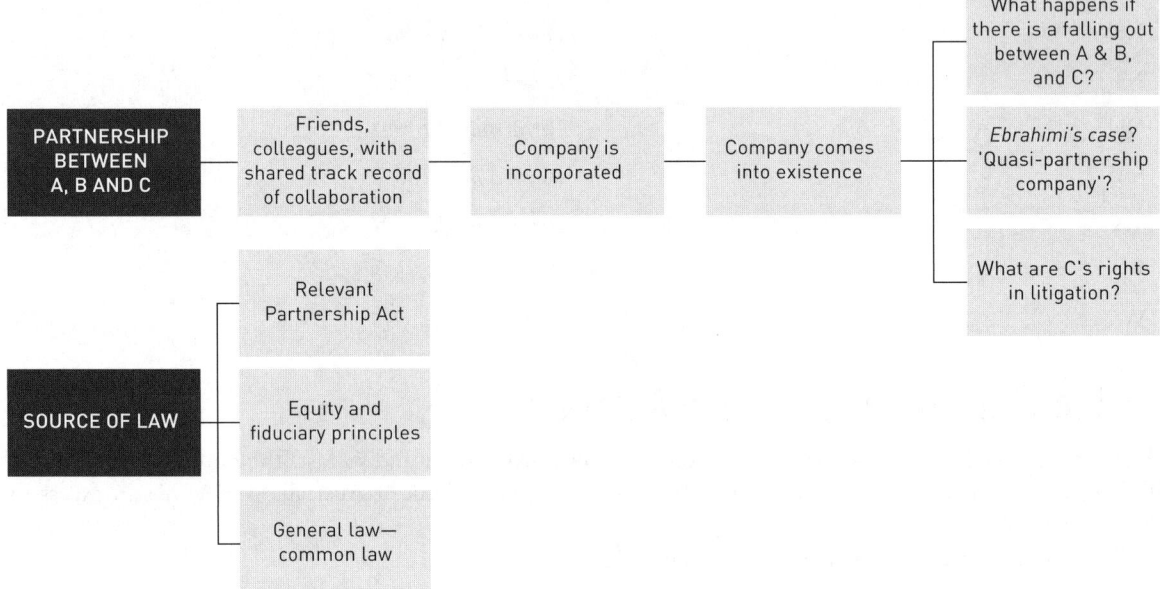

Activity 2.4

Look at Table 2.4 and consider the Partnership Act relevant to your home state or territory. What were the key steps or background issues that led to the Act coming into existence?

_____
_____
_____
_____
_____
_____
_____
_____

Figure 2.15 illustrates the transfer of ownership assets in the various business entities, ranging from 1 (relatively easy) to 4 (more complex with more obstacles). Partnerships have significant gateways and hurdles to effecting the sale.

FIGURE 2.15   Transfer of ownership assets in the various business entities

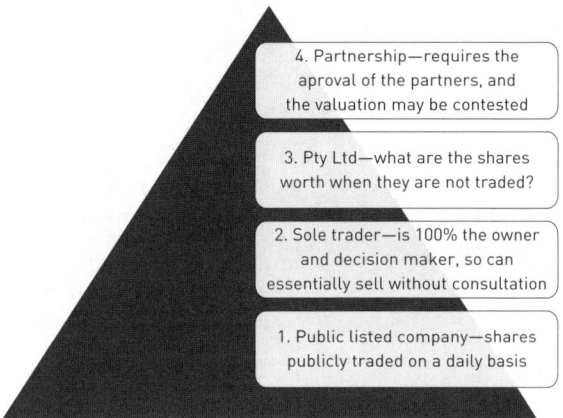

As with any classification system of business entities, there are some hybrid entities, including:

- limited partnerships, which provide a mechanism of limited liability for nominated partners on the basis that one or more partners bears the usual unlimited liability of a partner, and
- quasi-partnership companies, which are businesses displaying a particular history and two time phases: the first being unincorporated, and the second being incorporated. Quasi-partnerships were originally set up as partnerships and, given this structure, are 'high trust' and fiduciary as between the participants. Often, the issue for the courts to determine is: What are the remnant effects of the earlier unincorporated phase on the later incorporated entity?

FIGURE 2.16   Hybrid businesses feature elements of incorporated and unincorporated businesses

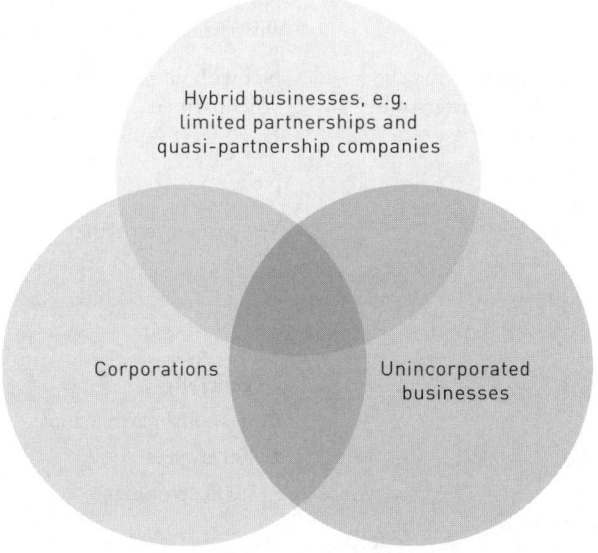

Table 2.5 compares the key features of the three main start-up, for-profit entities.

TABLE 2.5 Comparing sole traders, partnerships and companies

Comparative issue	Sole trader	Partnership	Company
Registration process	No	No	Yes, incorporation is confirmed by ASIC with the certificate of registration
Specialist regulator	No	No	Yes, ASIC
Comprehensive legislation	No	No, the Partnership Acts are limited in nature	Yes, CA2001
National coverage rules apply	No	No, each state and territory has its own Partnership Act	Yes, CA2001
Separate legal personality	No	No	Yes
Corporate veil	No	No	Yes
Necessity of having a constitution or internal rules	No	A commercial necessity, given the limitations of the Partnership Acts	Usually not: see s 134 of the CA2001; replaceable rules may be used
Might the entity be confused with another type of entity?	No, a one-person business is 'all risk' and 'all reward'	Perhaps, it may be a joint venture/contractual relationship as opposed to a fiduciary relationship	No, it is an incorporated business
Delegated management under a board structure	No	No, but there may be managing partner, e.g. in a law firm	Yes
Limited liability	No	No, but also depends on any partnership agreement	Yes
Transferable shares	The business may be sold or transferred by the owner	Not without permission of other partners	Yes
Investor ownership	No	No	Yes
Fiduciary duties within the entity	No	Yes, partner to partner	Yes, director to company
Minimum number of owners	1	2	1
Scale: maximum number of members	1	20 generally Professional partnerships: • 400 lawyers • 1,000 accountants	For a Pty Ltd: 50 non-employee shareholders For a public company: no limit

Comparative issue	Sole trader	Partnership	Company
Basic tax arrangements	The sole trader pays tax as an individual	Partners pay tax as individuals based on the consolidated partnership tax return. The individual returns align with the partnership return (note the partnership is not a separate entity; this is just for administration of tax purposes).	The company pays corporate tax on profits

The relative position of partnerships and Pty Ltds in relation to the adoption of internal rules are shown in Fig 2.17. The internal rules for companies are discussed in Chapter 4.

FIGURE 2.17   Internal rules

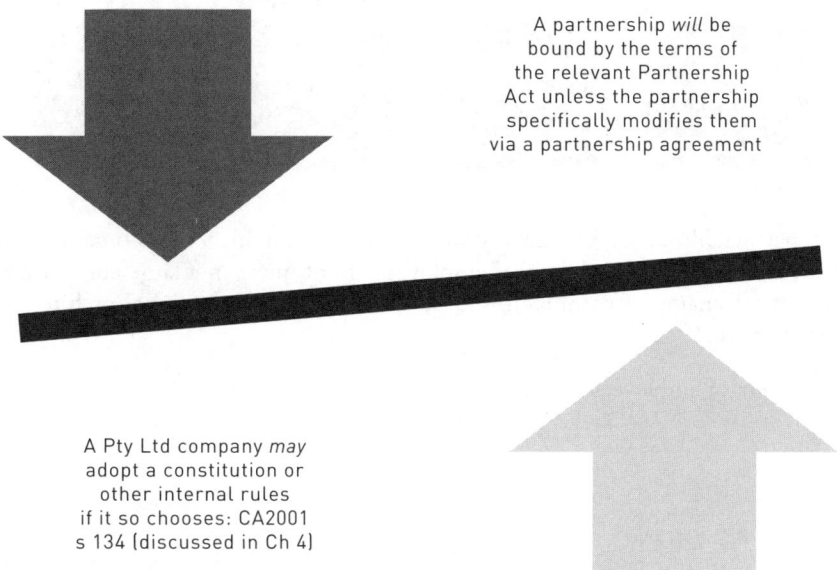

Professional partnerships like law firms are essentially flat structures with teams coalesced around partner expertise. For example, the firm may have a managing partner, E. The usual model of management adopted by law firms is to 'second' the managing partner from within the ranks of the partnership. That is, managing partner E is shifted away from the partnership's fee-earning function and their own client base to take on the management role for a limited time period.

FIGURE 2.18   The flat structure of a professional partnership—comprised of multiple, mini-teams with partners at the fulcrum of each

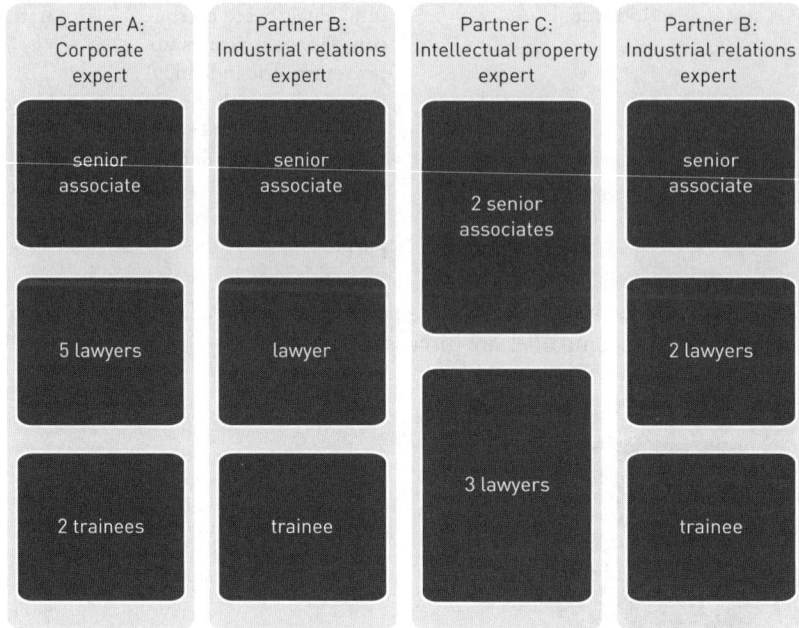

By contrast to partnerships, a large company will be more hierarchical in its organisational structure, as shown in Fig 2.19. There may be five 'layers' of employees, if not more, in a large company. Such businesses typically exhibit vertical chains of command and authority. This organisational architecture makes them distinct from partnerships.

FIGURE 2.19   The 'layers' of employees in a large company

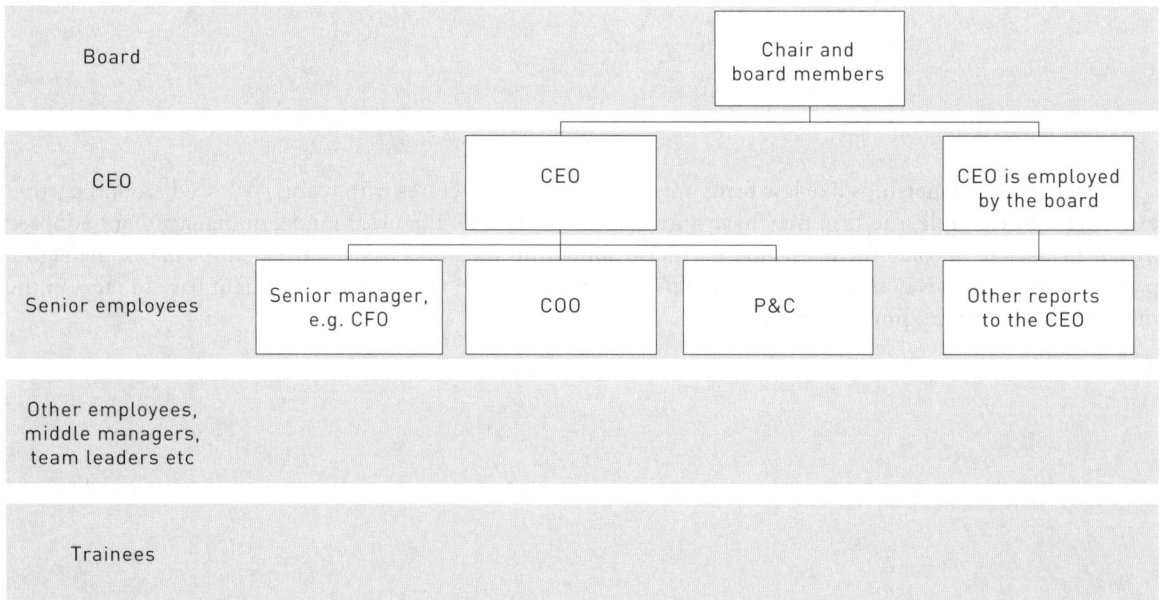

Table 2.6 compares the transactional nature of the main business entities other than companies.

TABLE 2.6 Partnerships and sole traders: a comparison of key transactions

Transaction	Sole trader	Partnership
Adding a new owner to the business	Will, by default, likely be treated as a partnership	Subject to the partnership agreement
Selling the business	A decision of the business owner	Depends on the Partnership Act or any agreement
Ceasing the business	A decision of the business owner	Depends on the Partnership Act or any agreement
Liability of the owners	The business owner has sole liability	Depends on the Partnership Act or any agreement
Separate entity status	No	No
Continuity: in perpetuity?	The business ceases on the death or bankruptcy of the owner or the sale of the business	Unless there is an agreement, the business can be terminated under the Partnership Act

Other ways of conducting a for-profit business

Other ways of conducting a for-profit business might variously involve specialist entities, including:

- trusts
- joint ventures, or
- syndicates.

It should be noted that these entities may still adopt/use some or all of the underlying business entities, or 'vehicles', in order to carry on the business; the deployment of the Pty Ltd company is particularly common.

TABLE 2.7 Comparing the key features of a joint venture with a trading trust

Feature	Joint venture	Trading trust
Type of arrangement	Contractual between the partners Usually a single enterprise, e.g. a mining operation	Comprises a trust arrangement Fiduciary as regards the role of the trustee The trustee is usually a company (Pty Ltd)
Owners	The contracting parties split the profits as per their contractual arrangement	Beneficiaries
Separate legal entity status	No, each party owns assets	The trust is not a separate entity
Parties	Two or more joint venture parties bound by contract	Settlor Trustee: legal owner Beneficiaries
Third party	Deals with each joint venture party	Deals with the trustee company

TABLE 2.7 Comparing the key features of a joint venture with a trading trust (continued)

Feature	Joint venture	Trading trust
Application of legal principles or rules	*United Dominions Corporation Ltd v Brian Pty Ltd* (1985)—a joint venture may, depending on the facts and circumstances, be found to be a partnership (and thereby bound by fiduciary principles)	Relevant state or territory Trustee Act: see Table 2.8

Trusts

The relevant state and territory Trustee Acts are set out in Table 2.8.

TABLE 2.8 The state and territory Trustee Acts

State or territory	Relevant Trustee Act
ACT	*Trustee Act 1925*
NSW	*Trustee Act 1925*
NT	*Trustee Act 1893*
Qld	*Trustee Act 1973*
SA	*Trustee Act 1936*
Tas	*Trustee Act 1898*
Vic	*Trustee Act 1958*
WA	*Trustee Act 1962*

Trust arrangements are popular trading and family devices. They potentially allow the splitting of income among the beneficiaries. The basic structure, subject to many permutations, is set out in Figs 2.20 and 2.21.

FIGURE 2.20 The basic structure of a trading or family trust

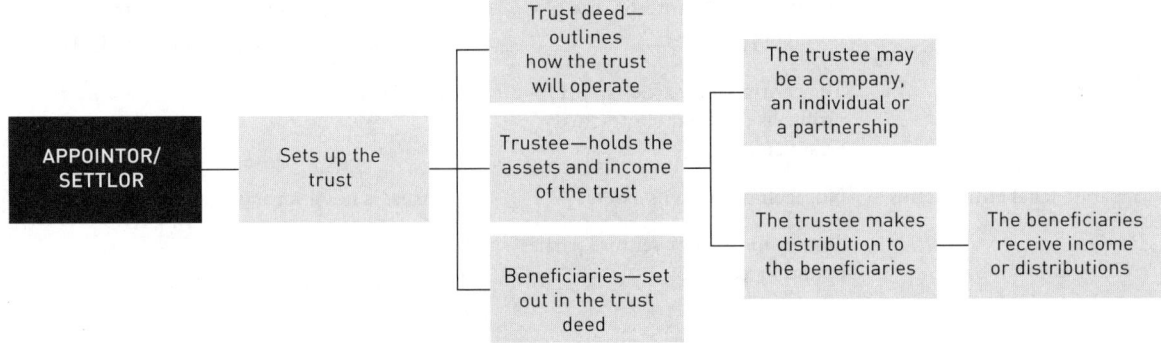

FIGURE 2.21   The participants in a trust

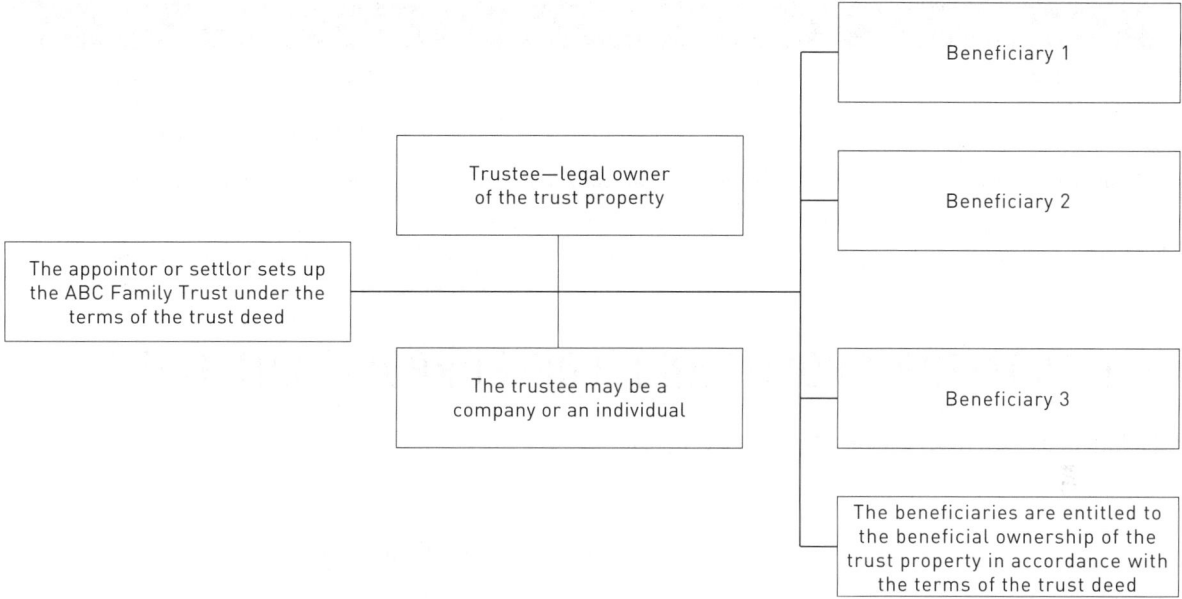

The trustee may be either an individual or a company. Each is bound by trust law to act in the best interests of the beneficiaries: see Fig 2.22.

FIGURE 2.22   The advantages and disadvantages of choosing a company or an individual as trustee

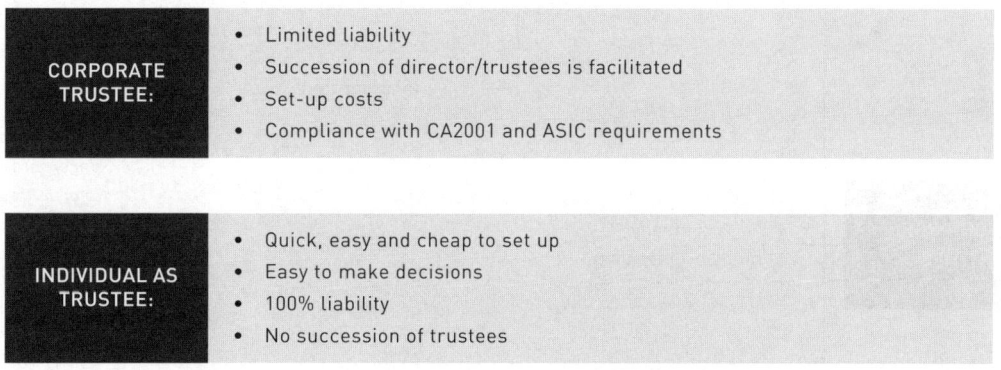

TABLE 2.9   A comparative analysis of the key features of entities other than companies

Relevant characteristics	Sole trader	Partnership
Is the entity established to make a profit?	Yes	Partnership Acts require the intention to make a profit
The basic structure	One-person business	May have an agreement; otherwise the relevant Partnership Act applies
Control of the business	Full-time or '24/7' control and responsibility	May have an agreement; otherwise the relevant Partnership Act applies

TABLE 2.9 A comparative analysis of the key features of entities other than companies (continued)

Relevant characteristics	Sole trader	Partnership
Financial returns and profit from the business	100%	Depends on the partnership agreement; otherwise the relevant Partnership Act applies
Main legislative oversight	*Business Names Registration Act 2011* (Cth)	Relevant Partnership Act
How is the business set up?	Informally, quickly	Can be quick; depends whether there is an agreement drafted

2.5 'NOT-FOR-PROFIT' AND 'FOR-PURPOSE' ENTITIES

FIGURE 2.23 An overview of NFP entities/associations

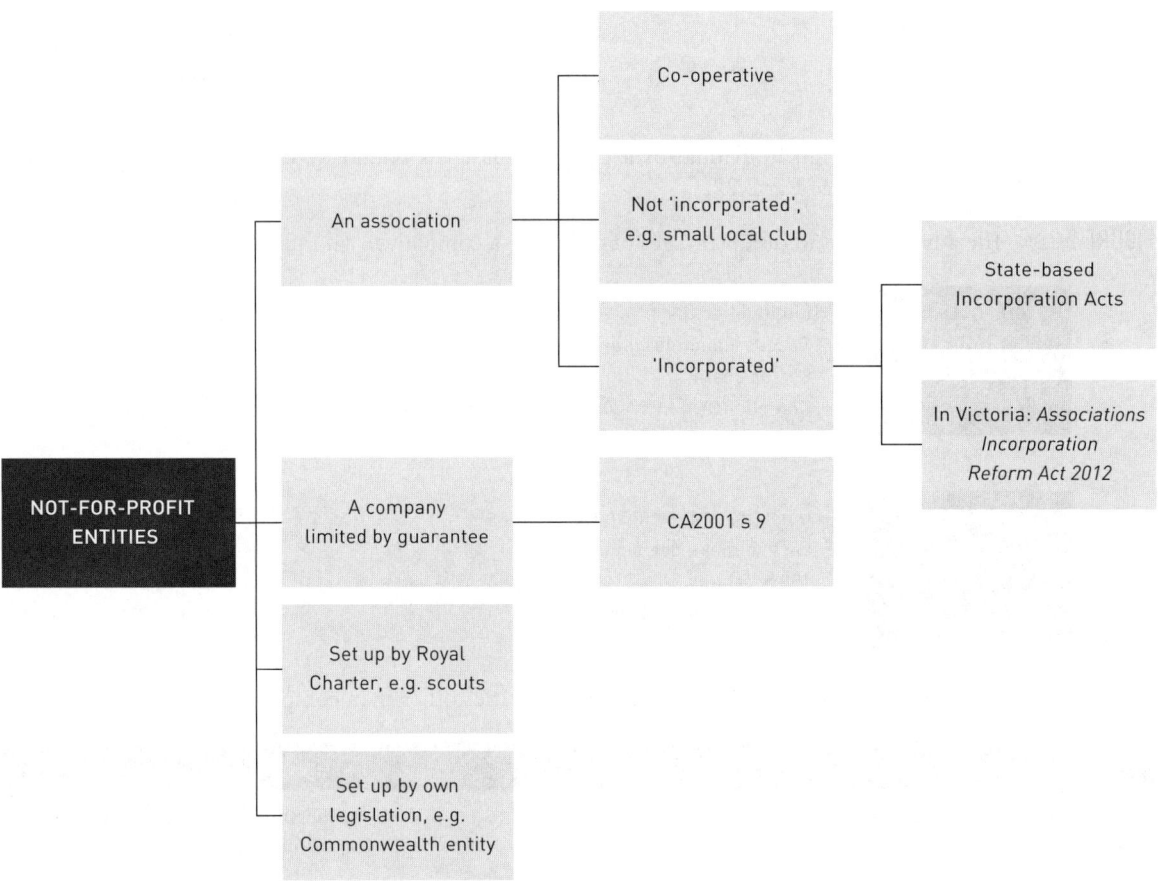

TABLE 2.10 A comparative analysis of the key features of associations

Relevant characteristics	Unincorporated association	Incorporated association
Is the entity established to make a profit?	No	No
The basic structure	Small, informal, community or other purpose—not for business purposes	Depends on the relevant state or territory legislation
Control of the business	The members collectively	The members collectively
Financial returns and profit from the business	Not set up for profit	Set up as a not-for-profit entity
Main legislative oversight		The relevant Act of the state or territory
How is the business set up?		Under the relevant Act of the state or territory

Relevant rules for NFPs include:
- their internal constitution, and
- if relevant, the Trustee Act (see Table 2.8).

NFPs are characterised by 'heterogeneity'—a range of differences in terms of size and scale, structure, focus etc. They vary greatly both in terms of size and type.

By contrast, companies, whatever their size and type, are governed by the CA2001 (although they may have limited replaceable/internal rules). Hence companies are characterised by 'homogeneity'.

Business entities by reference to legislation—whether NFP or for-profit

Figure 2.24 illustrates the centrifugal nature of statute in relation to business entities. Assume the business (entity, vehicle, organisation) is based in Victoria.

FIGURE 2.24 The centrifugal nature of statute in the contemporary consideration of business entities

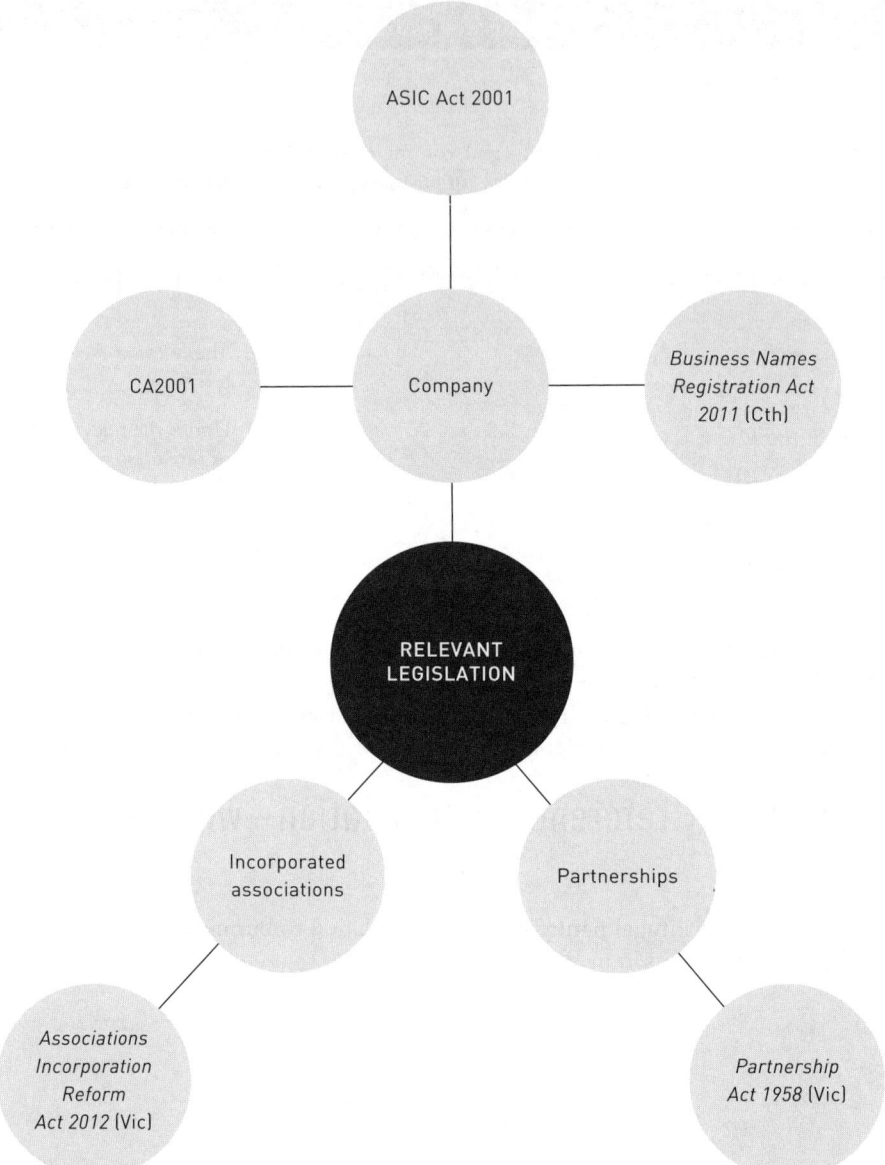

The Australian Charities and Not-for-profits Commission (ACNC)

The ACNC provides a registration system for NFPs. Entities do not have to register, but it is beneficial for profile building and tax status.[3]

---

3   https://www.acnc.gov.au/for-charities/start-charity/before-you-start-charity/.

FIGURE 2.25   The scope of the ACNC

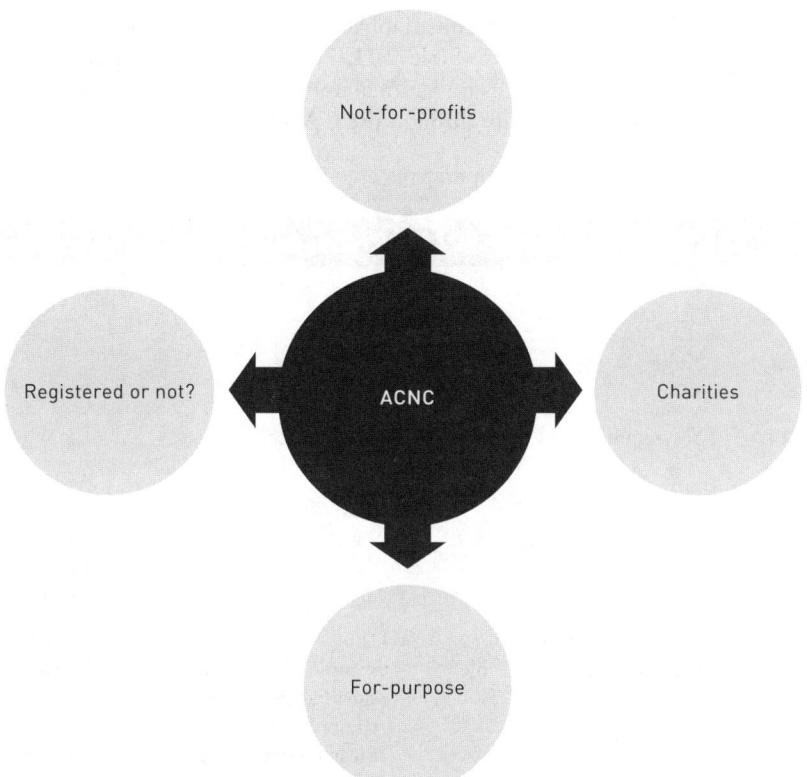

Activity 2.5

Investigate the ACNC website: https://www.acnc.gov.au/.

1. How many entities have registered?
   _____

2. What is the link between registration and charitable tax status?
   _____
   _____
   _____

Associations and co-operatives

Social and community-based organisations will invariably be NFP or 'for-purpose', and will therefore often be set up as associations or co-operatives: see Table 2.11. For these entities, there are state and territory provisions; so that—like partnerships—there is no national uniformity of approach. Companies, on the other hand, enjoy the benefits of national uniformity through the CA2001.

TABLE 2.11   Comparing associations and co-operatives

Feature	Association	Co-operative	Notes
Minimum number of members	5	5	
Ability to distribute profits to members	None	None	
Requirement to reinvest moneys into the organisation	Yes, required	Yes, required	
Tax treatment	Not a separate entity	Not a separate entity	May be given tax-exempt status if it is registered as a charity
Registration	See relevant Associations Incorporation Act (Table 2.12)	Using Victoria as an example, the co-operative registers with Corporate Affairs Victoria (CAV). If it is seeking to operate beyond the founding state, it must register with ASIC: see CA2001 s 9: 'Registrable Australian bodies' and s 57A: 'corporation' includes incorporated associations, co-operatives, building societies and credit unions	On 3 March 2014, the *Co-operatives Act 1996* (Vic) was replaced in Victoria by the Co-operatives National Law (CNL).

The relevant state and territory Associations Incorporation Acts and Co-operatives Acts are set out in Tables 2.12 and 2.13 respectively.

TABLE 2.12   The state and territory Associations Incorporation Acts

State or territory	Relevant Incorporated Associations Act
ACT	*Associations Incorporation Act 1991*
NSW	*Associations Incorporation Act 2009*
NT	*Associations Act 2003*
Qld	*Associations Incorporation Act 1981*
SA	*Associations Incorporation Act 1985*

State or territory	Relevant Incorporated Associations Act
Tas	*Associations Incorporation Act 1964*
Vic	*Associations Incorporation Reform Act 2012*
WA	*Associations Incorporation Act 2015*

TABLE 2.13 The state and territory Co-operatives Acts

State or territory	Relevant Co-operatives Act
ACT	*Co-operatives National Law (Tasmania) Act 2017*
NSW	*Co-operatives (Adoption of National Law) Act 2012* NSW is the lead or host jurisdiction of the CNL
NT	*Co-operatives Act 1997*
Qld	*Co-operatives Act 1997*
SA	*Co-operatives Act 1997*
Tas	*Co-operatives National Law (Tasmania) Act 2015*
Vic	*Co-operatives Act 1996*
WA	*Co-operatives Act 2009*

There is an emerging use of the term 'for-purpose' by both NFPs and for-profit businesses. This signals the need for businesses to satisfy a range of aims, objectives and stakeholders.

FIGURE 2.26 'For-purpose' entities

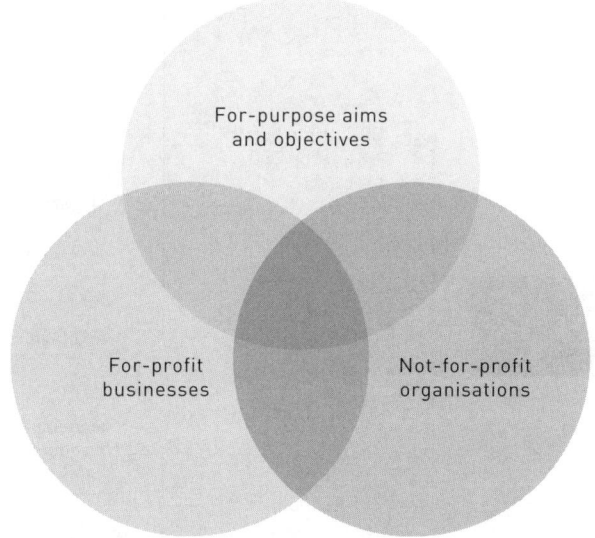

2.6 THE ROLE AND RATIONALE OF BUSINESS

The term 'business' is broad and amorphous. The aims of business are similarly multi-faceted. The main distinction is around the profit intention—to intend to make a profit or not. Hence, we can draw a broad and basic organisational distinction between 'for-profit' and NFP or 'for-purpose' entities: see Fig 2.27.

FIGURE 2.27   'For-purpose' and 'for-profit' entities

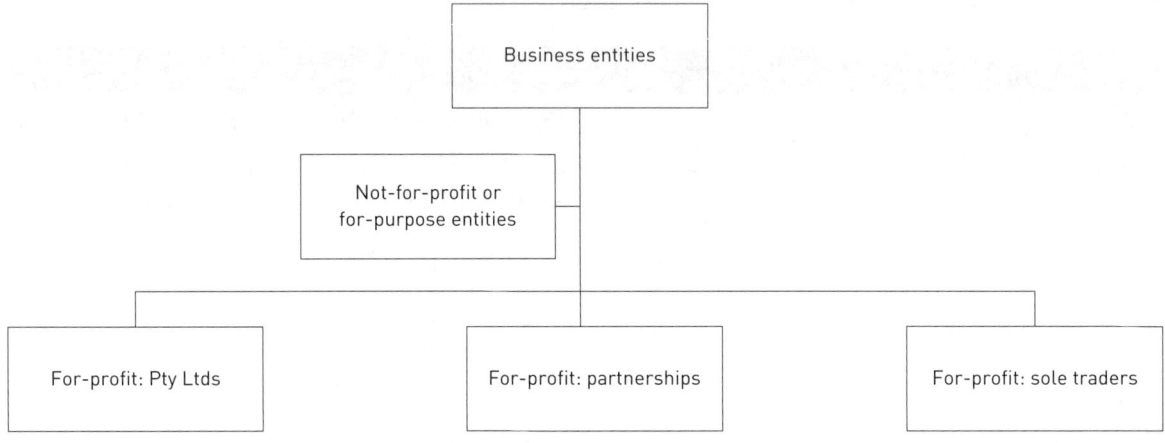

In broad terms, we can focus on two models: economic or CSR (corporate social responsibility): see Fig 2.28.

FIGURE 2.28   The aims and purpose of a business: economic or CSR?

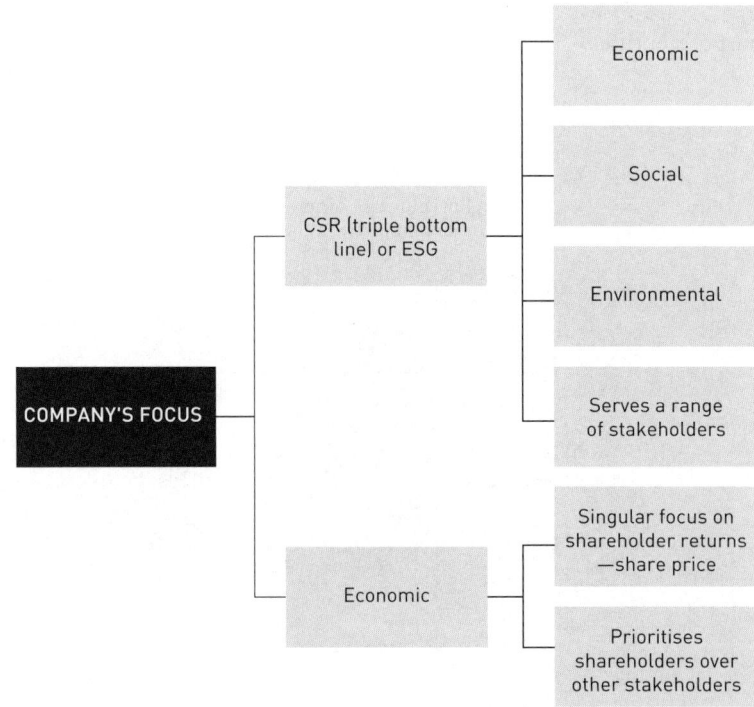

Activity 2.6

Read the following and then answer the questions below.

IN THE NEWS: RESTAURANT BUSINESSES

The brand name: George Calombaris

The context: Calombaris was well known as a judge on *MasterChef*, the reality television program. He had a chain of restaurants. In 2017, it became apparent that the restaurants were underpaying their staff. After an investigation, the total amount owed to staff was found to be in the vicinity of $8 million.

Issues: Calombaris had a series of companies, but the corporate brand and his personal brand are symbiotically linked. (This is similar to Jamie Oliver, the well-known UK-based chef, and his group of companies; Oliver's situation is referred to in Chapter 15 in terms of financial and solvency issues.)

QUESTIONS

1. What issues does Calombaris face in terms of his own business brand?

2. What issues did his group of companies face?

Activity 2.7

Read the following, conduct your own research, and then answer the questions below.

IN THE NEWS: PARTNERSHIPS INCORPORATING

The corporation: Slater and Gordon

The context: Slater and Gordon is a longstanding law firm and partnership.

Issues: Slater and Gordon listed on the stock exchange and expanded internationally by setting up in the UK.

QUESTIONS

1. What issues did Slater and Gordon face as a listed company?

2. What were the reasons behind the listed company's fall in share price?

WORKBOOK CHAPTER 2 REVIEW

An illustrative summary of the key points

Figure 2.29 contextualises for-profit and NFP entities, while Fig 2.30 provides a link between the topics covered, and their relationship to each other—hence, they form the basis of foundation issues relevant to for-profit entities such as the corporation.

FIGURE 2.29   For-profit and NFP entities contextualised

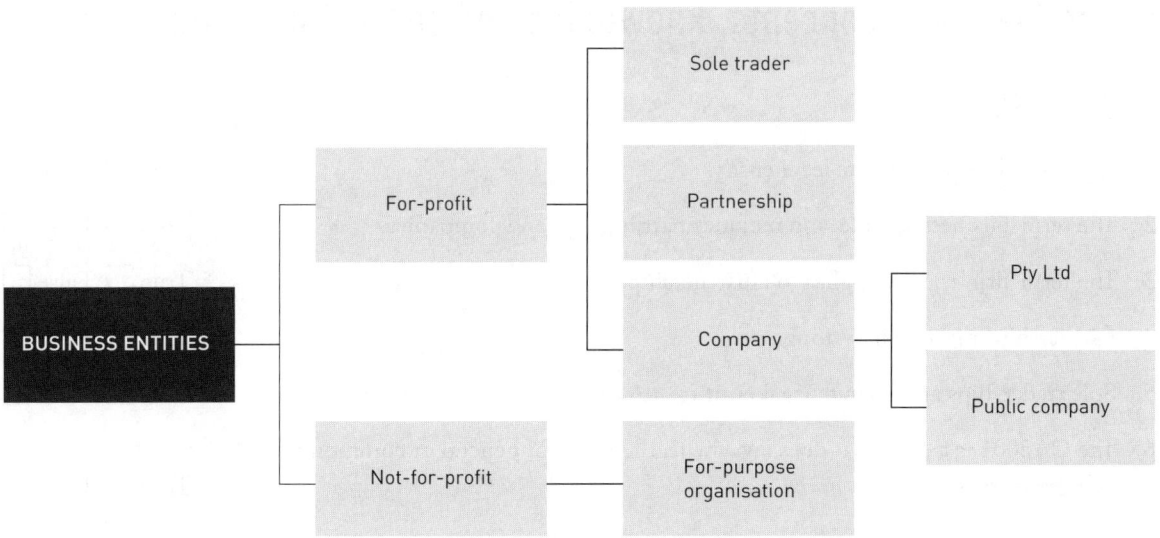

FIGURE 2.30 The topics covered, and their relationship to each other

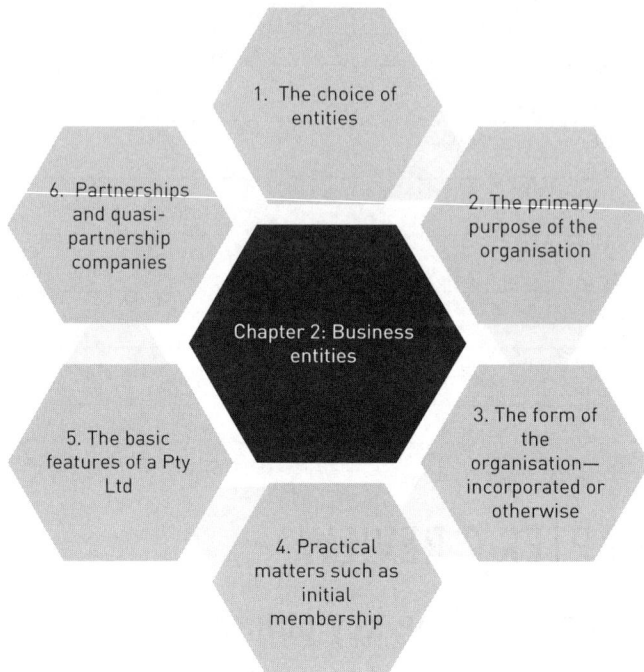

CHAPTER 2 REVISION ACTIVITIES

Consolidation of concepts, knowledge and content activities

TRUE OR FALSE?

1. A partnership is a separate legal entity. True ☐ False ☐
2. The term 'business' is wide, and includes partnerships and companies. True ☐ False ☐
3. The term 'firm' usually applies to a partnership. True ☐ False ☐
4. Partnerships must be in writing. True ☐ False ☐
5. Sole traderships are separate legal entities. True ☐ False ☐
6. The CA2001 is a code that does away with the need for general or common law as regards corporations. True ☐ False ☐

QUESTIONS

FILL IN THE GAPS

1. A partnership comprises two or more people carrying on a business in common with a view to making _____

2. A public company requires _____ directors, of which _____ must be Australian citizens.

3. Profit-sharing arrangements between business owners can be partnerships or _____

4. A law firm in Australia can have a maximum of _____ partners.

5. A partnership under the relevant state Act can be terminated by a partner giving _____

6. The various state and territory Partnership Acts are based on _____

MULTIPLE CHOICE

1. Partner liability under the relevant Act is usually:
   A. Joint
   B. Several
   C. Joint and several
   D. Nil

2. Shares in a company limited by guarantee are:
   A. Always $1
   B. Freely tradable
   C. Readily redeemable
   D. Not transferable

3. The AFL is:
   A. Limited by guarantee
   B. A registered charity
   C. An NFP
   D. Listed on the ASX

4. The liability of members of an associated incorporation is usually:
   A. Unlimited
   B. Limited
   C. $1
   D. Zero

5. The local netball club is most likely to be:
   A. A trust
   B. An association

C. A partnership
D. A public company

6. In Australia, small businesses:

   A. Number over 5 million and make up 80 per cent of the workforce
   B. Number over 1 million and make up 10 per cent of the workforce
   C. Number 100,000 and make up 2 per cent of the workforce
   D. Number over 2 million and make up 50 per cent of the workforce

SHORT ANSWER QUESTIONS

1. What is a business organisation?

2. What are the main forms of business other than a company?

3. What is a sole trader?

4. What is a partnership?

5. How is a partnership established?

6. What is a trust and how does it operate?

7. What are the main types of corporation chosen to conduct a business seeking to make a profit?

Higher order thinking activities

Consider the following questions and provide detailed discussion and analysis.

TOPIC A

What liability attaches to a partnership?

TOPIC B

How is property—both personal and real—treated in partnerships?

TOPIC C

How do you terminate/dissolve a partnership in Victoria?

TOPIC D

Provide an analysis of the main differences between associations—incorporated and unincorporated.

QUESTIONS

CHAPTER 3

ESTABLISHING THE CORPORATION—PRACTICALITIES OF REGISTRATION

Chapter synopsis and links to Textbook Chapter 3

This Workbook Chapter deals with six topics:

- 3.1 Registration of the company
- 3.2 The company as a separate legal entity
- 3.3 The 'corporate veil': maintaining it; piercing it
- 3.4 Company record keeping and reporting
- 3.5 The types of corporations
- 3.6 Specialist corporations.

Each of these topics is constructively aligned with, and linked to, the same topics in Chapter 3 of the Textbook.

Chapter executive summary

This Chapter examines the practical set of issues regarding the corporation, including:
- its registration, separate entity status and corporate veil
- the preliminary and ongoing forms required to be lodged with ASIC
- the different types of company, including the CATSI or Indigenous corporation.

CHAPTER 3 ESTABLISHING THE CORPORATION—PRACTICALITIES OF REGISTRATION

CHAPTER DIAGRAMMATIC OVERVIEW

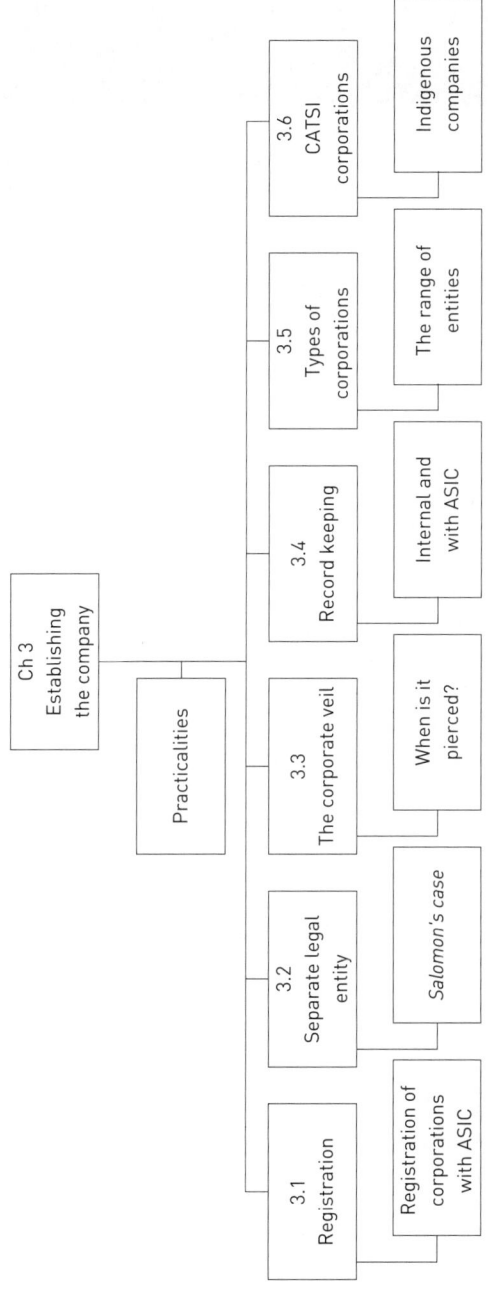

FIGURE 3.1   An overview of Chapter 3

3.1 REGISTRATION OF THE COMPANY

TABLE 3.1 The six potential stages of the corporation life-cycle

	Pre-registration	Registration	Operation	'Going concern' issues	External administration	Deregistration
Overview of the stage	Planning for the company Promoters are involved	Incorporation of the company	The company is a separate legal entity. Directors act for and on behalf of the company.	Is the company able to pay its debts as they fall due?	The company is in financial difficulty. An external administrator has been appointed. External administration is covered in Chapter 14.	The company comes to an end. This may be by choice, due to financial difficulty, or due to a court order.
What is involved in this stage?	Planning by the promoters Purchasing a ready-made/shelf company or starting a company 'from scratch'	Documents are lodged by the company. A certificate of incorporation is issued by ASIC.	Transactions are entered into by the company.			The company is wound up and formally deregistered by ASIC. Winding-up is covered in Chapter 15

Activity 3.1

Refer to Table 3.1. What further information could you add to the 'registration' column? Summarise it below.

_____
_____
_____
_____

The process of registration

The process of registration encompasses the second of the phases above. Registration is process-driven and document-dependent, as Table 3.2 shows.

TABLE 3.2 The steps, processes and documents involved in the registration of the company

Step	CA2001	Detail
Company type:	s 112	Chosen by the promoters or the purchasers of a shelf company
(a) Proprietary company	s 113	Limited by shares (most common)—the liability of the members is limited to amounts not paid on shares Unlimited with share capital
(b) Public company	s 9	Limited by shares Limited by guarantee Unlimited with share capital No-liability company—mining purposes
Company name	s 148	Promoters or buyers of shelf company select a name, subject to the following issues: • s 147: availability of the name • s 147(1): identical or unacceptable names • s 148(1)(b): ACN (Australian Company Number): see s 9 • s 152: reservation of name (optional)
Consent of the members	s 117(5)	s 117(2)(c): the name and address of each *proposed* member is supplied As per s 117(5), the consents must be in place before the application is lodged with ASIC
Consent of the directors and secretary	s 117(5)	s 117(2)(d): the name and address of each *proposed* director is supplied As per s 117(5), the consents must be in place before the application is lodged with ASIC
Registered office of the proposed company	s 142	s 100: may require consent, e.g. from a landlord
Consent of the proposed members to the proposed constitution	s 136(1)(a)	
Constitution is drafted	s 136(1)(a)	The constitution is adopted on registration of the company
Alternatively, the company may adopt any or all of the replaceable rules	s 135	s 135(2): a replaceable rule can be displaced or modified by the company's constitution
Lodge the relevant bundle of documents with ASIC	s 117(1)	The registration fee is paid to ASIC
Certificate of registration	s 118	Certificate is issued by ASIC An ACN is issued s 118(1)(c)(iii): the company's type is included

3.2 THE COMPANY AS A SEPARATE LEGAL ENTITY

The company, once registered, is a separate legal entity. It carries the full potential suite of rights and liabilities of a legal body, including the ability to sue and to be sued, and to own property as per s 124 of the CA2001.

Section 124 of the CA2001 confirms that the company can own property, and the case law previous to this sets out the principles.

TABLE 3.3 Cases relevant to establishing property ownership by the company

Year	Case	Court	Principle
1901	*Borland's Trustee v Steel Bros and Co Ltd*	UK	
1948	*Archibald Howie Pty Ltd v Commissioner for Stamp Duties (NSW)*	High Court of Australia	

Other company powers in the CA2001, and confirmed at common law, are set out in Table 3.4.

TABLE 3.4 The main powers of the company

Power or capacity of the company	CA2001	Case law
Limited liability		
The company can sue and be sued		
Perpetual succession		
Transfer of shares		
Formalities, publicity and expense		
Execution of documents		

> ## Activity 3.2
> Fill in the gaps in Tables 3.3 and 3.4.

3.3 THE 'CORPORATE VEIL': MAINTAINING IT; PIERCING IT

The liability of the members of a company is, for the most part, limited. All they need to do is to pay for their shares. Ordinarily, the company structure protects them from any further liability.

The courts have drawn the analogy with a 'veil' or barrier between the company and its owners. It is a membrane or construction that separates the company as a legal entity from the owners; it is a legal device to provide separation between the company as an entity and others acting in or through it. This is the usual situation and will apply in most cases.

The veil has proven to be durable, but also permeable. It may be penetrated or pierced, essentially as a fiction, where particular issues of justice or fairness require it; for example, where the company has been misused for dishonest, inappropriate or illegal purposes.

In summary, the veil can be pierced in certain circumstances that render the separate entity status unjustifiable. These exceptions are found in the CA2001 and in case law.

FIGURE 3.2   The three main exceptions relevant to piercing the corporate veil

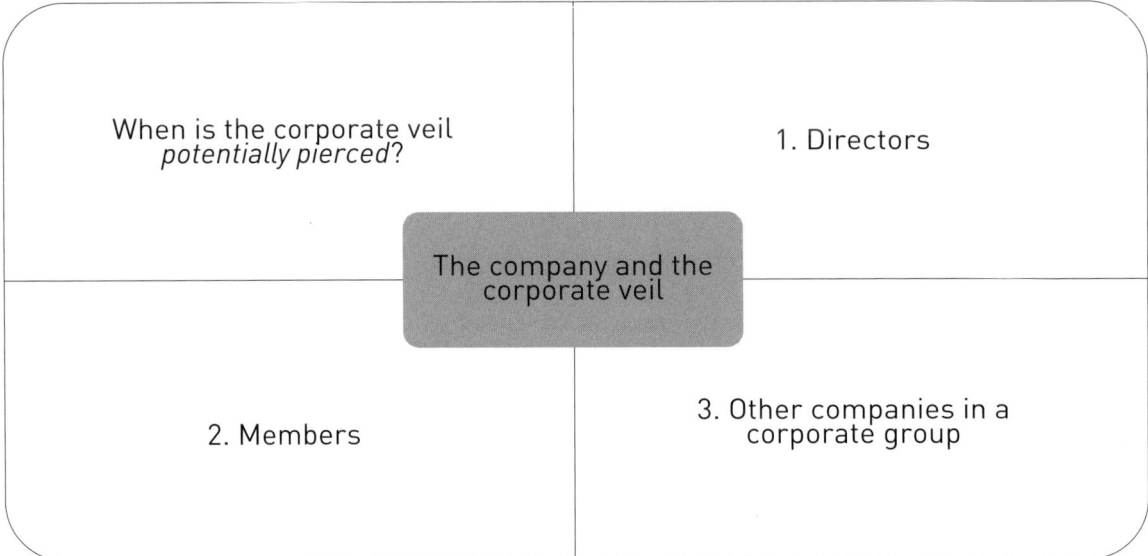

TABLE 3.5   Case law from the UK and Australia that has considered the corporate veil, and the potential piercing of the corporate veil

Year	Case	Court	Principle
1911	*Re Darby*	UK	
1925	*Macaura v Northern Assurance Co Ltd*	UK	
1933	*Gifford Motor Co Ltd v Horne*	UK	

CHAPTER 3 ESTABLISHING THE CORPORATION—PRACTICALITIES OF REGISTRATION

Year	Case	Court	Principle
1963	*Malyon v Plummer*	UK	
1965	*Gorton v Federal Commissioner of Taxation*	High Court of Australia	
1989	*Briggs v James Hardie and Co Pty Ltd*	NSW Supreme Court	
1997	*Repatriation Commission v Harrison*	Federal Court	

Activity 3.3

Refer to Table 3.5. Add any relevant cases, and complete the right-hand column.

Piercing the corporate veil: common law and statute

The common law has grappled for more than a century (and since *Salomon's case*) with the theoretical complexities of the corporate veil, and if and when it should be pierced. The statutory position in relation to the issue is, by contrast, relatively simple and straightforward. In effect, it becomes a standard matter of statutory interpretation.

FIGURE 3.3 Piercing the corporate veil—comparing the common law approach with statutory provision

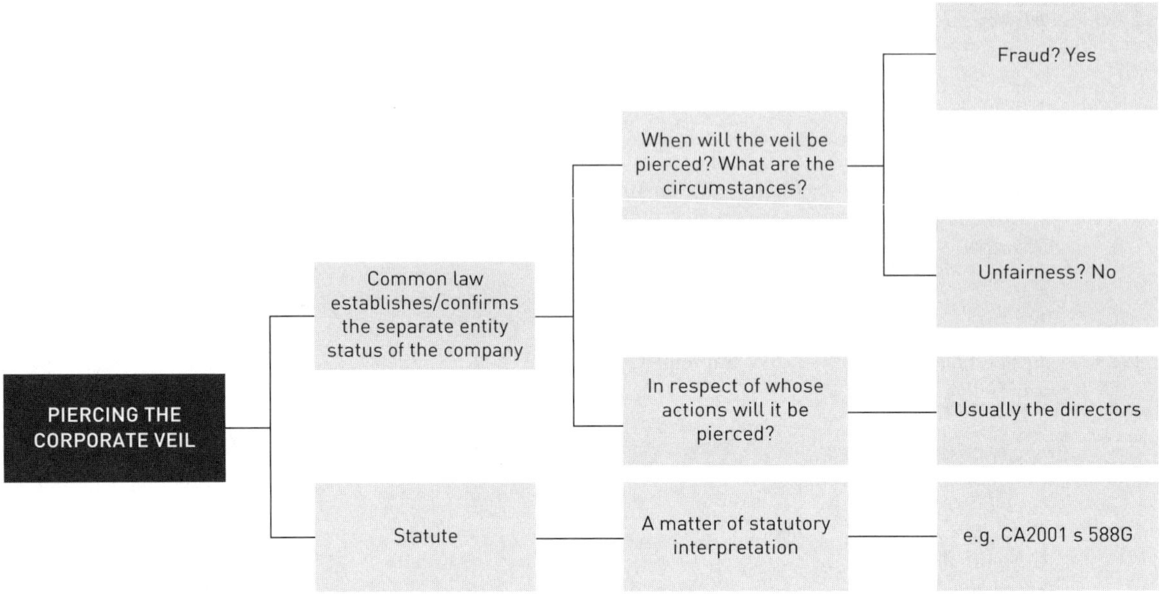

```
PIERCING THE          Common law                    When will the veil be           Fraud? Yes
CORPORATE VEIL        establishes/confirms          pierced? What are the
                      the separate entity           circumstances?                  Unfairness? No
                      status of the company
                                                    In respect of whose
                                                    actions will it be              Usually the directors
                                                    pierced?

                      Statute                       A matter of statutory           e.g. CA2001 s 588G
                                                    interpretation
```

3.4 COMPANY RECORD KEEPING AND REPORTING

After the company has been registered, the communication process with ASIC will be carried out by the company secretary or other officer.

TABLE 3.6 Reporting by the company to ASIC

Step	CA2001	Detail
Financial records	s 286	
Minute books of meetings	s 251A	
Appointment of auditor	s 327(1)	Required for large Pty Ltds and public companies
Keeping of various registers	s 168	s 169: Members s 170: Option holders s 171: Debenture holders
Common seal	s 123	This is optional, as per s 123(1)
Issue of shares by the company	Various: see next column	s 169: the members' register must be kept up to date s 254X: the company must lodge details within 28 days s 1071H: the company must issue a share certificate or other title document within 2 months

Step	CA2001	Detail
Directors appointed after registration	s 201G	Resolution in general meeting
Alternate directors	s 201 H	Alternate directors—to make up a quorum
Company secretary	s 204D	Appointed by the directors
Public officer—a 'natural person' appointed by the relevant corporation	As may be required by the ATO (Australian Tax Office)	For taxation purposes, see s 112 of the *Taxation Administration Act 1996* (Cth)

Activity 3.4

Are small companies required to report too much information to ASIC? If so, what are the consequences of this for the company?

3.5 THE TYPES OF CORPORATIONS

The types of corporations by reference to the liability of members can be illustrated as shown in Fig 3.4.

FIGURE 3.4   Classifying companies

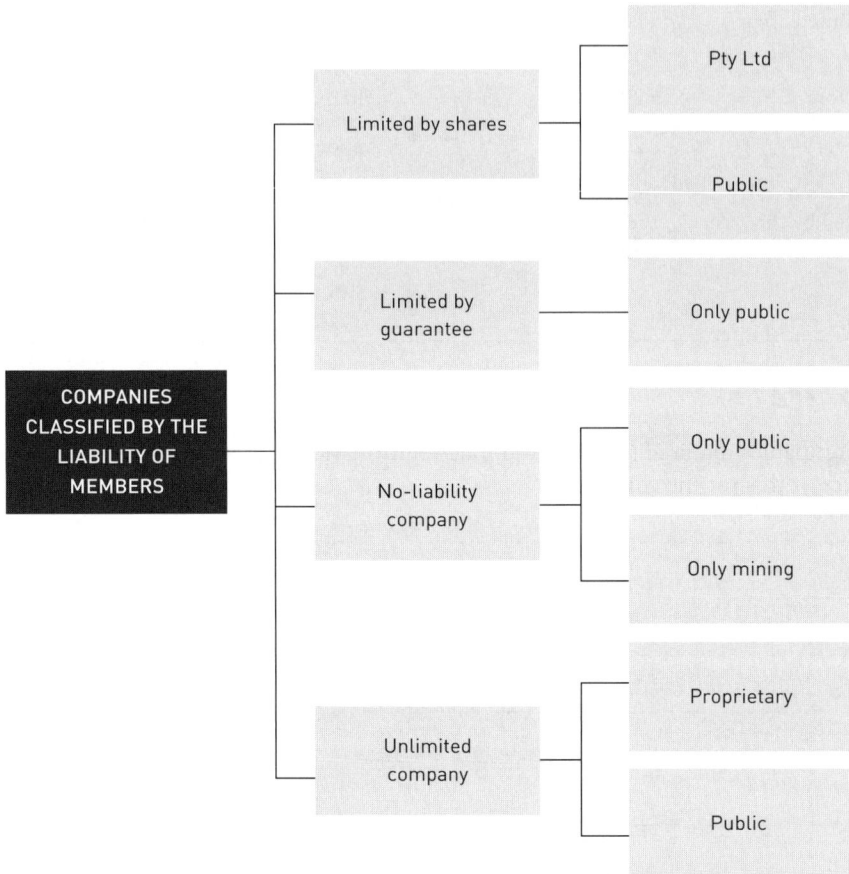

Based on Fig 3.4, no-liability companies can be visualised as shown in Fig 3.5. The no-liability type of company is a specialist one, often designed to encourage investment in high-risk intensive-capital-investment mining companies

FIGURE 3.5   No-liability companies

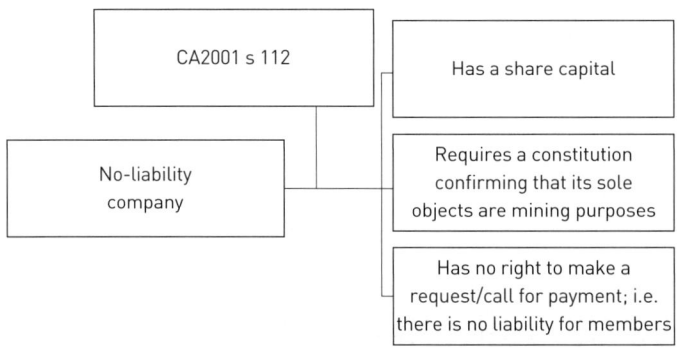

Activity 3.5

What is the genesis and history of the no-liability company?

_____
_____
_____
_____
_____
_____
_____
_____

The last-named company type—the unlimited company—is similar to the partnership in that liability is not limited. Figure 3.6 illustrates the hybrid nature of both the unlimited company and the quasi-partnership company.

FIGURE 3.6   The hybrid nature of the two types of entities sitting between partnerships and companies

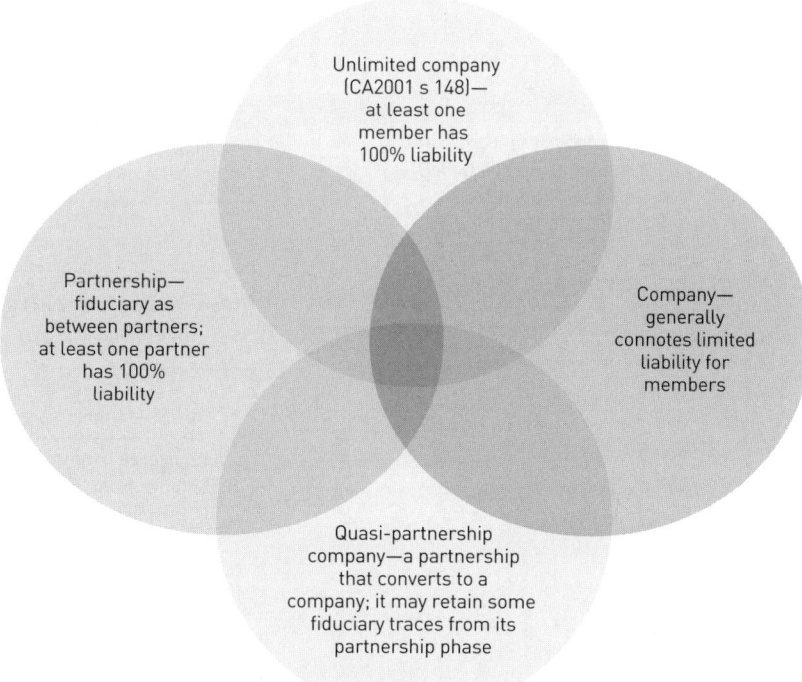

Table 3.7 sets out elements of financial reporting.

TABLE 3.7 The elements of financial reporting, depending on the company size and type, under the CA2001

Aspect of financial reporting	Public	Large proprietary	Small proprietary
To keep 'true and fair' financial records	Yes, s 286	Yes, s 286	Yes, s 286
Annual financial reports required	Yes, s 292	Yes, s 292	Only if directed to do so by: • shareholders with 5% of votes (s 293), or • ASIC (s 294)
Audited reports required	Yes, s 301	Yes, s 301	
Copies of reports to be sent to members	Yes, s 314	Yes, s 314	
Reports to be lodged with ASIC	Yes, s 319	Yes, s 319	

3.6 SPECIALIST CORPORATIONS

Indigenous corporations, or 'CATSI corporations' have their own legislation, registration and regulation requirements under the *Corporations (Aboriginal and Torres Strait Islander) Act 2006* (Cth) (CATSI Act), as shown in Figs 3.7 and 3.8.

FIGURE 3.7 An overview of CATSI corporations

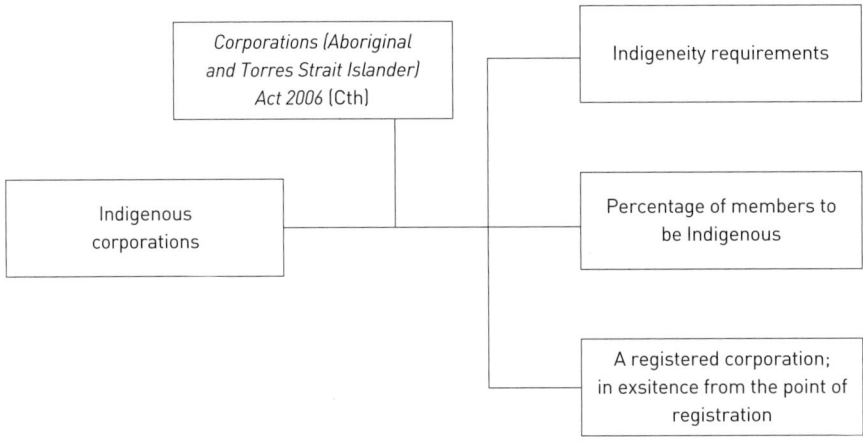

FIGURE 3.8 An overview of CATSI incorporation

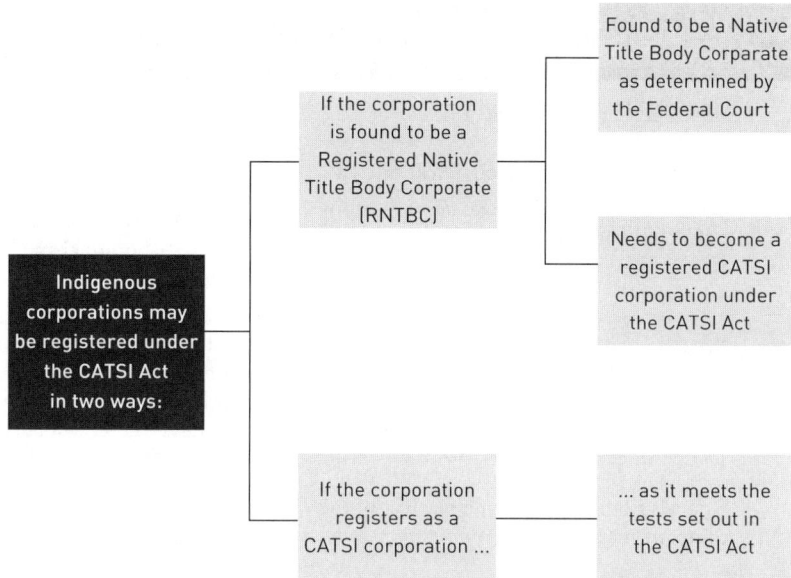

Section 57A of the CA2001 outlines the meaning of the term 'corporation', and s 57A(3) provides as follows:

(3) To avoid doubt, an Aboriginal and Torres Strait Islander corporation is taken to be a **corporation** for the purposes of this Act.

Note: Various provisions of this Act that generally apply to corporations do not apply to Aboriginal and Torres Strait Islander corporations because of express provisions to that effect: see section 190B, subsection 197(5), section 206HB and subsections 599(2), 1309(6), 1318(5) and 1335(3).

The issues raised in the Note are addressed below:

TABLE 3.8 Explanation of references in the Note to s 57A(3)

Section/subsection of the CA2001	Effect of the section/subsection of the CA2001	Application of the CATSI Act
190B	Chapter: Ch 2D: Officers and employees Part: Pt 2D.1: Duties and powers Division: Div 1: General duties (ss 180–190C) Effect of s 190B: Div 1 *does not* apply to CATSI corporations (see Note to s 190B)	Division 265 of the CATSI Act deals with the general duties of directors, secretaries, officers and employees of Aboriginal and Torres Strait Islander corporations.
197(5)	Directors liable for debts and other obligations incurred by corporation as trustee Section 197(5) *does not* apply to CATSI corporations	Section 271-1 of the CATSI Act deals with the liability of directors of Aboriginal and Torres Strait Islander corporations for debts and other liabilities incurred by those corporations as trustee.

TABLE 3.8 Explanation of references in the Note to s 57A(3) (continued)

Section/subsection of the CA2001	Effect of the section/subsection of the CA2001	Application of the CATSI Act
206HB	Chapter 2D deals with officers and employees Part 2D.6 deals with disqualification Effect of s 206HB: Pt 2D.6 *does not* apply to CATSI corporations	Note 1: Section 279-5(5) of the CATSI Act provides that a person who is disqualified from managing corporations under CA2001 Pt 2D.6 will be automatically disqualified under Pt 6-5 of the CATSI Act from managing Aboriginal and Torres Strait Islander corporations. Note 2: Similarly, s 206B(5) of the CA2001 provides that a person who is disqualified from managing Aboriginal and Torres Strait Islander corporations under Pt 6-5 of the CATSI Act will be automatically disqualified from managing corporations.
599(2)	Appeals from decisions of a receiver of the company may be made	Similar provision is made in relation to Aboriginal and Torres Strait Islander corporations under s 576-10 of the CATSI Act.
1309(6)		
1318(5)		
1335(3)		

TABLE 3.9   CATSI corporations and other corporations compared

	CATSI Act	CA2001
Type of legislation		Commonwealth
Minimum number of members	5	1
Maximum number of members		For a Pty Ltd, 50 non-employee shareholders
Age of directors	Directors must be 15	Directors must be 18
Background of members		
Minimum number of directors		
The regulator		
The types of corporation		
Own and trade shares	No	Members can
Issuing debentures to borrow funds		
Splitting profits	Up to the entity	
Registration		
Rules—internal		
Reporting		

Adapted from https://www.oric.gov.au/sites/default/files/documents/06_2013/Factsheet_CorporationsAct_Jun2010.pdf/.

Activity 3.6

Conduct some research (see, for example, https://www.oric.gov.au/), and then complete Tables 3.8 and 3.9.

Activity 3.7

Conduct some research and then answer the following question.

How do the Office of the Registrar of Indigenous Corporations (ORIC) and the CATSI Act provide corporations that are appropriate business vehicles for Indigenous entrepreneurs?

WORKBOOK CHAPTER 3 REVIEW

An illustrative summary of the key points

FIGURE 3.9 The range of companies and the basic features of the company

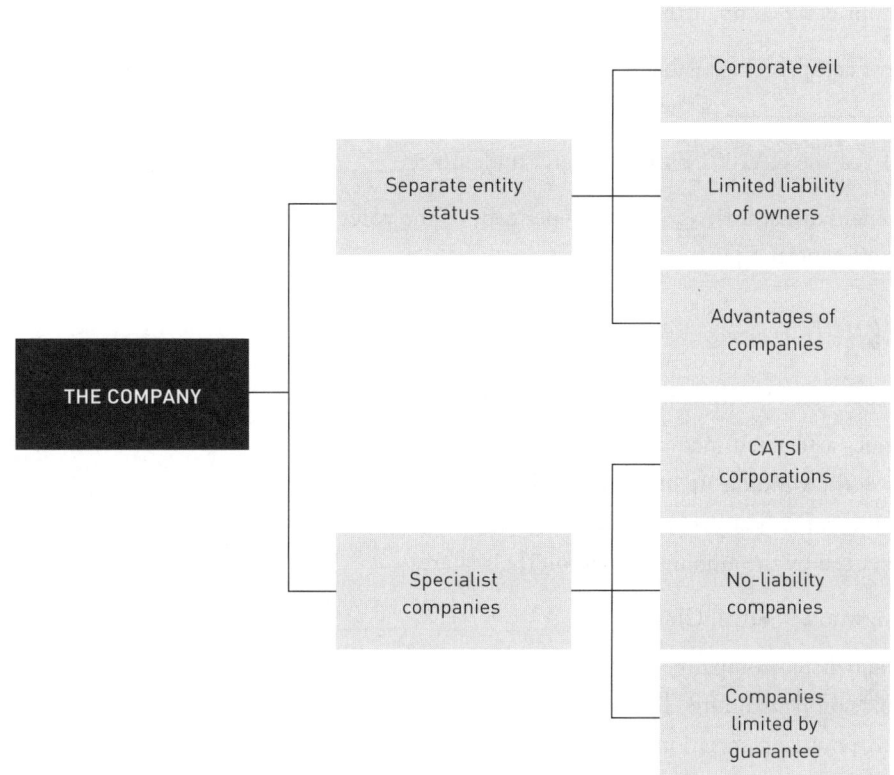

CHAPTER 3 REVISION ACTIVITIES

Consolidation of concepts, knowledge and content activities

TRUE OR FALSE?

1. Pty Ltd companies comprise more than 99 per cent of companies in Australia. True ☐ False ☐
2. No-liability companies are available in the agricultural sector. True ☐ False ☐
3. An unlimited company requires at least two members to bear unlimited liability. True ☐ False ☐
4. A limited partnership is illegal in Australia. True ☐ False ☐
5. A public company can convert to a Pty Ltd. True ☐ False ☐

FILL IN THE GAPS

1. A company is a separate entity and requires a minimum of _____ shareholder(s).

2. Companies cannot engage in misleading or deceptive conduct as set out in section _____ of the Australian Consumer Law.

3. A small proprietary company has a maximum of _____ employees.

4. The types of companies available to be registered in Australia are set out in section _____ of the CA2001.

5. Section 116 of the CA2001 provides that a trade union _____

6. A shareholder with at least _____ per cent of the votes in a small Pty Ltd can direct the company to prepare a financial report.

MULTIPLE CHOICE

1. For a member of a Pty Ltd company, their liability:

    A. Continues after their membership ceases

    B. Starts on the winding-up of the company

    C. Is payable in the first year of their membership

    D. Is referenced by the amount unpaid on their shares

2. The Collingwood Football Club is:

    A. A publicly listed company

    B. A public company limited by guarantee

    C. An incorporated association

    D. An unincorporated association

3. To be appointed as a director, a person must:

    A. Be at least 21 years of age

    B. Have completed secondary education

    C. Have completed 12 months' work experience

    D. Be at least 18 years of age

4. A company that is registered needs to conduct business within:

    A. 1 week

    B. 1 month

    C. 6 months

    D. 1 year

5. A public company must have at least:
   A. 1 director and 1 secretary
   B. 2 directors and 1 secretary
   C. 4 directors and 2 secretaries
   D. 3 directors and 1 secretary

SHORT ANSWER QUESTIONS

1. What is the difference between a company limited by shares and a company limited by guarantee?

2. What does 'no liability' mean in relation to a corporation?

3. What is an unlimited company?

4. Can a company, once registered, change to a different type or form of company?

5. What is the separate legal entity status of a one-person company?

6. What is the separate legal entity status of a company within a corporate group?

7. To whom do the directors of a company that is part of a corporate group owe their duties?

Higher order thinking activities

Consider the following questions and provide detailed discussion and analysis.

TOPIC A

Explain the veil of incorporation concept, its effects, and how it may be lifted.

QUESTIONS

TOPIC B

What are the registration processes for a company, including the steps before and after incorporation?

QUESTIONS

CHAPTER 4

THE RULES OF THE CORPORATION AND THE ROLE OF STATUTE

Chapter synopsis and links to Textbook Chapter 4

This Workbook Chapter deals with four topics:

- 4.1 The relationship between statute and internal rules
- 4.2 The corporate constitution
- 4.3 The replaceable rules
- 4.4 Statutory interpretation regarding companies.

Each of these topics is constructively aligned with, and linked to, the same topics in Chapter 4 of the Textbook.

Chapter executive summary

This Chapter examines the rules of the corporation including:

- the basic features of the provisions in the CA2001 relevant to the rules of the corporation
- the linkage between the corporation's own rules and the rules as set out in the CA2001
- internal rules the company may adopt
- model or replaceable rules that companies may adopt to streamline their processes
- mandatory rules that form part of the CA2001 and cannot be altered
- the principles of statutory interpretation inherent to this exercise and to corporate law more generally.

This Chapter also refers to a basic framework of statutory interpretation and analysis relevant to corporations.

CHAPTER 4 THE RULES OF THE CORPORATION AND THE ROLE OF STATUTE

CHAPTER DIAGRAMMATIC OVERVIEW

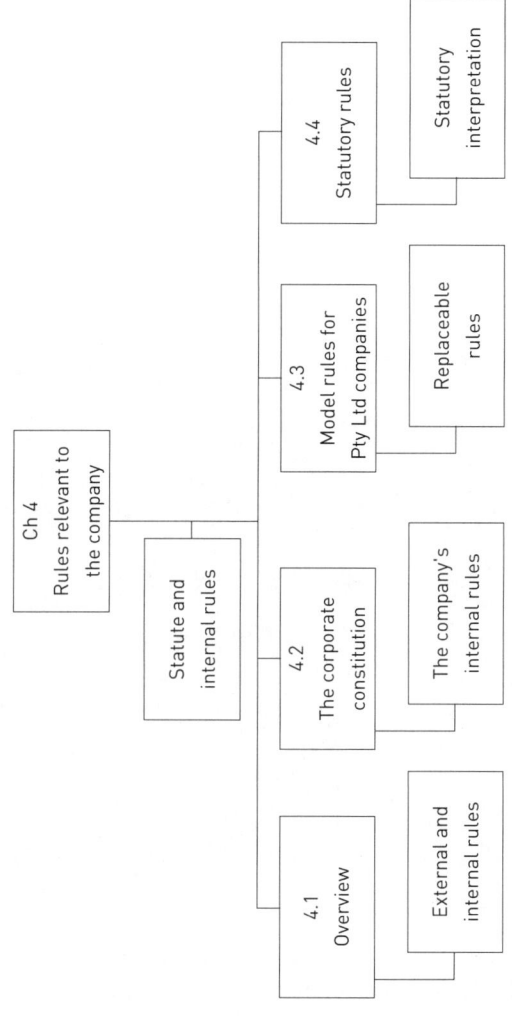

FIGURE 4.1 An overview of Chapter 4

4.1 THE RELATIONSHIP BETWEEN STATUTE AND INTERNAL RULES

The governance of a company involves reference to the relevant statute—the CA2001—and to the company's own internal rules. If there is a conflict between them, the statute prevails. These sources can be represented as shown in Fig 4.2

FIGURE 4.2 The overlap and interplay between internal rules and external statute; statute prevails

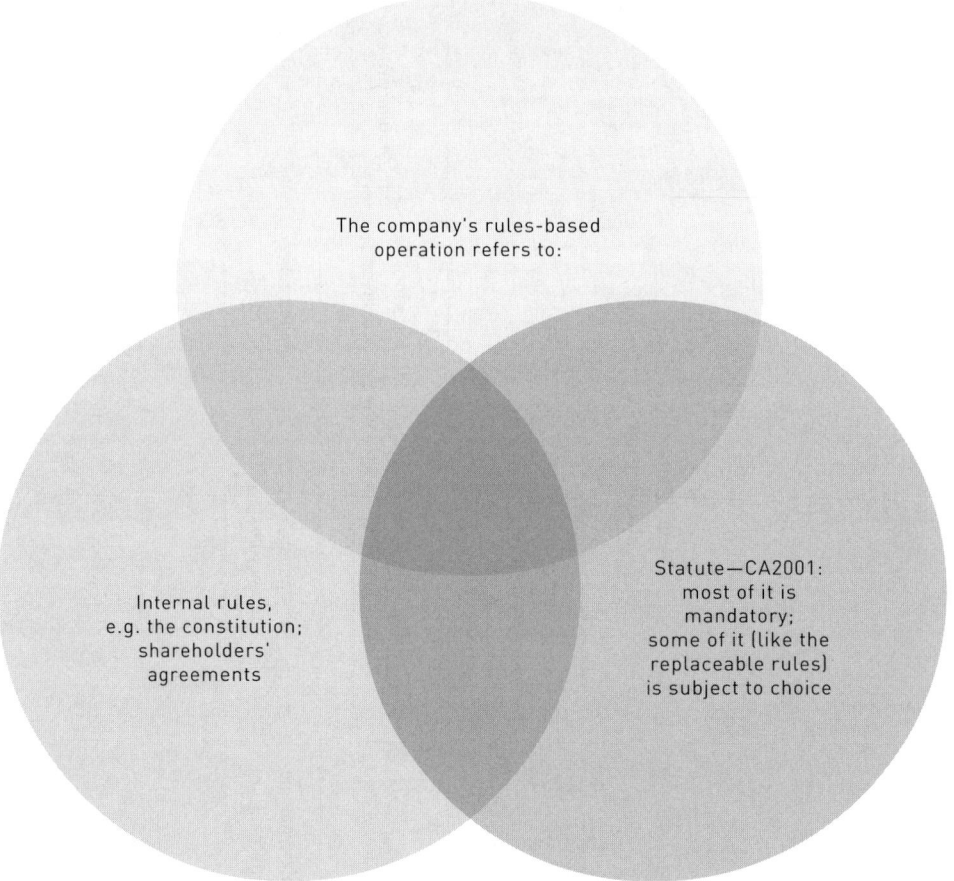

Statute is itself complex and multi-layered in the context of Australian corporate law, and includes the CA2001 and the ASIC Act 2001. The term 'corporations legislation' is defined in s 9 of the CA2001. The project of corporate law more broadly includes the matters set out in Fig 4.3.

FIGURE 4.3 The CA2001 sits atop the potential multi-layered search for legislative effect

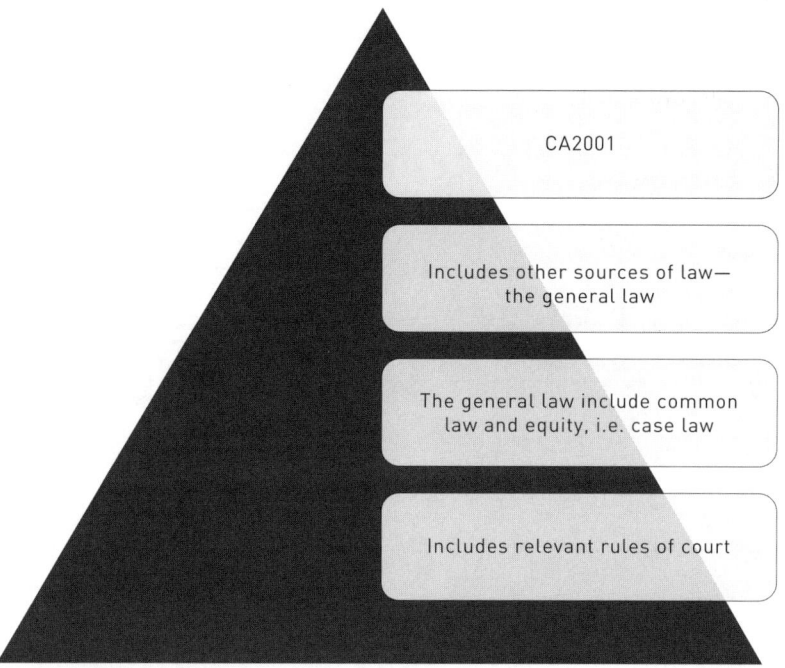

As noted, the CA2001 prevails over inconsistent rules in the company's own constitution; that is, most of the provisions in the CA2001 are mandatory/obligatory as opposed to discretionary/optional. (This is a version of the same principle of legislative primacy as between legislation and the common law generally.) The hierarchy of authority is illustrated in Fig 4.4.

FIGURE 4.4 The mandatory provisions of the CA2001 sit atop the hierarchy of rules applicable to a company

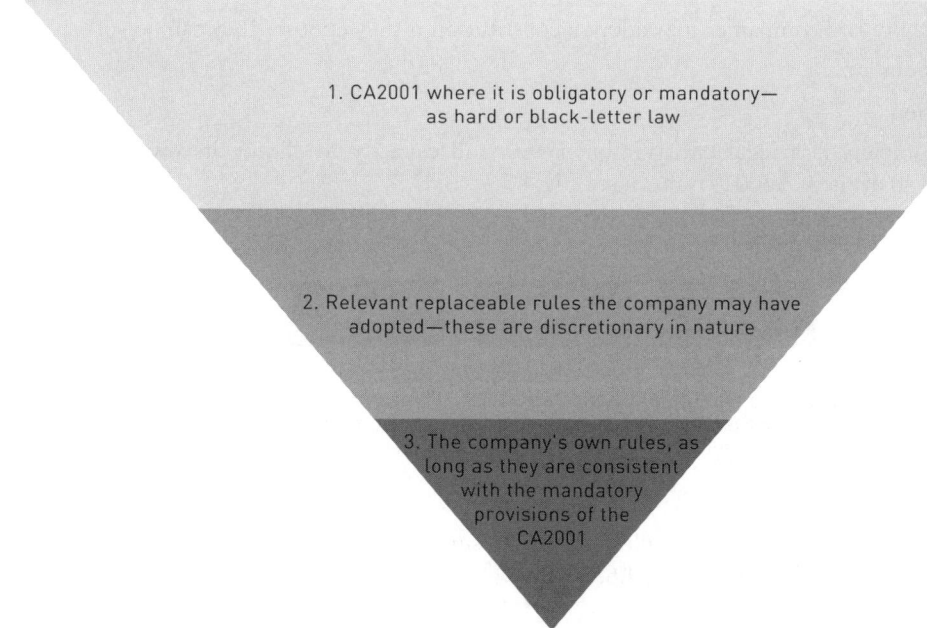

Activity 4.1

Referring to Figures 4.2 and 4.3, ascertain and describe the connection and links between the various sources of Australian corporate law.

4.2 THE CORPORATE CONSTITUTION

Adoption of the constitution

Under the CA2001, Pty Ltd companies may adopt a constitution if they choose. They can do so:
- as part of incorporation, or
- after incorporation.

The Pty Ltd company is a legal entity imbued with full capacity to choose its own internal rules, as ss 124, 134 and 140 of the CA2001 confirm: see Fig 4.5.

FIGURE 4.5 A company has powers flowing from s 124 of the CA2001

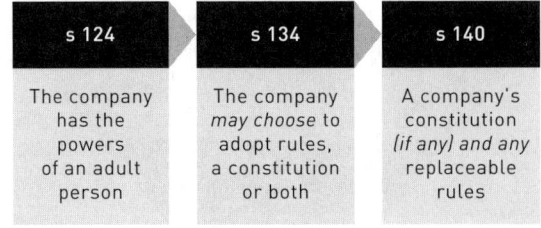

A Pty Ltd can therefore design its own rules in a way to suit its business, subject to compliance with the mandatory provsions of the CA2001: see Fig 4.6.

FIGURE 4.6 The company still needs to comply with the CA2001

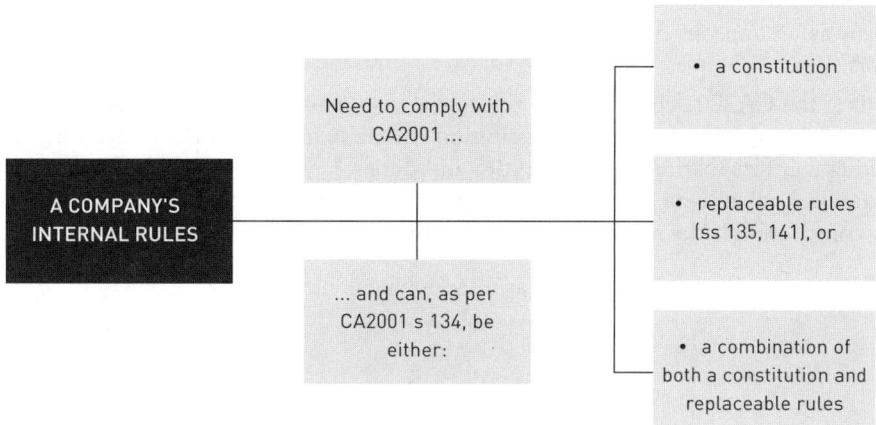

The process and rules relevant to adopting a constitution and the various options are set out in s 136 of the CA2001. Figure 4.7 provides an overview of the options set out in s 136. (Note that changing or adopting a constitution after incorporation is considered a key proposal; hence the need for a special resolution—75 per cent of the votes cast.)

FIGURE 4.7 An overview of the options set out in CA2001 s 136

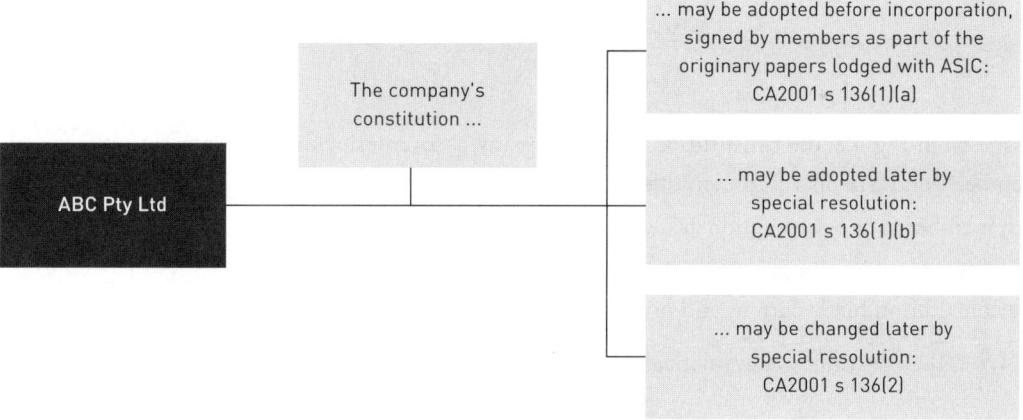

The constitution as an interlocking contract

Companies are legal entities that can only act through and by their agents. This is where the need for internal rules comes in—to regulate the acts, behaviours, duties, rights, and liabilities of three parties/groups who by necessity have to interact if the company is to function; hence the interlocking nature of the relationship between the three groups:

- The directors as the main agents and operatives of the company. They are its guiding mind, and are responsible in law for its financial solvency. They need to act in the best interests of the company—which is, in effect, the current membership collectively.
- The owners/members/shareholders who have contributed share capital. This allocation of capital is by its nature risk capital; the owners are, in economic terms, 'rent seekers'—they seek a return on investment. They place

their reliance on the directors to provide stewardship of the company—there is the so-called 'agency gap' between them and the directors. The directors have the day-to-day knowledge; hence their responsibility.
- The company as 'an unpeopled vessel' that by its nature can only be steered and navigated, principally by the directors.

Section 140 of the CA2001 confirms that the company constitution is a series of interlocking contracts between parties within the company. The constitution is a particular type of contract—it is a group-based, group-connecting contract that links, via liabilities and duties, key parties or stakeholders operating within the company and in legal existence as the result of the incorporation process. The effect and outcome of the contemporary constitution is the result of historical common law cases and the CA2001.

FIGURE 4.8   The constitution of the company as interlocking contracts

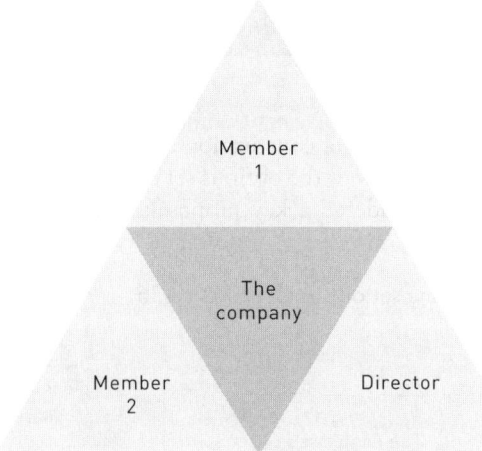

As shown in Fig 4.8, the constitution of the company, as an interlocking contract, simultaneously binds:
- Member 1 and Member 2 to each other
- each member to the corporation as a separate entity, and
- the directors to 'the company', which is essentially the current membership.

The constitution binds current and potential members, as illustrated in Fig 4.9.

FIGURE 4.9   The constitution automatically binds new members D and E as per CA2001 s 140

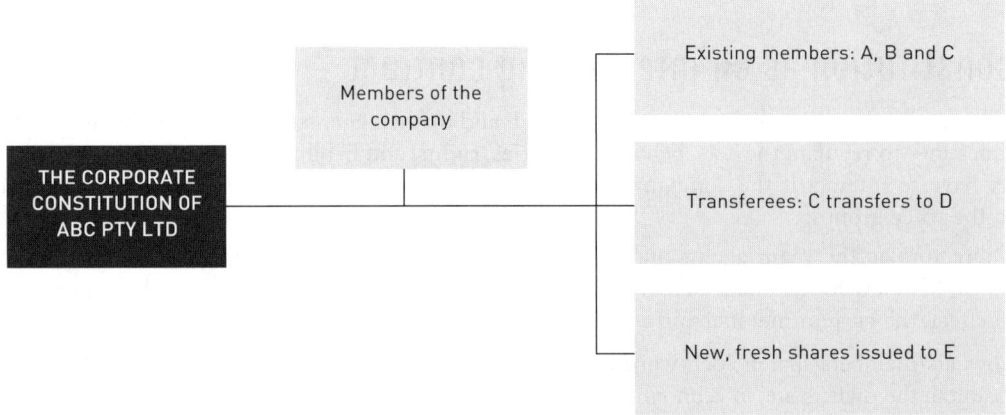

Case law relevant to constitutions

We can divide relevant cases as pre- and post-1961.

TABLE 4.1 Case law relevant to companies prior to 1961: generally from the UK

Year	Case	Court	Principle
1884	*London Financial Association v Kelk*	UK	Interpret the whole of the company's constitution; do not look at it in an artificially narrow manner
1900	*Borland's Trustees v Steel Bros & Co Ltd*	UK	
1915	*Hickman v Kent or Romney Marsh Sheep-Breeders' Association*	UK	The capacity of the rights to be asserted by members is linked to membership, not beyond membership
1938	*Beattie v E & F Beattie Ltd*	UK	
1958	*Rayfield v Hands*	UK	

By contrast, most relevant cases since 1961 have an Australian origin.

TABLE 4.2 Case law relevant to companies since 1961

Year	Case	Court	Principle
1975	*Re Caratti Holdings Co Pty Ltd*	WA Supreme court and Privy Council	The court may find that to enforce the provisions of the constitution would be unfair
1979	*Santos Ltd v Pettingell*	NSW Supreme Court	Third parties may want to rely on the terms of the constitution, especially with a public company

TABLE 4.2 Case law relevant to companies since 1961 (continued)

Year	Case	Court	Principle

Shareholder agreements governed by the rules of contract

By contrast to constitutions, shareholder agreements do not have the same formal legal recognition as provided by the CA2001. Nor do they have the enforcement underwritten by s 140 of the CA2001 as between the parties. The question, therefore, with a shareholder agreement is: Who is bound?

This can be illustrated as shown in Fig 4.10.

FIGURE 4.10 The problematic nature of shareholders' agreements—limited binding application

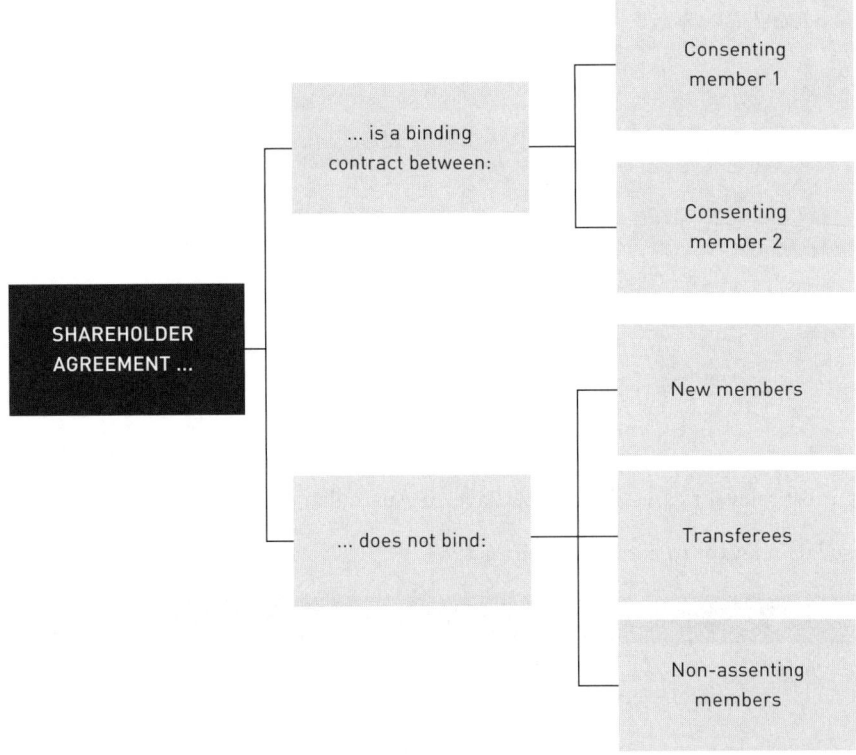

> ### ACTIVITY 4.2
> Refer to Tables 4.1 and 4.2 and fill in the gaps.

AMENDING THE CONSTITUTION: THE LEGALITY OF THE PROPOSAL

Amending the company's constitution is possible, as set out in s 136 of the CA2001. However, the proponents of the amendment (usually the directors, the majority shareholders, or both) cannot simply act for any purpose whatsoever. Their action is proscribed by basic notions of fairness as set out in Fig 4.11 by reference to case law and the CA2001.

FIGURE 4.11   The tests for, and potential consequences of, a proposal to amend the constitution

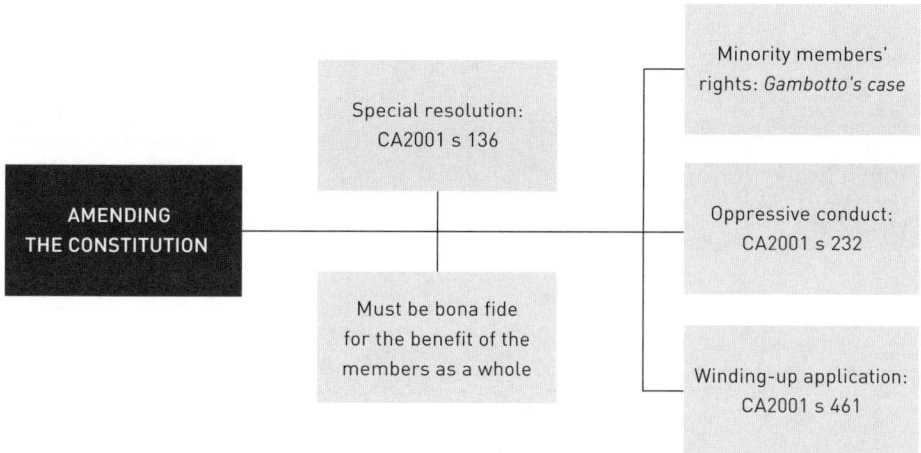

TABLE 4.3   Case law regarding amendment of the constitution of a company

Year	Case	Court	Principle
1900	*Allen v Gold Reefs of West Africa Ltd*	UK	• The amendment of the constitution must be for the benefit of the company as a whole • Changing the constitution to avoid contractual liabilities (under a separate contract) relevant to a director was not lawful
1919	*Brown v British Abrasive Wheel Co*	UK	
1920	*Sidebottom v Kershaw Leese & Co*	UK	

TABLE 4.3 Case law regarding amendment of the constitution of a company (continued)

Year	Case	Court	Principle
1938	*Peter's American Delicacy Co Ltd v Heath*	High Court of Australia	
1951	*Greenhalgh v Arderne Cinemas Ltd*	UK	
1995	*Gambotto's case*	High Court of Australia	• The purpose of the change must not be to aggrandise the majority and oppress the minority by expropriating their shares by compulsory acquisition • The proposed change must be for a proper purpose with commercial aims in mind • Changing the constitution to force out a minority shareholder was not lawful

> ### Activity 4.3
> Refer to Table 4.3 and fill in the gaps.

4.3 THE REPLACEABLE RULES

Pre-July 1998 companies

Companies incorporated under the pre-1998 law were required to adopt:
- a Memorandum of Association with an objects clause setting out the main business of the company, and
- Articles of Association.

They were bound by the *ultra vires* doctrine, which could render void acts made outside the scope of the company's main objects.

Post-July 1998 companies

Companies incorporated under the post-1998 law could, if they chose, adopt a constitution. They did not have to do so.

They were no longer bound by the *ultra vires* doctrine'. Section 125 of the CA2001 largely removed the effects of this doctrine.

Potential choices after 1998 for pre-1998 companies

These companies could change their old rules and adopt a constitution, or they could maintain their former rules. Section 125 of the CA2001 applied to them, as it did to all companies after July 1998.

FIGURE 4.12 Requirements for companies registered pre- and post-July 1998

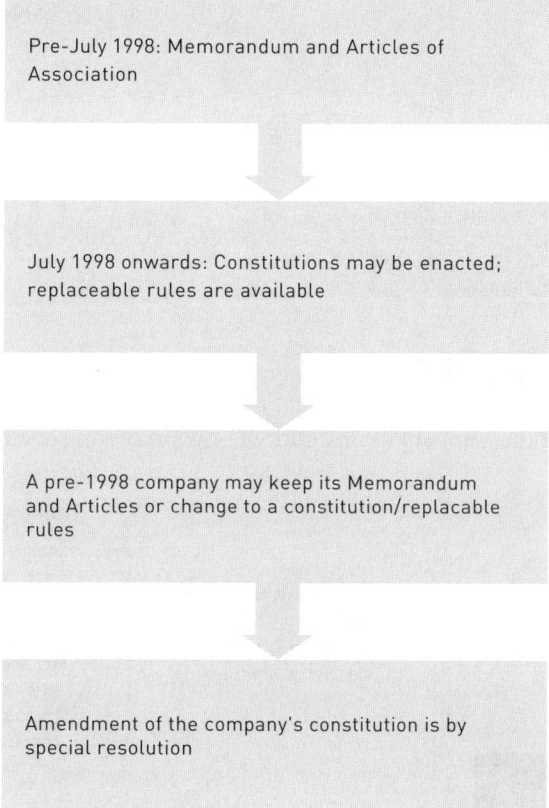

Adopting a constitution can take place in two basic ways, as shown in Fig 4.13.

FIGURE 4.13 The process of adopting a constitution can occur as part of registration, or at some point afterwards

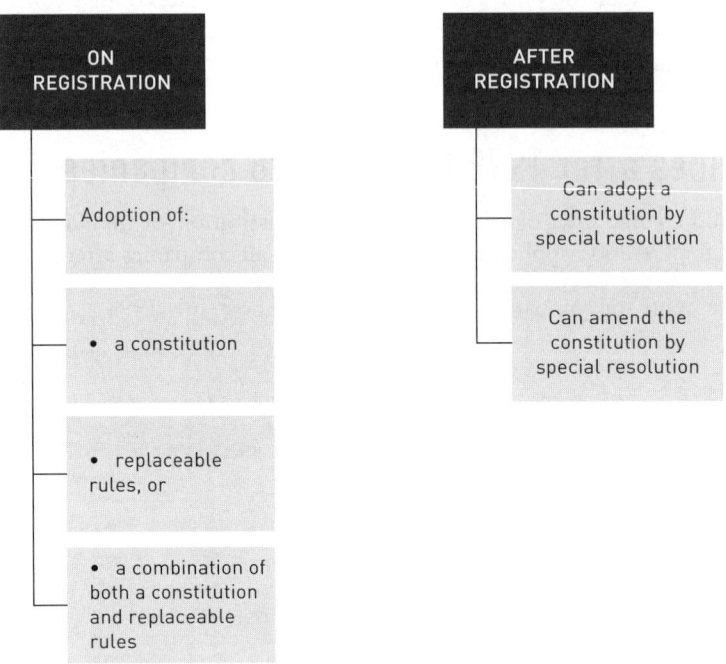

Amending the constitution

FIGURE 4.14 Amendment of the company's constitution—the process is set out in CA2001 s 136

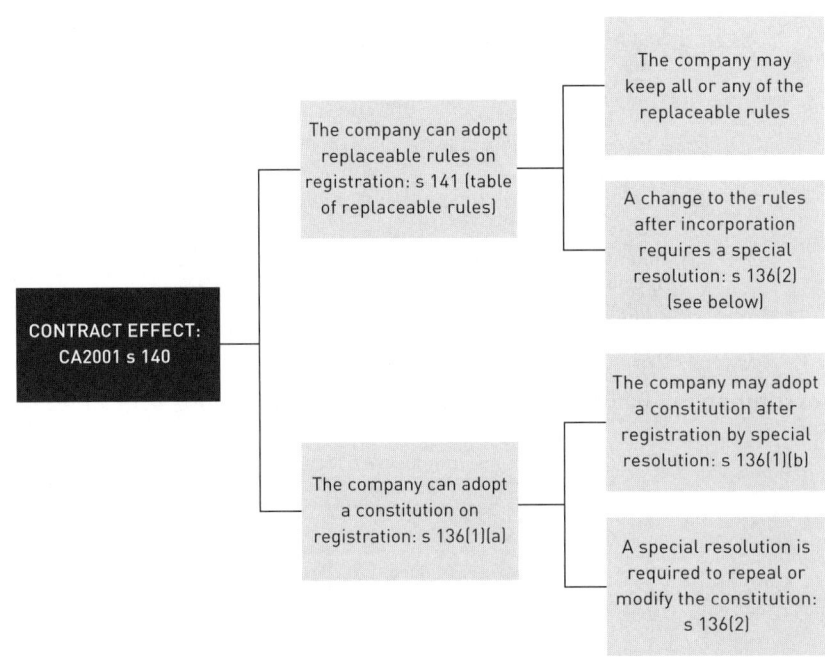

Activity 4.4
What are the choice of rules for a new Pty Ltd?

4.4 STATUTORY INTERPRETATION REGARDING COMPANIES

Given that corporate law is heavily influenced by statute, the rules of statutory interpretation apply. There are basic steps, as shown in Fig 4.15.

FIGURE 4.15   Statutory interpretation of the CA2001 proceeds by reference to the literal rule as a first step

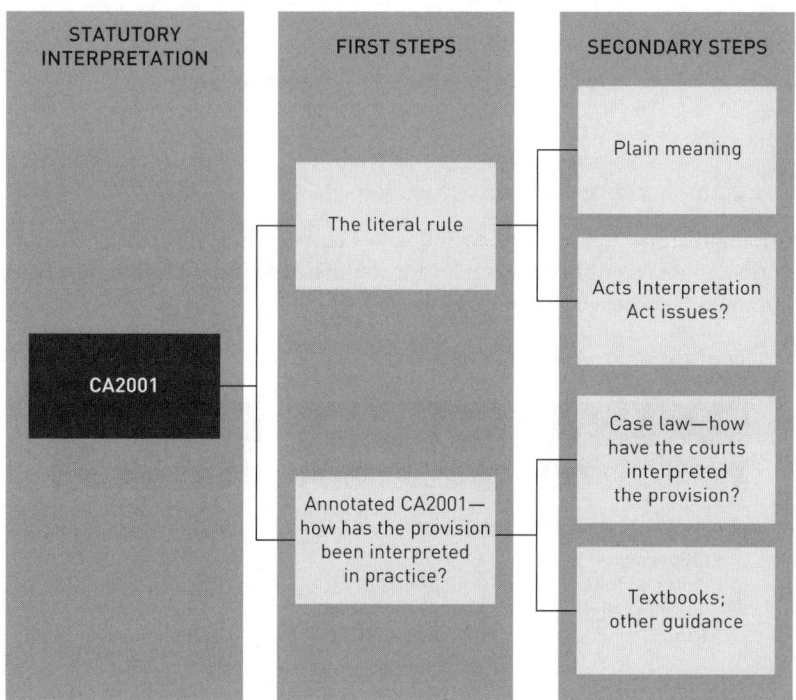

CORPORATIONS LAW: CONCEPTS, CASES AND CULTURE WORKBOOK

As the problem-solving methods in law demonstrate, whatever the subject matter, there is a link between:

- issues
- research
- argument, and
- conclusion.

These are variations on a theme that can be represented in basic form relevant to corporate law as shown in Fig 4.16.

FIGURE 4.16 A method for proceeding in corporate law problem solving

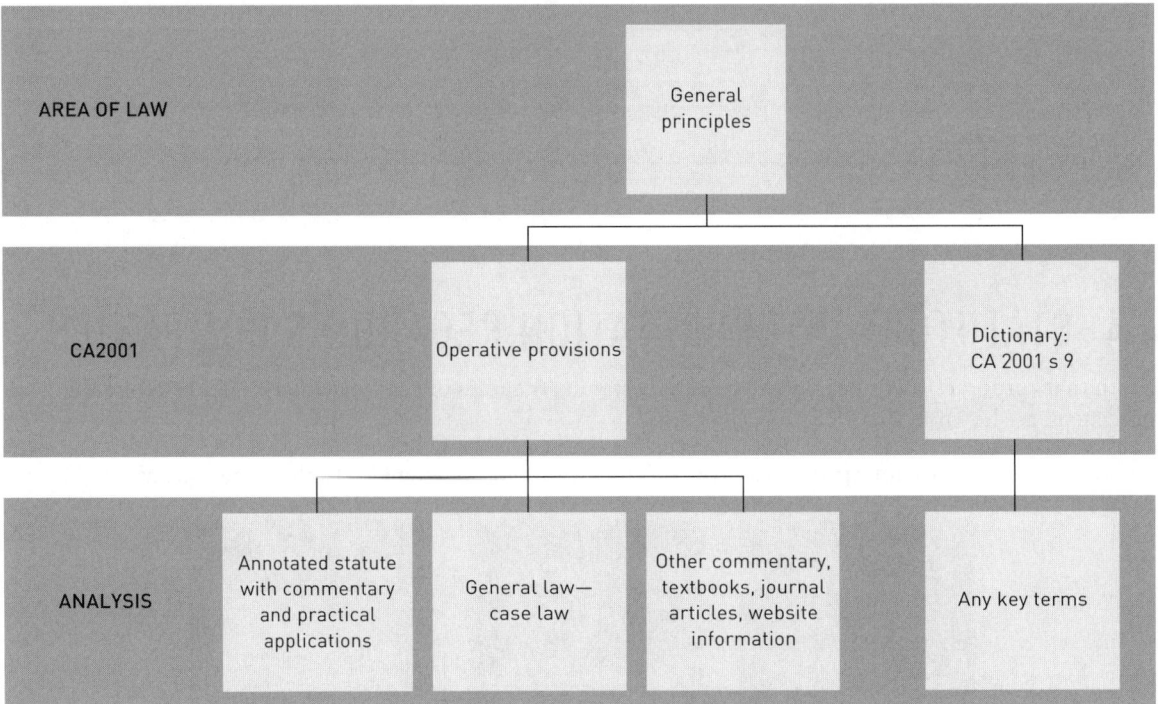

Just as constitutional history was relevant to the issues surrounding the power lacuna in s 51(xx) of the Australian Constitution, more recent history is relevant to the fact that the High Court has been the guardian of the Australian common law since 1986: see Fig 4.17.

FIGURE 4.17 The effect of the *Australia Act 1986* (Cth)

Case law is also important in the wider lexicon of interpretation. In terms of first principles, these matters were raised in Chapter 1. The decisions of other courts beyond the jurisdiction of Australia may be of interest or influence, but they occupy an informal position. No other court can bind the High Court of Australia.

FIGURE 4.18   The High Court sits at the apex of the Australian court system

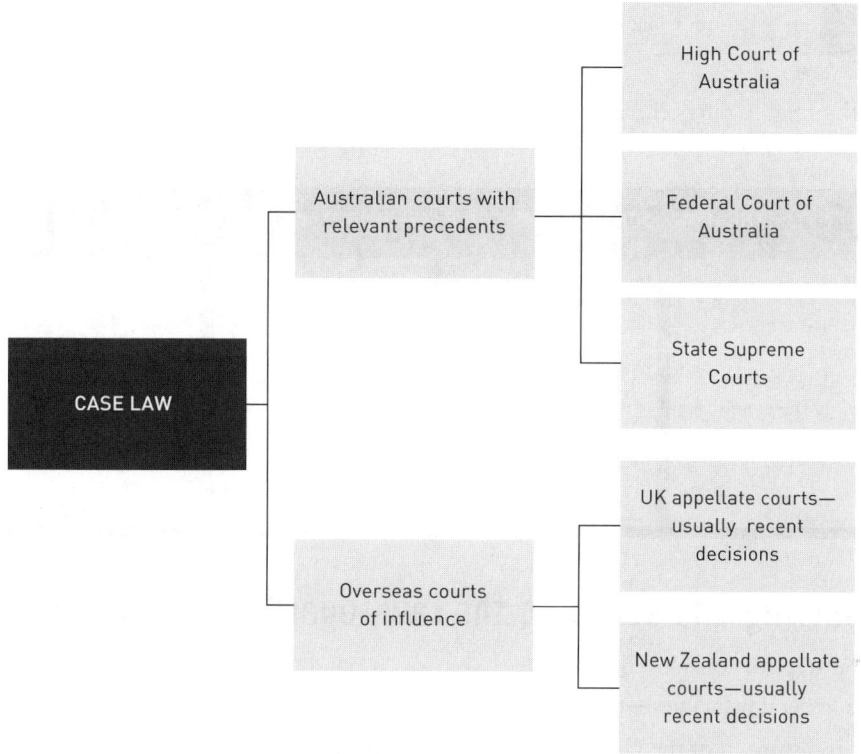

The position of the High Court relative to other courts is reflected in approaches to legal research relevant to Australian corporate law, as shown in Fig 4.19.

FIGURE 4.19   Courts dealing with commercial and corporate law

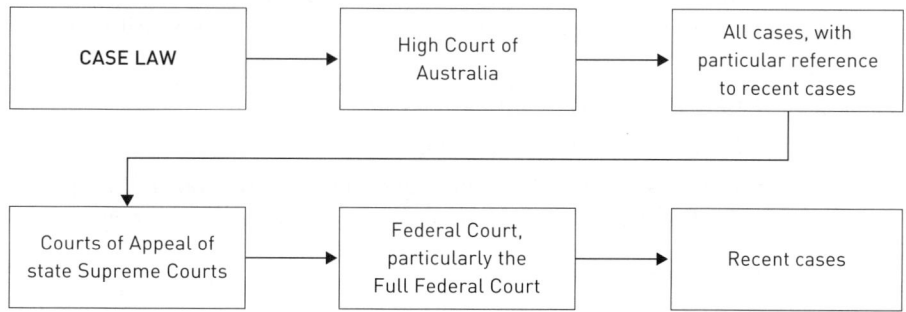

FIGURE 4.20 *Stare decisis* in practice[1]

THE HIGH COURT OF AUSTRALIA	• Is the final appellate court for all state and federal law • Is the guardian of Australian common law • Has original jurisdiction regarding the Constitution • Provides binding precedent to all other courts • Is governed by the *stare decisis* principle; may overrule one of its own prior decisions.

FIGURE 4.21 The High Court's theoretical ability to overturn a prior decision involves consideration of several issues

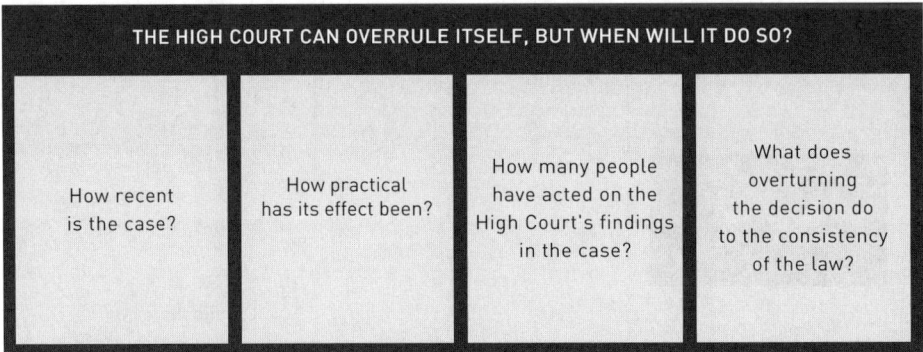

Problem solving and sourcing the law regarding corporations

There are several steps to consider including:

- reference to general principles—the location of the particular area of law
- the defined terms in s 9 of the CA2001—the gateway to the analysis
- sections of the CA2001—provides structure to the analysis; look for key words/terms
- subsections and paragraphs of the CA2001—gives the answer particularity
- case law, particularly decisions from the High Court of Australia, the Federal Court of Australia, and the Victorian and New South Wales Supreme Courts—adds weight to the analysis and statutory interpretation; provides clarity of application (and recency and/or seniority of the court adds weight, too)
- other sources, e.g. refereed articles, monographs, textbooks—adds depth
- websites, e.g. ASIC, ASX, other research—adds textual depth.

Remember to use terms such as 'usually', 'typically', 'generally', 'likely', 'mostly', 'it appears'; that is, be careful with your use of emphatic language and terms such as 'will', 'always', etc—they may be correct, but be sure.

---

[1] C Cook, R Creyke, H Geddes and D Hamer, *Laying Down the Law*, 7th ed, LexisNexis, 2009.

The development of corporate law in Australia

The development of corporate law in Australia can be seen to have happened in various phases. This includes an earlier emphasis on case law, but with legislation now at the forefront. Legislation is now the starting point for research into a point of corporate law; while the case law and other sources may inform its interpretation and practical effect.

FIGURE 4.22   Legislation is now the starting point for research into a point of corporate law

Much of corporate law is now statutory, but the case law (general law) remains important.

FIGURE 4.23   The case law can provide important contextual understanding to the statutory provisions

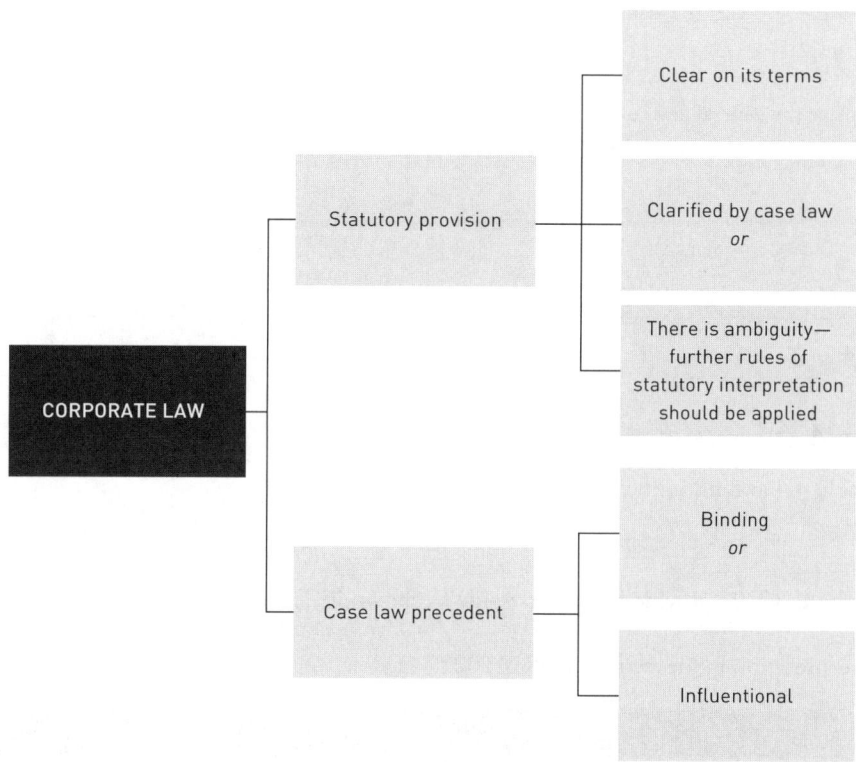

Given the breadth and volume of the CA2001, and its historical lineage and development, it is a document comprised of different drafting techniques, and across various epochs of parliamentary drafting. It is classic consolidation—'cut and paste', and the bringing together of disparate ideas and styles. The different drafting styles in the CA2001 are illustrated in Table 4.4.

CORPORATIONS LAW: CONCEPTS, CASES AND CULTURE WORKBOOK

TABLE 4.4 The various styles of certain provisions of the CA2001

Style	Example from CA2001	Significance for courts, regulators and others interpreting the law
Open-textured and broad principles	s 180: Directors' duties	Provides scope for interpretative discretion, e.g. CA2001 s 179
Lengthy, detailed and technical	s 256A and Ch 2J: transactions affecting share capital	Reduces the scope for interpretative discretion
Intended to supplement/add to the general law	ss 236 and 237: the statutory derivative provisions	Removes the strictures of *Foss v Harbottle*
Intended to work alongside the general law		
Intended to replace the general law	s 125(2): replaces the former common law *ultra vires* doctrine	

Activity 4.5

Refer to Table 4.4 and fill in the gaps.

Some parts of the CA2001 provide their own guide as shown in Table 4.5.

TABLE 4.5 Interpretation guides within the CA2001

CA2001 guide	Focus of the guide
s 7	Pt 1.2
s 9	The Dictionary
Provisions at the start of each Chapter	
Sections may have their own interpretation provisions	

The *Acts Interpretation Act 1901* (Cth) applies to the CA2001:

TABLE 4.6 The *Acts Interpretation Act* and Commonwealth legislation

Acts Interpretation Act 1901 (Cth)	Applies to CA2001	Applies to ASIC Act 2001
s 15AA	The words of the statute provide the first step Interpret the CA2001 to promote the underlying purpose or object	The words of the statute provide the first step
s 15AB	If there are ambiguities, obscurities, or absurdities, then material outside the text may be used	
s 15AB(2)		Does not refer to the regulatory guides published by ASIC

ACTIVITY 4.6

What are the main rules of statutory interpretation relevant to the CA2001 and the ASIC Act 2001?

ACTIVITY 4.7

Read the following and then answer the question below.

IN THE NEWS: BUYING A BUSINESS

Consider the issue of a client buying a business.[2]
The context: Things to consider when buying an existing business.

---

2 See https://www.business.gov.au/planning/new-businesses/buy-an-existing-business/.

As a prospective business owner, you should determine the current worth of the business and its future prospects. You should think about the following:

- Vendor—Why is the business being sold?
- Sales—Can you see any patterns or trends? What is the business's customer base? Who are the current suppliers?
- Costs—What are the fixed and variable costs? Are there any staff costs?
- Profits—Have you looked at previous financial records? Is the business profitable?
- Assets—What assets does the business have? Does it have any intellectual property or leasing arrangements?
- Inventory—Is the inventory on-hand being included in the purchase? How is the inventory managed, stored and distributed currently? Are there systems in place? What is the turnover rate?
- Liabilities—Does the business have any outstanding debts? What refunds and warranties still exist for the business? Are there debts owing on assets that are registered on the Personal Property Securities Register?
- Purchase agreement—Have you reviewed the purchase agreement carefully?
- Tax—What kinds of tax will apply? Consider GST, capital gains tax, and stamp duty implications.
- Legal issues—What are the legal agreements on leases?
- Business structure—What is the business structure? Do you need or want to change the business structure to suit your business needs? Do you know the different legal, tax and record-keeping requirements of your current business structure, or the one you want to change to?
- Partnerships—Are you buying a business with a business partner? Do you have a partnership agreement in place before you purchase?
- History—What has and hasn't worked in the business for the previous owner?
- Expectations—Do you have an idea of what expectations you'll need to manage as a franchisee or business owner?
- Planning—Have you written your business plan and marketing plan to help you document your business objectives and identify how this business will meet your goals?

QUESTION

What would be on the checklist of legal issues to look out for?

_____

_____

_____

_____

_____

_____

_____

WORKBOOK CHAPTER 4 REVIEW

An illustrative summary of the key points

Figure 4.24 illustrates that the corporate constitution is a flexible concept for Pty Ltd companies, which has replaced the previous system of the Memorandum of Association and the Articles of Association, together with the restrictive nature of the *ultra vires* doctrine.

FIGURE 4.24 The corporate constitution is a flexible concept for Pty Ltd companies

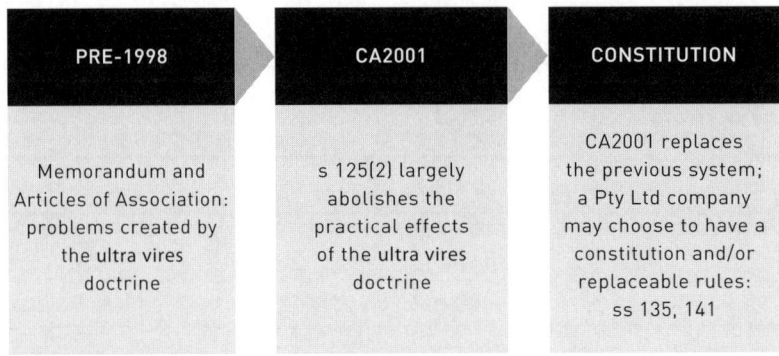

CHAPTER 4 REVISION ACTIVITIES

Consolidation of concepts, knowledge and content activities

TRUE OR FALSE?

1. Companies formed before 1998 have been required to change their rules to a constitution. True ☐ False ☐
2. The replaceable rules apply automatically to Pty Ltds. True ☐ False ☐
3. The company's constitution can be changed by a majority vote of the owners. True ☐ False ☐
4. The contractual effect of the company's constitution binds Member A to Member B in relation to their capacity as members. True ☐ False ☐
5. The replaceable rules in the CA2001 apply equally to Pty Ltd and public companies. True ☐ False ☐

FILL IN THE GAPS

1. The relevant provision of the CA2001 providing the replaceable rules is _____

2. The effect of the company's constitution is to bind the directors to the _____

3. A public company must lodge its constitution with _____ under section _____ of the CA2001.

4. The replaceable rules do not apply to a single _____ company as per s 135 of the CA2001.

5. The Mason High Court (1987–95) is known for its overall approach of _____ and implying _____ in relation to interpreting the Constitution.

6. The first Uniform Companies Legislation in Australia was adopted in _____

MULTIPLE CHOICE

1. The *ultra vires* doctrine:
    A. Is relevant for all companies
    B. Applies to pre-1998 companies
    C. Is largely abolished by s 125 of the CA2001
    D. Is totally abolished by s 130 of the CA2001

2. The company's capacity to conduct business as if it were equivalent to an individual is:
    A. Established by equity
    B. Conferred by customary principles
    C. Confirmed by *Salomon's case*
    D. Confirmed by s 124 of the CA2001

3. A pre-1998 Pty Ltd company needed to have:
    A. A constitution
    B. A shareholders' agreement
    C. A minimum of three directors
    D. A Memorandum and Articles of Association

4. A post-1998 company must have:
    A. A constitution
    B. A shareholders' agreement
    C. A Memorandum and Articles of Association
    D. A minimum of one director

5. To amend a company's constitution requires a members' meeting to approve the proposal by:
   A. 50 per cent plus one vote
   B. 25 per cent of votes
   C. 75 per cent of votes
   D. 100 per cent of votes

6. To amend a company's constitution requires the company after the members' meeting to lodge documents with ASIC:
   A. As soon as is practical
   B. As soon as possible
   C. Within five business days
   D. Within 14 days

SHORT ANSWER QUESTIONS

1. Do all of the replaceable rules need to be included in a corporation's constitution?

2. What does s 141 of the CA2001 provide?

3. What purpose do the replaceable rules fulfil?

4. Are replaceable rules used 'across the board' for all types of corporations?

Higher order thinking activities

Consider the following question and provide detailed discussion and analysis.

TOPIC A

Provide a memorandum setting out the situation pre-1998 and post-1998 concerning a company's constitution.

TOPIC B

What is the contractual effect of a company's constitution under the CA2001 and what is the relevance of the replaceable rules?

CHAPTER 5

THE CORPORATION'S DEALINGS WITH THIRD PARTIES AND POTENTIAL LIABILITY ISSUES

Chapter synopsis and links to Textbook Chapter 5

This Workbook Chapter deals with five topics:

- 5.1 Third parties dealing with the company
- 5.2 Corporate contracts
- 5.3 Pre- and post-incorporation contracts and liabilities
- 5.4 Company liability in tort
- 5.5 Company criminal responsibility.

Each of these topics is constructively aligned with, and linked to, the same topics in Chapter 5 of the Textbook.

Chapter executive summary

This Chapter provides an overview of the following topics:

- that a company has contractual capacity; as such, it can enter contracts, and can sue and be sued, on such promises
- the fact that contracts are made for and on behalf of the company by its directors, senior managers and others, depending on the company's rules
- the key provisions of the CA2001 relevant to the topic of the contractual capacity of the corporation
- the vicarious model of liability for corporate tort law liability
- the attributive model of statutory liability in terms of criminal law.

CHAPTER 5 THE CORPORATION'S DEALINGS WITH THIRD PARTIES AND POTENTIAL LIABILITY ISSUES

CHAPTER DIAGRAMMATIC OVERVIEW

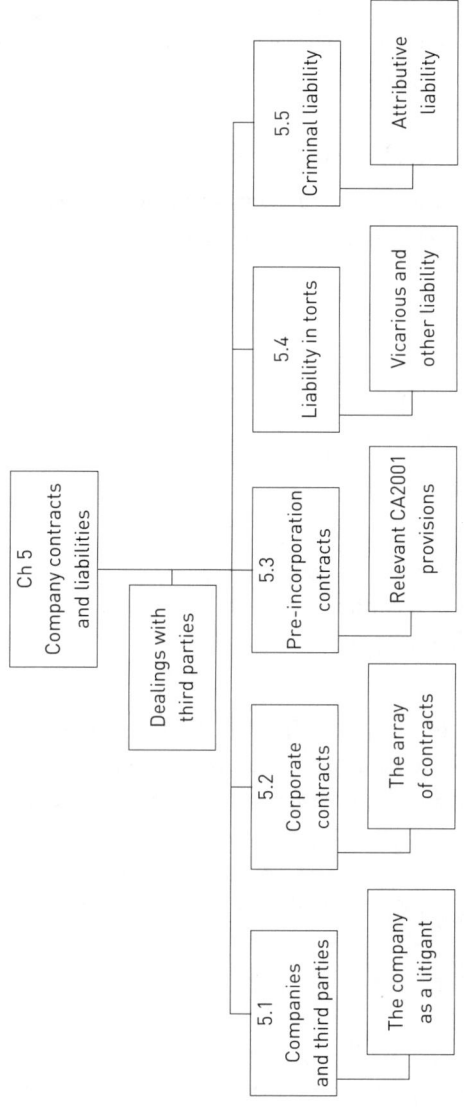

FIGURE 5.1 An overview of Chapter 5

5.1 THIRD PARTIES DEALING WITH THE COMPANY

Contractual foundations

The corporation is a separate entity; a legal person in its own right. As such, the company has contractual capacity.

Contracts that are enforceable in law go beyond mere social arrangements or informal understandings. They are enforceable in court as legal agreements with the necessary hallmarks to create binding legal rights and obligations. These ingredients include:

- two or more parties
- agreed terms and a 'meeting of minds' between the parties
- something of value or consideration exchanged between the parties.

Contracts usually have a set of certain core or irreducible elements in each case that give rise to legally enforceable commitments:

- offer and acceptance
- contractual subject matter
- an intention to create legal relations
- consideration—something of value
- an arm's-length bargain
- certainty of terms.

A non-binding contract, on the other hand:

- lacks the essential ingredients of a contract
- may be 'a domestic' or non-legal matter
- is not legally enforceable.

It is not always easy to identify a contract. The legal relationship must meet certain threshold tests or contain certain ingredients, as outlined above. This is assisted by evidence provided by the parties.

Identifying the contract will depend on the facts and circumstances. The contract may be:

- in writing
- oral, or
- partly written and partly oral.

The terms may be:

- express, or
- implied.

This will depend on the knowledge of the parties, former dealings (if any), and other relevant factors.

The company contracting with third parties

As an artificial legal entity, the company deals with third parties and enters into contracts through its directors in their capacity as agents of the company as principal: see Fig 5.2.

FIGURE 5.2   Provides the agency relationship between the directors and the company

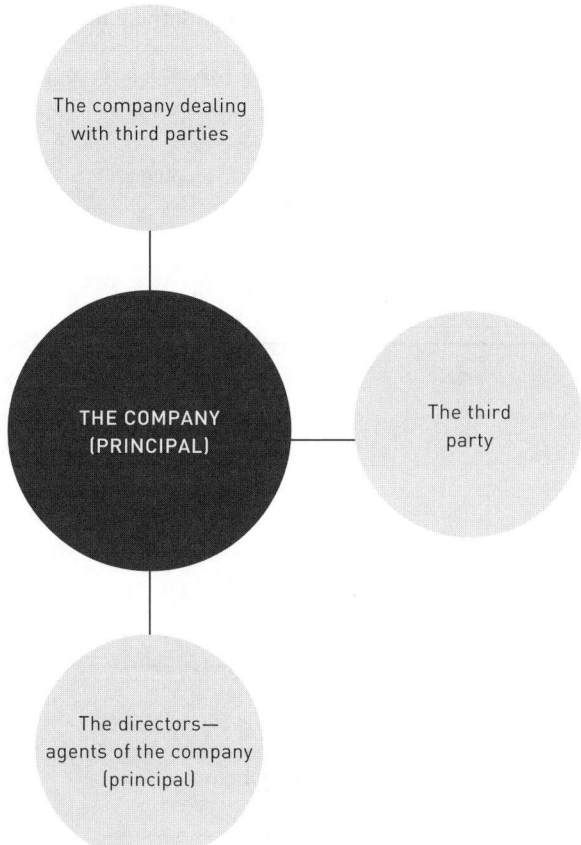

THE DEVELOPMENT OF COMMON LAW PRINCIPLES

TABLE 5.1   The 'indoor management rule' was originally developed in the UK case, *Royal British Bank v Tuquand*

Year	Case	Principle
1856	*Royal British Bank v Turquand* (UK)	Developed the so-called 'indoor management rule'
1990	*Northside Developments v Registrar-General of New South Wales* (High Court of Australia)	Provides an exception to the indoor management rule

THE MODERN STATUTORY POSITION

What inquiries of the company does the third party need to undertake under the CA2001?

FIGURE 5.3 The statutory position is set out in CA2001 ss 128 and 129

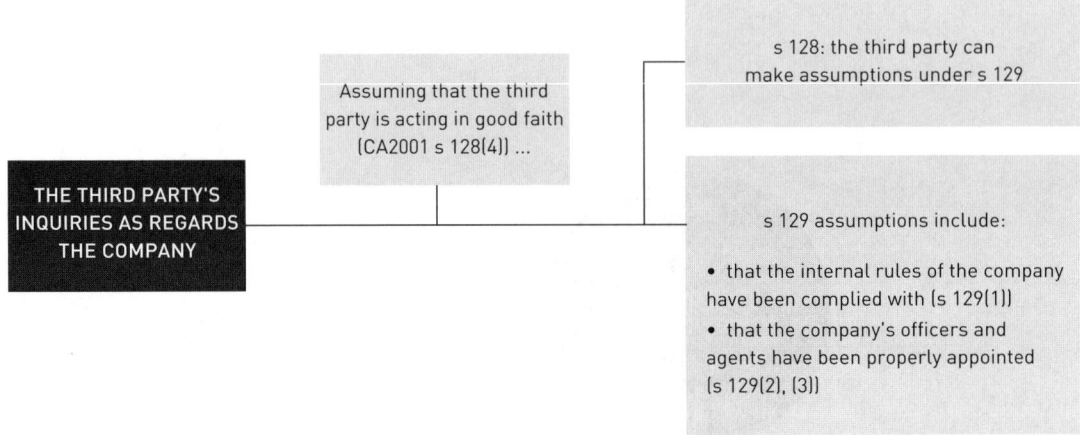

Activity 5.1

Add another case to Table 5.1. Set out its facts briefly below.

5.2 CORPORATE CONTRACTS

The corporation, as a bundle of contracts, is based on an economic model of business. We can break this into several standardised types of contract that align with the various phases of the business: see Fig 5.4.

FIGURE 5.4   The company as a series of negotiated contracts relevant to various phases

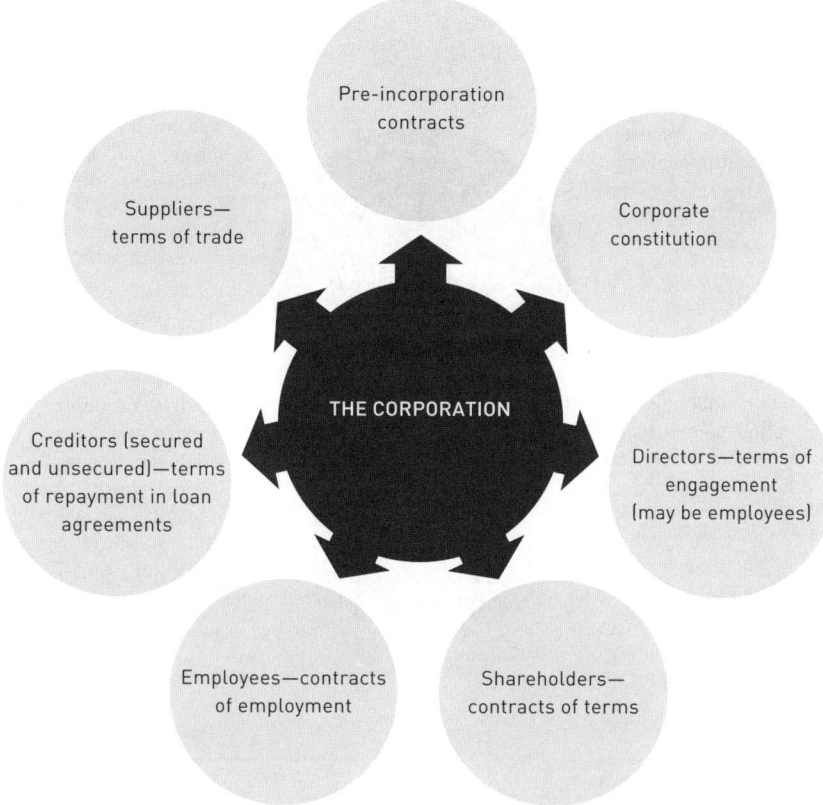

Key corporate contracts

Corporate law and its intersection with key aspects of commercial law can be represented as shown in Fig 5.5.

FIGURE 5.5 Corporate law intersects with several other areas of law

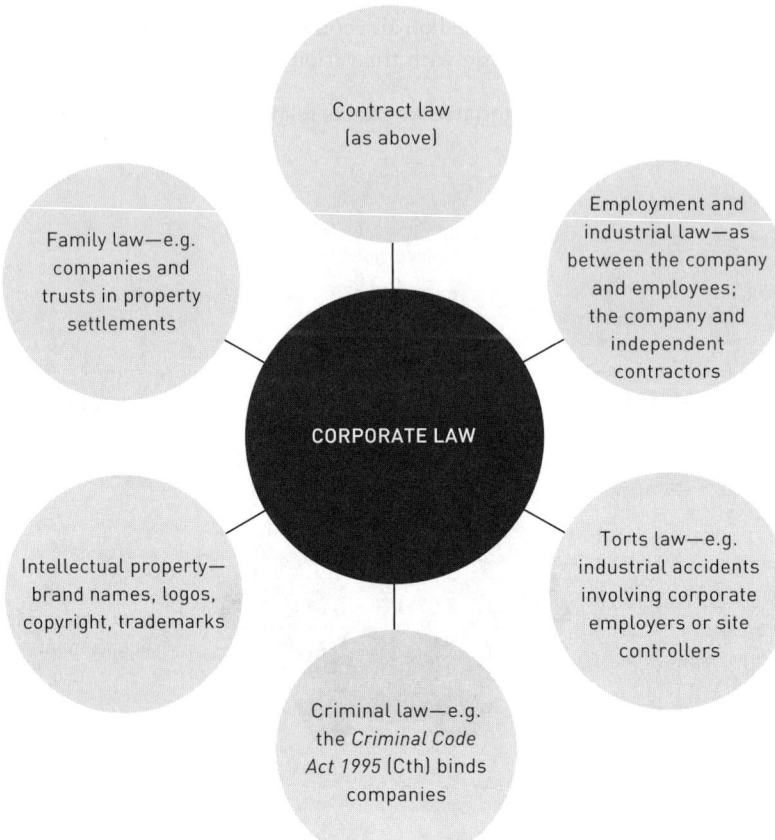

Activity 5.2

Outline the types of contract a new Pty Ltd is likely to negotiate in its first year of business.

_____
_____
_____
_____
_____
_____
_____

5.3 PRE- AND POST-INCORPORATION CONTRACTS AND LIABILITIES

There are two basic time elements in terms of the company's contractual capacity:
- before the company is in existence, and
- after the company is incorporated.

FIGURE 5.6   The pre- and post-incorporation context

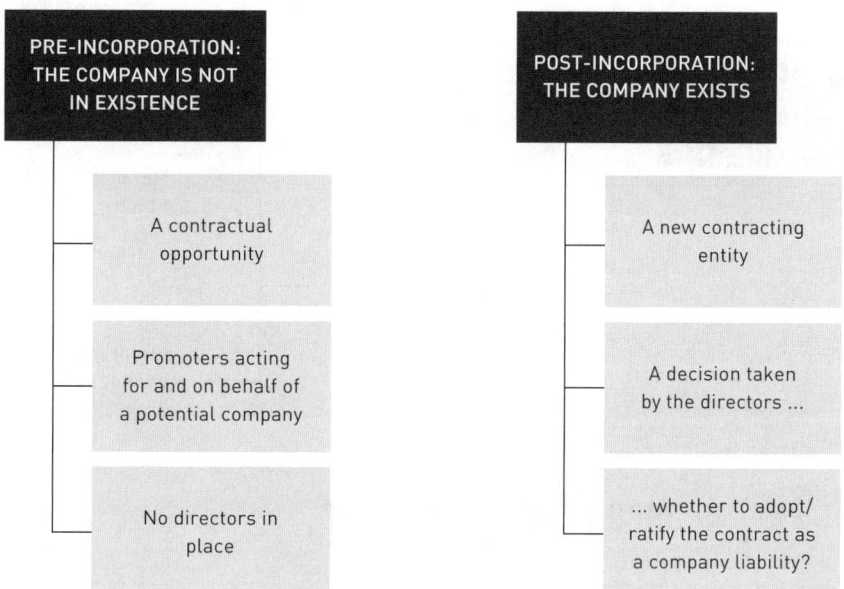

The incidence of pre-incorporation contracts

The common law regarding pre-incorporation contracts is from an earlier time, when it could take weeks to incorporate a company.

For practical purposes nowadays, it may well be that a shelf company can be purchased and used within a day or two. This probably means that the incidence of pre-incorporation contracts is reduced. Another factor is that a third party dealing with a company yet to be set up, or a new company with no track record and no assets, may require personal guarantees. This reduces the risk for the third party.

In any event, the common law principles remain important in terms of determining the risks and liabilities of the company and the third party.

THE ROLE OF THE PROMOTER REGARDING PRE-INCORPORATION CONTRACTS

Promoters are the people behind the setting up of the company. They can include:
- business people intending to become the first shareholders and directors
- professional advisers, including accountants and solicitors.

Promoters are usually involved in pre-incorporation contract negotiations. As such, they are likely to be active participants as regards these types of contracts.

FIGURE 5.7 The role of promoters

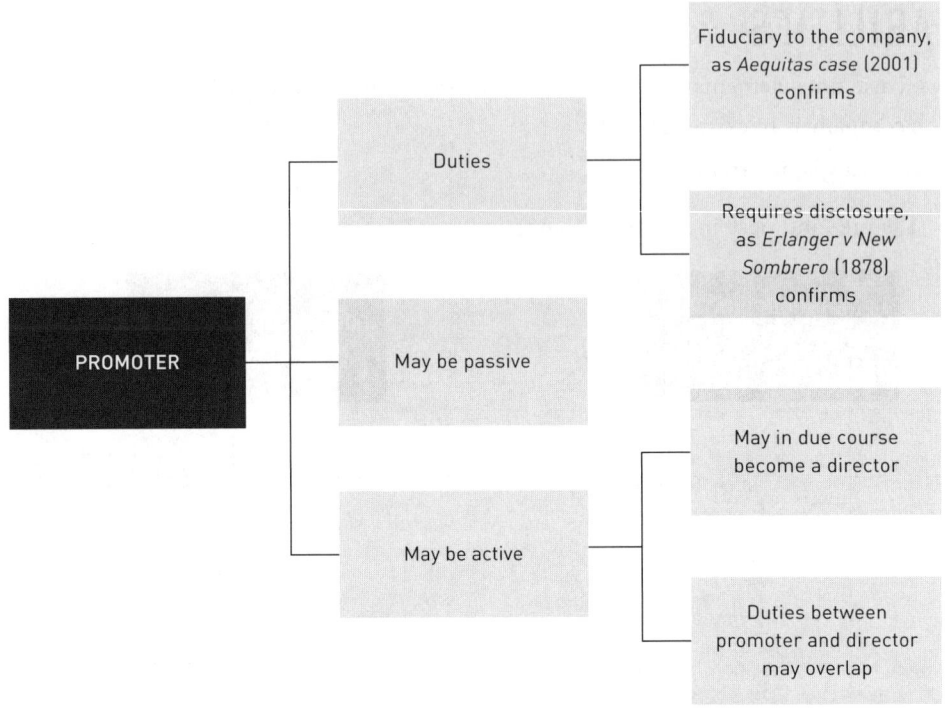

ANALYSIS OF PRE-INCORPORATION CONTRACTS

Activity 5.3

Outline the role and duties of the promoter of a company.

CHAPTER 5 THE CORPORATION'S DEALINGS WITH THIRD PARTIES AND POTENTIAL LIABILITY ISSUES

FIGURE 5.8 The statutory provisions relevant to pre-incorporation contracts

```
                    ┌─────────────────┐      ┌─────────────────┐
                    │ Potential       │      │ Potential       │
                    │ personal        │      │ personal        │
                    │ liability       │      │ liability       │
                    └─────────────────┘      └─────────────────┘
                             │                        │
┌─────────────┐   ┌──────────────────┐   ┌──────────────────┐
│ Company     │   │ Company does not │   │ ... so the       │
│ ratifies    │   │ ratify the       │   │ contract is      │
│ the contract│   │ contract         │   │ is not ratified  │
└─────────────┘   └──────────────────┘   └──────────────────┘
        │                 │                        │
        └────────┬────────┘                        │
                 │                                 │
        ┌─────────────────┐              ┌─────────────────┐
        │ Company comes   │              │ Company never   │
        │ into existence  │              │ comes into      │
        │                 │              │ existence ...   │
        └─────────────────┘              └─────────────────┘
                 │                                 │
                 └────────────┬────────────────────┘          ┌─────────────────┐
                              │                               │ Potential       │
                              │                               │ personal        │
                              │                               │ liability?      │
                              │                               └─────────────────┘
                     ┌─────────────────┐                              │
                     │ Potential       │                      ┌─────────────────┐
                     │ company         │                      │ CA2001 ss       │
                     └─────────────────┘                      │ 131-133         │
                              │                               └─────────────────┘
                              │                                       │
    ┌──────────────────┐  ┌──────────────────┐  ┌──────────────────┐
    │ Concepts and     │  │ Litigation;      │  │ Source of law    │
    │ principles:      │  │ third party      │  │                  │
    │ promoters/       │  │ rights?          │  │                  │
    │ others enter into│  │                  │  │                  │
    │ the contract     │  │                  │  │                  │
    └──────────────────┘  └──────────────────┘  └──────────────────┘
              │                   │                    │
              └───────────────────┼────────────────────┘
                                  │
                        ┌─────────────────┐
                        │ PRE-INCORPORATION│
                        │ CONTRACTS        │
                        └─────────────────┘
```

OXFORD UNIVERSITY PRESS

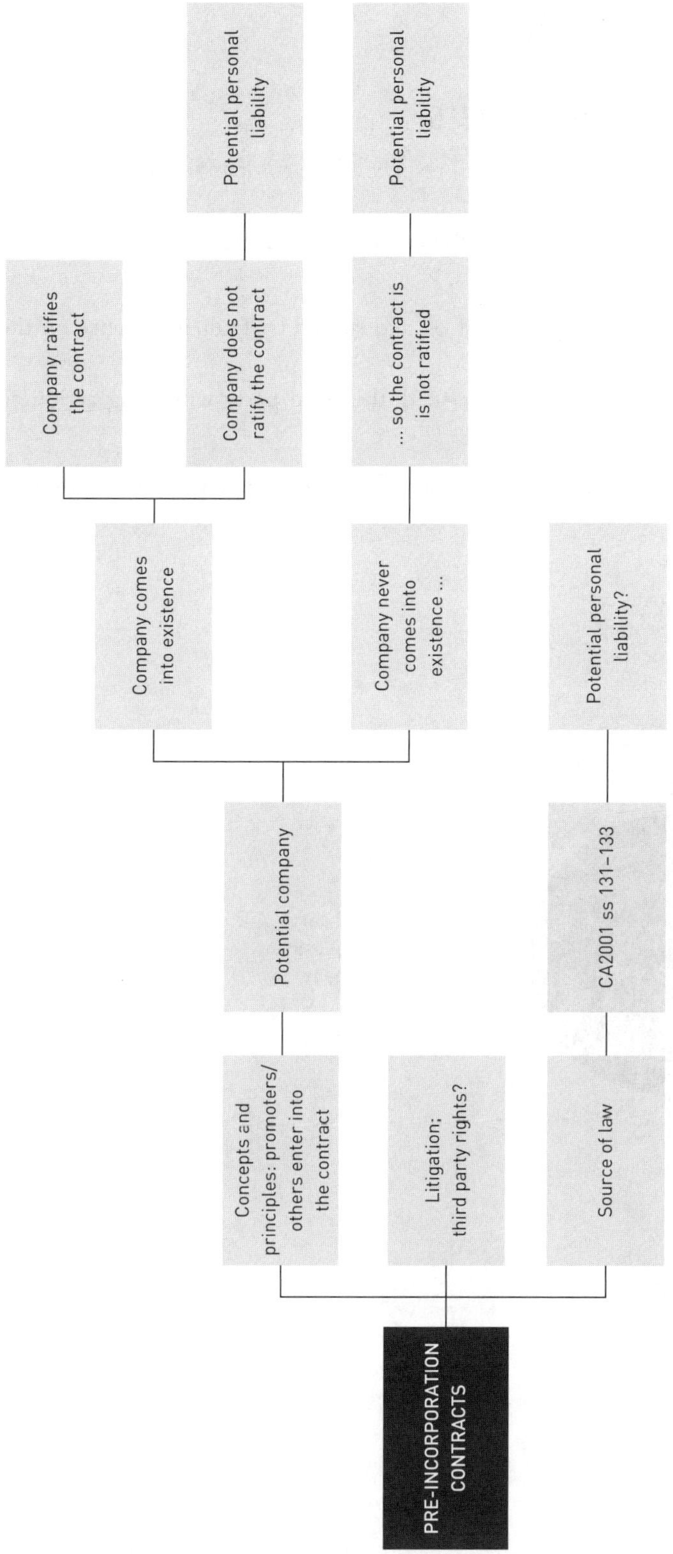

5.4 COMPANY LIABILITY IN TORT

Vicarious liability of company employers

A practical dimension of potential company liability arises in respect of the company's employees. Vicarious liability is predicated on:

- an employment relationship between the employee and the company/employer
- the employee acting in the course of their employment
- the third party being injured or suffering loss as a result of, and caused by, fault/negligence on the part of the employee.

Given that the company is a separate entity able to be sued, the third party will bring action against the company.

FIGURE 5.9   An overview of the vicarious liability of the company for the negligence of an employee

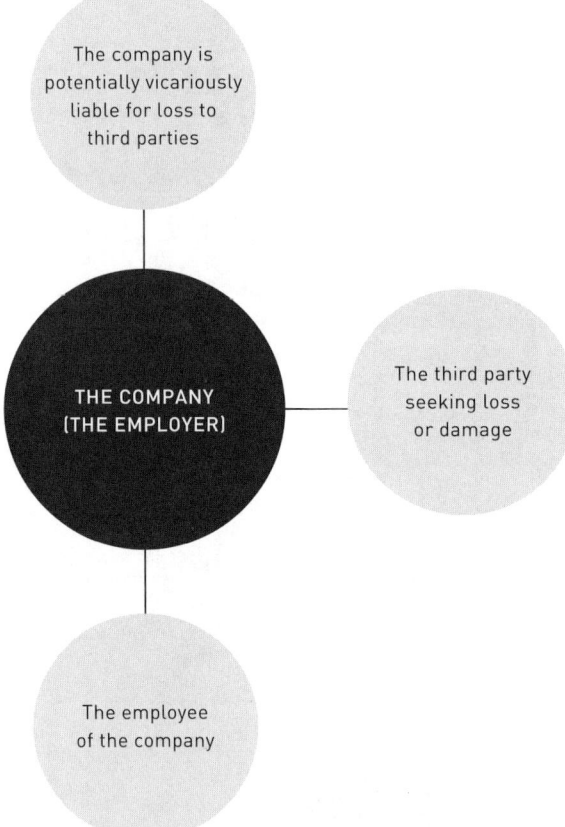

INDEPENDENT CONTRACTOR STATUS

Alternatively, the company may argue that there is no employment relationship; instead, the person is characterised as an independent contractor, and therefore it is an arm's-length relationship. As such, the company is not vicariously liable. So the analysis in Fig 5.10 is an important foundational inquiry.

FIGURE 5.10   Is the person an employee or an independent contractor?

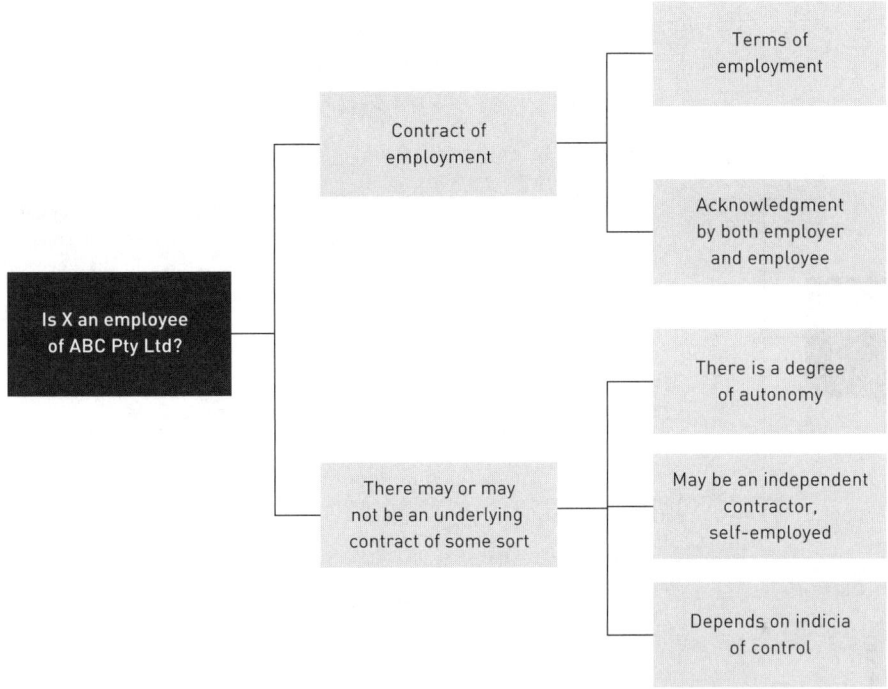

Activity 5.4
A delivery rider for Deliveroo wants advice about an injury they suffered while working. Are they an employee or independent contractor?

5.5 COMPANY CRIMINAL RESPONSIBILITY

As we have seen, the company can be liable as a defendant in terms of contract law and torts law. These areas of civil law are not so problematic. The company is a separate legal entity, and it has contractual capacity and the ability to sue and be sued. This can occur directly or via relationships, as set out in Fig 5.11.

FIGURE 5.11   Sheeting home criminal liability to companies via the so-called 'organic theory'

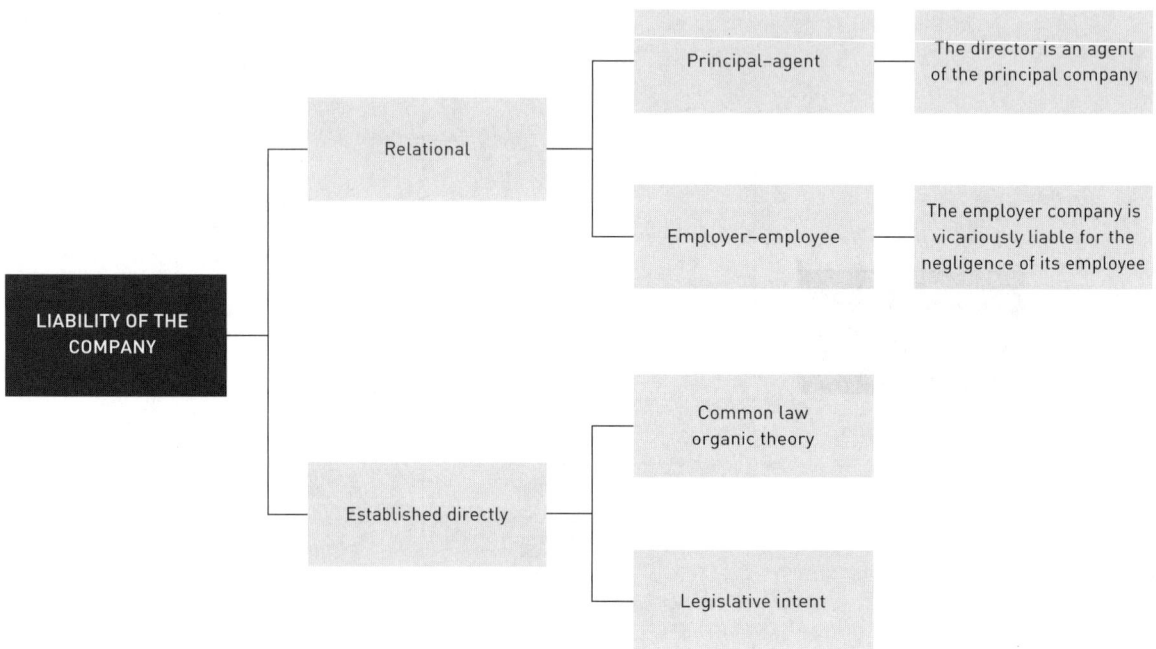

What of a crime? The company is like a human, but it is not a human. It, of itself, cannot have a guilty mind. The common law developed the organic theory to overcome this. The corporation is an artificial legal entity, and the organic theory is regarded as a legal fiction. It proceeds on the basis of metaphor. The corporation is like a human; given this, the board is like the brain; it is the 'guiding mind'.

Organic theory at common law: the mind of the company

FIGURE 5.12 Organic theory and criminal liability

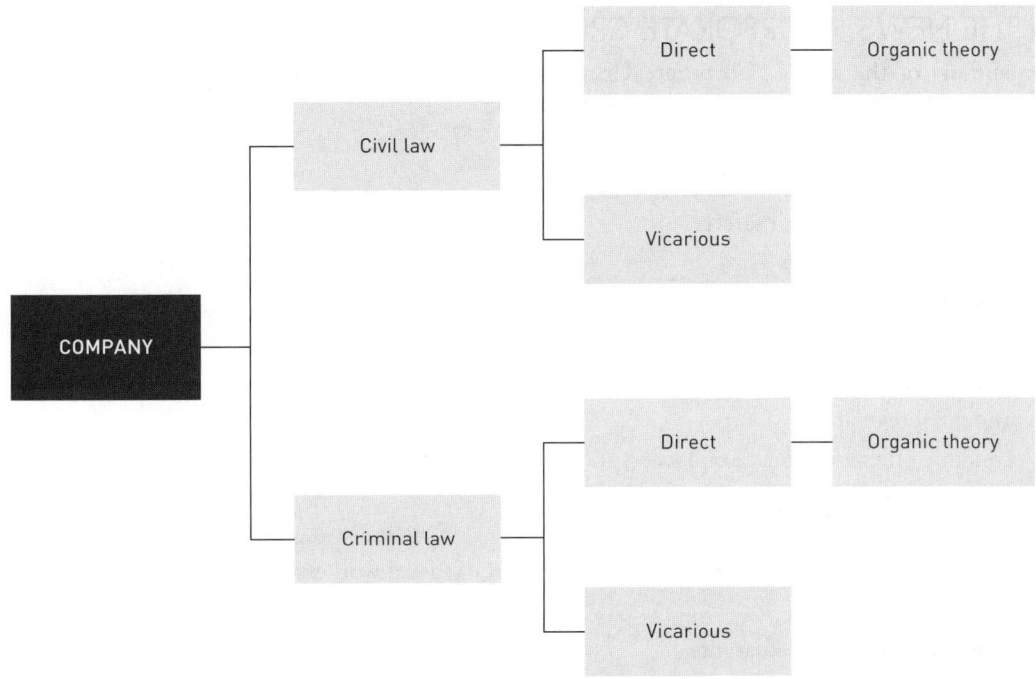

FIGURE 5.13 Legislative attribution of liability to corporations

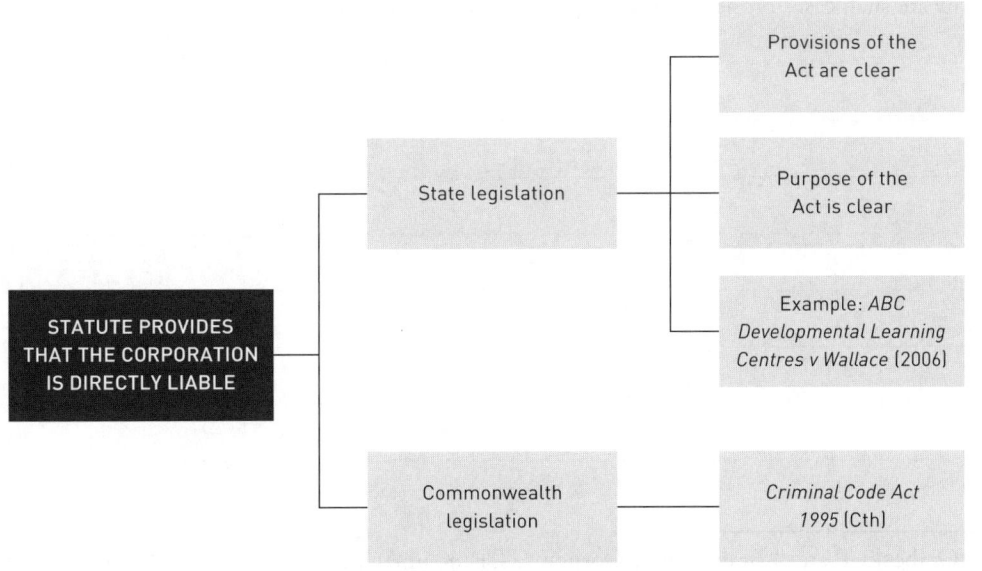

Activity 5.5

Research the following issues online and then answer the questions below.

IN THE NEWS: 'CORPORATE CRIME IN AUSTRALIA'

The authors of the article, 'Corporate Crime in Australia'[1] define and outline 10 major areas of corporate conduct in which the law may be breached:

- companies and securities offences
- taxation
- occupational health and safety
- environmental offences
- consumer affairs
- restrictive trade practices
- food standards
- prudential regulation
- economic offences against employees, and
- discriminatory practices.

The context: Underpayment of workers

Issues: Refer to the recent examples of underpayment of casual workers in:

- 7-Eleven
- George Calombaris' restuarants
- Rockpool restaurants.

QUESTIONS

1. Why are such cases prone to occurring in hospitality and retail?

_____
_____
_____
_____
_____
_____
_____
_____
_____

---

1 P Grabosky P and J Braithwaite, 'Corporate Crime in Australia' in *Trends & Issues in Crime and Criminal Justice No 5*, Australian Institute of Criminology, 1987.

2. Why are they still occurring more than 30 years after the article referred to above?

WORKBOOK CHAPTER 5 REVIEW

An illustrative summary of the key points

FIGURE 5.14 An overview of the corporation's contractual capacity

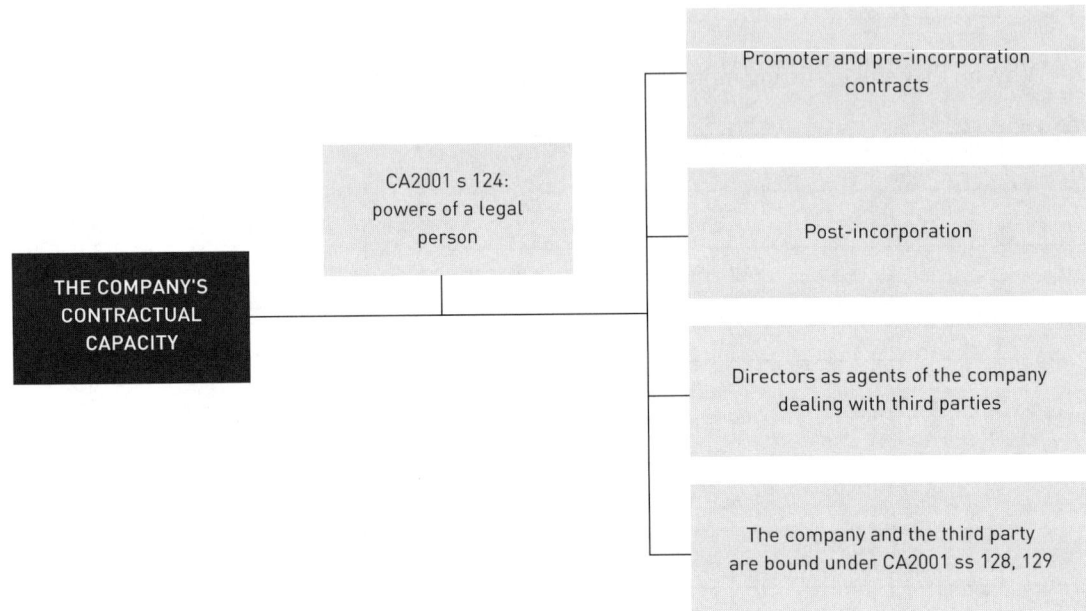

CHAPTER 5 REVISION ACTIVITIES

Consolidation of concepts, knowledge and content activities

TRUE OR FALSE?

1. An officer of a partnership is a partner, as confirmed by the CA2001. True ☐ False ☐

2. Companies registered under the CA2001 need to be registered before they enter contracts. True ☐ /False ☐

3. The New South Wales case of *Aequitas v AEFC* (2001) confirmed that promoters are fiduciaries to the corporation. True ☐ False ☐

4. A third party dealing with a company can always rely on s 128 of the CA2001. True ☐ /False ☐

5. Shareholders in general meeting can ratify a pre-incorporation contract by special resolution. True ☐ /False ☐

FILL IN THE GAPS

1. The relevant provision of the CA2001 dealing with the so-called 'indoor management rule' is _____

2. A company can be _____ liable for the torts committed by its employees in the course of _____

3. The organic theory of the corporation undermines the principle that the company is _____

4. The managing director of a company usually has authority to bind the company in _____

5. A company can execute a contract signed by _____ and with or without a common seal depending on the company's _____

MULTIPLE CHOICE

1. The rule in *Royal British Bank v Turquand* (1856) has been:
   A. Overruled by Australian common law
   B. Overruled and replaced by s 129 of the CA2001
   C. Adopted by s 140 of the CA2001
   D. Adopted and replaced by s 129 of the CA2001

2. Promoters of the company are:
   A. Officers of the company
   B. Fiduciaries to the company
   C. Both (a) and (b)
   D. Neither (a) nor (b)

3. The High Court decision in *Northside Developments* (1990) was:
   A. Decided under common law rules
   B. Before the introduction of ss 128–130 of the CA2001
   C. An exception to the rule in *Turquand's case* (1856)
   D. All of the above

4. The current exceptions to the rule in *Turquand's case* (1856) are found in:
   A. *Northside Developments*
   B. Section 128 of the CA2001
   C. Section 129 of the CA2001
   D. Section 124 of the CA2001

5. A pre-incorporation contract principally commits:
   A. The company
   B. The third party
   C. The majority shareholder
   D. The promoter
   to personal liability.

SHORT ANSWER QUESTIONS

1. Who is an officer of the company?

2. Is a senior executive of a company an officer?

3. What is the legal significance of being an officer of the company?

4. Can individuals contract on behalf of the company?

5. How are documents executed for and on behalf of companies?

Higher order thinking activities

Consider the following questions and provide detailed discussion and analysis.

TOPIC A

A client, Danni, has been offered the role of 'senior manager and head of marketing' in a public company. She wants to know what her liabilities would be under the CA2001, given these proposed roles.

TOPIC B

Discuss how (a) organic theory and (b) vicarious liability impact upon the principle that the company is a separate legal entity.

FOUNDATIONAL CASE STUDIES

Maximum word length for these case studies: 2,500 words *(this word limit excludes footnotes and bibliography)*

REQUIREMENTS FOR THESE ASSIGNMENTS:

- comprehensive footnotes
- a bibliography of all research and related sources and resources
- memorandum of advice in the following format:

| To: (recipient) |
| From: (trainee) |
| Subject matter/heading: |

SCENARIO

You are a trainee solicitor in Delaney Williams, Lawyers and Consultants. You work for Jo Delaney, Lawyer.

CASE STUDY 1: HOMESMART RECYCLING

THE CLIENT MATTER

Long-time university friends, Renae, Wendy and Jacqui, have set up a business providing smart recycling bins for homes in the western suburbs of Melbourne.

The business has been operating for six months and is enjoying great success. (The friends have deferred their studies for a year.)

They have registered a business name, HomeSmart Recycling. They have developed a new recycling method from Wendy's home in Footscray. It allows them to rapidly decompose food and plastic scraps so that they can be broken down and used for a variety of purposes (on home gardens etc).

They have made a business pitch to Footscray City Council (FCC). This innovation will allow FCC to drastically reduce the weekly kerbside collection down from three weekly bins—general rubbish (red lid), garden waste (green lid) and recyclable plastics (yellow lid)—to just one bin. The friends are planning to further adapt their process so that in due course there will be no kerbside collections; that is, all of the general waste will be recycled too.

They have sought to register the intellectual property of the work-in-progress process called 'HomeSmart EcoTransfer' (the process).

FCC wants to enter a contract with HomeSmart on an urgent basis to replace the yellow and green bins for its 20,000 homes/ratepayers.

FCC will pay HomeSmart a sign-on fee of $300,000 plus $50 per household in the first year to remove the bins and oversee the installing of 20,000 HomeSmart bins using the process.

The COO of FCC has sent a draft contract to HomeSmart for consideration. If the FCC deal is signed, HomeSmart will also need to lease factory premises as soon as possible, on a one year plus one year plus one year lease.

REQUIRED

Provide a memorandum of preliminary advice on the client file referred to above.

The memorandum is written by you in your capacity as a legal trainee, and addressed to your supervisor Jo Delaney, Lawyer.

It should contain comprehensive advice on the legal and related matters pertinent to the issues referred to above.

To: (recipient)
From: (trainee)
Subject matter/heading:
Feel free to use subheadings and navigation guides for the reader

CASE STUDY 2: FINE ART FACTORY

THE CLIENT MATTER

Gene and Hedley, two long-time friends, have been running a pop-up art gallery in various locations across Melbourne for three years. They have run the business on a 50/50 basis, splitting all costs and profits. They are keen on moving into a permanent location and have spotted a warehouse that looks suitable.

- They have informally been using a business name Fine Art Factory.
- The proposed building is owned by Gene's Aunt Fay.
- They are considering setting up a Pty Ltd company.

LEGAL ISSUES

Gene seeks your legal advice on the following issues:

1. What can they do to secure and protect the business name?
2. Is Gene obliged, given these circumstances, to disclose that Fay is her aunt? What should she do?
3. What is involved in setting up the company?
4. Can the business enter a contract to buy the land before the company is set up? What is the process?
5. Gene would like a first right of refusal if Hedley wants to sell her share in the company. How can this be achieved?

REQUIRED

Provide a memorandum of preliminary advice on the five issues referred to above.

The memorandum is written by you in your capacity as a legal trainee addressed to your supervisor Jo Delaney, Lawyer.

It should contain comprehensive advice on the legal and related matters pertinent to the five issues referred to above.

| To: (recipient) |
| From: (trainee) |
| Subject matter/heading: |
| *Feel free to use subheadings and navigation guides for the reader* |

CASE STUDY 3: SEAFOOD BOUNTY CAFÉ

THE CLIENT MATTER

Sam and Ida run a café as a Pty Ltd, trading under the business name 'Seafood Bounty Café', and have done so for three years. Sam and Ida are the only members and shareholders of the company, SBC Pty Ltd.

Ida's mother, Rowena, lent the company start-up capital of $50,000.

The two long-time friends ran a café business previously without paperwork, but split everything 50/50. They discussed a partnership, but never formalised anything.

Ida has just found out that Sam has secretly set up another business with Patrick.

ADVICE SOUGHT

- Rowena wants to know how she can recover her loan.
- Ida wants to know what she can do, given Sam's actions.

REQUIRED

Provide a memorandum of preliminary advice on the client file referred to above.

The memorandum is written by you in your capacity as a legal trainee addressed to your supervisor Jo Delaney, Lawyer.

It should contain comprehensive advice on the legal and related matters pertinent to the issues referred to above.

To: (recipient)
From: (trainee)
Subject matter/heading:
Feel free to use subheadings and navigation guides for the reader

CHAPTER 6

STAKEHOLDERS OF THE CORPORATION

Chapter synopsis and links to Textbook Chapter 6

This Workbook Chapter deals with four topics:

- 6.1 The stakeholders of the corporation
- 6.2 The regulation of companies
- 6.3 The role and function of ASIC
- 6.4 The Banking Royal Commission and its aftermath.

Each of these topics is constructively aligned with, and linked to, the same topics in Chapter 6 of the Textbook.

Chapter executive summary

This Chapter examines the corporation by reference to:

- the stakeholder concept, both internal and external
- the evolving and contested nature of the stakeholder concept
- the role of corporate regulation in general and ASIC in particular
- the recent Banking Royal Commission and some of its effects and consequences (also examined in Chapter 16)
- it being a 'creature of statute' and, in particular, the main legislation relevant to all Australian corporations: the CA2001, and
- its practical operating context subject to the relevant law, comprising the CA2001 and the general or case law.

CHAPTER DIAGRAMMATIC OVERVIEW

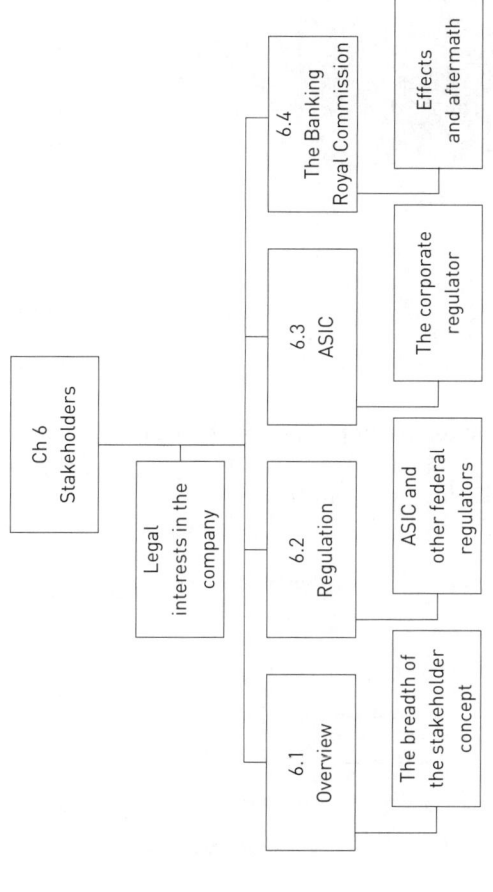

FIGURE 6.1 An overview of Chapter 6

6.1 THE STAKEHOLDERS OF THE CORPORATION

The four broad groups of stakeholders can be visualised as shown in Fig 6.2.

FIGURE 6.2 The operating context of the company

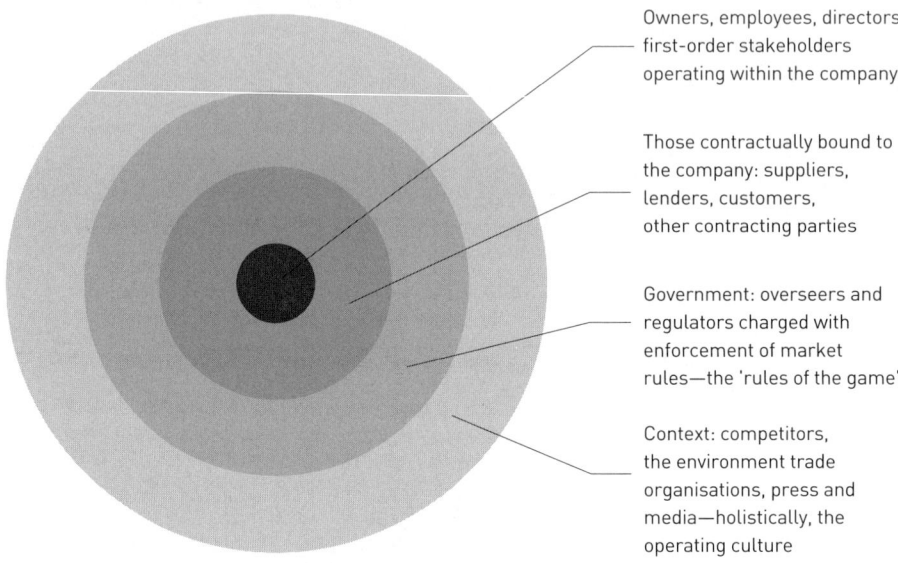

Owners, employees, directors: first-order stakeholders operating within the company

Those contractually bound to the company: suppliers, lenders, customers, other contracting parties

Government: overseers and regulators charged with enforcement of market rules—the 'rules of the game'

Context: competitors, the environment trade organisations, press and media—holistically, the operating culture

The basic choice for a start-up for-profit business is shown in Fig 6.3.

FIGURE 6.3 A review of the basic for-profit entities

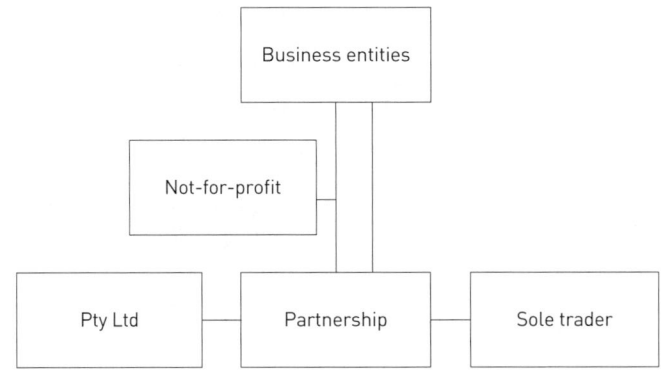

The focus of a for-profit business will be on owner returns. In the case of companies, this means shareholder returns. In broad terms, the focus can be economic or may be broader, as shown in Fig 6.4.

FIGURE 6.4   The focus of a company: the two key models

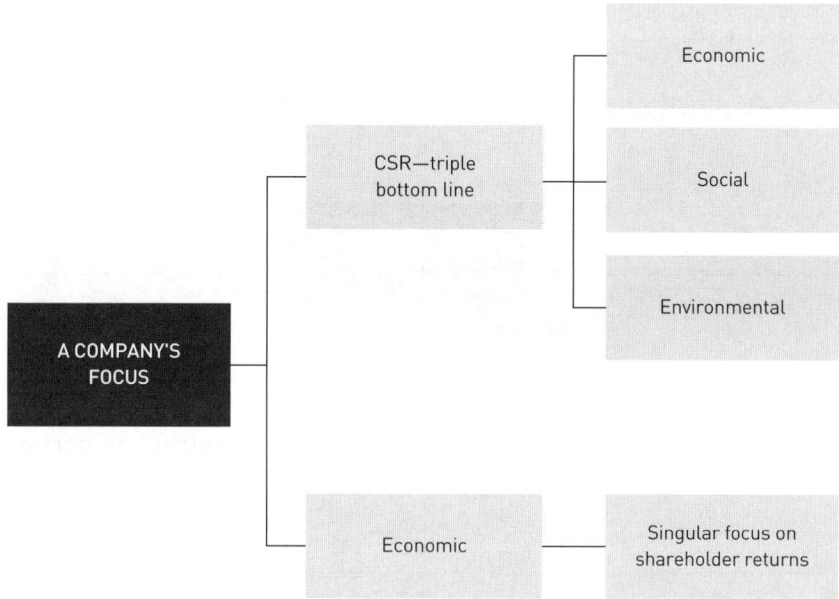

Stakeholders can be broadly defined as either internal or external: see Fig 6.5.

FIGURE 6.5   An overview of the company's stakeholders

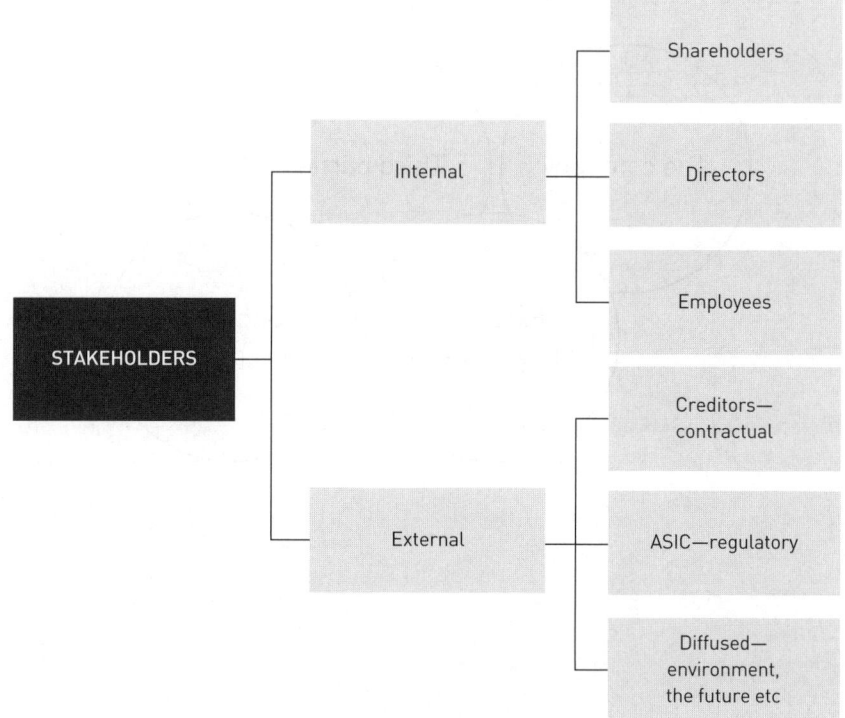

The main parties are linked by contract to the corporation as a separate entity, as shown in Fig 6.6.

FIGURE 6.6 The link between the main parties and the corporation

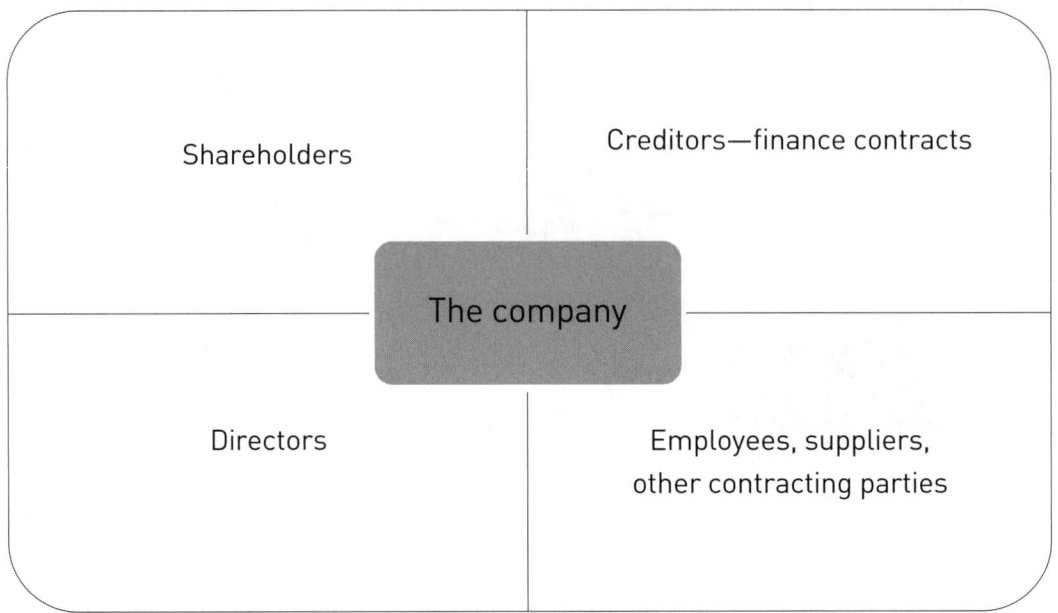

External stakeholders can include third parties with particular rights or interests in the corporation, and these interests can overlap and intersect depending on the nature of the connnection to, or interest in, the company.

FIGURE 6.7 The main actors external to the company

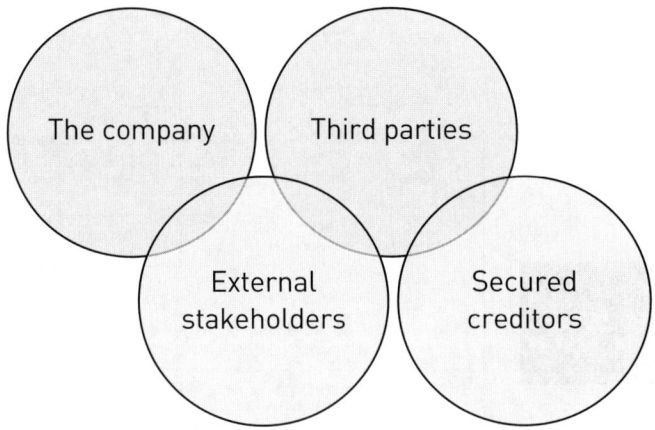

CHAPTER 6 STAKEHOLDERS OF THE CORPORATION

A secured creditor has rights under contract law, and additionally a security interest that may be enforceable (for example, by appointing a receiver: see Chapters 14 and 15).

FIGURE 6.8 The multiple potential roles of a secured creditor in relation to the company

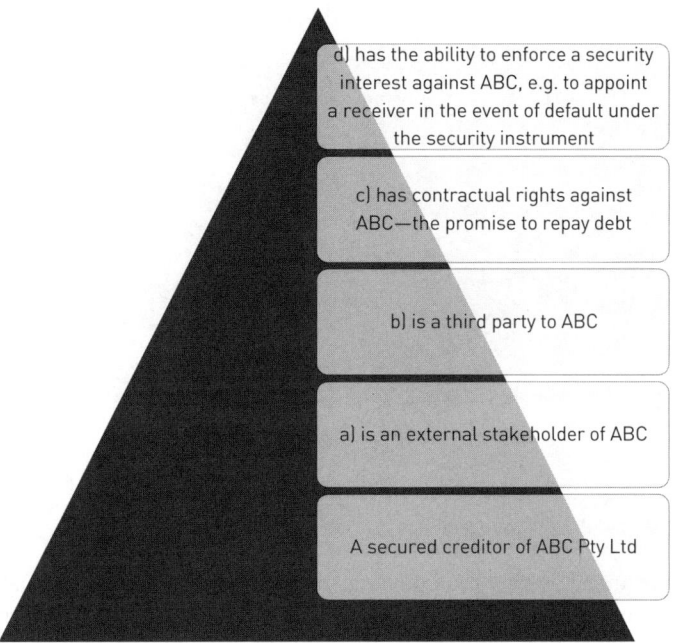

FIGURE 6.9 An overview of stakeholders

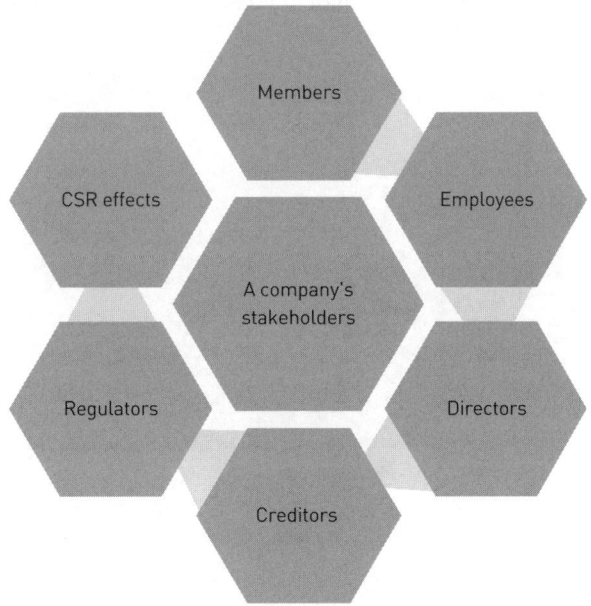

In a corporate law system such as Australia's, in which the current shareholders are the prime stakeholders, they sit at the top of the pyramid, as shown in Fig 6.10.

FIGURE 6.10   Stakeholders internal and external

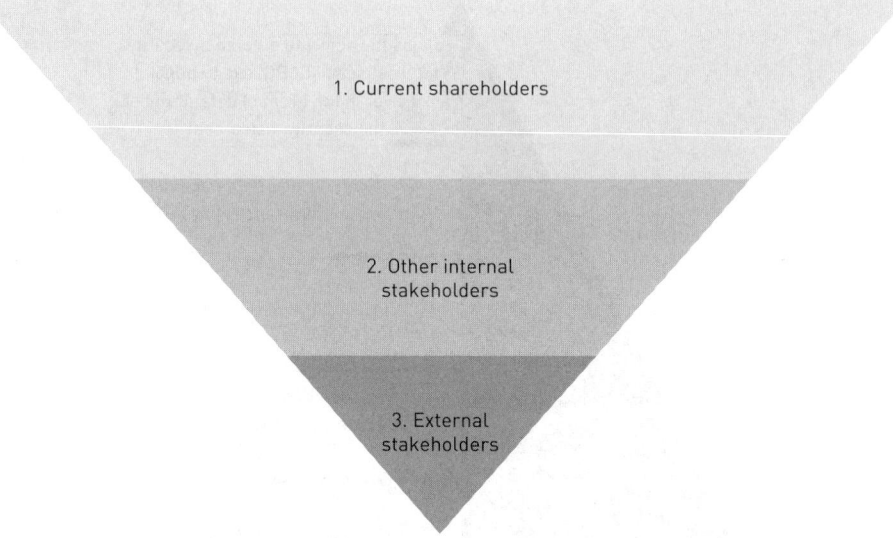

By contrast, in some countries, rather than putting shareholders first, other internal stakeholders may rank ahead of the current shareholders. For example, in Germany and Japan, both modern, advanced economies, employees rank ahead of shareholders, as shown in Fig 6.11. These systems are often referred to as 'stakeholder models'.

FIGURE 6.11   The stakeholder model, where the shareholders are not the prime internal stakeholders

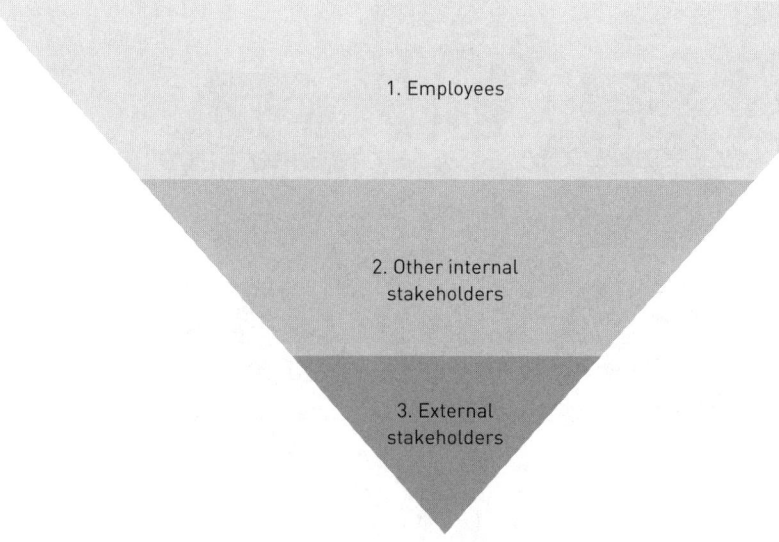

Figure 6.12 sets out three of the basic models regarding how a business is run. These include corporate social responsibility (CSR) and environmental social governance (ESG).

FIGURE 6.12   Three of the basic models of how businesses are run

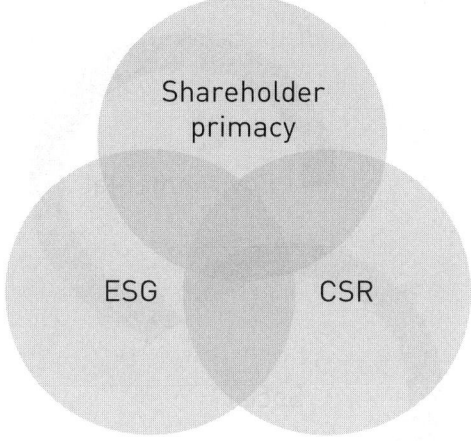

FIGURE 6.13   CSR models

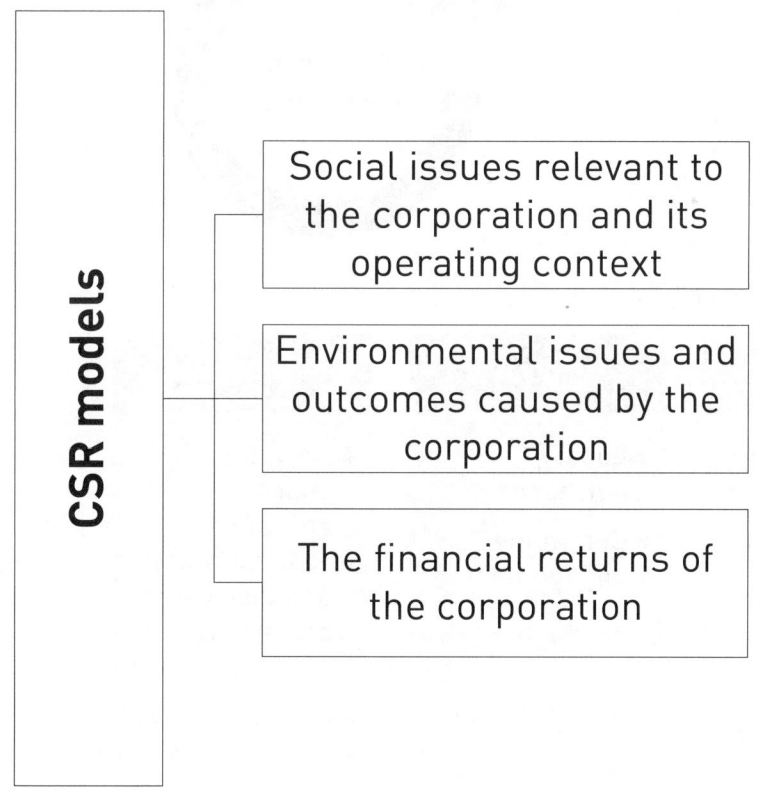

CSR models give rise to the 'triple bottom line' concept of corporations. This puts environmental performance, social outcomes and financial metrics on an essentially equal footing.

ESG is a variation of CSR.

FIGURE 6.14 The main elements of ESG

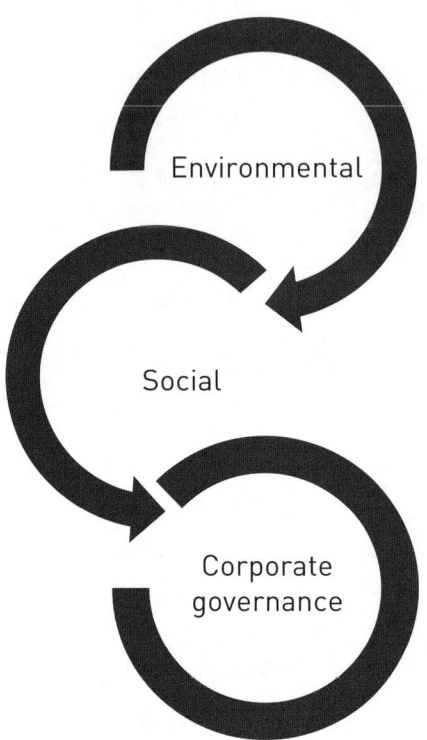

FIGURE 6.15 The ESG pillars

Environmental	Social	Governance
• Sustainability • Emissions	• Local outreach • Community engagement	• How the board operates • Transparency and disclosure practices

Activity 6.1

Explain and expand on the main features of two models of the corporation—the so-called shareholder model versus the so-called stakeholder model. What are their relative virtues and vices?

_____
_____
_____
_____
_____
_____
_____

6.2 THE REGULATION OF COMPANIES

A corporation's stakeholders are those groups with a stake, commitment to, or interest in the company. Regulators are external stakeholders.

TABLE 6.1 Stakeholders of a corporation

Internal stakeholders	External stakeholders
• Employees • Shareholders • The board • The senior managers • The CEO	• Customers • Suppliers • Creditors • Regulators • Competitors? Other intangible/emerging stakeholders: • The environment? • The future? • The community? • The competitive context?

FIGURE 6.16 The oversight role of regulators

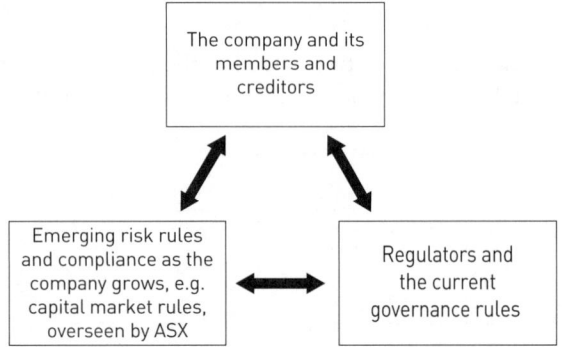

The stakeholder regulators in the corporate sphere are:
- ASIC
- Takeovers Panel
- ASX
- APRA
- ACCC
- ATO
- accounting-related groups, including:
  - CPA
  - CAANZ
  - Auditing and Assurance Standards Board (AuASB)
  - Australian Accounting Standards Board (AASB)
  - Financial Reporting Council (FRC).

A company will interact with, or be influenced by, several regulators, as shown in Fig 6.17.

FIGURE 6.17 The range of regulators relevant to a public company

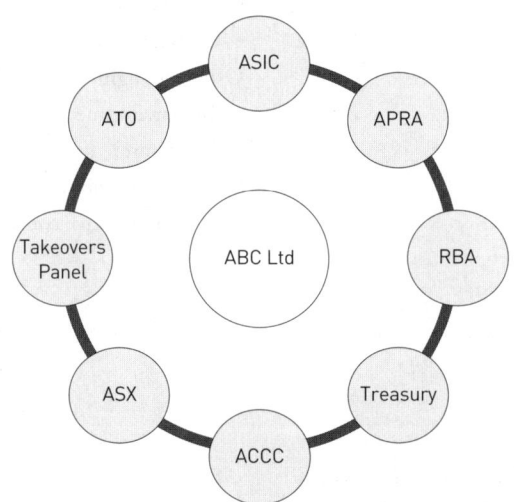

Other federal regulation includes:
- intellectual property
- the franchise code.

State regulation includes:
- property law
- contracts.

Key related documents include:
- ASX Listing Rules.

Activity 6.2

Think of an international company that is of interest to you, and operating in Australia; for instance, Google, Apple, Facebook or Amazon.

What are some of the current and emerging regulatory challenges relevant to the oversight of these companies in terms of their activities within Australia?

6.3 THE ROLE AND FUNCTION OF ASIC

FIGURE 6.18 An overview of ASIC's role

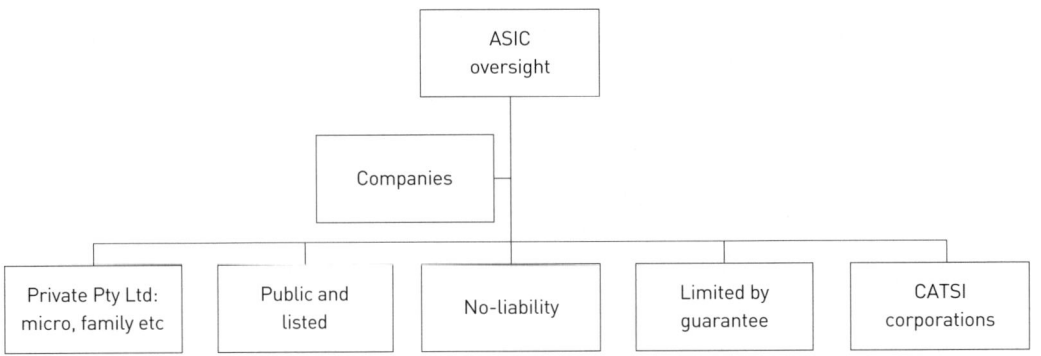

TABLE 6.2 The genesis of the ASIC Act 2001

Date	Event
1989	*Corporations Act* (Cth) Australian Securities Commission (ASC)
1990	*New South Wales v Commonwealth* ('*Incorporation case*') (High Court): invalidates the 1989 Act
1991	ASC and the Corporations Law Scheme
1998	ASC changes its name to ASIC A cross-vesting scheme is deployed
1999	*Re Wakim* (High Court): the cross-vesting scheme is declared invalid
2000	Alice Springs Agreement: state and Commonwealth laws are passed
2001	CA2001 and ASIC Act 2001 come into existence Locked in by sunset renewal clauses every five years and state control—a scheme in the gift of the states

FIGURE 6.19   ASIC: the main corporate regulator

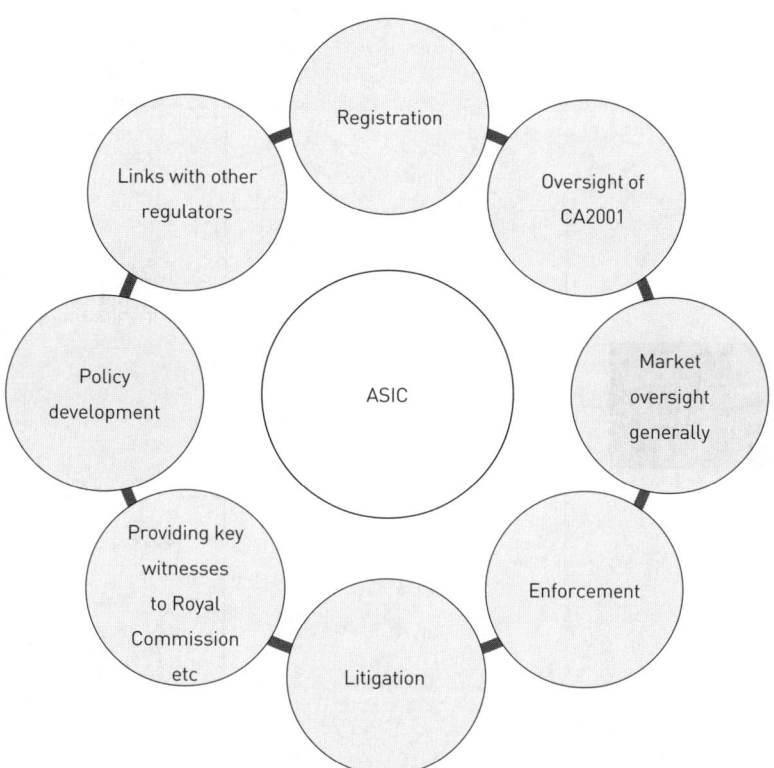

The role of ASIC includes enforcing 'the rules of the game' and dealing with market misconduct: see Fig 6.20.

FIGURE 6.20   ASIC's oversight of market misconduct

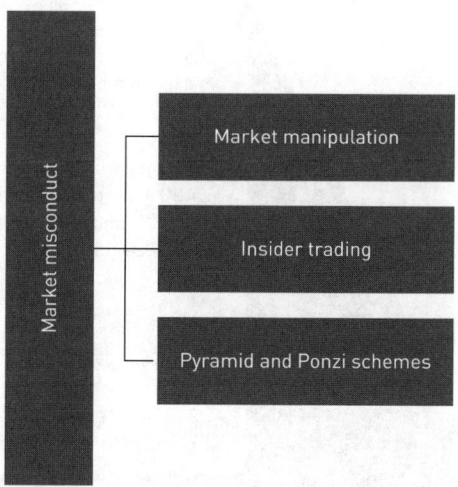

Note what ASIC does not regulate—this includes barrels of whisky: see Fig 6.21.

FIGURE 6.21　What ASIC does not regulate

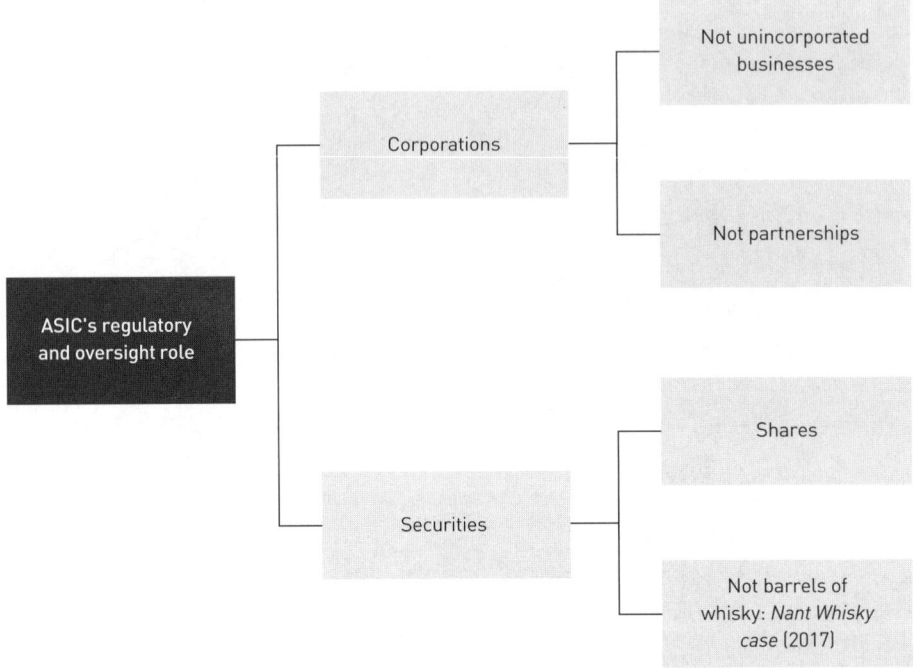

Figure 6.22 sets out the role of ASIC in relation to a company, ABC Pty Ltd.

FIGURE 6.22　The multi-faceted nature of the relationship between a company and ASIC

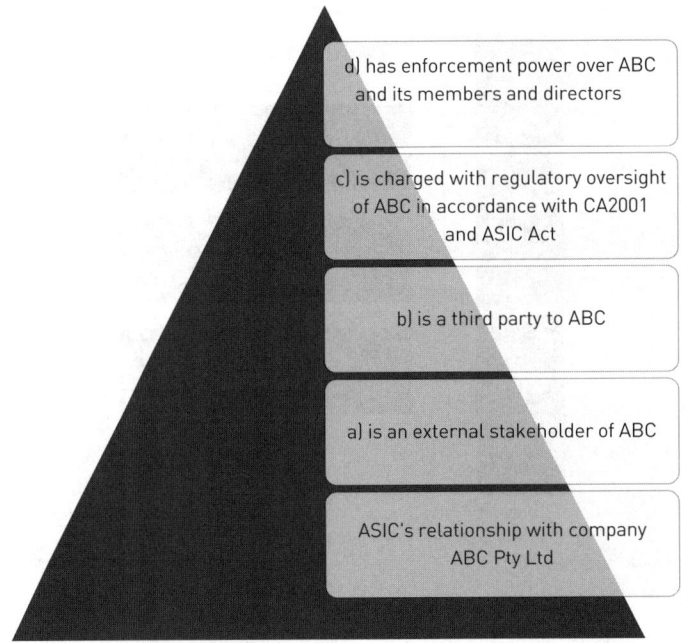

ASIC v Vizard (2005) 145 FCR 57 illustrates the significant disconnection between ASIC's apparently lenient approach, and the judge's harsher, more salutary one.

TABLE 6.3 *ASIC v Vizard*: the disconnection between ASIC's approach and that of the judge

Issue	ASIC recommendation	The judge's decision
The amount of the fine	$130,000 for each of three instances	Would have preferred a higher amount per instance
The period of disqualification from being a director	5 years	10 years

The ASIC Act 2001 established several specialist bodies with particular oversight roles, as shown in Table 6.4.

TABLE 6.4 Bodies and related entities established under the ASIC Act 2001

Body provided for under the ASIC Act 2001	Role of the body
Corporations and Markets Advisory Committee (CAMAC)	Formed under Pt 9 of the ASIC Act 2001 Provided expertise on corporate law review Now disbanded
Takeovers Panel	Formed under Pt 10 of the ASIC Act 2001 An expert panel dealing with takeovers
Companies Auditors Disciplinary Board	Formed under Pt 11 of the ASIC Act 2001 Deals with registration and potential suspension of auditors
Financial Reporting Council (FRC)	Formed under Pt 12 of the ASIC Act 2001 Provides advice on the process for determining accounting and auditing standards
Australian Accounting Standards Board (AASB)	Formed under Pt 12 of the ASIC Act 2001 Provides advice on the process for determining accounting and auditing standards
Parliamentary Joint Committee on Corporations and Financial Services	Formed under Pt 14 of the ASIC Act 2001 Examines the annual reports and activities of ASIC and the Takeovers Panel Undertakes inquiries and provides reports as required by either Commonwealth chamber: the House of Representatives or the Senate

> **Activity 6.3**
>
> Fill in the final row of Table 6.4.

6.4 THE BANKING ROYAL COMMISSION AND ITS AFTERMATH

The Banking Royal Commission (BRC) is one of several royal commissions that have been held in Australia in recent times. It was headed by retired High Court justice, Kenneth Hayne. Three other recent or ongoing royal commissions include investigations of aged care, disability care, and issues of institutional sexual abuse.

Royal commissions are instituted due to widespread community concern, and political and other pressure. The BRC is no different. It was resisted for a period of time by the Federal Government, as it was considered to be potentially destabilising of the financial and banking sectors.

An example of this political resistance is as follows:

Malcolm Turnbull admits trying to stave off the Banking Royal Commission was wrong

Malcolm Turnbull says commentators arguing it was a mistake not to set up a Royal Commission into the banking sector 'are all right', and that the government 'would have had less political grief if it had set up a royal commission two years ago'.

The revelations of wrongdoing in banks at the Royal Commission have had Turnbull's ministers scrambling to explain their resistance to the idea.

The Prime Minister argues the government was working on regulatory measures and the Royal Commission threatened to delay that process.[1]

> **Activity 6.4**
>
> Read the following, conduct your own research, and then answer the questions on the next page.
>
> ### IN THE NEWS: AFTER THE BRC
>
> **The corporation:** AMP
>
> **The context:** AMP is a long-established financial services and advisory business listed on the S&P/ASX 200. AMP (previously the Australian Mutual Provident Society) received particular attention during the course of the BRC, and in the *Final Report*.[2] AMP has, arguably, been the most excoriated financial institution as a result of the BRC. Its chair, its CEO and its chief legal officer were all forced to resign.[3]

---

1   Phillip Coorey, afr.com, 23 April 2018, https://www.businessinsider.com.au/malcolm-turnbull-royal-commission-wrong-to-resist-2018-4/.
2   Royal Commission into Misconduct in the Banking, Superannuation and Financial Services Industry, *Final Report*, 1 February 2019, https://financialservices.royalcommission.gov.au/Pages/default.aspx/.
3   https://www.smh.com.au/business/banking-and-finance/amp-chair-catherine-brenner-steps-down-20180430-p4zcd9.html/.

The damage to the reputation and brand of AMP has been significant. The company's stock price has fallen substantially, halving in the last two years, and it has recorded large operating losses in the wake of the BRC. It is now described as a 'former blue chip company'.

AMP's business focus is on financial advice, and life and other insurances.

QUESTIONS

1. Why is AMP more vulnerable to after-shocks from the BRC than the banks?

2. What is the strategy of AMP, as discerned from business reports and related online information?

WORKBOOK CHAPTER 6 REVIEW

An illustrative summary of the key points

FIGURE 6.23 An overview of the main stakeholders relevant to the corporation and the oversight of Australian corporate law

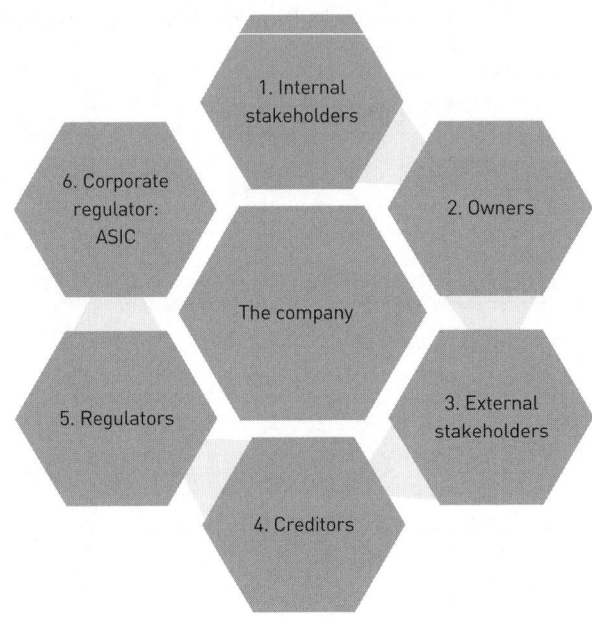

CHAPTER 6 REVISION ACTIVITIES

Consolidation of concepts, knowledge, and content activities

TRUE OR FALSE?

1. Australian companies prioritise shareholders.   True ☐ False ☐
2. German companies prioritise employees.   True ☐ False ☐
3. ASIC is funded by each state and territory.   True ☐ False ☐
4. ASIC's use of enforceable undertakings was seen as cost-effective and efficient by the Banking Royal Commission.   True ☐ False ☐
5. Corporate social responsibility promotes the environment as a stakeholder.   True ☐ False ☐

FILL IN THE GAPS

1. ASIC was criticised in the *Vizard case* (2005) for suggesting a disqualification period of _____ years.

2. In the *Vizard case* (2005), the Court imposed a disqualification period of _____ years.

3. The case of *ASIC v Rich* (2009), which ASIC _____, involved the business _____ rule.

4. ASIC appealed the *Forrest* decision to the _____ and won, but lost on appeal to the _____.

5. The case ASIC pursued against Andrew Forrest to the High Court involved the continuous _____ rules of the CA2001.

MULTIPLE CHOICE

1. ASIC stands for:
    A. Australian Shares, Investors and Corporations
    B. Association of Shareholders, Investors and Corporates
    C. Australian Securities and Investments Commission
    D. Australian Securities and Insurance Corporation

2. APRA stands for:
    A. Australian Professional Relationships Agency
    B. Australian Primary Regulatory Association
    C. Administrative Portfolio for Regional Australia
    D. Australian Prudential Regulation Authority

3. ASX stands for:
    A. Australasian Stock Exchange
    B. Asian Stock Exchange
    C. Australian Securities Exchange
    D. Australian Share Exchange

4. ACCC stands for:
    A. Australian Consumer Credit Council
    B. Australasian Council for Corporate Credit
    C. Australasian Competition and Consumer Commission
    D. Australian Competition and Consumer Commission

5. The Banking Royal Commission *Final Report* was:
   A. Critical of ASIC
   B. Critical of ACCC
   C. Praiseworthy of ASIC
   D. Praiseworthy of APRA

SHORT ANSWER QUESTIONS

1. Why are shareholders important stakeholders?

2. What is meant by the phrase 'triple bottom line'?

3. What does CAMAC refer to?

4. What is the Takeovers Panel and what is its function?

5. What is the scope and purpose of the ASX Listing Rules?

Higher order thinking activities

Consider the following questions and provide detailed discussion and analysis.

TOPIC A

What is the function, purpose and scope of ASIC, and what challenges does it face in the next five years?

TOPIC B

What is the function and purpose of the ASX?

CHAPTER 7

COMPANY LEADERSHIP AND THE BOARD OF DIRECTORS

Chapter synopsis and links to Textbook Chapter 7

This Workbook Chapter deals with five topics:

- 7.1 Directors, officers and managers
- 7.2 The board and its strategic role
- 7.3 Corporate governance
- 7.4 The chair
- 7.5 The CEO.

Each of these topics is constructively aligned with, and linked to, the same topics in Chapter 7 of the Textbook.

Chapter executive summary

This Chapter examines the leadership of the corporation:

- the board of directors acts as the strategic overseer of the company—what the company does and why
- the board is responsible for the steerage or governance of the company—accountability, oversight and compliance
- the board is comprised of individual directors, each bearing responsibility under the CA2001
- the board is chaired by the chair—a director regarded as 'first among equals'—and employs the CEO.

CHAPTER 7 COMPANY LEADERSHIP AND THE BOARD OF DIRECTORS

CHAPTER DIAGRAMMATIC OVERVIEW

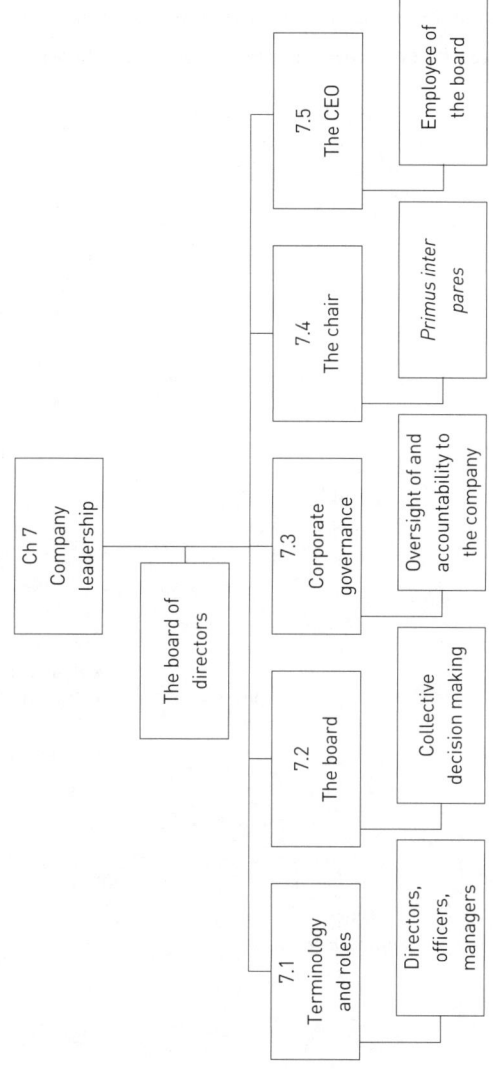

FIGURE 7.1 An overview of Chapter 7

7.1 DIRECTORS, OFFICERS AND MANAGERS

The terminology of this Chapter links to Chapter 8, which focuses on directors. The terms 'directors', 'officers', 'executives', 'employees' and 'senior employes' may get used in different, flexible and potentially inconsistent ways.

The terms 'director' and 'officer' are defined in the CA2001. They prioritise:

- legal substance or content

  over

- the title, form or labels that may be applied to a particular person or role.

Directors and officers will often be employees of the corporation; however, that is not necessarily the case.

FIGURE 7.2   An overview of potential employees of the firm

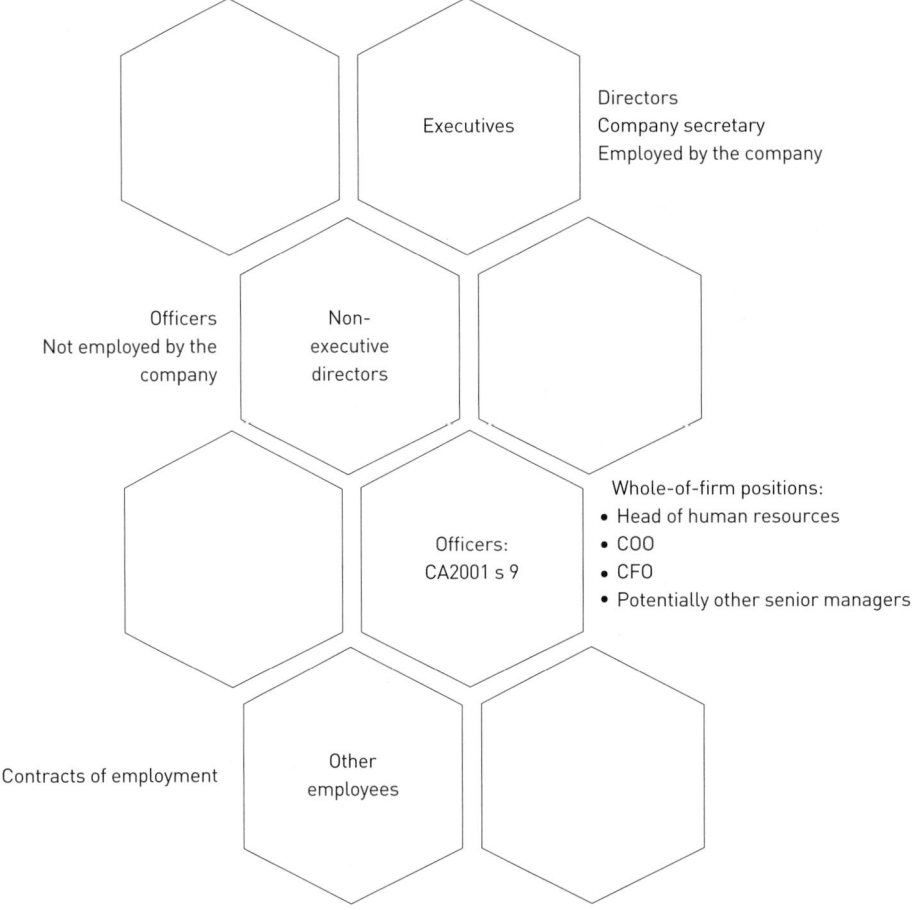

The tests for whether a person is an employee are found in employment law, torts law and contract. These are outlined in Fig 7.3.

FIGURE 7.3 Ascertaining whether A is an employee of the company

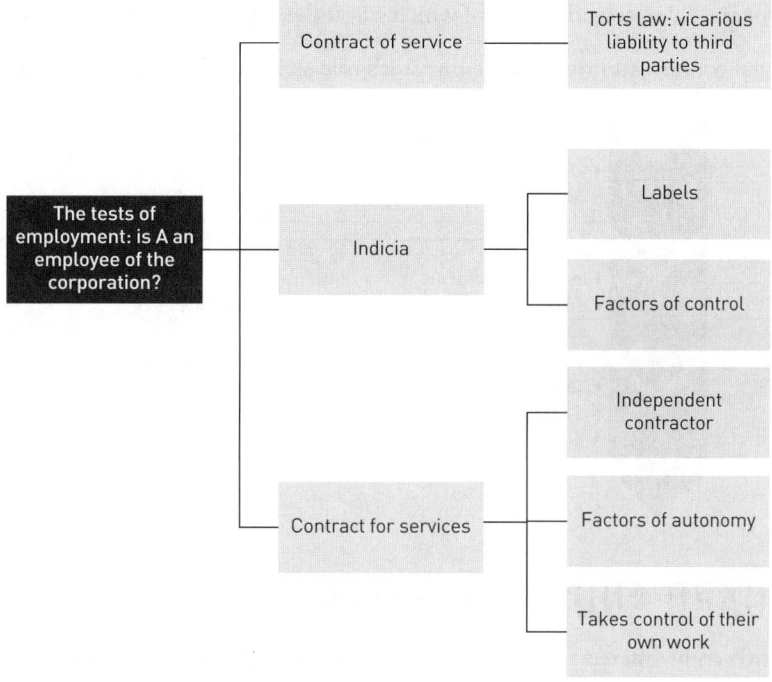

Figure 7.4 gives guidance on how to ascertain whether a person is a director of a company.

FIGURE 7.4 The rubric for the appointment of, or the finding that, a person is a director

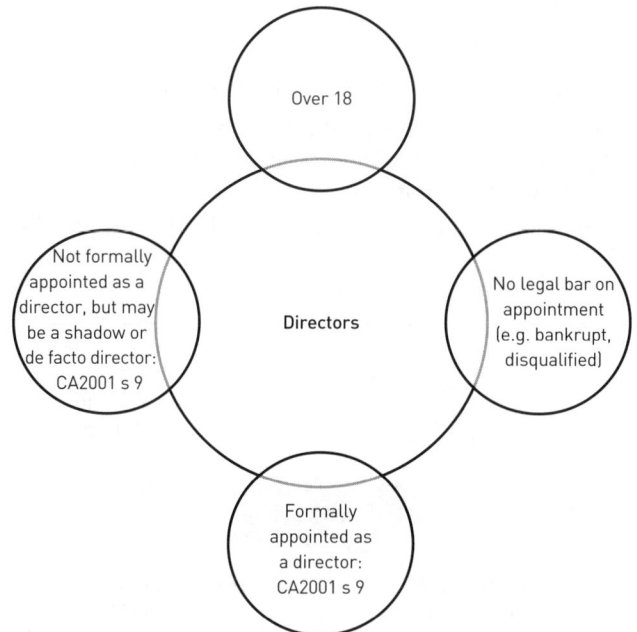

The role of director carries with it core responsibilities and duties; it is foundational to the efficient, fair and accountable conduct of the company's business. The assumption or imposition of the term 'director' therefore freights legal content and rules, consideration of which sits at the apex of corporate considerations: see Fig 7.5.

FIGURE 7.5 The legal content and rules in the director's role sit at the apex of the corporation

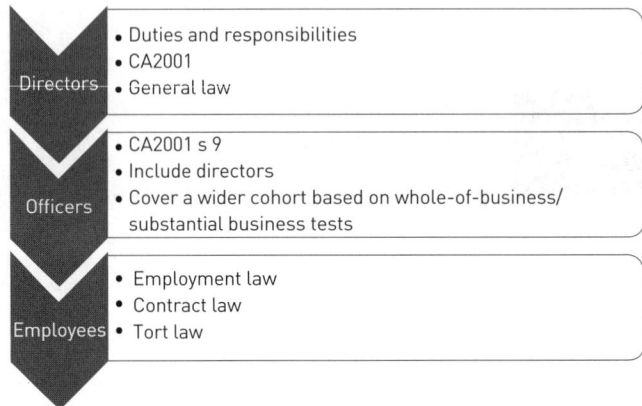

7.2 THE BOARD AND ITS STRATEGIC ROLE

The role of the board can be diluted to a relatively simple set of high-level responsibilities.

What boards do and what they are required to do at law was addressed in the New South Wales case of *AWA v Daniels* (1992) 7 ACSR 759. Rogers CJ found that the board's functions are four-fold:

- setting the goals for the company
- appointing the company's CEO
- overseeing the plans of the managers
- reviewing, at reasonable intervals, the goal setting of the company.

Of course, the theoretical statement of these precepts belies the fact that they can give rise to so-called 'wicked problems' (that is, very complex problems) and 'black swan events' (that is, unexpected or unpredictable events that are low in probability, but high in impact) in practice.

From the perspectives of law and management, we could surmise that the board's role is as shown in Fig 7.6.

FIGURE 7.6 The role of the board in theory

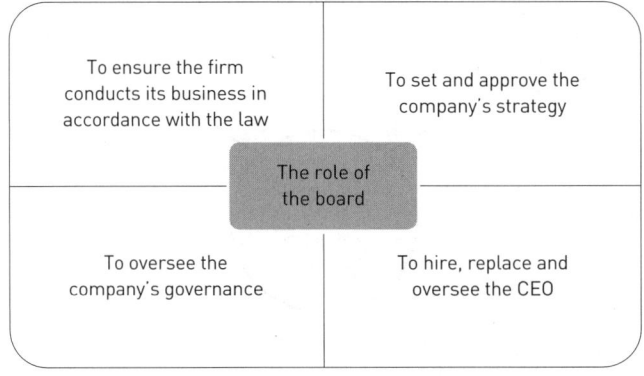

Ascertaining the concept and content of the word 'strategy' can be difficult because it is multi-faceted in its use and application. In this regard, it is somewhat like the word 'capital', which we unpack in Chapters 12 and 13. Strategy is variously:

- higher order thinking and analysis
- 'big picture' (a macro-view) problem solving
- what the firm seeks to do (aims, objects, purposes) and why (meaning, rationale)
- multi-faceted, as required
- flexible and responsive—it covers the short and long term, as may be necessary.

Boards may play somewhat different roles, depending on the context: see Fig 7.7.

FIGURE 7.7 The potentially varied role of the board in different settings

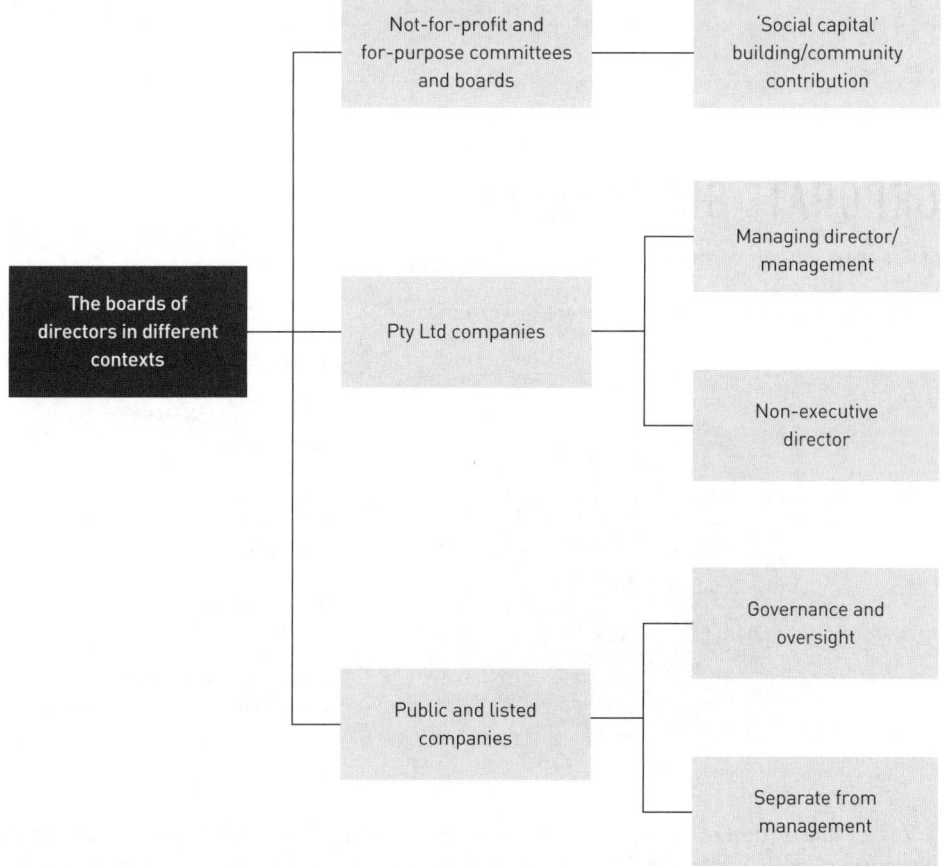

Activity 7.1
Outline some of the features of the concept of 'strategy' as it applies to corporations.

7.3 CORPORATE GOVERNANCE

The elements of corporate governance are illustrated in Fig 7.8.

FIGURE 7.8 The elements making up corporate governance[1]

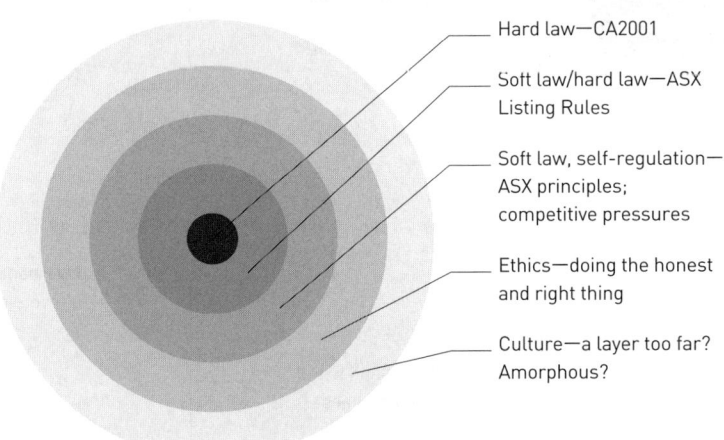

Figure 7.9 is an illustration of corporate governance as cascading responsibilities—six aligned layers with people at the centre of each, while Fig 7.10 builds on this to show contractual and related liability.

---

1 Adapted from John Farrar, *Corporate Governance: Theories, Principles and Practice*, OUP, 2005, 4.

FIGURE 7.9 Corporate governance as cascading responsibilities

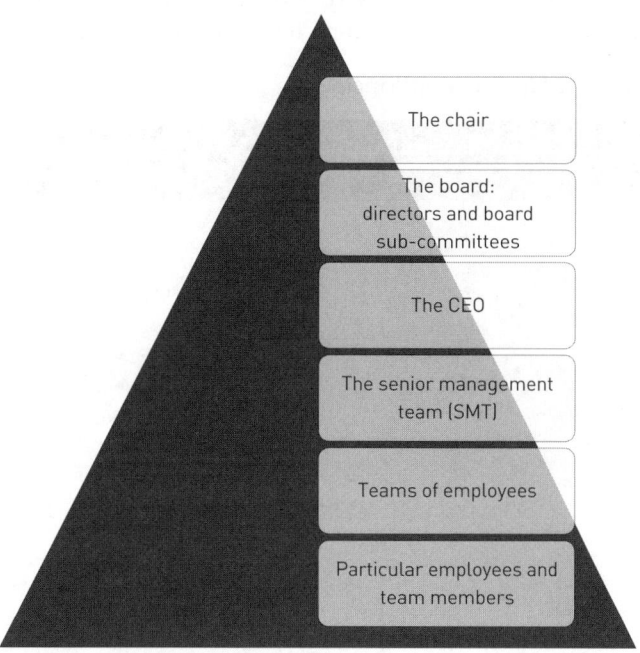

FIGURE 7.10 The various aspects of corporate governance

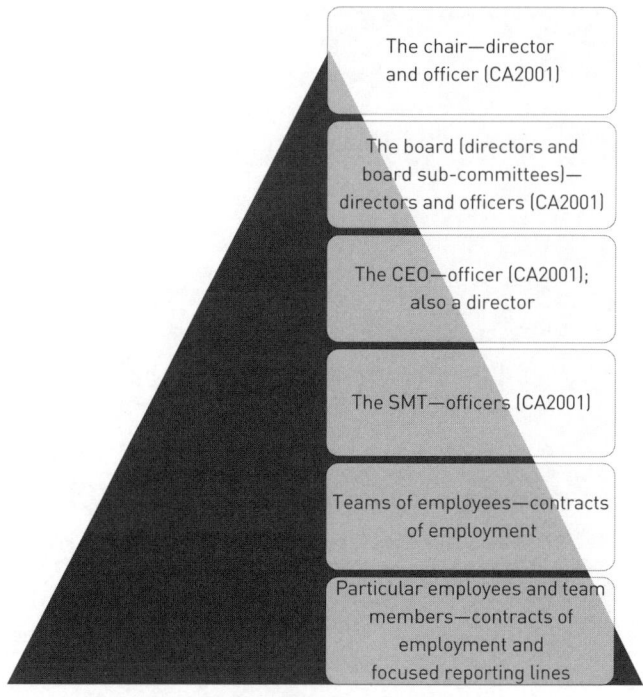

The main focus of corporate governance for listed companies in Australia is the set of ASX Corporate Governance Principles, which are now in their fourth iteration. They operate on an 'if not, why not' basis; that is, they are not mandatory, but require explanation if they are not adopted.

TABLE 7.1 The ASX Corporate Governance Principles

Corporate Governance Principle	Relevance and application
Lay solid foundations for management and oversight	
Structure the board to add value	
Act ethically and responsibly	
Safeguard integrity in corporate reporting	
Make timely and balanced disclosure	

CHAPTER 7 COMPANY LEADERSHIP AND THE BOARD OF DIRECTORS

Corporate Governance Principle	Relevance and application
Respect the rights of security holders	
Recognise and manage risk	
Remunerate fairly and responsibly	

Activity 7.2

Go to the ASX website, find the Corporate Governance Principles and provide a brief analysis of each, using the spaces in Table 7.1.

Corporate governance is also an international project. This has arisen in response to globalisation and the increasing importance of global trade, and the need to set standards of accountability. There have been several major reviews, particularly from the UK.

TABLE 7.2 The development of corporate governance as an international project particularly informed by, and provided impetus through, UK initiatives and reform processes

Date	Major corporate governance reviews	Outcome and effect
1992	Cadbury	

TABLE 7.2 The development of corporate governance as an international project particularly informed by, and provided impetus through, UK initiatives and reform processes (continued)

Date	Major corporate governance reviews	Outcome and effect
1995	Greenbury	
1998	Hampel	
2003	Higgs	
2003	Smith	
2018	UK Corporate Governance Code[2]	The Code sets out standards of good practice in relation to issues such as leadership, effectiveness, accountability, remuneration and relations with shareholders.

---

2   See https://www.frc.org.uk/directors/corporate-governance-and-stewardship/uk-corporate-governance-code/.

Activity 7.3

Look at Table 7.2, which deals with UK corporate governance reviews and developments. Add to and complete the table.

7.4 THE CHAIR

Table 7.3 lists cases relevant to the role of the chair (and the board).

TABLE 7.3 The role of the chair and board: significant cases

Date	Case	Outcome and effect
1966	*Colorado Constructions Pty Ltd v Platus*	
1991	*Kelly v Wolstenholme*	
1992	*AWA Ltd v Daniels*	
2000	*Woonda Nominees Pty Ltd v Chng*	

TABLE 7.3   The role of the chair and board: significant cases (continued)

Date	Case	Outcome and effect
2003	*ASIC v Rich*	
2003	*Whitlam v ASIC*	

Activity 7.4

Look at Table 7.3. Complete the table by making notes as to the outcome and effect of each case.

7.5 THE CEO

The term 'chief executive officer' (CEO) has overtaken the former term 'managing director' in the contemporary Australian business environment.

The CEO may or may not be a director of the company. They will be an officer, as defined in s 9 of the CA2001, by virtue of their 'whole of organisation' role. The role of the CEO within the business has several aspects to it, as illustrated in Fig 7.11.

FIGURE 7.11   The various internal demands (within the company) on the CEO

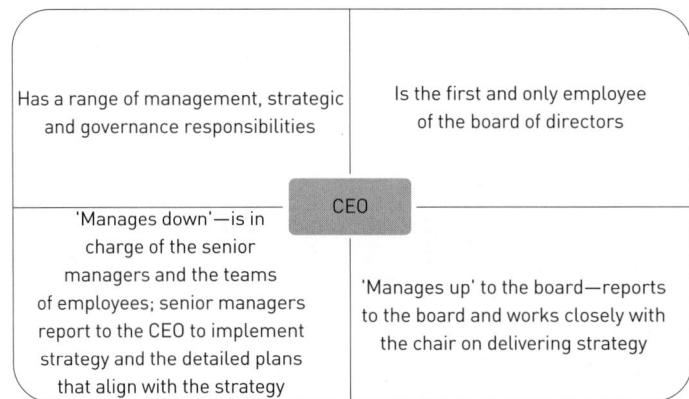

The CEO needs to be able to effectively manage the diverse range of stakeholders of the business, both internal and external: see Fig 7.12. Obviously, this becomes more complex with large listed entities.

FIGURE 7.12 The CEO's potential range of internal and external stakeholders

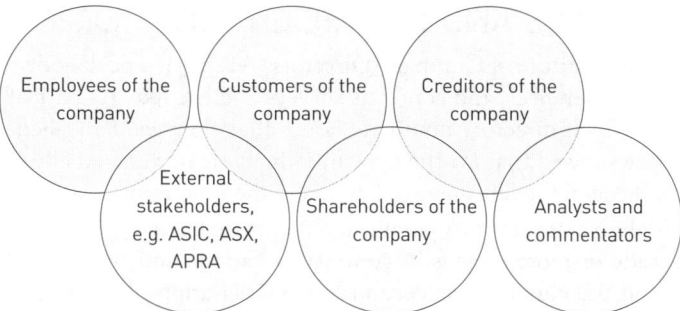

The CEO also has an important role in working with the board on delivering effective corporate governance for the particular organisation they lead, whether it is for-profit, not-for-profit, or for-purpose.

Finally, the CEO is at the centre-point of the flow of information—both up and down within the organisation; for example, the CEO is both a receiver of reports from senior managers, and a deliverer of information and summaries to the board.

FIGURE 7.13 The complex two-way nature of the CEO role

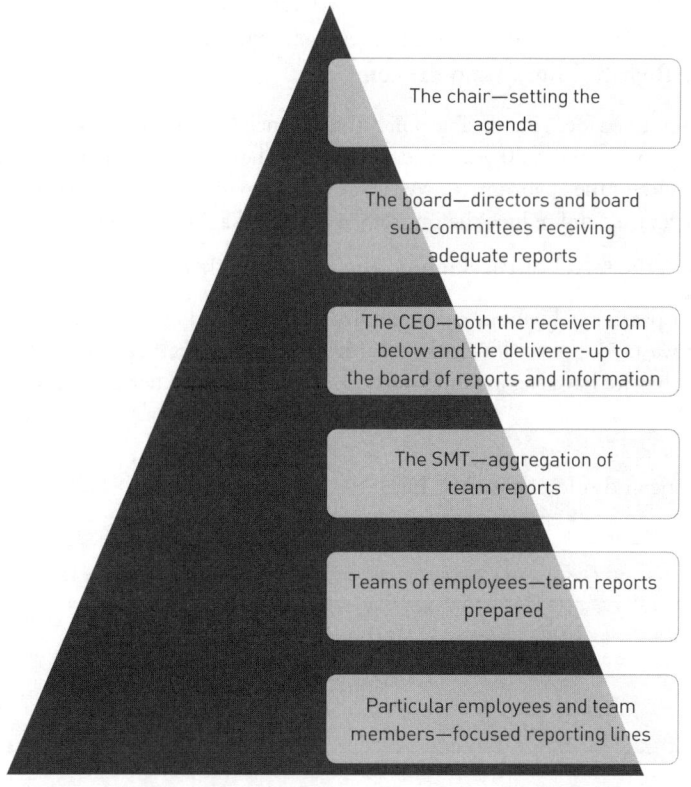

Activity 7.5

Read the following and answer the questions below.

IN THE NEWS: BOARDS AND CLIMATE CHANGE CORPORATE CULTURE[3]

The issue: The Australian Institute of Company Directors (AICD) is a peak body for directors; it offers short courses, provides conferences, and conducts surveys and the like. As part of its work, it releases 'sentiment indexes', in which directors nominate issues that they want the Federal Government to address. A recent report 'showed that for the first time, directors nominated climate change as the top issue they wanted the Federal Government to address in the long term'.

The context: There is always debate in Australia about climate change, given it has been a politicised issue for the past decade or more. This is in contrast to Europe and the UK, where there has been broad consensus around the climate science, and less politicisation of the issue. An example of this politically charged environment in Australia is one of the responses to the AICD report—provided by another peak body, the Business Council of Australia (BCA), through a former head, Tony Shepherd. Mr Shepherd offered a differing view:

> At the end of the day the prime requirement of boards and directors is to optimise the long-term return to investors while being responsible and living within the law.

Michael Fraser, Chair of APA (a gas pipeliner), said:

> Climate change being a top concern was a statement that would not be made across all sectors.

By contrast, the heads of other major companies took a view more aligned with the AICD findings. JB Hi-Fi CEO Richard Murray said the company:

> …supported a continued focus on sensible policy that balanced economic growth and the environment. None of us want to wake up in 20 years and find that we haven't made the right decisions today for the long-term health of the environment. We want to work with suppliers to work out ways to reduce packaging, do it smarter and reduce the impact [of] our packaging, for example.

Richard Henfrey, the CEO of Blackmores, the vitamin maker, said:

> the company felt passionately about sustainability generally and climate change in particular. It is something that we talk about a lot in the boardroom. We source ingredients from nature, so it's important to us that we have sustainable sources of those wild and natural ingredients.

QUESTIONS

1. What is the scope and role of the AICD?

---

3 All quotes taken from Sarah-Jane Tasker and Paul Garvey, 'Former BCA chief cool over climate focus', *The Australian*, 25 October 2018.

2. What is the scope and role of the BCA?

3. What is meant by 'strategy' for the board?

4. Is climate change a strategic issue for all boards, or is it 'sector dependent', as noted above?

CORPORATIONS LAW: CONCEPTS, CASES AND CULTURE WORKBOOK

WORKBOOK CHAPTER 7 REVIEW
An illustrative summary of the key points

FIGURE 7.14 The operating context of corporate governance for a company

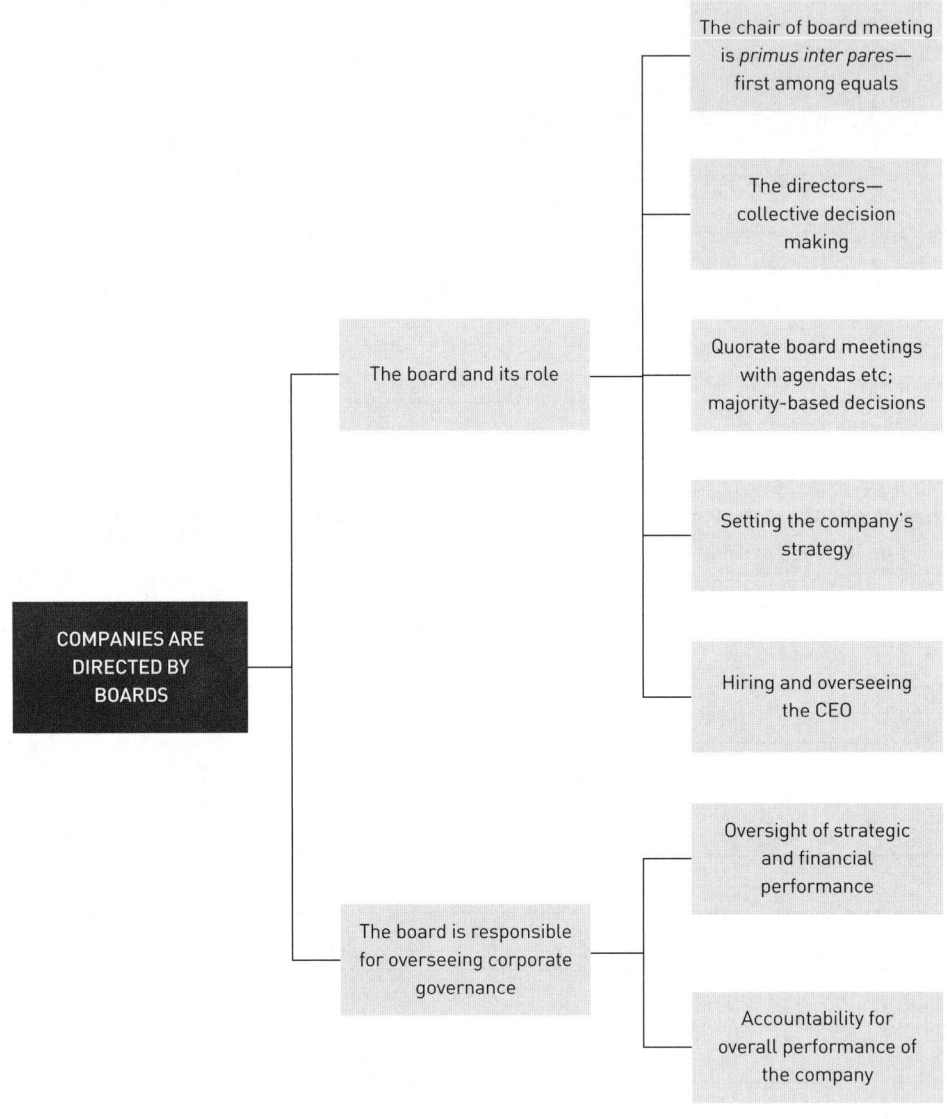

QUESTIONS

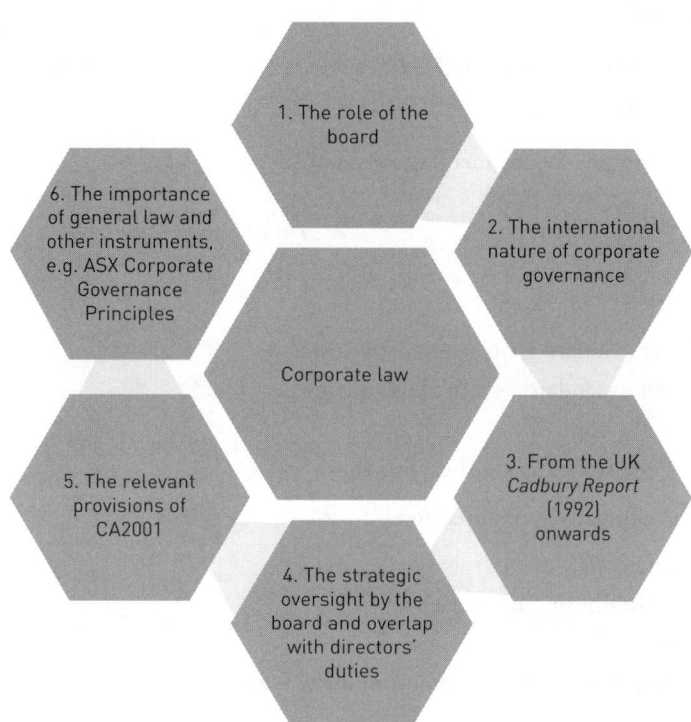

FIGURE 7.15 The international project of corporate governance: 30 years of iterative development

CHAPTER 7 REVISION ACTIVITIES

Consolidation of concepts, knowledge, and content activities

TRUE OR FALSE?

1. Public companies require three directors, all of whom reside in Australia.   True ☐ False ☐
2. Pty Ltd companies require a company secretary.   True ☐ False ☐
3. Executive directors are required to hold shares in the company.   True ☐ False ☐
4. A chair needs to be appointed to conduct business at board meetings.   True ☐ False ☐
5. The chair automatically receives a casting vote.   True ☐ False ☐

FILL IN THE GAPS

1. A director can be formally appointed to the role or may be adjudged as fulfilling the role as defined in section _____ of the CA2001.

2. The chair is regarded as the _____ among equals or *primus inter* _____

3. The 1995 High Court case _____ provided an overview of the role of the board.

4. The High Court case *Hospital Products Ltd v United States Surgical Corporation* in the year _____ considered the subject of _____.

5. A director not able to attend a board meeting can appoint an _____ director.

MULTIPLE CHOICE

1. A non-executive director:
   A. Is judged by a lesser standard than an executive director
   B. Is judged by the same standard as a shadow director
   C. Is not an officer of the company
   D. Is judged by the same standard as other directors

2. A director of a public company is required to:
   A. Have a law or business degree
   B. Have at least five years' business experience
   C. Be 18 years of age
   D. Have served an apprenticeship as a director of a Pty Ltd

3. The ASX Corporate Governance Principles are:
   A. Obligatory
   B. Discretionary
   C. Based on the 'if not, why not' principle
   D. Mandatory

4. The CEO of a company is:
   A. The only employee of the board
   B. One of several equal-ranking members of the executive team
   C. Necessarily a director
   D. On an equal footing with the chair

5. Modern international corporate governance relevant to Australia dates from:
   A. 1960s (Milton Friedman)
   B. 1992 (UK *Cadbury Report*)
   C. 2001 (ASIC Act (Cth))
   D. 2019 (Banking Royal Commission)

SHORT ANSWER QUESTIONS

1. How are directors appointed?

2. What is a shadow director?

3. What is a de facto director?

4. What is the role of the chair?

5. What are the key features of the relationship between the CEO and the chair?

6. Can directors be disqualified from acting?

Higher order thinking activities

Consider the following questions and provide detailed discussion and analysis.

TOPIC A

What is the scope of the term 'director'?

QUESTIONS

TOPIC B

What is the role and function of the board?

QUESTIONS

CHAPTER 8

DIRECTORS AS AGENTS OF THE CORPORATION— ROLES AND RESPONSIBILITIES

Chapter synopsis and links to Textbook Chapter 8

This Workbook Chapter deals with six topics:

- 8.1 Laws and rules relevant to directors
- 8.2 The roles undertaken by directors
- 8.3 Directors as agents and fiduciaries of the company
- 8.4 Duties owed by the directors
- 8.5 Issues of skill, competence and negligence relevant to directors
- 8.6 Issues of disclosure, honesty and good faith relevant to directors.

Each of these topics is constructively aligned with, and linked to, the same topics in Chapter 8 of the Textbook.

Chapter executive summary

This Chapter examines the nature and role of directors by reference to:

- the titles, if any, assigned to people carrying out these roles
- the pervasive requirement to act in the best interests of the company as a whole
- the fiduciary nature of the role of the director in terms of the general law and its historical development
- the relevant statutory provisions covering both matters of competence (civil) and honesty (potentially criminal).

CHAPTER DIAGRAMMATIC OVERVIEW

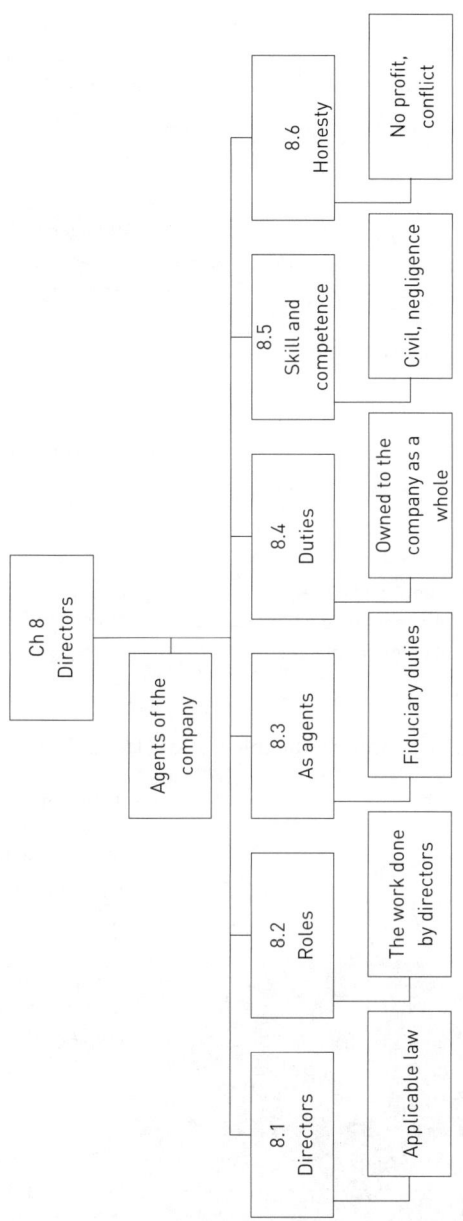

FIGURE 8.1 An overview of Chapter 8

8.1 LAWS AND RULES RELEVANT TO DIRECTORS

The scope and range of directors is set out in Fig 8.2, while Fig 8.3 shows directors' duties.

FIGURE 8.2 The scope and range of directors

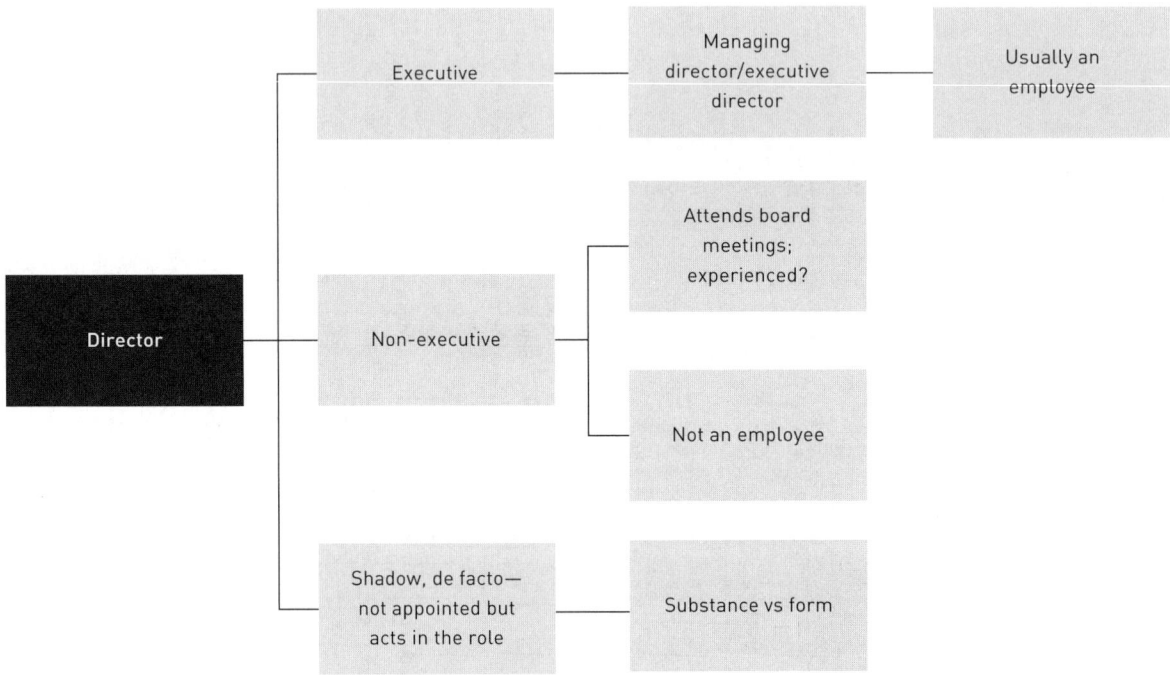

FIGURE 8.3 Directors' duties: the core and irreducible duties (Items 1 and 2) are fiduciary in nature

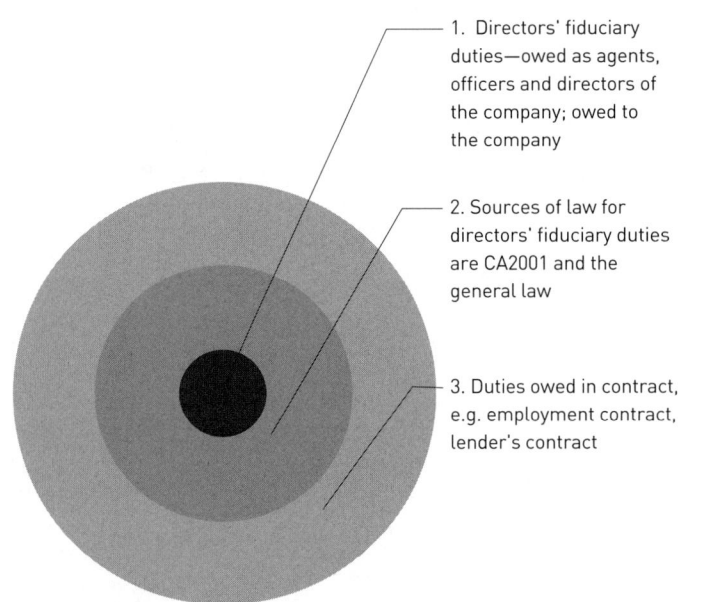

The role of the director is multi-faceted. It can be broken down into three categories of action, as shown in Fig 8.4.

FIGURE 8.4   Three categories of action relevant to directors

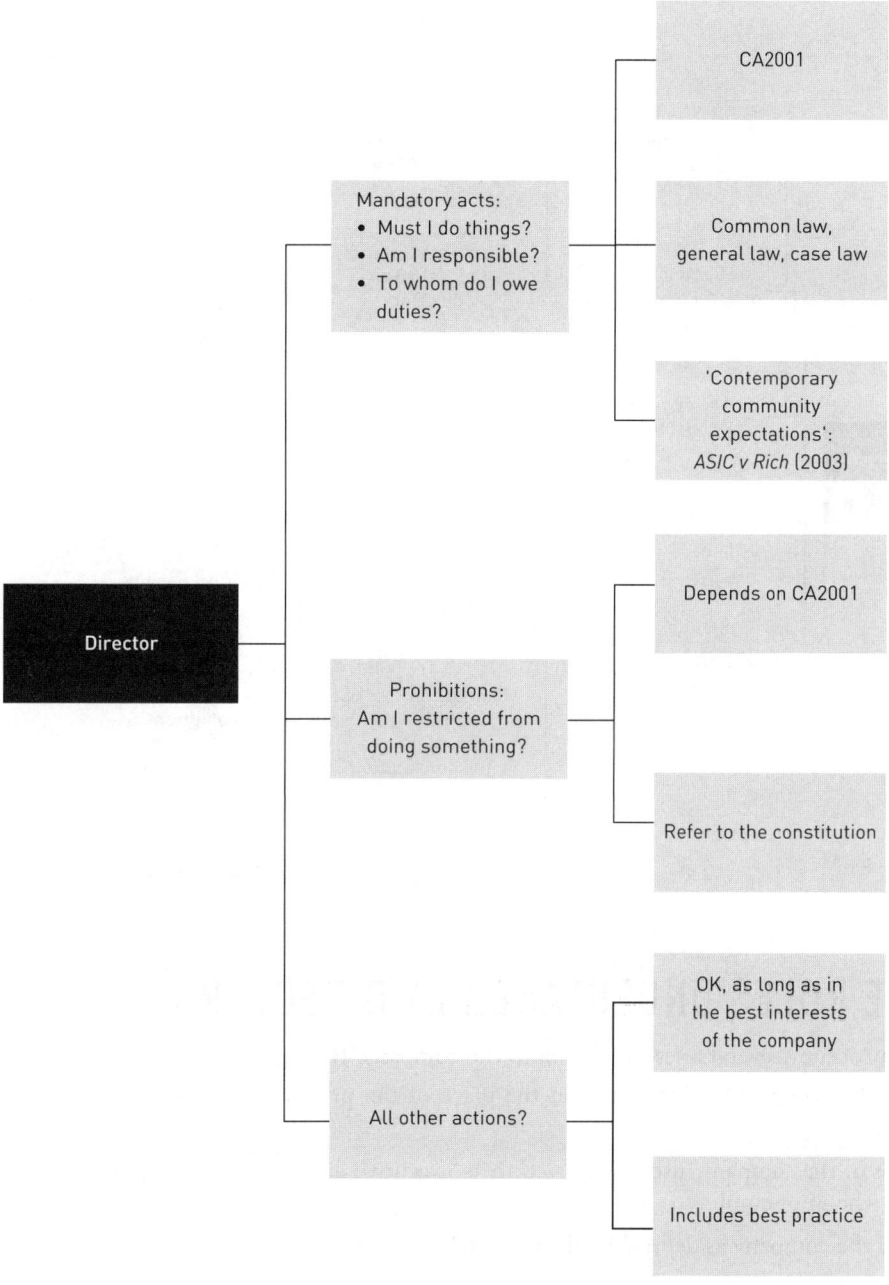

Figure 8.5 gives an overview of issues relevant to directors.

FIGURE 8.5   An overview of directors: the key issues

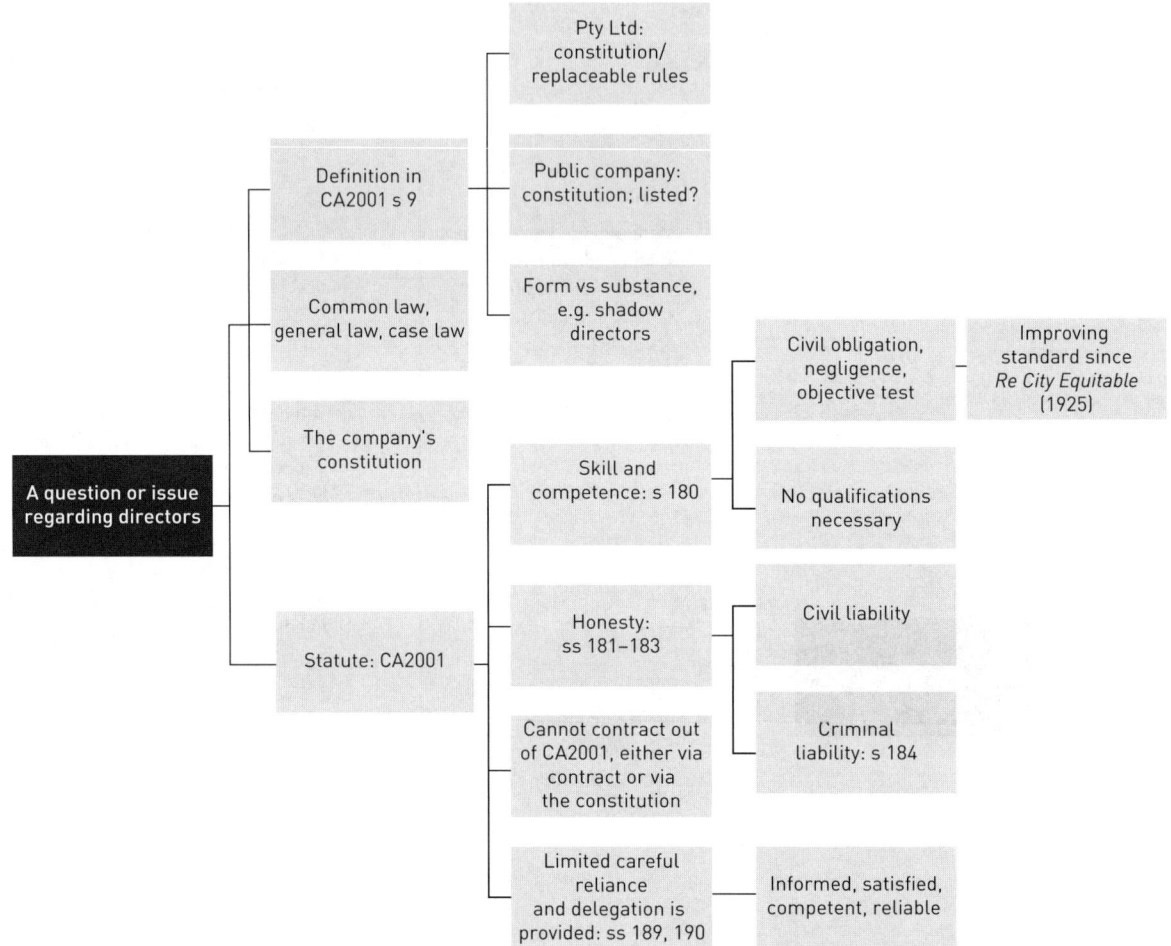

8.2 THE ROLES UNDERTAKEN BY DIRECTORS

Directors may occupy several roles in relation to the company. They are, or may be, variously:

- agents of the company, which stands in the place of the principal; this is a core commercial fiduciary relationship
- employees of the company (usually referred to as 'executive directors' when employed, and 'non-executive directors' when not employed)
- officers of the company as defined by the CA2001
- creditors of the company
- debtors to the company
- shareholders of the company
- guarantors to third parties of company debt (involving the pledging of the directors' personal assets).

CHAPTER 8 DIRECTORS AS AGENTS OF THE CORPORATION—ROLES AND RESPONSIBILITIES

In relation to the final point above, note that directors of start-up companies may, for practical purposes, be required to provide guarantees: see Fig 8.6.

FIGURE 8.6   The phases relevant to a new company's borrowing capacity

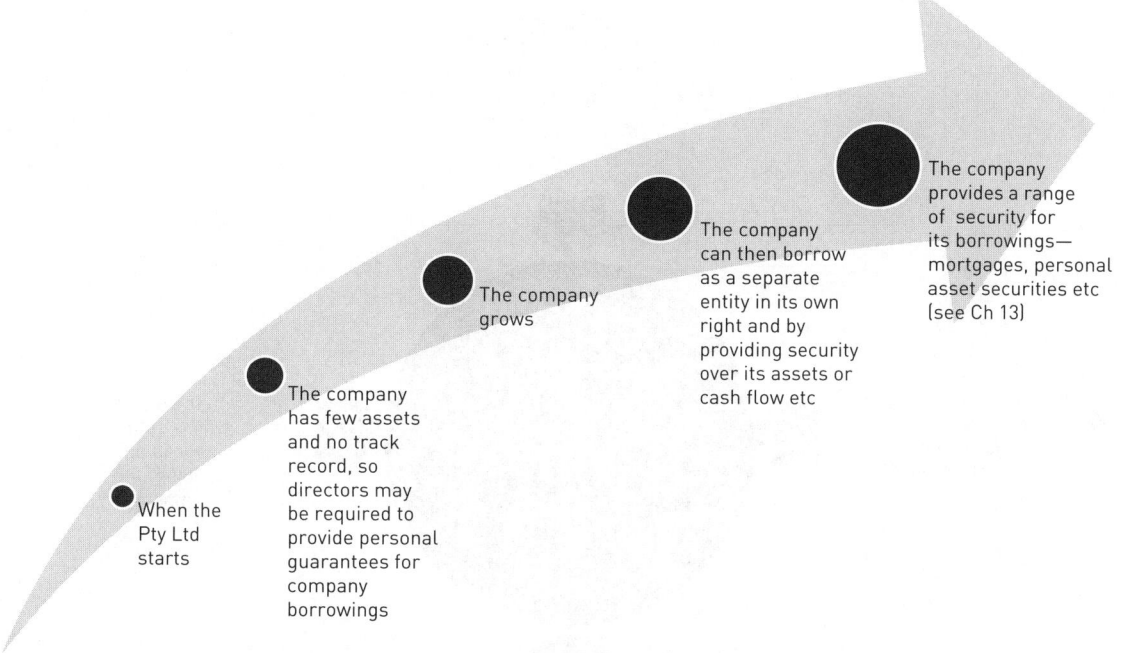

8.3 DIRECTORS AS AGENTS AND FIDUCIARIES OF THE COMPANY

The directors are agents of the company as principal: see Figs 8.7 and 8.8.

FIGURE 8.7   The directors are agents of the company as principal

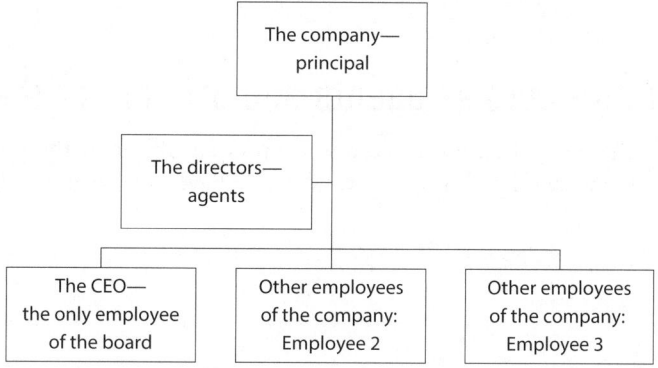

FIGURE 8.8 The principal–agent relationship relevant to the company, the director and the third party

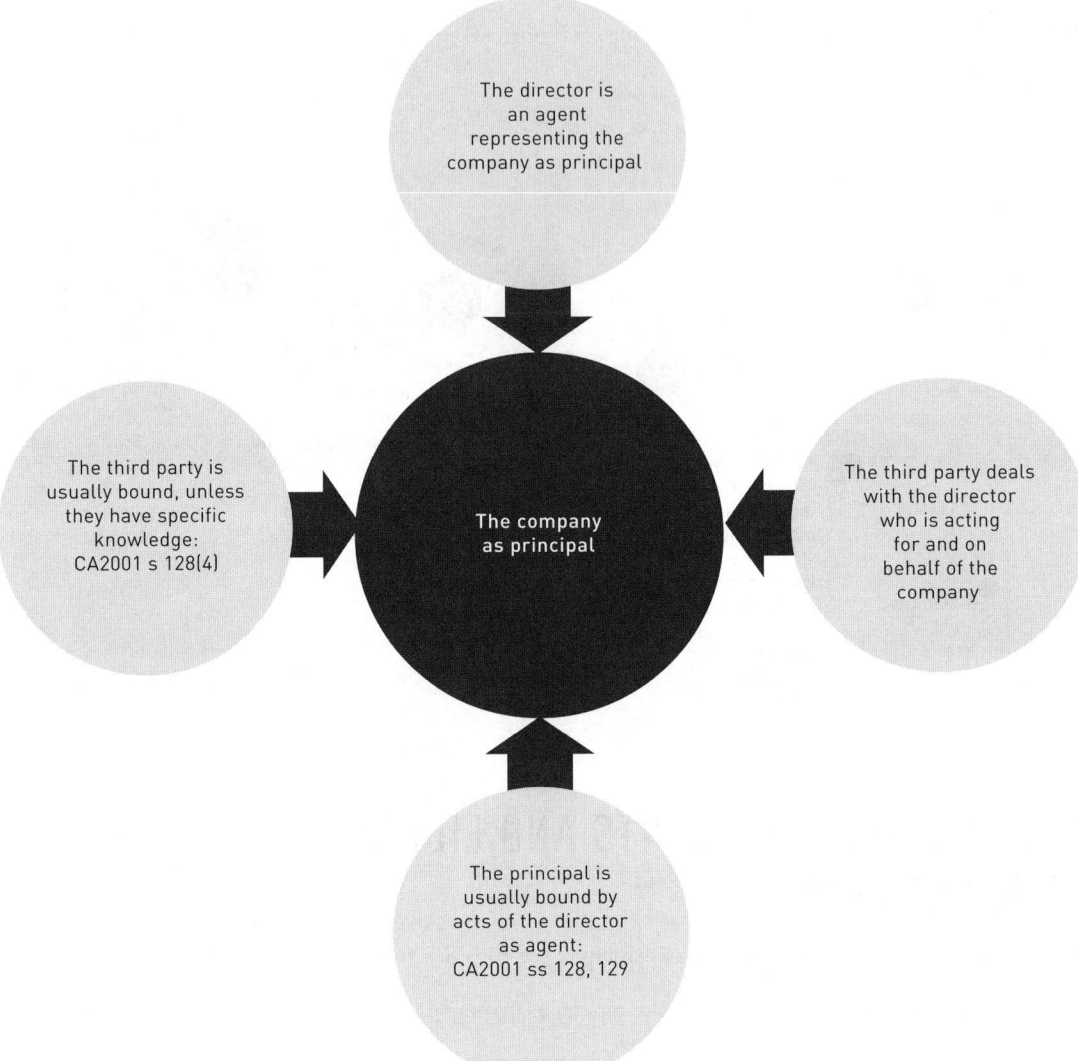

The authority of directors as agents and officers of the company

'Customary authority' is the general authority bestowed upon an officer in the position they occupy; for example, the CFO (chief financial officer) would be expected to have carriage of financial decisions on behalf of the company.

FIGURE 8.9 Authority of the agent/fiduciary to bind the principal to a third party contract

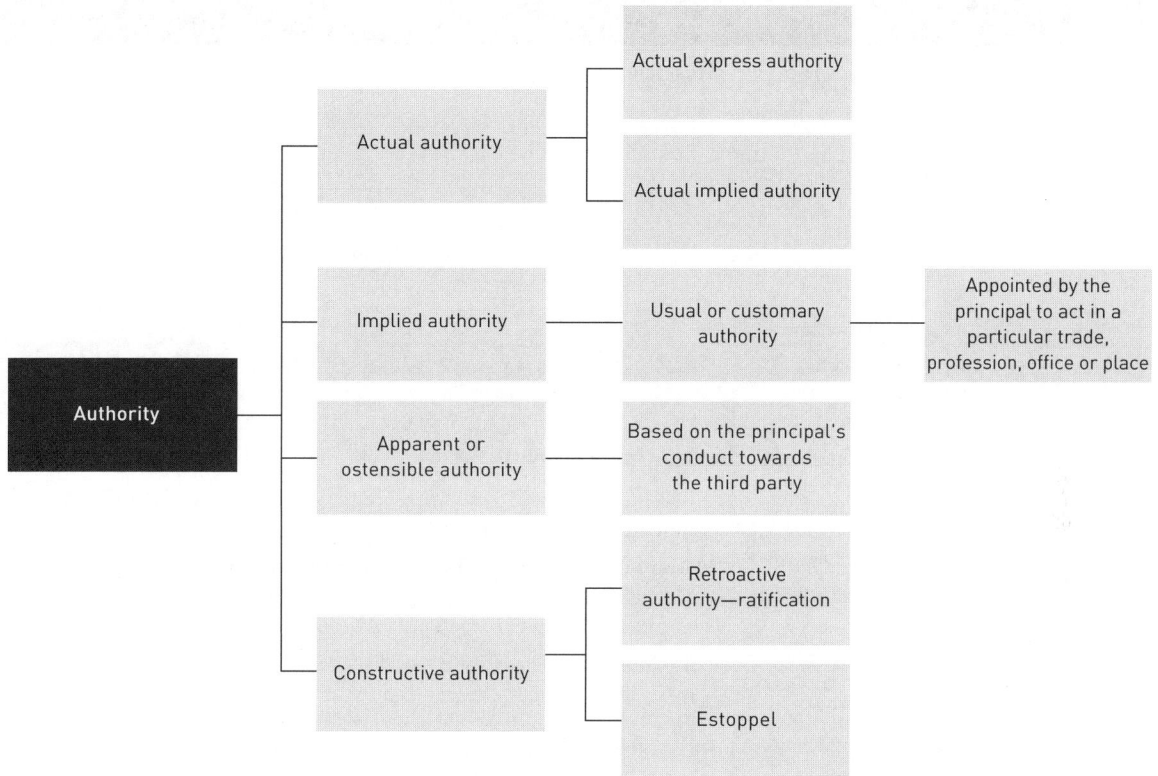

Frequently, individual directors are given the power to:
- witness the fixing of the company's common seal
- sign the company's negotiable instruments, including cheques.

Looking at the customary authority of officers by title:
- A managing director has the customary authority to make contracts related to the day-to-day management of the company's business.
- An individual director usually does not have customary authority to make contracts on the company's behalf. Directors can usually act only collectively as a board, and the function of an individual director is to participate in decisions of the board.
- The chair of the board does not have the customary authority to contract on the company's behalf.
- The customary authority of the company secretary is limited to matters of an administrative nature.

Directors as agents of the principal company

By reason of the fact that directors are agents of the company (as principal), they owe fiduciary duties. They owe these duties, additionally and in any event, in their capacity as directors vis-à-vis the company. There is a line of authorities relevant to the assertion of fiduciary relationships.

TABLE 8.1 Some key cases developing fiduciary duties in the context of company law

Date	Case	Areas of law, outcome and effect
1726	*Keech v Sandford*	Trust law
1984	*Hospital Products Ltd v US Surgical Corporation*	Commercial relationships Mason J (in dissent) found a fiduciary relationship
1984	*Chan v Zacharia*	Partnership

Activity 8.1

Review Table 8.1. Add cases and notes relevant to commercial fiduciary relationships.

Fiduciary relationships in the commercial context

Fiduciary relationships in the commercial context cover a potentially broad range of formal and informal relationships. At the central point of the concept and application, there are core and status-based relationships, which are presumptively fiduciary. Beyond this central point, there are non-core relationships that may be fiduciary, depending on the particular facts.

The various layers can be summarised as follows:

1. Core: trusts

2. Core: agents, partners, directors, solicitors

3. Core: senior employees

4. Non-core—depends on the facts; may include other commercial relationships on an ad hoc basis.

    Remember that the relationship between the director and the company is a core fiduciary relationship.

    Core commercial fiduciary relationships include the following (those in italics are relevant to the corporate context):

- trustee to beneficiary
- partner to partner
- agent to principal
- *director to company*
- *promoter to company*
- *senior employee to company*
- solicitor to client.

    Other potential commercial fiduciary relationships include:

- *general employee to company*
- receiver to creditor
- liquidator to creditor
- financial adviser to client
- stockbroker to client
- bank to customer
- manufacturer to distributor
- joint venture party to joint venture party.

A commercial relationship that is not a core or status-based relationship (carrying with it a presumption of being fiduciary) may be found to be fiduciary on an ad hoc, or case-by-case, basis. This is predicated on the dissenting judgment of Mason J in the 1984 High Court case *Hospital Products Ltd v United States Surgical Corporation*, in which he said that the list of potential fiduciary relationships was not necessarily closed.

The basis upon which a potential fiduciary relationship of this kind may be so characterised may cover one or several bases, including the following potentially relevant criteria:

- trust and confidence reposed by A in B
- mutual confidence

- control by B
- vulnerability on the part of A
- asymmetric knowledge and information; B knows far more than A
- reliance by A on B, given B's expertise.

8.4 DUTIES OWED BY THE DIRECTORS

Duties owed by directors to the company are basically of two types:
- fiduciary: honesty and fidelity, and
- skill, competence and care.

FIGURE 8.10 The basic bifurcation of directors' duties

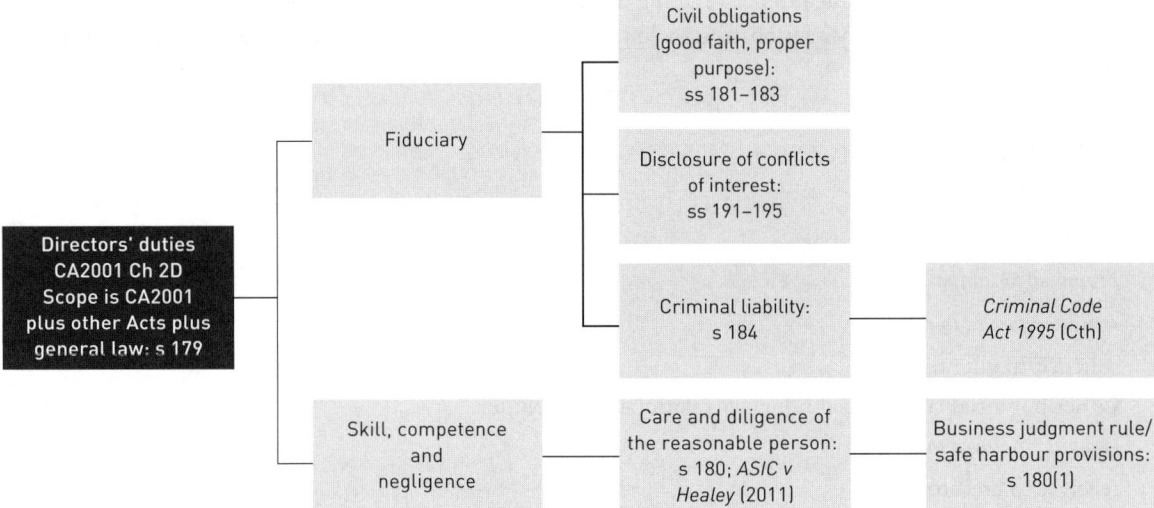

To whom do directors owe their duties? The usual principle is that directors owe their duty to the company as a separate entity.

FIGURE 8.11 The usual principle is that directors owe their duty to the company

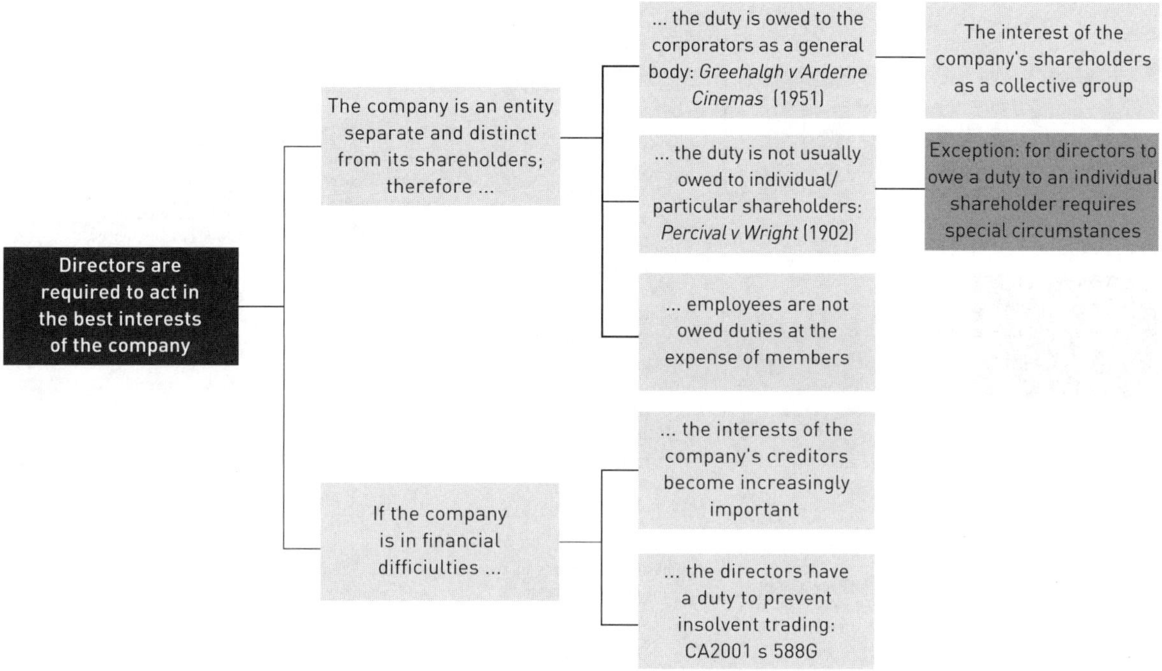

```
Directors are required to act in the best interests of the company
├── The company is an entity separate and distinct from its shareholders; therefore ...
│   ├── ... the duty is owed to the corporators as a general body: Greehalgh v Arderne Cinemas (1951) ── The interest of the company's shareholders as a collective group
│   ├── ... the duty is not usually owed to individual/particular shareholders: Percival v Wright (1902) ── Exception: for directors to owe a duty to an individual shareholder requires special circumstances
│   └── ... employees are not owed duties at the expense of members
└── If the company is in financial difficiulties ...
    ├── ... the interests of the company's creditors become increasingly important
    └── ... the directors have a duty to prevent insolvent trading: CA2001 s 588G
```

Exceptions to the general principle

In some special circumstances, a director may owe fiduciary duties to an individual shareholder. For such circumstances to arise, the UK case of *Peskin v Anderson* [2001] 1 BCLC 372 confirms that three factors are necessary:

- the director must have been in direct and close contact with the individual shareholder/member
- so that the director caused the member to act in a certain way
- which turned out to be detrimental to the shareholder.

These exceptions can be represented as shown in Fig 8.12.

FIGURE 8.12   The potential additional parties to whom a duty may be owed

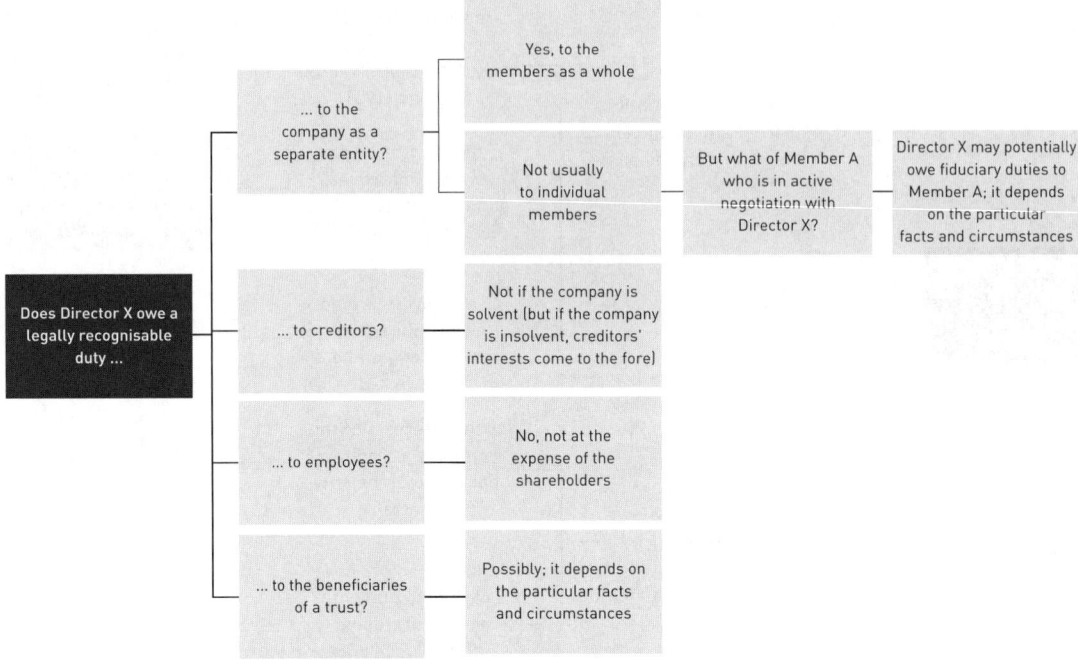

The focus of the directors' duties is on the company, which translates, in effect, to the current membership. In some cases, particular shareholders may be owed a duty: see Fig 8.13.

FIGURE 8.13   Directors' duties are owed to the company

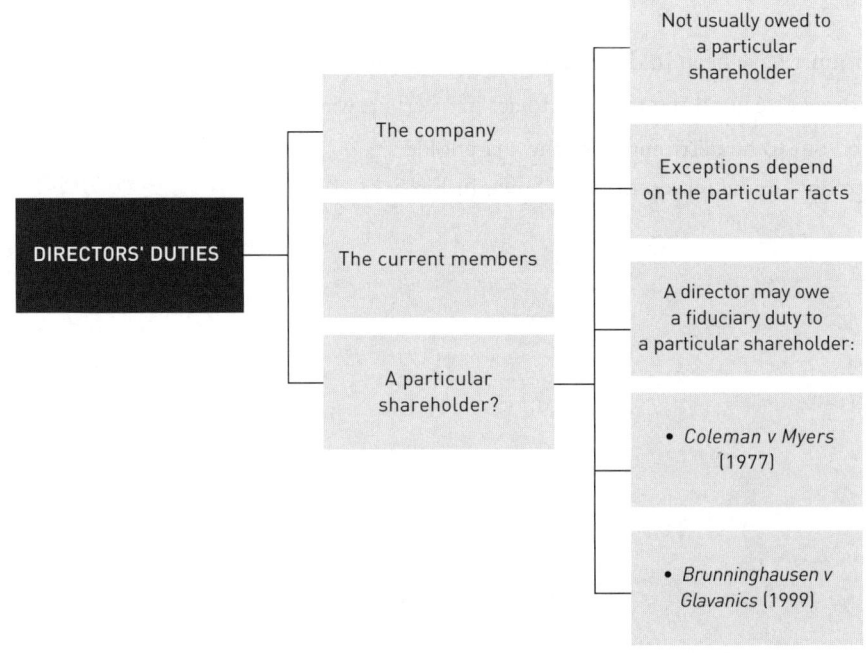

TABLE 8.2 The general principle that a director owes a duty to the company and the potential exceptions

Duty	Case	Notes
The duty is owed to the company	*Percival v Wright* (1902) Applied in/see also: • *Greenhalgh v Arderne Cinemas Ltd* (1951)	This is the usual situation/general principle
Exceptions to the general principle:		
A particular member asserts that a duty is owed to them	*Coleman v Myers* (1977) Applied in/see also: • *Brunninghausen v Glavanics* (1999) • *Crawley v Short* (2009) • *McClymont v Critchley* (2011) • *Peskin v Anderson* (2000)	An exception to the general principle Will depend on particular facts and context Usually involves a negotiation for a share sale in which the director withholds information from the member, to the member's detriment
A beneficiary asserts that a director of the trustee company owes them a duty directly	*Hurley v BGH Nominees Pty Ltd (No 2)* (1984) Applied in/see also:	

Activity 8.2

Review Table 8.2 and complete the final row.

Figure 8.14 illustrates the correlative relationship at the core of the corporation.

FIGURE 8.14 The symbiotic link between the directors and the members when the corporation is a going concern

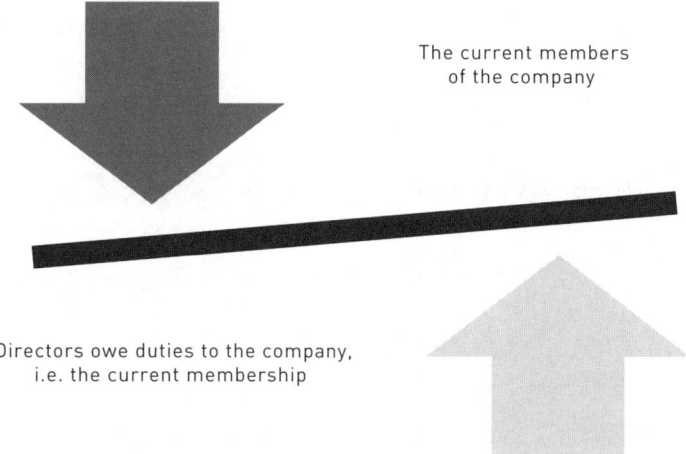

TABLE 8.3 Key cases regarding directors

Date, country	Case law relevant to directors	Outcome and effect
1901, UK	*Dovey v Cory*	
1902, UK	*Percival v Wright*	
1925, UK	*Re City Equitable Fire Insurance Co Ltd*	
1951, UK	*Greenhalgh v Arderne Cinemas Ltd*	
1967, UK	*Regal (Hastings) Ltd v Gulliver*	

Date, country	Case law relevant to directors	Outcome and effect
1992, Australia	*AWA Ltd v Daniels*	
1995, Australia	*Daniels v Anderson*	
2003, 2009, Australia	*ASIC v Rich*	
2011, Australia	*ASIC v Healey*	

Activity 8.3

Review Table 8.3 and add notes to the third column.

8.5 ISSUES OF SKILL, COMPETENCE AND NEGLIGENCE RELEVANT TO DIRECTORS

Refer to Fig 8.5, which gives an overview of the competence of directors.

8.6 ISSUES OF DISCLOSURE, HONESTY AND GOOD FAITH RELEVANT TO DIRECTORS

Consequences of contravention of directors' duties

Where wrongs are done to the company by its directors, as a general rule, the company is the proper plaintiff, because the directors' duties are owed to the company.

The company may seek the following remedies:

- compensation
- account of profits
- rescission of a contract
- injunction
- an order for property to be returned.

ASIC may also seek various remedies. Civil penalties may apply under the CA2001; for example:

- s 180: care and diligence
- s 181: good faith and proper purpose
- s 182: improperly using position
- s 183: improperly using information
- s 588G: insolvent trading.

Civil penalties include:

- s 1317G: fine of up to $200,000
- s 1317H: compensation for damage suffered
- s 206C: disqualification from management.

Criminal penalties may apply under the CA2001. Section 184 provides for criminal penalties under ss 181–183 if there was:

- recklessness, or
- intentional dishonesty.

Criminal penalties include:

- up to 2,000 penalty units (one unit is $180): $360,000
- five years' imprisonment, or
- both.

Note that breach of s 180(1)—the duty of care and diligence—is not a criminal offence.

The possibilities of forgiving a breach of duty by a director

The company has the ability to confirm some directorial breaches, subject to the CA2001: see Fig 8.15.

FIGURE 8.15 The company's ability to confirm some directorial breaches

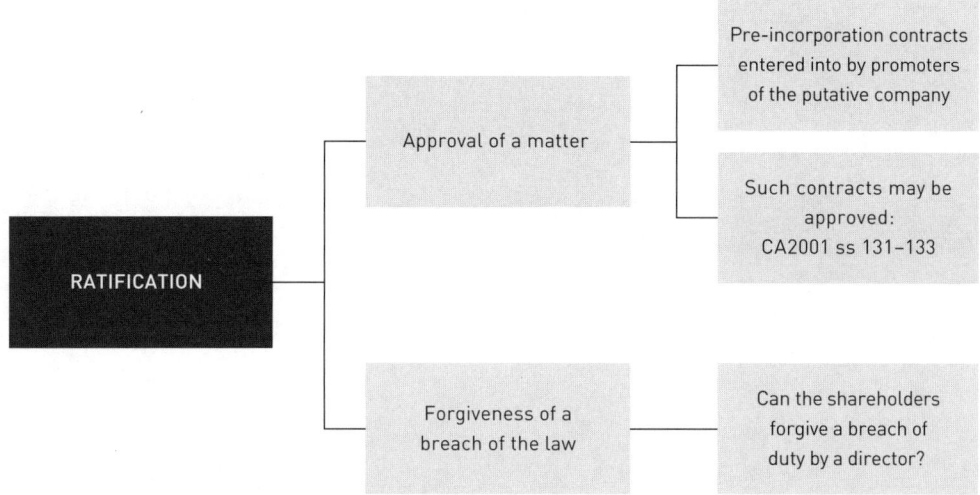

Table 8.4 sets out cases dealing with ratification.

TABLE 8.4 Case law relevant to ratification

Case	Date	Outcome and effect
Cook v Deeks	1916	
Furs Ltd v Tomkies	1936	

TABLE 8.4 Case law relevant to ratification (continued)

Case	Date	Outcome and effect
Regal (Hastings) v Gulliver	1942	
Bamford v Bamford	1969	
Winthrop Investments Ltd v Winns Ltd	1975	
Queensland Mines Ltd v Hudson	1978	
Kinsela v Russell Kinsela Pty Ltd	1986	

Activity 8.4

Review the cases in Table 8.4 and add notes to the third column.

Activity 8.5

Read the following and answer the question below.

IN THE NEWS: *GENDER BALANCE ON AUSTRALIAN GOVERNMENT BOARDS REPORT 2017–18*[1]

The Gender Balance on Australian Government Boards Report is prepared annually by the Australian Government Office for Women, and reports on the Government's performance against its gender diversity target.

On 1 July 2016, the Government's target of women holding 50 per cent of Government board positions overall, and men and women each holding at least 40 per cent of positions on individual boards, came into effect. This target replaced the previous gender diversity target of women holding 40 per cent of Australian Government board positions overall.

This Report includes details of both whole-of-Government and individual portfolio performance against the Government's gender diversity target in 2017–18. As at 30 June 2018, women held 45.8 per cent of Australian Government board positions. This is the highest outcome since public reporting on the gender balance of Government boards began.

Statistics on new appointments made in 2017–18 show how individual portfolios have progressed towards meeting the target. Of the 542 new appointments made in 2017–18, 53.1 per cent of appointees were women. This is higher than the 2016–17 figure of 46.2 per cent. The individual portfolio results as at 30 June 2018, women comprised 50 per cent and over of new appointments made by 11 of the 16 portfolios.

In addition, the number of women across portfolios that hold Chair and Deputy Chair roles are reported. Specifically reporting on the number of women who hold these senior positions is important in understanding women's representation at higher levels of leadership.

---

[1] https://www.pmc.gov.au/sites/default/files/publications/gender-balance-report.pdf/.

QUESTION

Why do government boards at the Commonwealth level appear to be nearly 20 per cent ahead of corporate boards (the S&P/ASX 200, referred to in the Textbook)?

WORKBOOK CHAPTER 8 REVIEW

An illustrative summary of the key points

FIGURE 8.16 The foundation issues and topics providing an overview of directors' duties

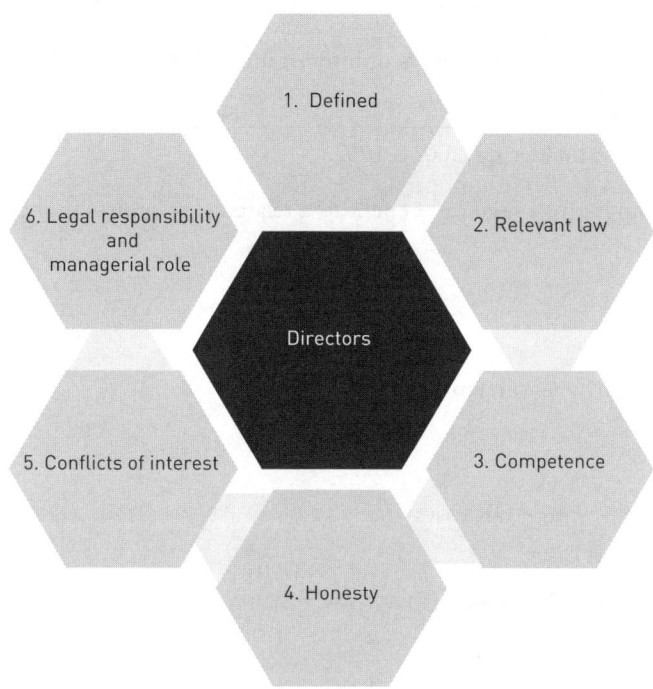

CHAPTER 8 REVISION ACTIVITIES

Consolidation of concepts, knowledge and content activities

TRUE OR FALSE?

1. The CA2001 codifies the duties of directors. True ☐ False ☐
2. Directors appointed to public companies must have relevant experience and qualifications. True ☐ False ☐
3. Executive directors are not held to a higher standard than non-executive directors. True ☐ False ☐
4. The business judgment rule sets a high standard for directors to meet. True ☐ False ☐
5. The CA2001 provides detailed provisions dealing with CEOs and chairs. True ☐ False ☐

FILL IN THE GAPS

1. Under CA2001 section _____ a director may rely on information or advice from a person, but they need to satisfy themselves of that person's _____

2. Directors can delegate under CA2001 section _____ so long as they have _____ that the delegate is _____ of carrying out the delegated task.

3. Directors _____ declare conflicts of interest under CA2001 s 191.

4. Directors of public companies cannot _____ or _____ on a matter in which they have an interest under CA2001 s 195.

5. A public company cannot give a financial benefit to a related party unless it obtains _____

MULTIPLE CHOICE

1. The starting point for clarifying directors duties is:
   A. CA2001
   B. ASIC Act 2001
   C. The foundation 19th-century UK cases
   D. Post-1986 High Court cases

2. The general law in the CA2001 refers to:
   A. UK case law
   B. Australian case law
   C. Law Reform and Royal Commission reports
   D. Case law

3. *Percival v Wright* (1902) is precedent for the proposition that:
   A. The company is the proper plaintiff in a wrong done to it
   B. The directors owe their duties to each particular shareholder
   C. The company is a separate legal entity
   D. The directors owe their duties to the company

4. In terms of finding out the remuneration of directors, what percentage of members can seek this information?
   A. 1 per cent
   B. 5 per cent
   C. 10 per cent
   D. 20 per cent

5. Mason J in *Hospital Products Ltd v United States Surgical Corporation* (1984) principally confirmed that:
   A. Directors are fiduciaries
   B. Officers are fiduciaries
   C. Agents are fiduciaries
   D. The categories of commercial fiduciaries are not closed

SHORT ANSWER QUESTIONS

1. What are considerations relevant to the directors paying a dividend to members?

2. Do directors owe duties to particular shareholders?

3. Do the directors have exclusive rights to bring actions for and on behalf of the company?

4. Do directors have a duty to disclose personal profits that arise from their position?

5. What does s 182 of the CA2001 provide for/address?

Higher order thinking activities

Consider the following questions and provide detailed discussion and analysis.

TOPIC A

What assumptions can a third party make when dealing with a company?

QUESTIONS

TOPIC B

Eddy, a director of company ABC Pty Ltd, owns the commercial property that ABC is keen to purchase. Eddy wants to achieve top price. Advise Eddy.

How would your answer differ if the company were public?

TOPIC C

Put together a summary in table form of the corporate law topic 'directors', referring to key CA2001 provisions and cases.

TOPIC D

Directors are central to corporate law. Discuss.

CHAPTER 9

SHARES AND SHAREHOLDING: PROPERTY, OWNERSHIP AND INVESTMENT

Chapter synopsis and links to Textbook Chapter 9

This Workbook Chapter deals with five topics:

- 9.1 The nature of shares
- 9.2 The ownership of shares: shareholders
- 9.3 Different types of shares
- 9.4 Potential financial returns for shareholders
- 9.5 Shareholding as a risk investment.

Each of these topics is constructively aligned with, and linked to, the same topics in Chapter 9 of the Textbook.

Chapter executive summary

This Chapter examines:
- the nature of shares and share ownership as a form of risk capital
- shares as a tradable commodity or species of intangible personal property
- the monetisable benefits of share ownership, and
- the mechanisms providing for the transfer of shares.

CHAPTER 9 SHARES AND SHAREHOLDING: PROPERTY, OWNERSHIP AND INVESTMENT

CHAPTER DIAGRAMMATIC OVERVIEW

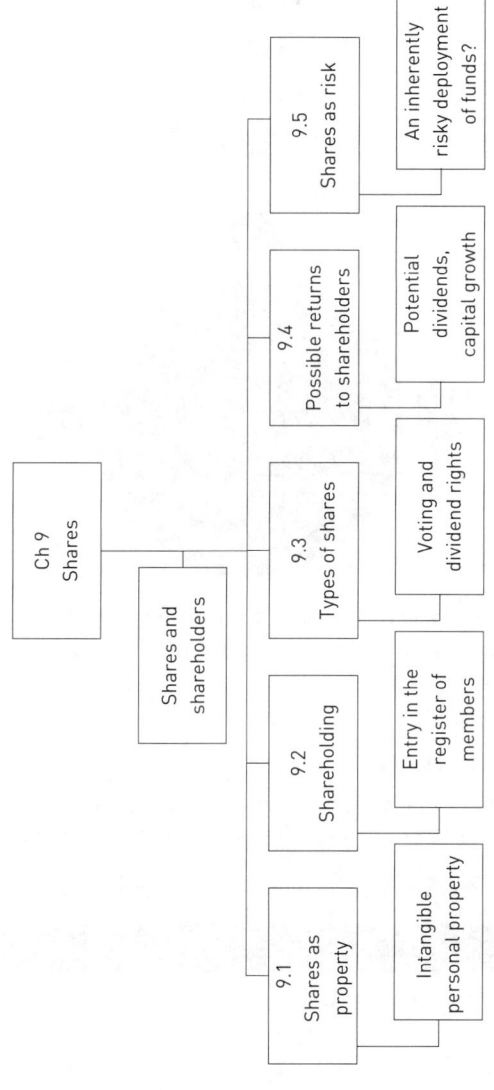

FIGURE 9.1 An overview of Chapter 9

9.1 THE NATURE OF SHARES

The terms 'shareholder', 'owner' and 'member' are interchangeable. Chapters 9–11 deal with various aspects of shares and membership rights, as shown in Fig 9.2.

FIGURE 9.2   An overview of Chapters 9–11

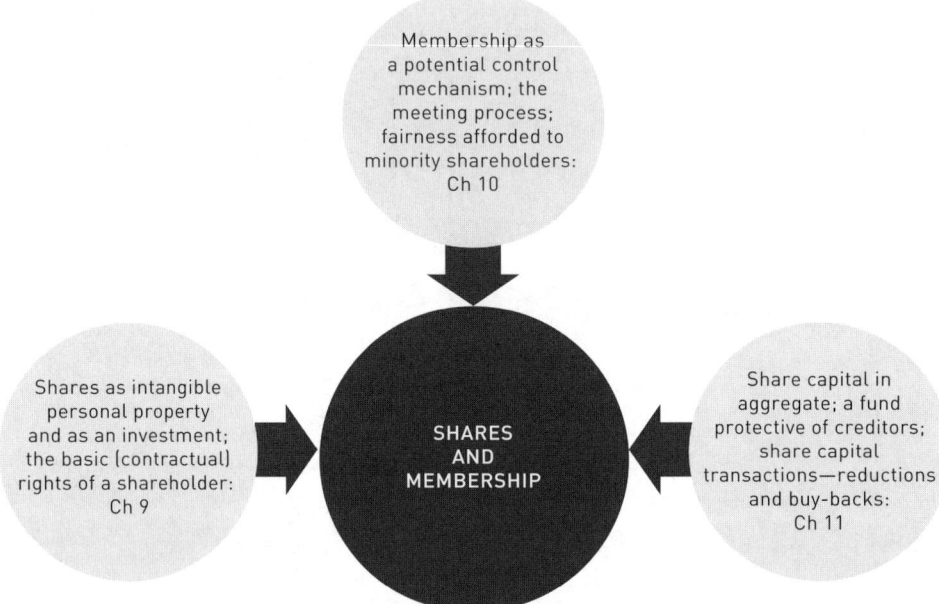

A share is intangible personal property. As such, it is transferred not by delivery, but by registration in the register of members. When shares are transferred, the question is: What is actually transferred? It could, in theory, be either:

- particular property belonging to the company, or
- the rights that attach to the shares in question.

Case law, both in the UK and Australia, has answered the question in favour of the latter proposition, reflects the underlying point that shares are a species of intangible personal property.

TABLE 9.1   Case law relevant to confirming the effect of share transfers

Year	Case	Principle regarding share transfers
1901	*Borland's Trustee v Steel Bros & Co Ltd* (UK)	The rights that attach to particular shares are transferred (UK common law)
1948	*Archibald Howie Pty Ltd v Commissioner for Stamp Duties (NSW)* (High Court of Australia)	The rights that attach to particular shares are transferred (Australian common law)

9.2 THE OWNERSHIP OF SHARES: SHAREHOLDERS

Company membership and its contractual nature

A shareholder has a contract with the company. The contract sets out the nature of the right, obligation, and potential rewards. Hence, in Fig 9.3, the three shareholders—A, B and C—each have a contract with the company ABC Pty Ltd.

FIGURE 9.3   Each shareholder has a share contract with the company

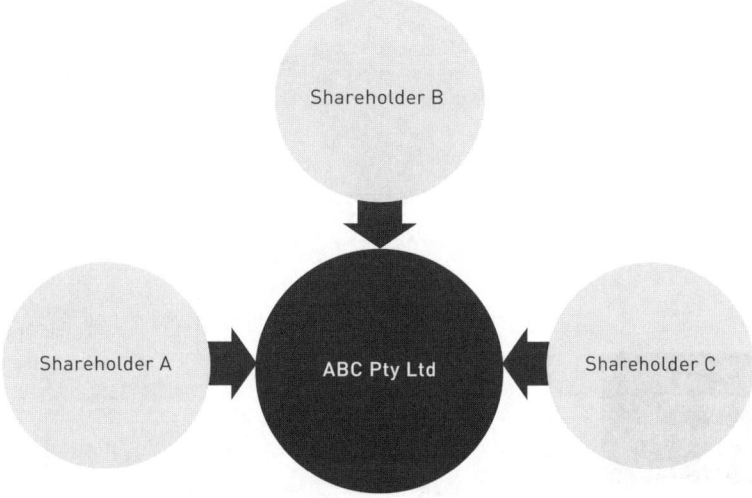

There are several ways by which a person can become a shareholder: see Fig 9.4.

FIGURE 9.4   The various ways of becoming a shareholder

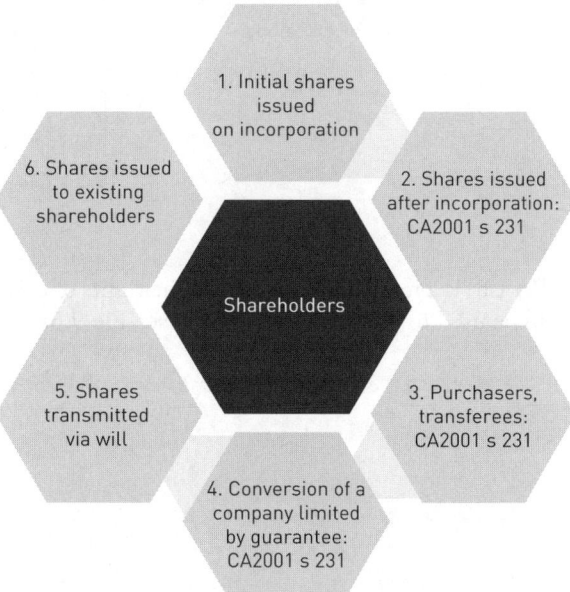

Corporate and non-person shareholders

This section looks at the relative issues extant to share transfers in Pty Ltd and listed companies. The value of shares is a comparative exercise as between private and public companies. Paradoxically, the value of shares is an easier concept—and process—in a publicly listed company than in a Pty Ltd. This is because the listed company has a public, day-by-day and up-to-date market price for its shares. By contrast, the Pty Ltd company does not usually generate a readily ascertainable market price. This may well need to be established on a transfer-by-transfer basis.

FIGURE 9.5   The issues relating to share transfers in public and Pty Ltd companies

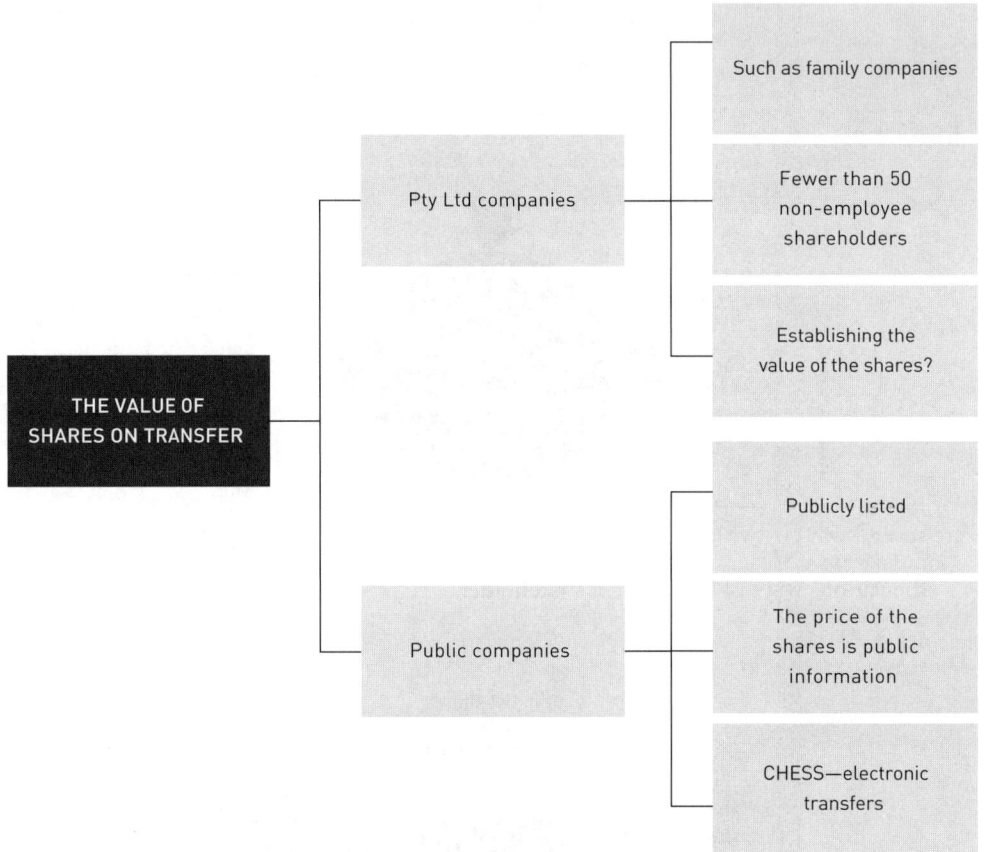

The transfer of shares in a Pty Ltd is a matter of considering the rights of existing shareholders, if any, and determining the mechanisms to be used to agree the share price: see Fig 9.6.

FIGURE 9.6 The need to establish the current value of shares in a Pty Ltd is critical

```
PRIVATE COMPANY
SHARE TRANSFER
├── Value the shares
│   ├── Financial performance of the company
│   ├── A multiple of recent earnings?
│   └── Other recent sales
└── Process
    ├── Rights of pre-emption and rights of first refusal for existing shareholders?
    └── Transfer to third party, i.e. to X, a new shareholder ── Directors to put X's name in the register of members
```

Pre-emption rights are a potential issue relevant to share transfers within corporations and other business entities. This is because they give current owners a right ahead of third parties or outsiders to the corporation or business. They are a mechanism for retaining control and maintaining the status quo; they provide a basis for continuity.

FIGURE 9.7 Pre-emption rights

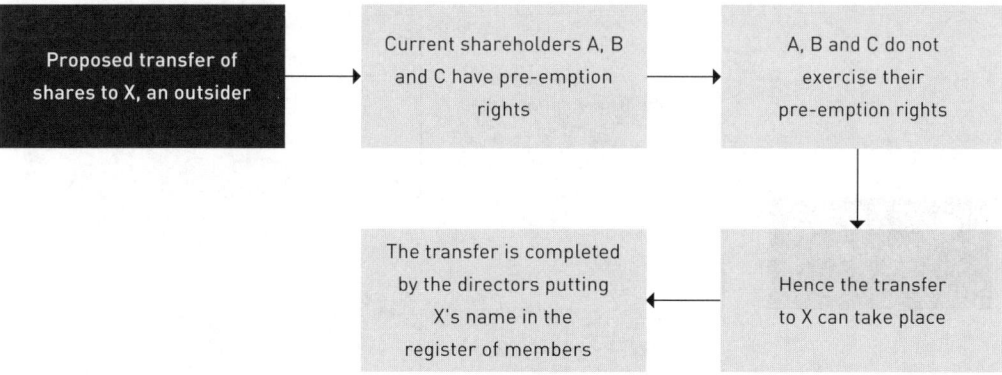

Activity 9.1
How are shares transferred in a Pty Ltd company?

9.3 DIFFERENT TYPES OF SHARES

The power of the company to issue shares is found in s 124 of the CA2001. This includes shares with particular rights attaching to them. Further, s 254A provides the company with specific power to issue particular types of shares; that is, it provides power to issue bonus, partly-paid, preference and redeemable preference shares: see Fig 9.8.

FIGURE 9.8   The basic schematic of shares that may be issued under CA2001 s 254A

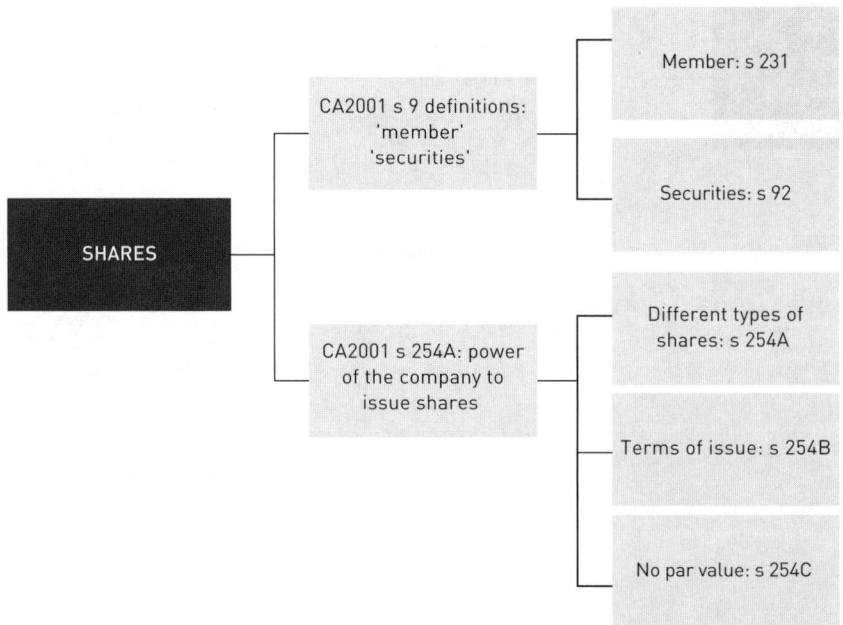

These four more specialised types of shares that may potentially be issued by the company are outlined in Table 9.2.

TABLE 9.2 The four types of shares referred to in CA2001 s 254A

Type of share	Features	Notes
Bonus	These are additional shares issued to existing shareholders.	Are these pro rata to existing shareholders? Note replaceable rules under CA2001 s 254D.
Partly-paid	This is where the shareholder still has money to pay on the shares as per the terms of issue.	These are covered by CA2001 ss 254–254R.
Preference	These attract the payment of any dividend in preference to other types of shares.	This depends on the company's constitution or other document, such as a shareholder's agreement
Redeemable preference shares	As with preference shares, these shares rank ahead of other shares in terms of the payment of any dividend. The shareholder has a right, as set out in the contract of issue, to have the company repurchase the shares. Hence, these shares are also a hybrid form of share finance and debt finance.	The shareholder provides share capital in the form of a specialised loan to the company. It combines this with a form of share repurchase by the company. The redemption by the company of redeemable preference shares is covered by CA2001 ss 254J, 254K, 254L.

The splitting of shares: converting the shares into larger or smaller number

A company is able to split shares by virtue of s 254H(1) of the CA2001:

> A company may convert all or any of its shares into a larger or smaller number of shares by resolution passed at a general meeting.

This works to the advantage of the shareholder, and is more advantageous based on two aspects:
- the number of shares initially held, and
- the number of the times the shares are split.

Examples of share splits have been seen in Walmart (USA) and Fortescue Metals (Australia).

A single share that is split 10 times results in the creation of more than 1,000 shares, as Table 9.3 demonstrates:

TABLE 9.3 A single share split 10 times, and the compounding effect

Number of shares	Number of splits	Total number of shares
1	1	2
2	2	4
4	3	8
8	4	16

TABLE 9.3 A single share split 10 times, and the compounding effect (continued)

Number of shares	Number of splits	Total number of shares
16	5	32
32	6	64
64	7	128
128	8	256
256	9	512
512	10	1,024

The CA2001 also provides for shares to be converted into smaller numbers.

> ### Activity 9.2
> Look at Table 9.3. If 10 had been the starting number of shares, what would 10 share splits come to?

9.4 POTENTIAL FINANCIAL RETURNS FOR SHAREHOLDERS

Shareholders seek an increase in the value of their shares. They seek monetary reward for their investment of risk capital in the company: see Fig 9.9.

FIGURE 9.9   The economics of shares

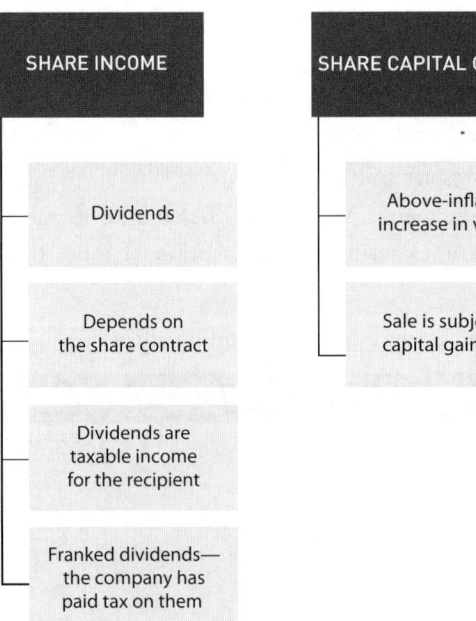

Members' financial returns are putatively dividends and capital gains. A dividend is an income stream for the member that is dependent on:

- the company making a profit, and
- the directors declaring a dividend.

Capital gains are the appreciation in value of the shares for the duration of their ownership by the member, by which the gain is over and above the percentage of inflation for the relevant period.

The general principles can be illustrated as shown in Fig 9.10, where a shareholder seeks a basic two-dimensional return on their investment.

FIGURE 9.10   Dividends and capital gains

Share dividends	Share capital gain
• Company needs to make a profit • Directors declare a dividend • Members receive the dividend as income • If tax has been paid by the company, it is referred to as a franked dividend • Members pay income tax on the dividend at their marginal rate, subject to any franking	• Shares are purchased for $X • Shares are held for a period of time in which inflation is 10% • The shares go up in value by 30% • Subject to particular tax rules, the capital gain is 20%, and the shareholders declare this as part of their income

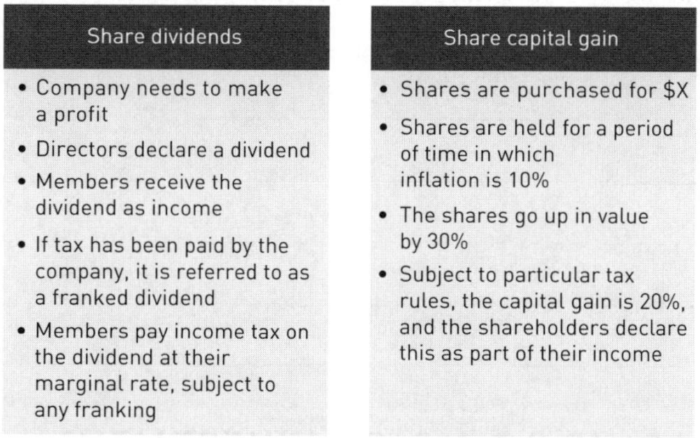

The payment of dividends by the company

A company's excess profit or capital can be either:

- reinvested in the business (e.g. on further capital expenditure, such as land, buildings and infrastructure, or research and development (R&D) etc), or
- paid out to the shareholders/owners as dividends.

This duality can be represented as shown in Fig 9.11.

FIGURE 9.11   The company's choice in terms of the use of company profits

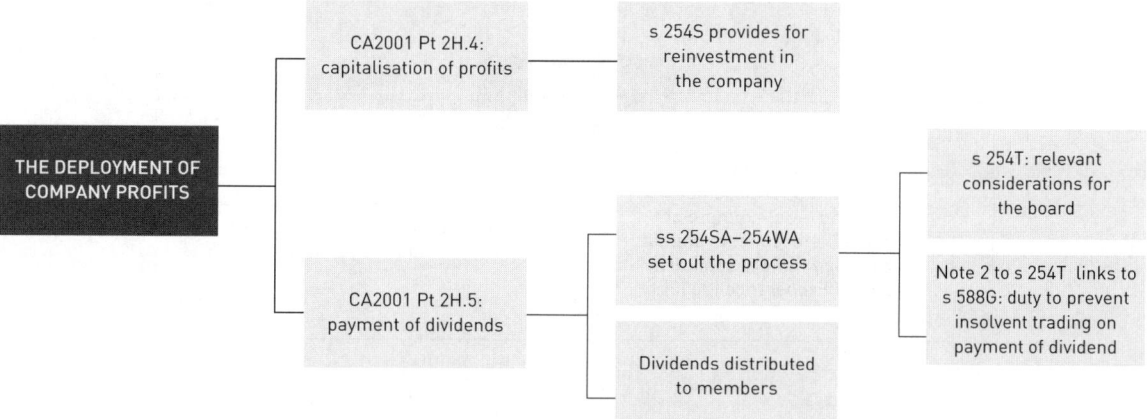

In regard to dividends, shareholders may either:
- receive a dividend out of profits, which has been recommended by the board, or
- have their shares bought back by the company as part of a share buy-back, and receive a payment for the shares followed by their cancellation.

These choices will be matters for the particular board, and part of its strategic decision making.

Activity 9.3
Outline the main issues for a board seeking to set a dividend payment.
_____
_____
_____
_____

9.5 SHAREHOLDING AS A RISK INVESTMENT

There has been much written about stock markets and investing. Shareholding is a form of investment 'currency' central to these markets. Investment decisions, including investing in shares, can be characterised in several ways: see Fig 9.12.

FIGURE 9.12   A basic classification of approaches to investment

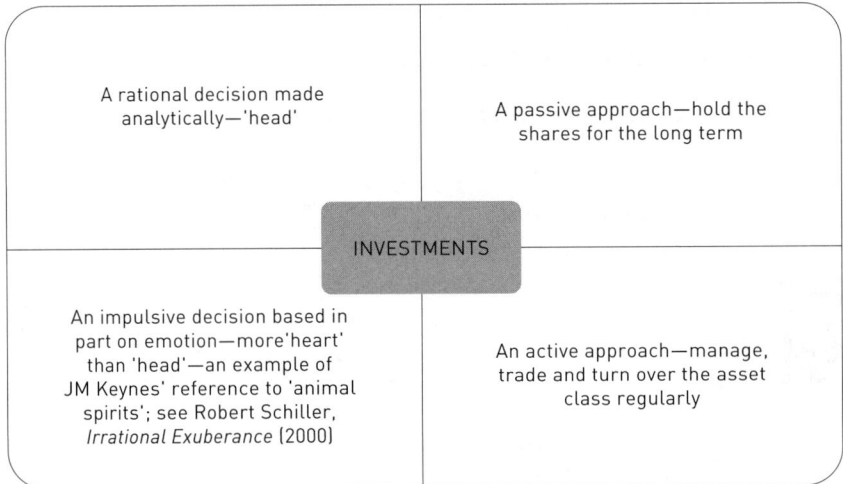

CHAPTER 9 SHARES AND SHAREHOLDING: PROPERTY, OWNERSHIP AND INVESTMENT

The value of shares is a current informed guess against future projections and trends and a range of unknowable factors. While income and capital may be the sought-after results by the hopeful shareholder, the opposite may in fact occur: see Fig 9.13.

FIGURE 9.13   The aims of the shareholder may not be achieved

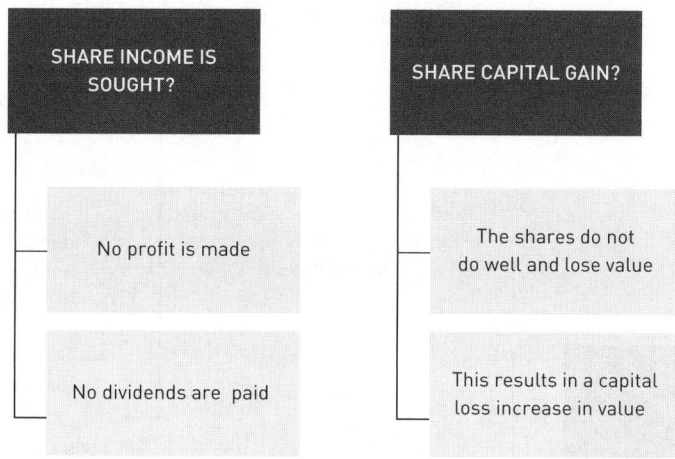

Activity 9.4

How are shares valued in a Pty Ltd?

_____
_____
_____
_____
_____
_____
_____
_____
_____
_____

WORKBOOK CHAPTER 9 REVIEW

An illustrative summary of the key points

FIGURE 9.14 Shares and their various uses and contexts for the company and the shareholder

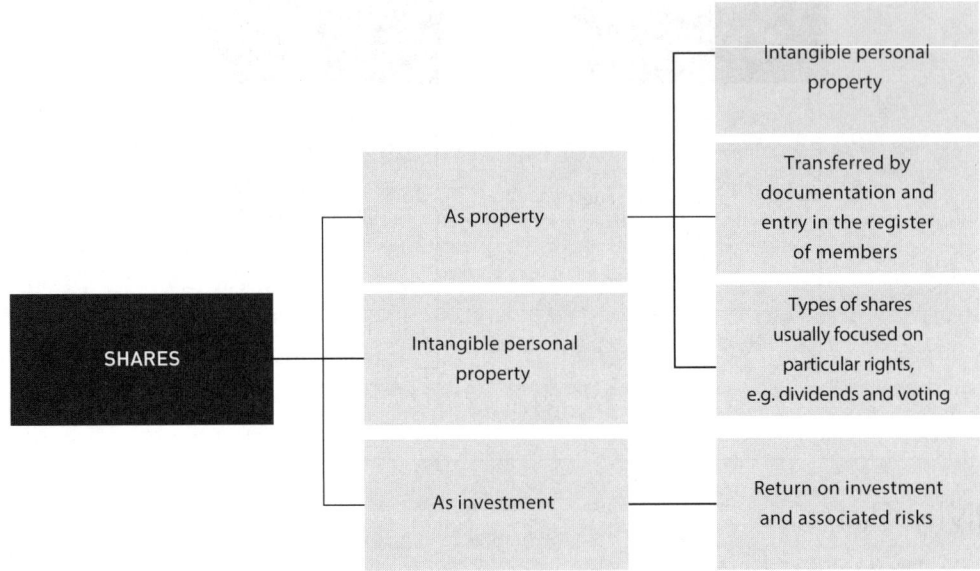

FIGURE 9.15 The links between key stakeholders, and between Chapters 9–11

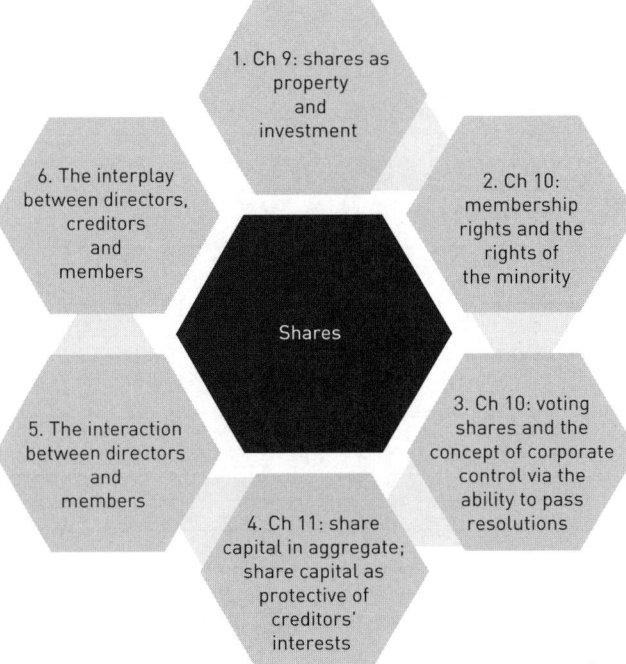

Figure 9.15 illustrates the link between key stakeholders, and the link with Chapters 10 and 11, which deal with issues relevant to company membership and share capital as an aggregate concept.

CHAPTER 9 REVISION ACTIVITIES

Consolidation of concepts, knowledge and content activities

TRUE OR FALSE?

1. Shares provide a percentage ownership in nominated assets of the company. True ☐ False ☐
2. Each share provides one vote. True ☐ False ☐
3. Shares are a form of intangible personal property. True ☐ False ☐
4. The completion of the transfer of shares in a Pty Ltd takes place by way of contract. True ☐ False ☐
5. The par value of shares is a matter to be determined when the company is first registered. True ☐ False ☐

FILL IN THE GAPS

1. Pre-emption rights are also referred to as rights of _____
2. The first members are appointed as a result of _____
3. Under the CA2001, a proprietary company limited by shares requires at least _____ member(s).
4. The payment of any dividend is payable as a priority to _____ shareholders.
5. A company is required to keep a register of members as required by _____
6. The main replaceable rule relevant to the role of the directors in the transfer of shares in a proprietary company is _____

MULTIPLE CHOICE

1. A company cannot issue:
   A. Stock
   B. Bearer shares
   C. Authorised share capital information
   D. Any of the above

2. A dividend can be paid by:
   A. A company limited by a guarantee
   B. An incorporated association
   C. A Pty Ltd
   D. All of the above

3. Ordinary shares usually carry:
   A. The right to vote
   B. The right to a dividend
   C. The right to be consulted
   D. No particular rights

4. Redeemable preference shares:
   A. Provide share capital to the company
   B. Entitle the shareholder to have them redeemed by the company
   C. Are a hybrid form of share and loan capital
   D. All three of the above

5. Dee has just been allotted 1,000 shares in ABC Pty Ltd. Each share is $10. Her share contract specifies a 50 per cent first-tranche payment within 30 days. Dee needs to pay ABC:
   A. $5,000
   B. $10,000
   C. $1,000
   D. $20,000

SHORT ANSWER QUESTIONS

1. What are shares?

2. How do you become a member of a corporation?

3. How do you cease to be a member?

4. Are details of members recorded/registered? What is recorded and where?

5. What are stapled securities?

6. What is CHESS?

7. What are 'redeemable preference shares'?

HIGHER ORDER THINKING ACTIVITIES

Explanatory notes to higher order question

Consider the following questions and provide detailed discussion and analysis.

TOPIC A

How are shares transferred, and what are the powers of the directors to prevent transfers?

QUESTIONS

TOPIC B

What responsibilities attach to substantial shareholders?

QUESTIONS

CHAPTER 10

MEMBERSHIP: MEETINGS, RIGHTS, RESPONSIBILITIES

Chapter synopsis and links to Textbook Chapter 10

This Workbook Chapter deals with five topics:

- 10.1 Company membership and its contractual nature
- 10.2 Membership rights and liabilities
- 10.3 Members' meetings
- 10.4 Potential remedies for members
- 10.5 Majority rule vs minority rights.

Each of these topics is constructively aligned with, and linked to, the same topics in Chapter 10 of the Textbook.

Chapter executive summary

This Chapter considers:

- the role and rights of members provided by the company by virtue of their relevant contract of membership
- linking the rights of the members with meetings and decision making within the company
- the primary importance of voting shares, and the potential premium for a controlling block of shares
- the principle of member decision making within the corporation: majority rule versus fairness to the minority, and
- the potential remedies under the CA2001 available to aggrieved minority shareholders.

CHAPTER DIAGRAMMATIC OVERVIEW

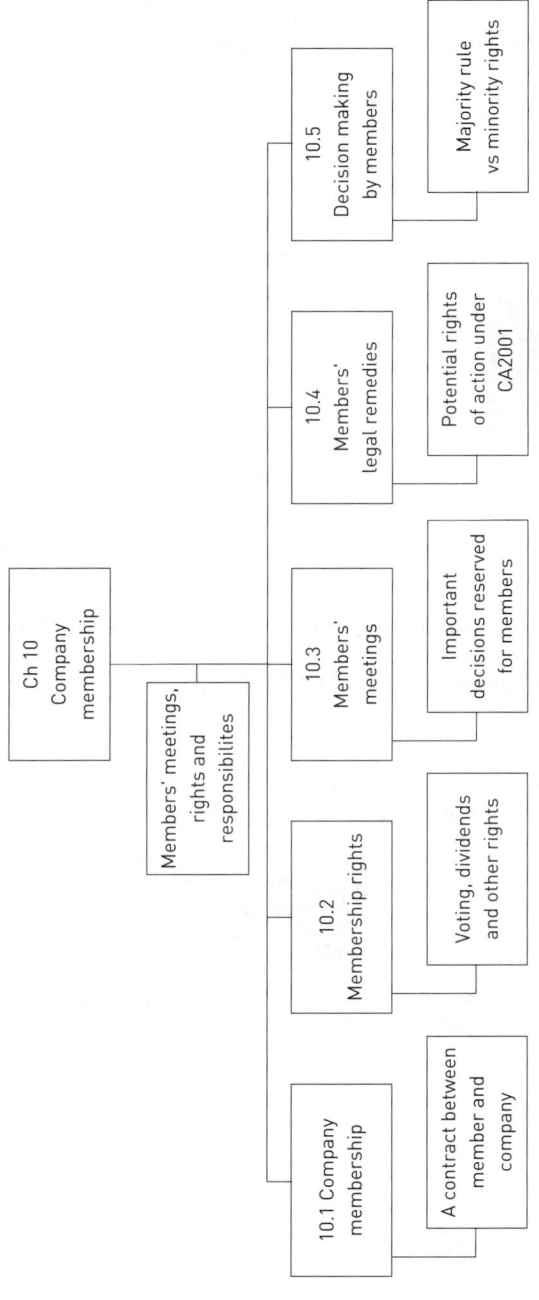

FIGURE 10.1 An overview of Chapter 10

10.1 COMPANY MEMBERSHIP AND ITS CONTRACTUAL NATURE

As noted in Chapter 9, the terms 'shareholder', 'owner' and 'member' are interchangeable. Contract informs the relationship between the company and the member: see Fig 10.2.

FIGURE 10.2 The contractual basis of share ownership

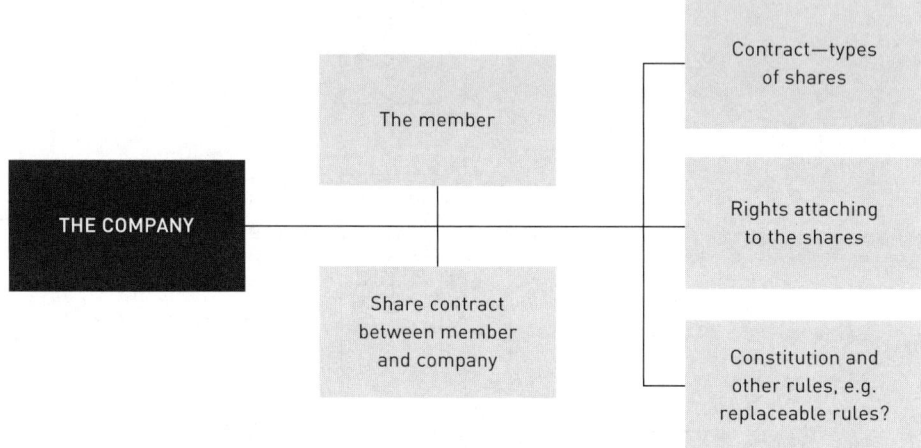

There are a related set of issues connecting shares with potential control: see Fig 10.3.

FIGURE 10.3 Company shares, potential control of the company

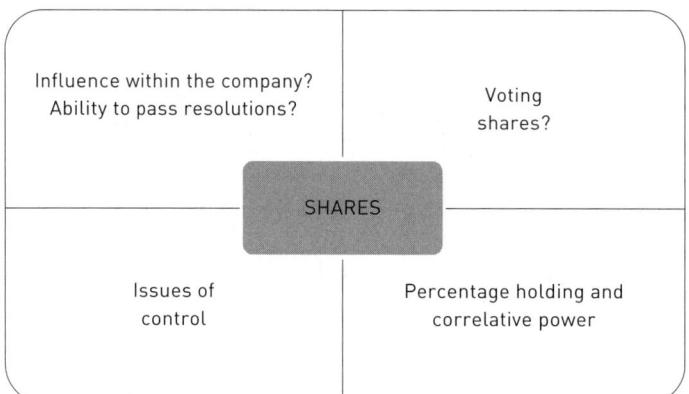

In addition, membership of Pty Ltd companies can range from one member to up to 50 non-employee shareholders. By contrast, public companies theoretically have no upper limit on the number of shareholders. Public companies require at least three directors, and Pty Ltds require at least one director.

> ### Activity 10.1
> When and why does a block of voting shares in a listed company attract a premium price?

10.2 MEMBERSHIP RIGHTS AND LIABILITIES

The rights attaching to the shares will depend on the share contract. The shares may carry a vote and a potential dividend. They are, in theory, transferable. The transfer of shares in a Pty Ltd company is, however, a matter of considering the rights of existing members, if any, and the mechanism to agree the share price.

The ability, at least in theory, to transfer shares is regarded as a basic feature of any corporation. It can be somewhat difficult in a small company, given the lack of a ready market of buyers and sellers, price history, or recent track record. This was also noted in Chapter 9, Section 9.2. It is an important point of basic practical control in a small company and will be of widespread effect, given that most companies in Australia are of this type and size.

FIGURE 10.4 The critical need to establish the current value of shares in a Pty Ltd

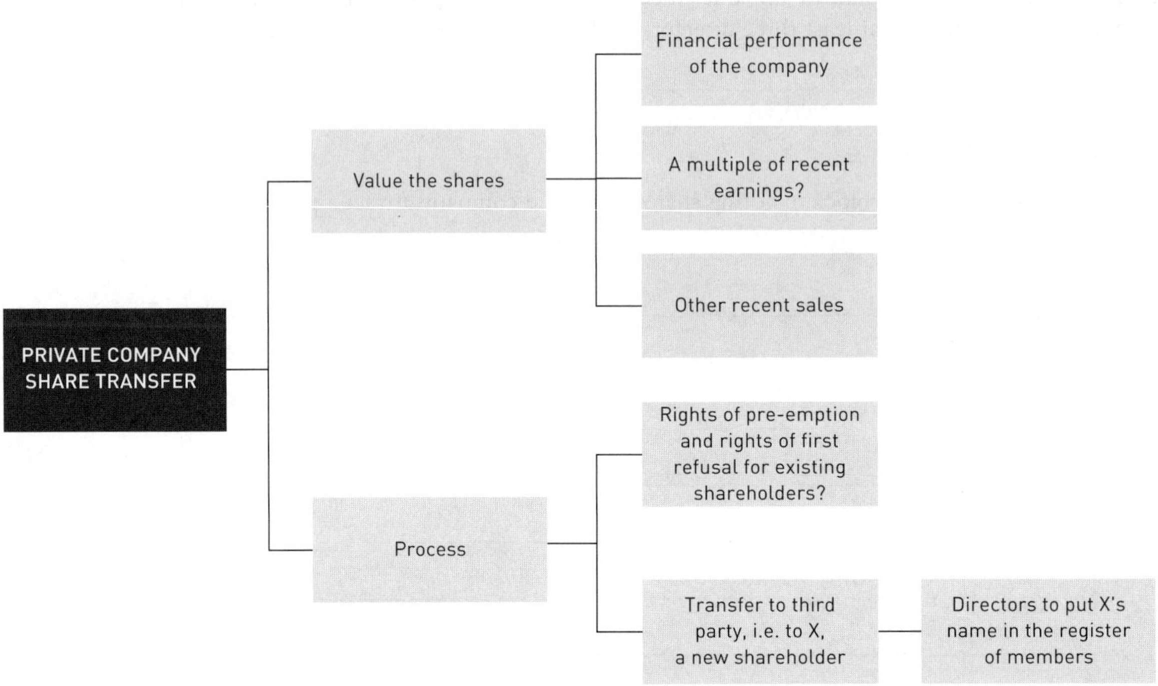

Pre-emption rights are a potential issue relevant to share transfers within corporations and other business entities. This is because they give current owners or members a right ahead of third parties or outsiders to the corporation or business.

FIGURE 10.5 Pre-emption rights are an important control mechanism, particularly for small Pty Ltd companies

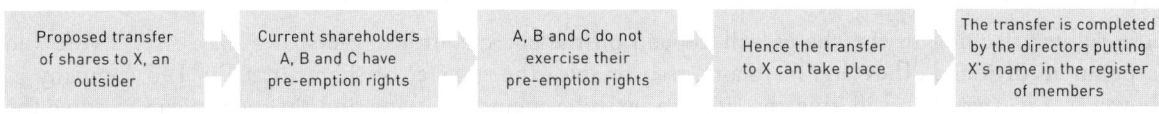

Case law relevant to members' rights

Cases develop over time, and between categories. Some cases can crossover or intersect with several areas of law. The precedent value can change, too. For example, *Gambotto v WCP Ltd* (1995) 182 CLR 432 was about unfairness by the majority members in the context of expropriation of the final small percentage of shares outstanding at the end of a takeover process.

While the particular law has changed as regards the takeover process, the underlying principle of unfairness relevant to the case applies. The issues relevant to members' rights that have been litigated are set out in Table 10.1.

TABLE 10.1 Development of common law principles relevant to members' rights

Year	Case	Principle
1874	*Menier v Hooper's Telegraph Works*	The majority are not able to expropriate property of the company to the detriment of the minority.
1887	*North-West Transportation Co v Beatty* (UK)	Owners of shares may vote in their own interests. Members may also be directors; when they vote at a members' meeting, they do so in their capacity as members. They need to have made any disclosure as directors.
1900	*Allen v Gold Reefs of West Africa Ltd*	'Fraud on the minority' was the key expression in this case. In some cases, the majority can amend the Articles of Association to the detriment of the minority.
1916	*Cook v Deeks* (UK)	Follows *Menier v Hooper's Telegraph Works* (1874).
1916	*Puddephatt v Leith* (UK)	Members can agree among themselves to vote in future in a particular way.
1927	*Shuttleworth v Cox Bros & Co Ltd*	In some cases, the majority can amend the Articles to the detriment of the minority.
1951	*Greenhalgh v Arderne Cinemas*	The minority needs to show that the change of Articles was not 'bona fide for the benefit of the company as a whole'.
1959	*Australian Fixed Trusts Pty Ltd v Clyde Industries Ltd*	Applies *Greenhalgh v Arderne Cinemas* (1951).
1966	*Re Five Minute Car Wash Service Ltd*	Oppression requires unfairness towards the complaining members.
1967	*Hogg v Cramphorn Ltd* (UK)	The issue is whether the matter in question can be ratified by the majority of members at a general meeting.
1969	*Hawkesbury Development Co Ltd v Landmark Finance Pty Ltd*	Applies *Greenhalgh v Arderne Cinemas* (1951).
1969	*Re Bright Pine Mills Pty Ltd*	Oppression requires unfairness towards the complaining members.
1970	*Bamford v Bamford* (UK)	The issue is whether the matter in question can be ratified by the majority of members at a general meeting.
1971	*Re Jermyn Street Turkish Baths* (UK)	The shareholder needs to show the conduct is part of a pattern.
1972	*Re Tivoli Freeholds Ltd*	The shareholder needs to show the conduct is part of a pattern.
1975	*Winthrop Investments v Winns Ltd*	The directors need to make disclosure to the general meeting. The members can authorise matters, but not those that amount to a fraud on the company.

TABLE 10.1 Development of common law principles relevant to members' rights (continued)

Year	Case	Principle
1976	*Clemens v Clemens Bros Ltd* (UK)	The minority needs to be treated fairly. (In this case, resolutions at a members' meeting targeted a shareholder (the niece of the proponent) who held 45% of the shares. The proposed changes would dilute the holding to less than 25%. This would prevent the shareholder being able to block a special resolution (75% of the votes cast). The proposed changes would also reduce the value of pre-emptive rights relevant to other members seeking to sell their shares.)
1977	*Cumberland Holdings Ltd v Washington H Soul Pattinson & Co*	
1995	*Gambotto v WCP Ltd*	Follows *Menier v Hooper's Telegraph Works* (1874)
2010	*Vadori v AAV Plumbing*	
2014	*Sumiseki Materials Co Ltd v Wambo Coal Pty Ltd*	

Activity 10.2

Complete Table 10.1.

10.3 MEMBERS' MEETINGS

Business decisions typically commence at the board level, and may be resolved at that point. In the case of issues requiring shareholder approval as the result of the CA2001 or the company's own rules, the decision may go to a members' EGM (extraordinary general meeting).

FIGURE 10.6   The process of members' meetings

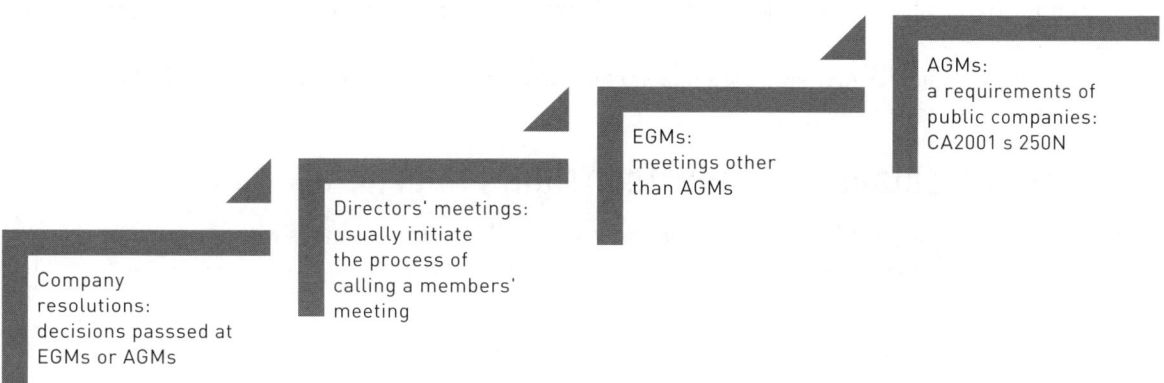

Owning just one share may bestow significant rights on the holder. It all depends on the terms of the contract between the owner and the company.

TABLE 10.2   The member's suite of rights as regard their shareholding

Company ABC Pty Ltd	Member A: the potential range of rights attaching to A's shareholding:
Usual rights	<ul><li>Right to attend meetings (and receive notices)</li><li>Right to vote (voting share)</li><li>Right to receive a dividend (if a dividend is announced)</li><li>Preferential right to a dividend</li></ul>
Other rights (depending on the share contract relevant to the share issue and ownership)	

The passing of resolutions by members: majority rule vs fairness

Assume that A, B and C have one share each in the company ABC Pty Ltd. A and B acting together are a majority, and can pass an ordinary resolution.

If A and B each have 40 per cent of the shares, leaving C with 20 per cent, this tips the voting balance completely in favour of A and B. Together, they have 80 per cent of the votes, which gives them the ability to pass a special resolution.

However, mere mathematical percentages are tempered by provisions relating to fairrness. The CA2001 contains provisions that potentially redress the balance in C's favour.

Assume again that A, B and C each have one share (it could be 10 or 100; the point is that they are equal shareholders). Potential transactions that may give rise to issues for C include:

- new shares being issued—C has a pro rata entitlement to participate, so as to not dilute their 33.3 per cent holding
- C wanting to transfer to a new shareholder, D—A and B can block the transfer, or may seek pre-emption rights to C's shares.

A minority shareholder may seek various remedies under the CA2001 (including ss 232, 233 and 461) such as court orders and winding-up.

Member percentages: shareholder rights in general

From a base of one share, further considerations flow. Generally, control increases with the number of shares held, because this translates into an increased percentage shareholding. Table 10.3 demonstrates the relative power of members as their shareholding increases.

TABLE 10.3   The relative power of members as their shareholding increases

Percentage of voting shares	Members' rights (potential rights)
1 share:	Receive information and notices May be able to vote at general meetings (GMs)—depends on the contract May be able to receive dividends
1% of shares:	
3% of shares:	

Percentage of voting shares	Members' rights (potential rights)
5% of shares:	**Topic: GMs—general** CA2001 s 249C and 249CA: the usual situation is that the directors call the GM. *Default situations for meetings* CA2001 s 249D covers the situation where the directors call the meeting only after members with 5% of the votes have requested the directors to call the meeting. CA2001 s 249E: directors fail to call a members' meeting. CA2001 s 249F: members with 5% of votes (substantial shareholder) may call an EGM without asking the directors, as per s 249F, but they have to pay the expenses of calling and holding the meeting; hence, this is not often used. **Topic: Resolutions at GMs** These are usually put by directors. *Default situations for resolutions to be considered at meetings* For members' resolutions to be tabled at GMs requires 100 members, or 5% of the voting shares, as per s 249N of the CA2001. **Topic: Members seeking details of directors' remuneration** CA2001 s 202B: 100 members, or those holding 5% of the votes, may seek details of the directors' remuneration.
10% of shares:	**Topic: Changing the class rights of members** CA2001 s 246D: members with 10% of the votes of the relevant class of shares may apply to the court to have a proposed variation of cancellation of rights attaching to shares set aside on the grounds of unfair prejudice. Timing: the application has to be within one month after the variation, cancellation or modification.
20% of shares:	
25% of shares plus 1:	*Can block a special resolution*
50% of shares plus 1:	Can pass an ordinary resolution
75% of shares:	Can pass a special resolution
90% of shares:	The shareholder is relevant in a takeover context. A shareholder with this percentage of shares can 'mop up' the rest of the shares to 100%. This particular change to the CA2001 (see s 664A) was inserted as a result of the particular facts of *Gambotto's case* (1995) (the principle of oppression, however, remains relevant from the case).
100% of shares:	Total control of the shares

Special resolutions signal that a decision of the members is an important one. Such resolutions carry significance requiring more than a simple majority of the votes—they require a 75 per cent approval; that is, an emphatic affirmation.

Figure 10.7 illustrates the gradations of shareholder control, depending on the percentage of votes that can be cast. Note that the value of a controlling shareholding would attract a premium price, given the assignation it carries.

FIGURE 10.7 The gradations of shareholder control

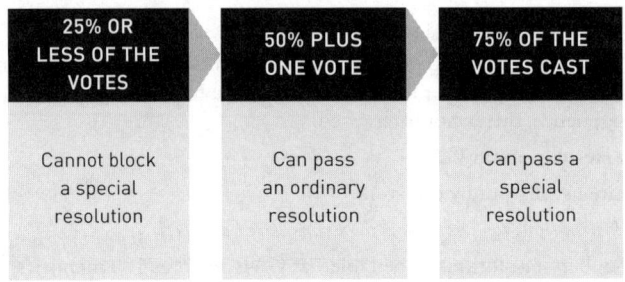

There are 13 special resolutions set out in the CA2001, which are set out in Table 10.4.

TABLE 10.4 Special resolutions required by the CA2001

	CA2001	Focus of the resolution
1	s 136	Change of constitution
2	s 157	Change of company name
3	s 162	Change from Pty Ltd to public; public to Pty Ltd
4	s 162	Change of company type
5	s 246B	Variation of rights
6	s 254N	Call-up decisions regarding share capital
7	s 256C	Selective (differentiated) reduction of share capital
8	s 260B	Financial assistance to the company to purchase its shares
9	s 461	Winding-up of the company
10	s 491(1)	Voluntary winding-up of the company
11	s 506(1A)	Powers of the liquidator in a members' voluntary winding-up
12	s 507(2)	Liquidator transferring business or property of the company
13	s 510	Approving an arrangement between the company and the creditors before winding-up

Based on Table 10.4, there are broadly four types of areas of corporate law for which special resolutions are required. These can be reconfigured as set out in Fig 10.8.

FIGURE 10.8 The various types of special resolution, as described in Table 10.4

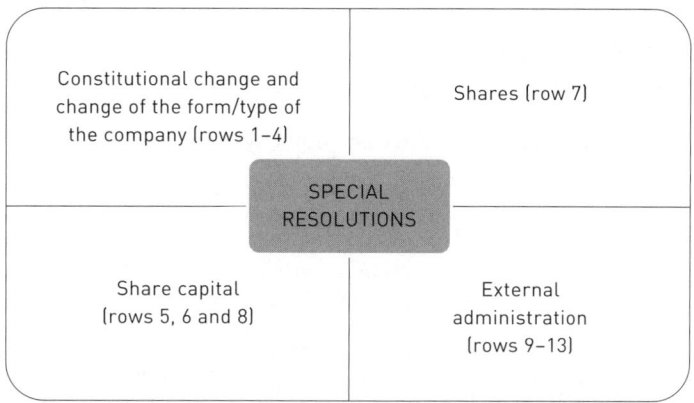

> ### Activity 10.3
> Look at Tables 10.2 and 10.3. Is there any further detail that can be added?

10.4 POTENTIAL REMEDIES FOR MEMBERS

Members of companies may all get along most of the time. There can, however, be disagreements that cannot be readily settled. Disputes are likely to involve certain types of issues, including:

- a lack of control
- a change in expectations
- a failure to act by the company
- a perception of a lack of clarity or fairness
- a belief that personal issues (self-dealing, animosity etc) are guiding events, rather than genuine business considerations
- a drop in value of the investment.

In terms of the last issue, financial considerations may be of certain types:

- dilution of a percentage shareholding
- expropriation—a forced sale—for an undervalue
- diminution in the value of the share parcel.

The dilution of a shareholder's interests: interim potential solutions

Take the example where A, B and C are equal members in XYZ Pty Ltd. A and B want to issue further shares, and to dilute C's holding. C's legal options may include:

- alternative dispute resolution (ADR), such as a meeting to clarify the motivations of A and B, negotiation and other non-litigious options, or
- formal litigation, including issuing proceedings.

C's rights potentially cover a series of bases, as set out in Fig 10.9.

FIGURE 10.9 The potential remedies to be explored by minority members

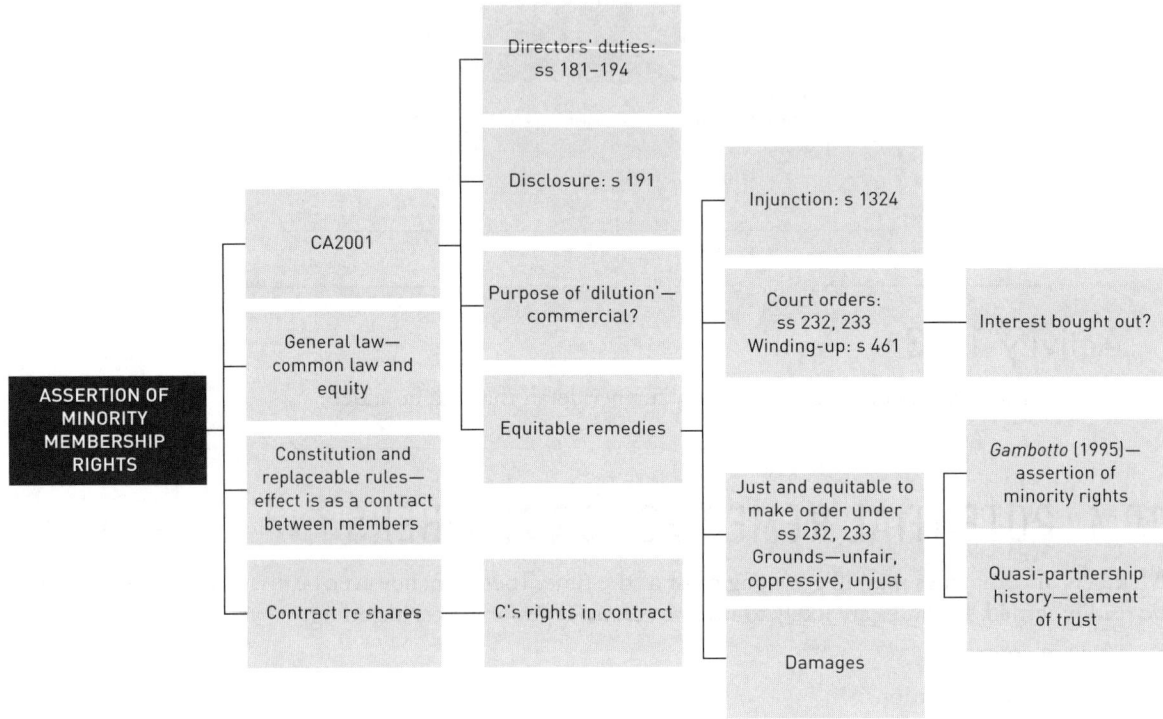

Statutory derivative actions

The usual situation is that a wrong done to the company is a matter for the company to pursue via a resolution of the directors.

TABLE 10.5 The CA2001 provides a statutory derivative action in ss 236 and 237

Date	Case	Relevant principle of corporations law	Ongoing relevance to CA2001
1843	*Foss v Harbottle*	The corporation is the proper plaintiff in a wrong done to the company	
		The majority of the company in general meeting makes decisions on the company's behalf	

Date	Case	Relevant principle of corporations law	Ongoing relevance to CA2001

Activity 10.4
Complete Table 10.5, and provide an outline of the statutory derivative action below.

_____
_____
_____
_____
_____
_____

10.5 MAJORITY RULE VS MINORITY RIGHTS

The concept of majority rule of the company by the directors acting together with the majority of members is a bedrock principle of corporations law. However, this core concept can be pitted against the rights of minority members to be treated fairly in the event of treatment that they can demonstrate is unfair or prejudicial in terms of their particular circumstances, such that their membership rights have not been properly observed.

The usual situation is that the majority vote is determinative, so long as it is done for commercial bona fide purposes. The majority needs to act in accordance with established principles of objective commercial considerations. The test is what is in the best interests of the company. This is somewhat vague on the one hand, but flexible and malleable on the other. As such, it is a widely used principle developed by the case law and adopted by the CA2001.

Figure 10.10 illustrates that corporations, much like democracies, operate on the basic principle of majority rule. That is, for the most part, they are not governed by, or operated via, resort to exceptionalism.

FIGURE 10.10   Corporations, much like democracies, operate on the basic principle of majority rule

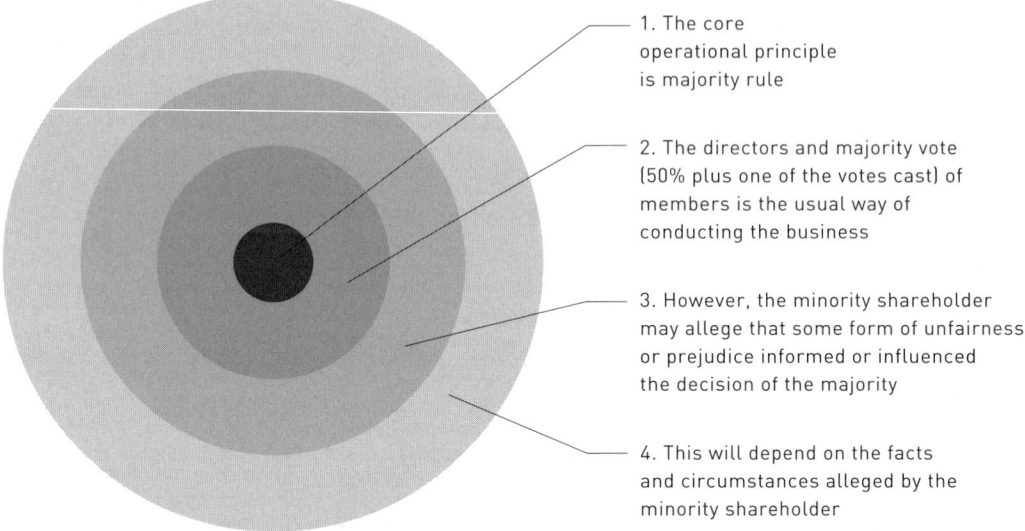

1. The core operational principle is majority rule

2. The directors and majority vote (50% plus one of the votes cast) of members is the usual way of conducting the business

3. However, the minority shareholder may allege that some form of unfairness or prejudice informed or influenced the decision of the majority

4. This will depend on the facts and circumstances alleged by the minority shareholder

The principle of majority control is enunciated by reference to the number and percentage of shares held and is informed historically by the development of commercial principles in common law. By contrast, the rights to be asserted by the minority shareholder are informed by notions of fairness, and principles historically developed by equity. The legal rights of the minority shareholders on the one hand, as opposed to the legal responsibility of the majority shareholders on the other hand, are competing considerations.

This potential tension between the minority and the majority can be remedied. It involves making business decisions with business criteria in mind. This, in turn, involves basic notions of fairness informing the decision, and of not 'targeting' (explicitly or implicitly) particular members for non-business reasons.

Majority behaviour can be characterised as shown in Fig 10.11. There is no necessary 'bright line' between the two; hence the incidence of litigation from time to time.

FIGURE 10.11   The characterisation of majority behaviour

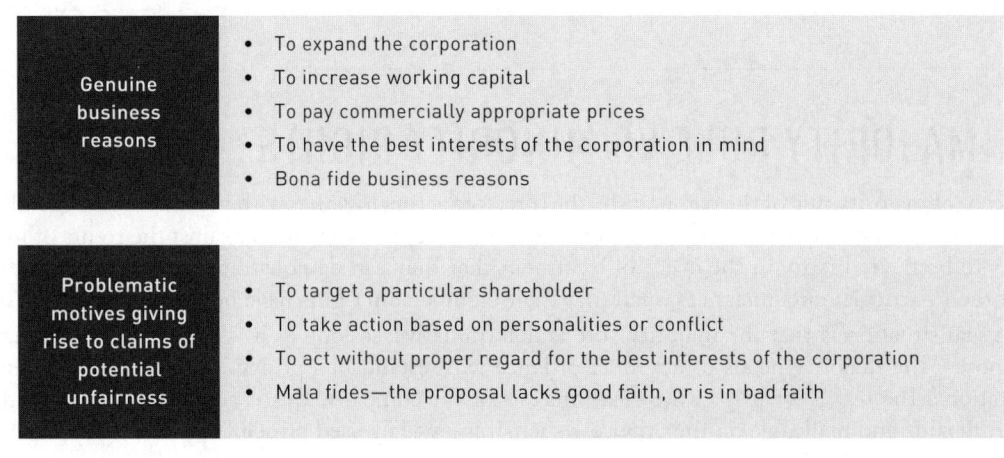

Genuine business reasons	• To expand the corporation • To increase working capital • To pay commercially appropriate prices • To have the best interests of the corporation in mind • Bona fide business reasons
Problematic motives giving rise to claims of potential unfairness	• To target a particular shareholder • To take action based on personalities or conflict • To act without proper regard for the best interests of the corporation • Mala fides—the proposal lacks good faith, or is in bad faith

In a small family or Pty Ltd company, there is a certain level of 'getting on' and healthy interpersonal relationships, which lie at the heart of the corporation being successful. Without this, the corporation will struggle. Personality-based and other issues need to be kept to one side. The focus of the directors and members is to act in the best interests of the company. This can become particularly apparent where there are just a few owners, and a subsequent falling out between the members.

Take the example of three members, A, B and C and the steps set out in Table 10.6 that act to isolate C, and to dilute C's shareholding.

TABLE 10.6 An example of the diminution of C's shareholding

Shareholder/event	Shareholder A	Shareholder B	Shareholder C	Notes
No 1: Issue of initial shares	10	10	10	
Percentage holding of shares	33.3%	33.3%	33.3%	
No 2: Issue of a further 10 shares, to be paid in full immediately for $1,000 each	10	10	0	Assume that C cannot take up the shares as they cannot meet the payment requirement
Resulting number of shares	20	20	10	
Percentage holding of shares	40%	40%	20%	C is now in a much weaker position with just 20% of the shares. Conversely, A and B are in a much stronger position with 80% of the shares and the ability to pass a special resolution. If C has been treated unfairly in this process, C can investigate the merits of an oppression action.

Expropriation of shares

In the case of *Gambotto v WCP Ltd* (1995) 182 CLR 432:

- After a successful takeover of WCP, the bidder acquired over 99 per cent of its share capital.
- It sought to alter the WCP constitution to allow any member with 90 per cent of the issued shares to compulsorily acquire all the other issued shares (i.e. the balance to 100 per cent).
- The bidder justified the alteration on the grounds of the potential taxation, and administrative cost savings.

It was held that the expropriation of shares owned by a minority is valid only if the majority of members can provide and demonstrate that it is:

- for a proper purpose, and
- fair, and not oppressive, in all the circumstances.

'Proper purpose' includes preventing the company suffering significant detriment or harm, for example:

- if the particular shareholder was competing with the company
- if the legislation requires particular shareholdings.

The ongoing effect of *Gambotto's case* is illustrated in Fig 10.12.

FIGURE 10.12 *Gambotto*-style unfairness

GAMBOTTO'S CASE (1995)
- Involved expropriation of shares within the context of a takeover
- Involved unfair treatment of the minority shareholder

CA2001 AMENDED
- Allows for the purchase of outstanding shares in the context of a takeover

GAMBOTTO-STYLE UNFAIRNESS
- Oppression of the minority
- The principle of unfairness remains

Activity 10.5
Outline the ongoing relevance of *Gambotto's case*.

WORKBOOK CHAPTER 10 REVIEW

An illustrative summary of the key points

FIGURE 10.13   The links between shares and shareholdings

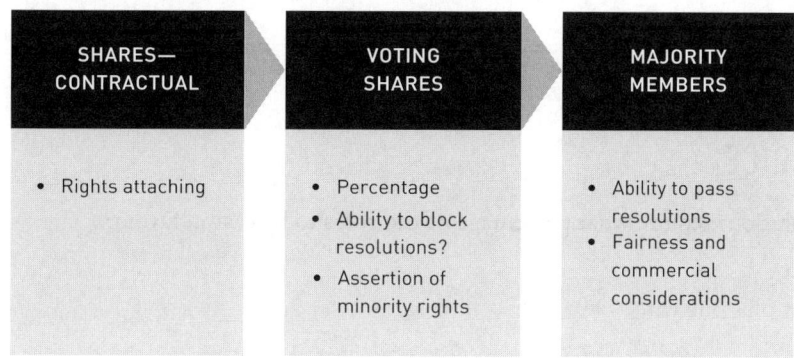

CHAPTER 10 REVISION ACTIVITIES

Consolidation of concepts, knowledge and content activities

TRUE OR FALSE?

1. A Pty Ltd must hold an AGM. — True ☐ False ☐
2. A court has the power to call a general meeting. — True ☐ False ☐
3. A public company must hold its first AGM within 18 months of incorporation. — True ☐ False ☐
4. Procedural irregularities will necessarily invalidate a members' meeting. — True ☐ False ☐
5. Ordinary resolutions require a simple majority vote. — True ☐ False ☐
6. The statutory derivative action is set out in s 140 of the CA2001. — True ☐ False ☐

FILL IN THE GAPS

1. A(n) _____ will be required to value the shareholding in a Pty Ltd in which shares have not been traded.

2. If C wishes to exit the company, A and B would be best protected by _____ allowing them to purchase C's shares.

3. The High Court case of *Sons of Gwalia Ltd v Margaretic* (2007) has been _____ _____ by the CA2001.

4. The main avenue for a minority shareholder alleging unfairness in relation to the majority members is section _____ of the CA2001.

5. The 1995 High Court decision of _____ is instructive as regards the content of and approach to s 232 of the CA2001.

MULTIPLE CHOICE

1. Ordinary resolutions require what percentage of the votes to be cast in favour?

   A. 25 per cent
   B. 50 per cent plus one vote
   C. 50 per cent
   D. 75 per cent

2. What is the usual notice period in days for a Pty Ltd having a meeting?

   A. 7
   B. 14
   C. 21
   D. 28

3. Special resolutions require what percentage of votes?

   A. 50 per cent
   B. 75 per cent
   C. 75 per cent plus one
   D. 90 per cent

4. A proxy is:

   A. A branch office
   B. A substitute shareholder
   C. A part-time director
   D. A professional adviser

5. Members in a Pty Ltd with what minimum percentage of shares may call a general meeting?

   A. 5 per cent
   B. 10 per cent
   C. 25 per cent
   D. 50 per cent

SHORT ANSWER QUESTIONS

1. How are company resolutions passed?

2. What does 'quorum' mean in relation to a company meeting?

3. Can irregularities invalidate the meeting?

4. What is the rule in *Foss v Harbottle* (1843), and what is its status?

5. What was the significance of the decision in *Jordan v Avram* (1997) as regards irregularities?

Higher order thinking activities

Consider the following questions and provide detailed discussion and analysis.

TOPIC A

What are the personal rights of members and how are they protected under statute?

QUESTIONS

TOPIC B

A, B and C have been in a Pty Ltd for several years. A and B want C out of the company. They issue further shares on the condition that they are fully paid, knowing C is short of finance. What are C's options?

QUESTIONS

CHAPTER 11

SHARE CAPITAL: TRANSACTIONS AND CONTROL

Chapter synopsis and links to Textbook Chapter 11

This Workbook Chapter deals with five topics:

- 11.1 Share capital and its maintenance
- 11.2 Share capital transactions: reductions and buy-backs
- 11.3 Transactions affecting control of voting shares: takeovers
- 11.4 Schemes of arrangement: an alternative to takeovers
- 11.5 Groups of companies and control issues.

Each of these topics is constructively aligned with, and linked to, the same topics in Chapter 11 of the Textbook.

Chapter executive summary

This Chapter examines:
- the company's share capital as an asset designed to protect the interests of the creditors
- the common law rules as to the maintenance of capital
- transactions relevant to the reduction of capital
- takeovers and the change of control of the company via the voting shares
- group companies and the issues of holding and subsidiary companies.

CHAPTER DIAGRAMMATIC OVERVIEW

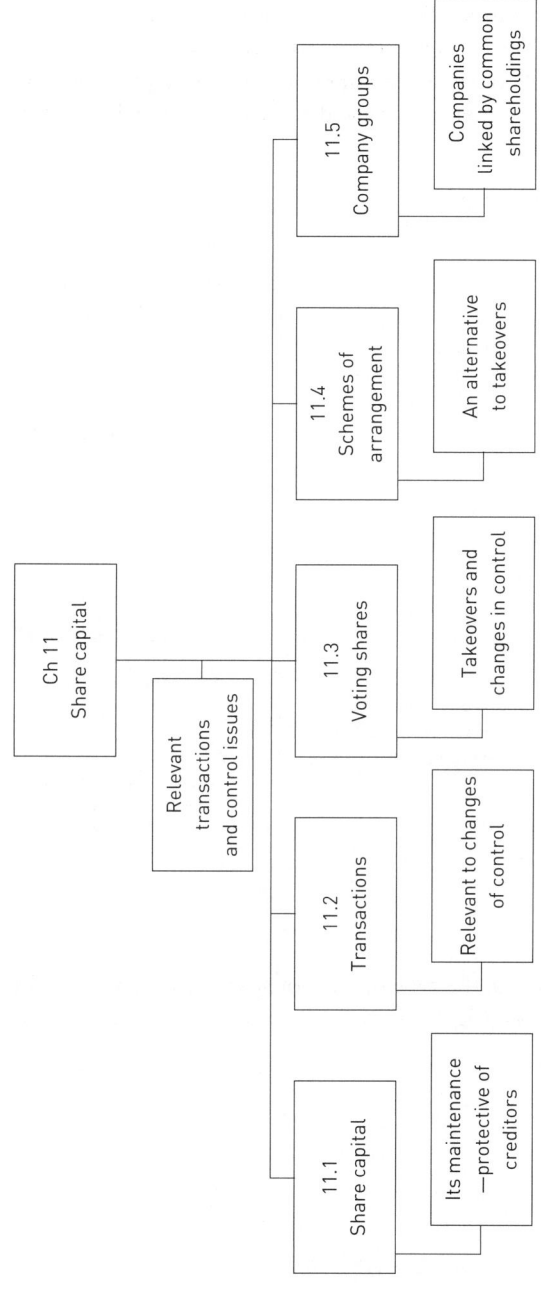

FIGURE 11.1 An overview of Chapter 11

11.1 SHARE CAPITAL AND ITS MAINTENANCE

'Share capital' refers to the aggregation of the value of the shares issued by the company. If the company has issued 100 $1 shares and they have been fully paid, it has share capital of $100. Likewise, if it issues 1,000 shares at $10 each and they are fully paid, the share capital is $10,000. The share capital is a fund to grow the business for members, and is protective of the interests of creditors. Given this latter need, the common law developed rules to prevent the company from reducing or decimating the value of this protective fund.

There are remnants of this common law approach in the contemporary corporate law. The CA2001 provides particular process requirements that need to be complied with by a company if it wishes to reduce its share capital: see Fig 11.2.

FIGURE 11.2   Reductions of share capital

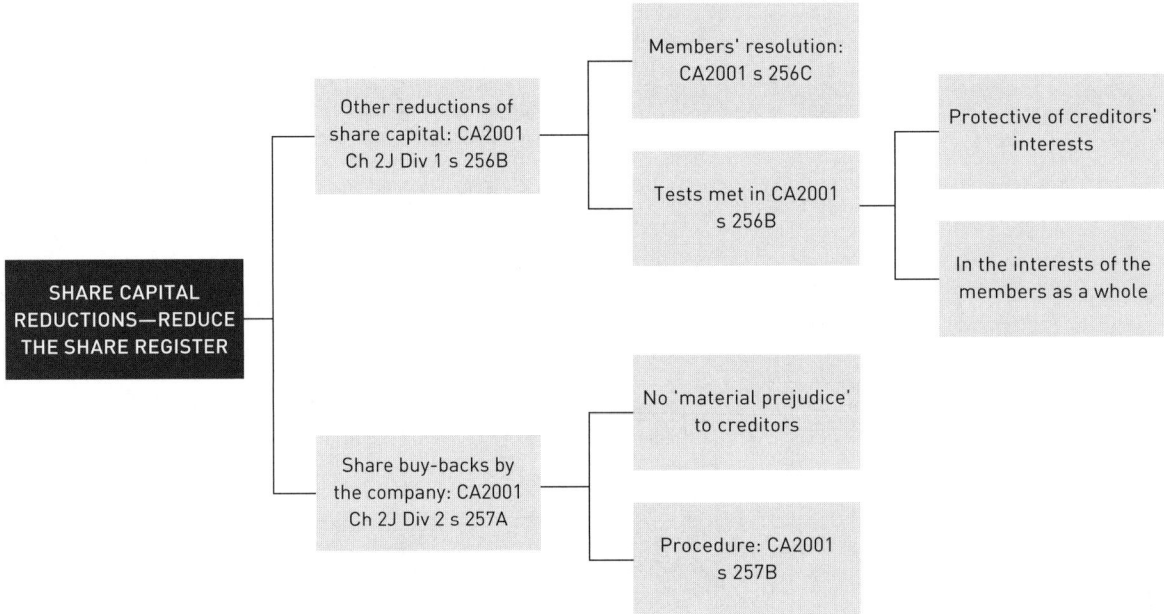

Classes of shares

As discussed in Chapters 9 and 10, the type or class of shares can vary according to the contract between the company and the shareholder: see Fig 11.3.

FIGURE 11.3 Voting rights and access to a dividend (if paid) tend to be key indicators of rights attaching to shares

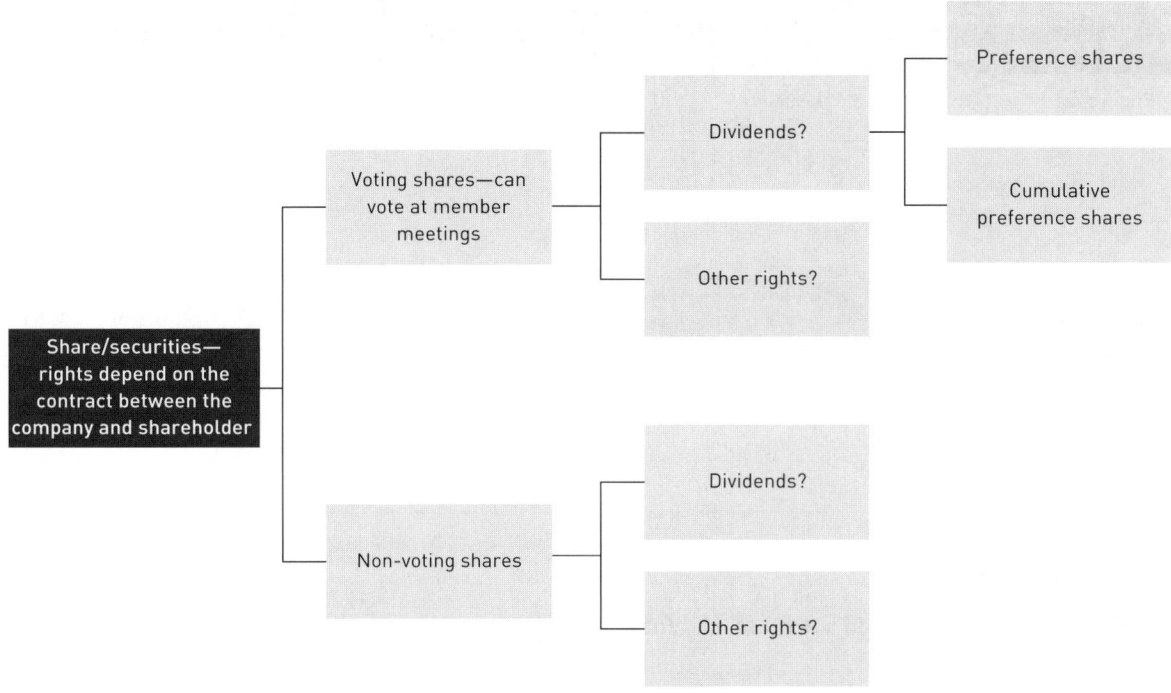

The rights attaching to shares will be determined by contract.

TABLE 11.1 The rights attaching to shares

Class of shares	Receive notice of meetings	Vote at members' meetings	Dividend receipt	Other rights
Non-voting ordinary shares	Yes	No		
Voting shares	Yes	Yes		

TABLE 11.1 The rights attaching to shares (continued)

Class of shares	Receive notice of meetings	Vote at members' meetings	Dividend receipt	Other rights
Preference shares	Yes	Usually	If declared, yes	
Cumulative preference shares	Yes	Usually	If declared, yes	

Activity 11.1

Review Table 11.1 and add any other relevant information.

11.2 SHARE CAPITAL TRANSACTIONS: REDUCTIONS AND BUY-BACKS

By way of background:
- Share capital is also called equity capital.
- Share capital is the total amount of money/property provided to the company in consideration for the shares issued to the members/shareholders.
- The principles and legislation are to ensure that the transactions do not materially prejudice the interests of:
  - the company
  - its shareholders, or
  - the ability of the company to pay its creditors.

The background to the modern law of share capital transactions is found in the common law in the rule in *Trevor v Whitworth* [1887] 12 App Cas 409 (UK):
- The principle is that a company is *generally prohibited* from reducing its issued share capital because a reduction could prejudice the rights of creditors.
- The reason is because the reduction would have the effect of reducing the amount of funds/share capital available to the company to pay its creditors.

The facts of the case were as follows:
- Whitworth, who was deceased at the time of the litigation, held shares in the company Schofield and Sons Ltd (SL).

- Whitworth's executors agreed to sell Whitworth's shares back to SL.
- Payment by SL was to be in two instalments.
- The first instalment was paid by SL.
- SL then went into liquidation.
- Whitworth's executors claimed the balance (the second instalment) from Trevor, the liquidator of SL.

The House of Lords held that even though the Articles of Association of SL purported to allow buy-backs, there was no power for SL to do so in this case. The buy-back was void. Hence, the claim failed.

The effect of the rule in *Trevor v Whitworth* can be summarised as shown in Fig 11.4.

FIGURE 11.4 The common law principle enunciated in *Trevor v Whitworth*

THE INTENDED EFFECT	The buy-back would have diminished the company's share capital available to its creditors
THE CREDITORS' RISK	Creditors take the risk that the company's capital may be diminished in the ordinary course of the company's business
THE COMMON LAW PRINCIPLE	The law does not expect that capital will be returned to shareholders ahead of creditors

Figure 11.5 gives an example of the common law principle.

FIGURE 11.5 The common law principle in practice

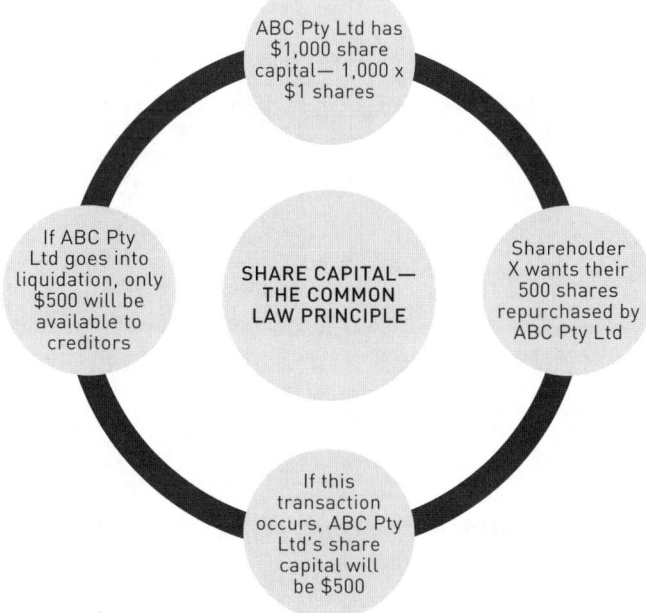

The statutory process that has replaced the common law

The strictures of the common law have been superseded by statute. The situation is now governed by s 259A of the CA2001, which provides the circumstances that allow for the company to buy back its shares. These circumstances are relatively limited, reflecting the common law context as set out in *Trevor v Whitworth* (1887).

A corporation's share capital is a critically important account within the company. There is a tension between the maintenance of the capital and transactions affecting it. In particular, share capital may be affected by three potential transactions, as shown in Table 11.2:

TABLE 11.2 Reasons for maintaining share capital, and the three potential transactions affecting share capital

Reasons for maintaining share capital	Transactions reducing share capital
• Solvency of the company • Retaining a strong balance sheet • For the benefit of creditors of the company • A reserve fund in case of an operating emergency	1. Payment of dividends—to shareholders out of profits and as determined by the directors 2. Share buy-backs—the purchase of issued shares in order to simplify the company's share register 3. Other reductions of capital

Figure 11.6 gives an overview of the legislative principles and processes regarding the reduction of capital.

FIGURE 11.6 An overview of share capital transactions under the CA2001

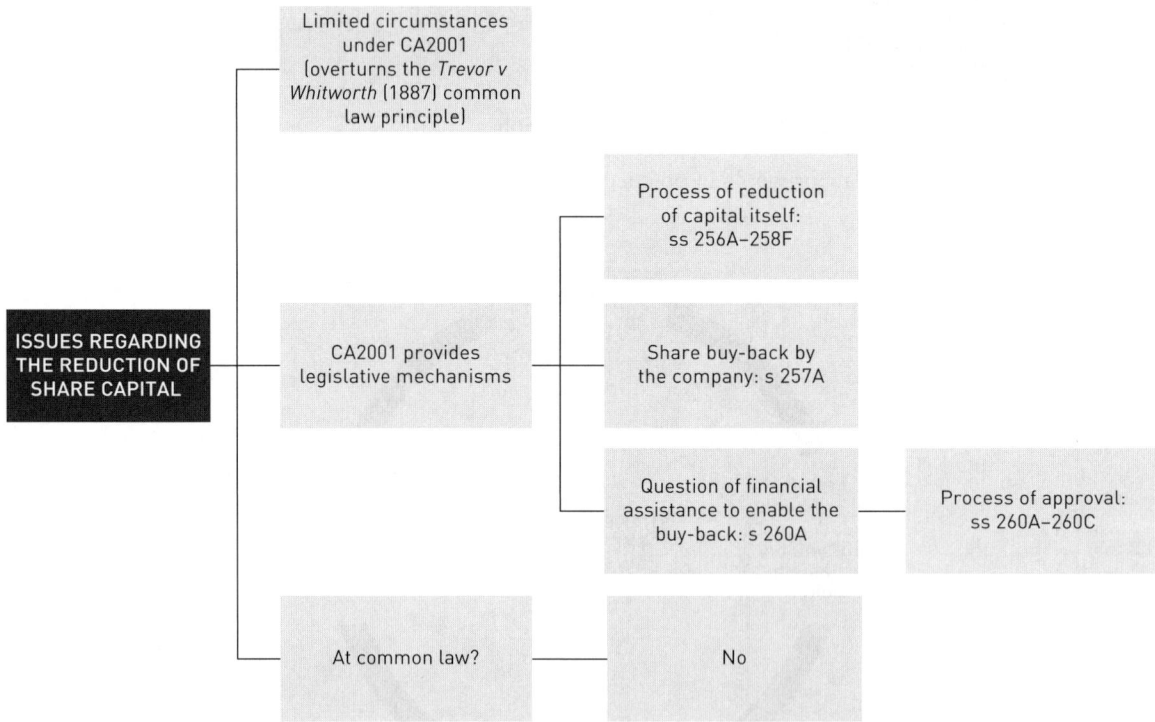

The issue of shares by the company, and the resultant share capital account, will affect three parties—directors, creditors and members:

- Directors—the directors play a role in the issuing of shares by the company and entering the new member in the register of members. They are charged with responsibility for transactions regarding the share capital and its maintenance, including reductions, buy-backs and so forth.
- Creditors—the common law principle is that, historically, share capital is maintained to protect the interests of creditors: *Trevor v Whitworth* (1887); the interests of creditors need to be borne in mind by the directors in this respect.
- Members—there may be competing rights of members to consider, e.g. the payment of dividends under s 254T of the CA2001 will provide a financial benefit to members, but will also have the effect of reducing capital, which may be detrimental to the interests of creditors.

Processes relevant to share capital transactions

TABLE 11.3 An overview of the key features of the transactions affecting share capital

Proposed process	Reduction of share capital: CA2001 ss 256B and 256C	Share buy-backs: CA2001 ss 257A–257J	Exceptions
Information required to be provided by the company	Notice of meeting Statement of material information	Notice of meeting Statement of material information	
Effect on the shareholders	Must be fair and reasonable to shareholders as a whole		
Shareholder approval if the effect of the proposal is equal among shareholders	Ordinary resolution required (50% plus one vote)	No resolution	Ordinary resolution may be required The so-called '10/12 rule' applies if more than 10% of the shares are proposed to be bought back in less than 12 months
Shareholder approval if the process is selective	Special or unanimous resolution	Special or unanimous resolution	
Effect on the share capital as a result of the process	Shares are cancelled	Shares are cancelled	
Effect on the creditors	Must not prejudice the company's ability to pay its creditors	Must not prejudice the company's ability to pay its creditors	
Effect on targeted members	Can be compulsory—i.e. mandatory to relevant class of shareholders	The affected shareholder must consent	

Statutory provisions relevant to the reduction of capital

TABLE 11.4 The main provisions relevant to a reduction: CA2001 ss 256B–256D

Requirements of the CA2001	Concept	Relevant case law
Fair and reasonable to shareholders: s 256B(1)(a)	A single expression to convey an overall meaning	*Re Rancoo Ltd* (1995) *Elkington v CostaExchange Ltd* (2011)
No material prejudice to creditors: s 256B(1)(b)	The original common law principle	*Trevor v Whitworth* (1887)
Approval by shareholders: ss 256B(1)(c) and 256C	s 256C(2) requires a special resolution	
Notices and lodgment with ASIC: s 256C(3)	s 256C(3) requires lodgment with ASIC within 14 days	
Consequences of failing to comply with s 256B: s 256D	s 256D makes it an offence by the company	

Share buybacks: their use and potential abuse

Share buybacks may be potentially 'gamed' or manipulated by the protagonists. The scenarios include those set out in Table 11.5.

TABLE 11.5 The potential misuse of the buy-back process

Potential issues	Context	Ramifications
Discriminate unfairly between shareholders	What is the price of the shares?	The control value may be higher than the minority basis value of the shares
Misused by directors to increase control	The share register may be manipulated to reduce the power of the minority	
As a would-be takeover tool	A shareholder (usually new) may use it as a strategy—in effect saying, buy these shares back, or a formal takeover will be launched	

Potential issues	Context	Ramifications
Market manipulation of the share price	If a listed company purchases a large tranche of its own shares, does this distort the share price?	

> **Activity 11.2**
> Look at Table 11.5 and complete the third column.

11.3 TRANSACTIONS AFFECTING CONTROL OF VOTING SHARES: TAKEOVERS

The Takeovers Panel produces an annual report, which is available on its website.[1]

The Takeovers Panel 'at a glance' 2018–19[2] is as follows:

- Applications: 30
  - (average 28.5 per year since 1 July 2000)
  - (average 23.7 per year since 1 July 2009)
- Matters the Panel conducted proceedings in/matters the Panel declined to conduct proceedings in: 15/10*
  - (*plus five applications withdrawn)
- Matters where the Panel accepted undertakings: 3
- Matters where the Panel made declarations and orders: 10*
  - (*plus two declaration and undertakings)
- Average calendar days between application and decision: 18.5
  - (average 16.2 since 13 March 2000)
  - (average 16.6 since 1 July 2009)
- Average calendar days between decision and publication of reasons: 23.3
  - (average 33.7 since 13 March 2000)
  - (average 14 since 1 July 2009).

---

1 https://www.takeovers.gov.au/content/resources/reports/annual_reports/2018-19/default.aspx/.
2 Ibid, 5.

Table 11.6 sets out the Panel's dispute resolution functions:

TABLE 11.6 The Takeovers Panel's dispute resolution functions[3]

	Unacceptable circumstances	Review of ASIC decisions
What	Deciding applications for a declaration of unacceptable circumstances is the main work of the Panel	The Panel may, on application, review ASIC decisions under Chapter 6 and, during a takeover bid, Chapter 6C
How	The Panel (comprising three members) considers the circumstances against the principles in section 602, the provisions and policy of Chapter 6 and the public interest	The Panel may exercise all the powers of ASIC under Chapters 6 and 6C
Guidance	Guidance Notes, Procedural Rules, legislative policy of Chapter 6, previous decisions	Regulatory Guides, ASIC policies, reasons for ASIC's decision, Panel policy
Outcomes	If a declaration is made, the Panel can make any orders to address the unacceptable circumstances, including a 'remedial order'[4]	Affirm, vary, set aside (and substitute/remit) the ASIC decision
Review	The Panel, on application, conducts a merits review of a decision of the initial Panel.[5] A review Panel comprises three different members to the initial Panel. There may be only one review of a Panel decision	As the Panel proceeding is the merits review, there is no review Panel
How often	In the current period, there were 22 applications for a declaration at first instance and six applications for review	In the current period, there were two applications for review of an ASIC decision

Activity 11.3

Who are the stakeholders relevant to a takeover, and what are some of the key issues for them?

_____
_____
_____
_____
_____

---

[3] Ibid, 7–8.
[4] Section 9. However, it cannot make an order directing a person to comply with a requirement of Chapters 6–6C.
[5] Only with consent of the President if the initial Panel did not make a declaration or orders. See generally section 657EA.

11.4 SCHEMES OF ARRANGEMENT: AN ALTERNATIVE TO TAKEOVERS

Schemes of arrangement (also referred to as schemes of compromise) have proven to be a popular mechanism to achieve a change in control of a corporation. They can involve a change in the rights and duties of:

- the members
- the creditors, or
- both the members and the creditors.

The process for finalising the proposed scheme of arrangement involves court approval. Court approval, being a litigation process, can be contested. This means that, depending on the context, obtaining approval may be somewhat difficult to predict. This, in turn, depends on the context of the application, and the surrounding facts and circumstances.

For an incisive examination of how a scheme of arrangement is used for the acquisition of a listed Australian company, read the article, 'How a Scheme of Arrangement Works', written by Michael Gajic from MinterEllison.[7]

11.5 GROUPS OF COMPANIES AND CONTROL ISSUES

The term 'groups of companies' refers to two or more companies that include a holding company and a subsidiary. The holding company has control of the subsidiary. This is the most simple type of group.

FIGURE 11.7   A simple corporate group: holding company and subsidiary company

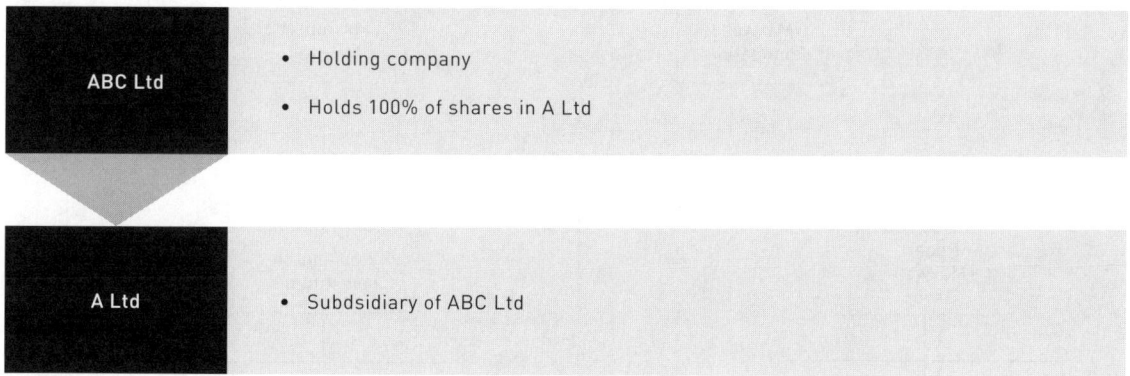

There can be multiple companies within the particular group structure, as shown in Figs 11.8 and 11.9.

---

6   https://www.minterellison.com/articles/how-a-scheme-of-arrangement-works/.

FIGURE 11.8   A more complex corporate group

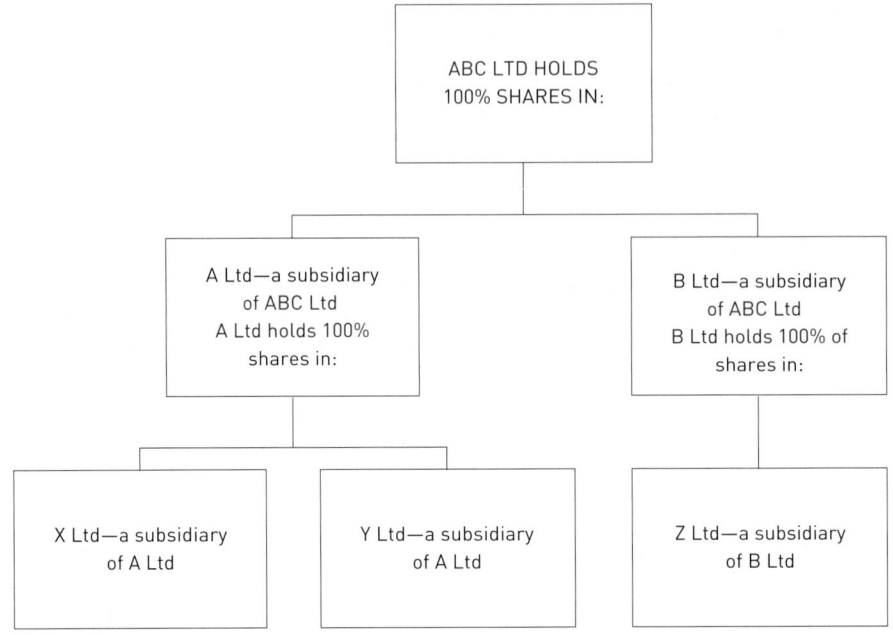

FIGURE 11.9   Maxwell Organisation in 1991

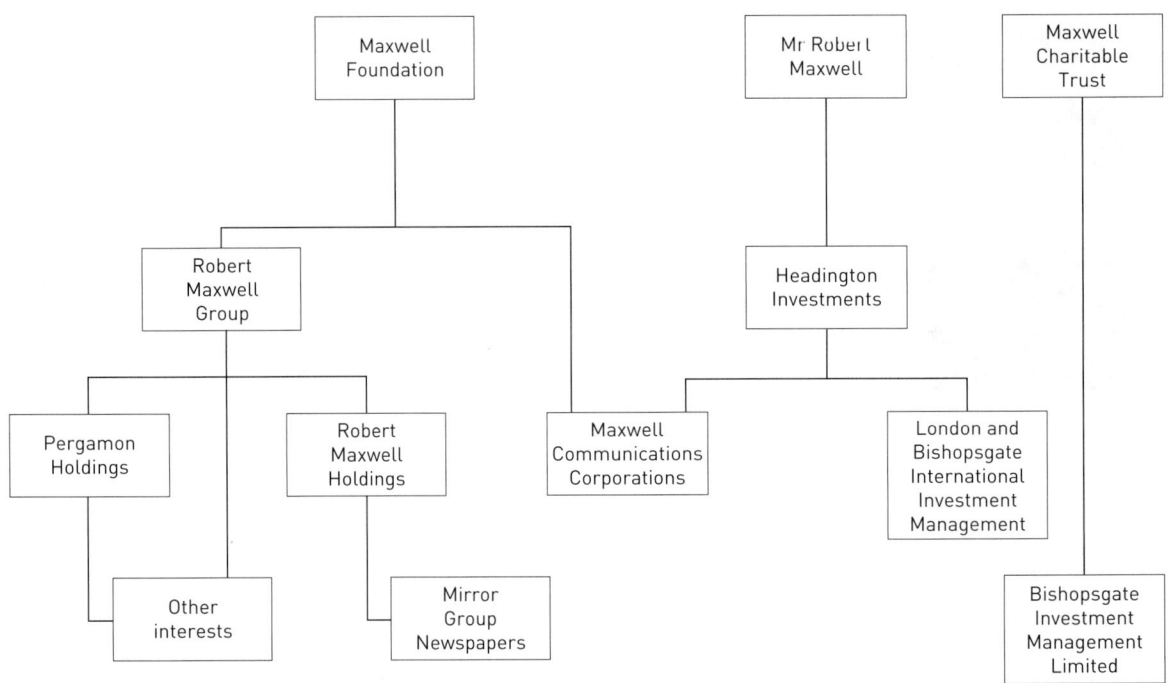

Source: Adapted from *Financial Times*, 31 March 2001, 7.

The structures can be very complex and interlocking. This raises the questions: Why have groups of companies, and for what purposes are they legitimate? The answers to these questions are discussed in the Textbook.

Generally, in Australian corporate law, each company within the group is treated as a separate legal entity as per the legal principles established in *Salomon v A Salomon & Co Ltd* [1897] AC 22.

Activity 11.4

Read the following, conduct your own research, and answer the question below.

IN THE NEWS: A PROPOSED TAKEOVER BID

The corporation: Bellamy's, an Australian food and infant milk company

The context: The bidder is an international company based in Hong Kong: China Mengniu Dairy. It is backed by a Chinese SOE (state-owned enterprise) Cofco, which has a 16 per cent stake in it. The takeover offer is valued at $1.5 billion. It puts a price of $12.65 a share, and Bellamy's will pay a special dividend of 65 cents a share, taking the bid to $13.25. The board of directors of Bellamy's has unanimously recommended that the takeover bid be accepted. The approval of the FIRB (Foreign Investment Review Board) will be required for the proposed bid to go ahead.

Question: What is involved in obtaining FIRB approval?

WORKBOOK CHAPTER 11 REVIEW

An illustrative summary of the key points

FIGURE 11.10 The interaction between the company, control, and corporate arrangements

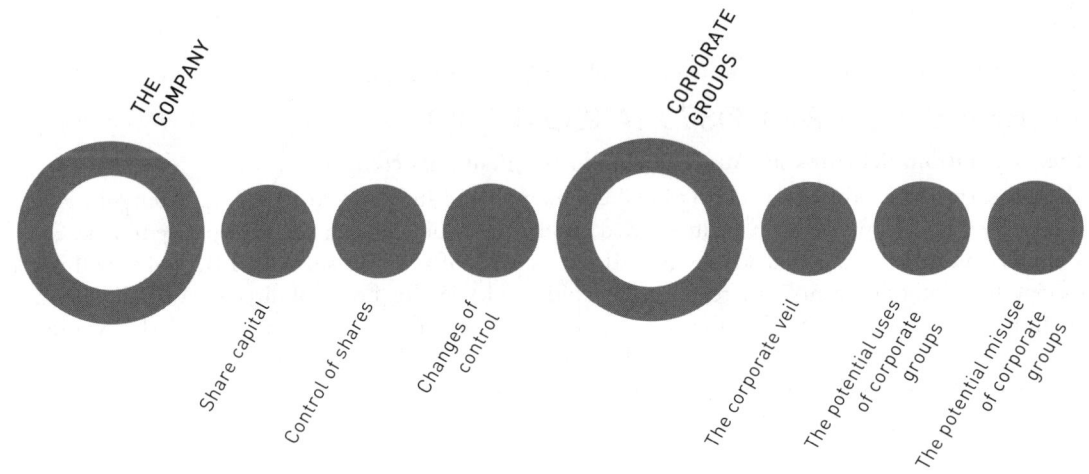

CHAPTER 11 REVISION ACTIVITIES

Consolidation of concepts, knowledge and content activities

TRUE OR FALSE?

1. The rule in *Trevor v Whitworth* (1887) applies to companies and bans the reduction of capital. True ☐ False ☐

2. The maintenance of capital principally protects employees. True ☐ False ☐

3. Share capital is the aggregate investment in the company by its shareholders. True ☐ False ☐

4. A company limited by guarantee can issue shares. True ☐ False ☐

5. Company A is a subsidiary of Company B if B controls the board of A. True ☐ False ☐

FILL IN THE GAPS

1. A takeover involves the change in control of _____ shares in the target company.

2. A company can provide financial assistance for acquiring shares in the company, as provided by section _____ of the CA2001.

3. The takeover provisions of the CA2001 are found in Chapter _____

4. The High Court *Engineers' case* (1920) established the model of _____ as the type of interpretation relevant to the Australian Constitution.

5. The alternative model or approach to interpreting the Australian Constitution is referred to as _____.

6. The takeover provisions are informed by the _____ principles, which balance economic efficiency with protection of the interests of the _____

MULTIPLE CHOICE

1. The rule in *Trevor v Whitworth* (1887) was principally designed to protect:

   A. Employees
   B. Debtors
   C. Directors
   D. Creditors

2. Takeover disputes are dealt with by:

   A. ASIC
   B. Supreme Courts
   C. The Takeovers Panel
   D. The Federal Court

3. The takeover provisions are triggered by what percentage acquisition of voting shares?

   A. 5 per cent
   B. 10 per cent
   C. 20 per cent
   D. 25 per cent

4. Schemes of arrangement are:

   A. An alternative to a takeover
   B. Commonly used in insolvency situations
   C. A necessary option to consider prior to a takeover
   D. A process controlled by creditors

5. The contemporary Australian law on corporate groups is best represented by which statement?

   A. The law reflects corporate reality
   B. The principle in *Salomon's case* (1897) is routinely ignored
   C. Corporate groups are a creature of the common law
   D. The law often does not reflect commercial reality

SHORT ANSWER QUESTIONS

1. What is share capital?

2. What do shareholders receive for their contribution of share capital?

3. What is a reduction of share capital?

4. Why would a company seek to reduce share capital?

5. What is the rule in *Trevor v Whitworth* (1887)?

6. What tests must a proposed reduction of capital meet, and for whose benefit?

7. What is an indirect self-acquisition?

Higher order thinking activities

Consider the following questions and provide detailed discussion and analysis.

TOPIC A

What types of buy-backs does the CA2001 provide for?

QUESTIONS

TOPIC B
Provide a case analysis of *Elkington v CostaExchange Ltd* (2011).

CHAPTER 12

CORPORATE FINANCE I: RAISING SHARE CAPITAL

Chapter synopsis and links to Textbook Chapter 12

This Workbook Chapter deals with five topics:

- 12.1 Corporate finance: the two options
- 12.2 Sources of share capital
- 12.3 Raising share capital from the public
- 12.4 Emerging methods of raising share capital
- 12.5 Hybrid share capital/loan capital arrangements.

Each of these topics is constructively aligned with, and linked to, the same topics in Chapter 12 of the Textbook.

Chapter executive summary

This Chapter analyses the corporation's ability and capacity to raise funds:

- from current and future shareholders (share capital)
- from lenders and others (loan capital)

CHAPTER 12 CORPORATE FINANCE I: RAISING SHARE CAPITAL

CHAPTER DIAGRAMMATIC OVERVIEW

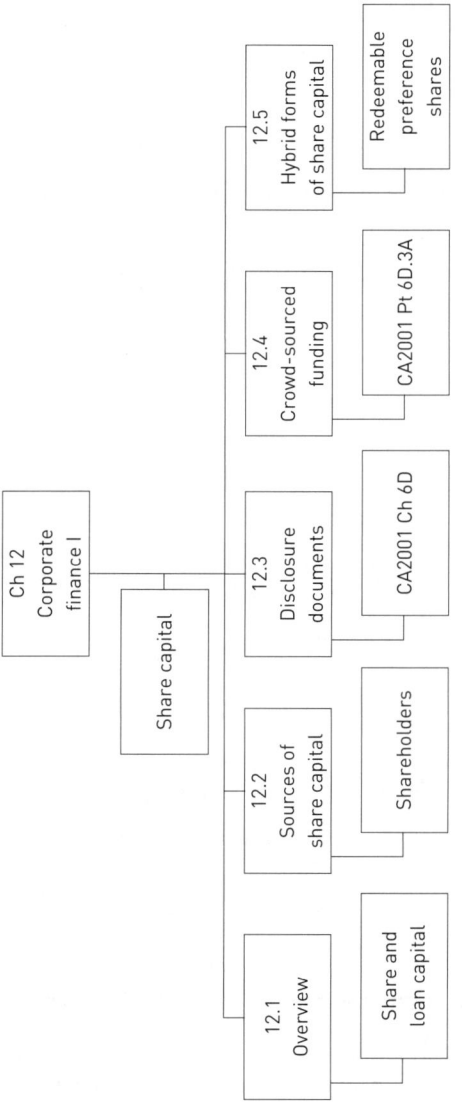

FIGURE 12.1 An overview of Chapter 12

12.1 CORPORATE FINANCE: THE TWO OPTIONS

Corporate finance revolves around two options:
- share capital (dealt with in this Chapter), and
- loan capital (dealt with in Chapter 13): see Fig 12.2.

FIGURE 12.2 The basic division between share and loan capital

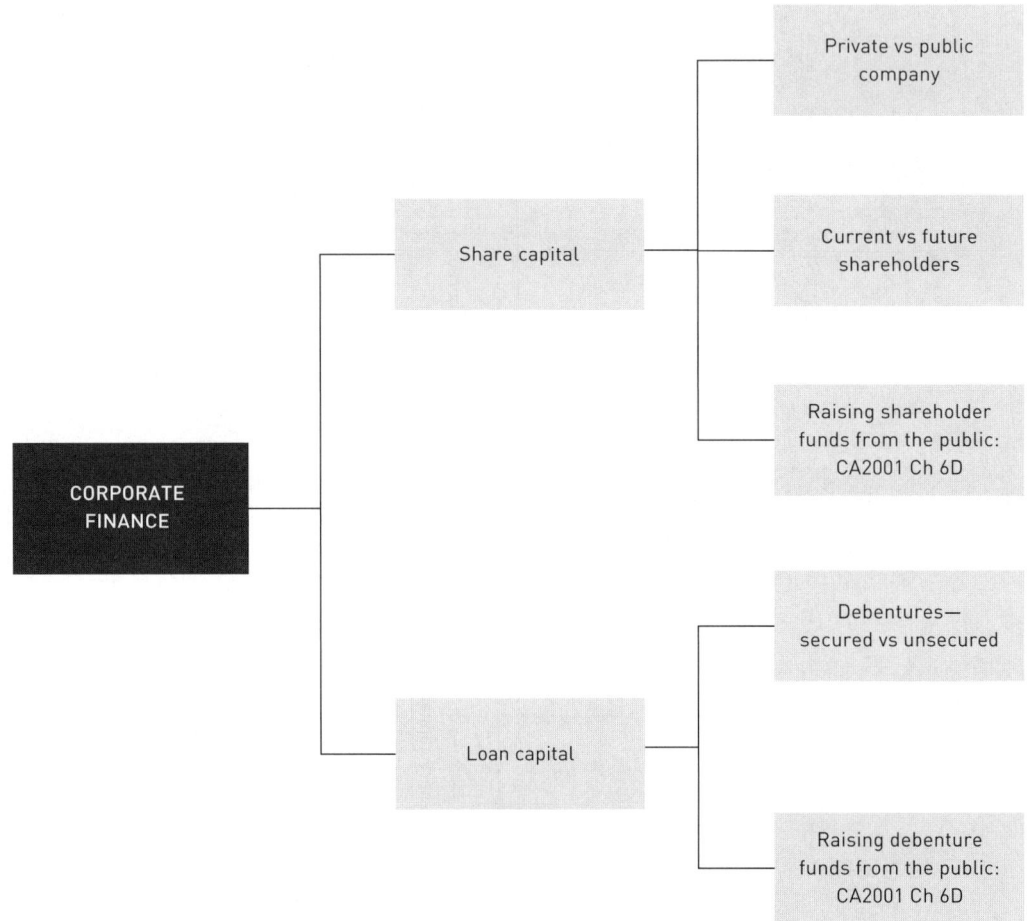

As a business entity in its own right, the company has a basic binary choice. It can:
- seek funds from its shareholders, or
- seek funds from a third party via a loan, which is usually secured against assets as required by the lender; or it may be unsecured.

From the perspective of the finance provider, the key questions will include those set out in Fig 12.3.

FIGURE 12.3   Fundraising from the perspective of the investing shareholder and the lender

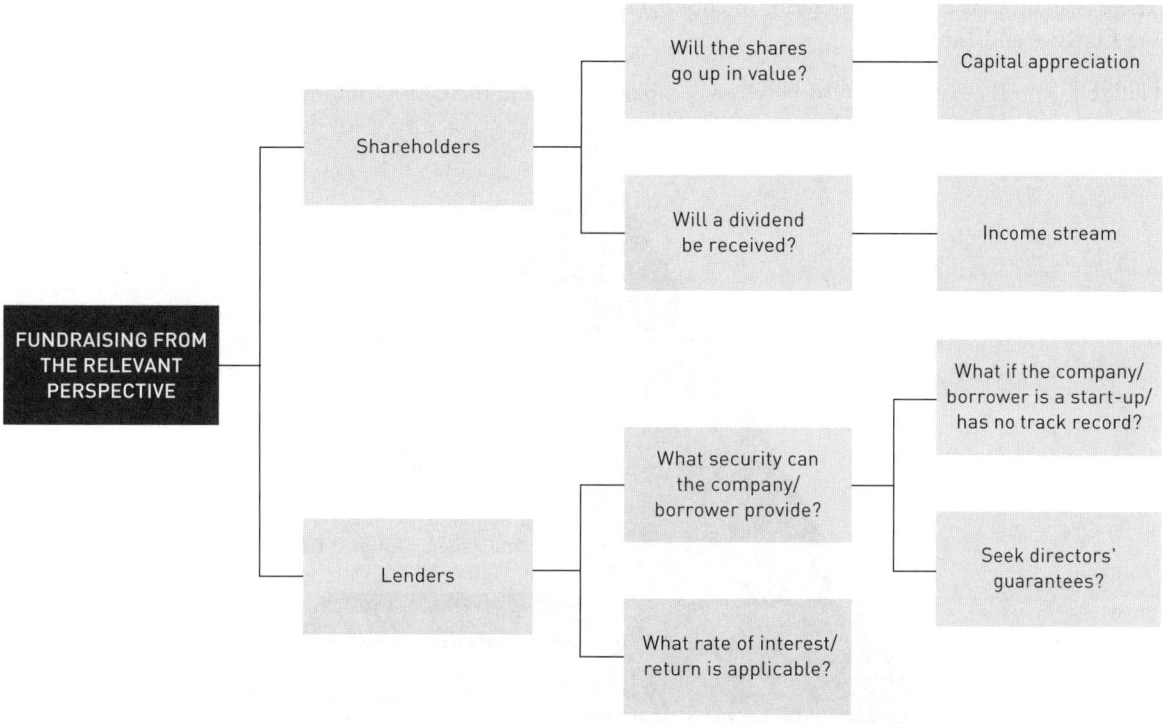

Activity 12.1

By reference to the ASIC website, provide a note on the basic differences between the methods of capital raising available to a Pty Ltd company.

_____
_____
_____
_____
_____
_____
_____

12.2 SOURCES OF SHARE CAPITAL

Generally speaking, the larger the company, the more options it has to raise funds on the capital markets. There is an upward trajectory in terms of choice, ranging from the small Pty Ltd to the listed public company: see Fig 12.4 and Table 12.1.

FIGURE 12.4 The basic hierarchy between company types and increasing fundraising choice and capacity

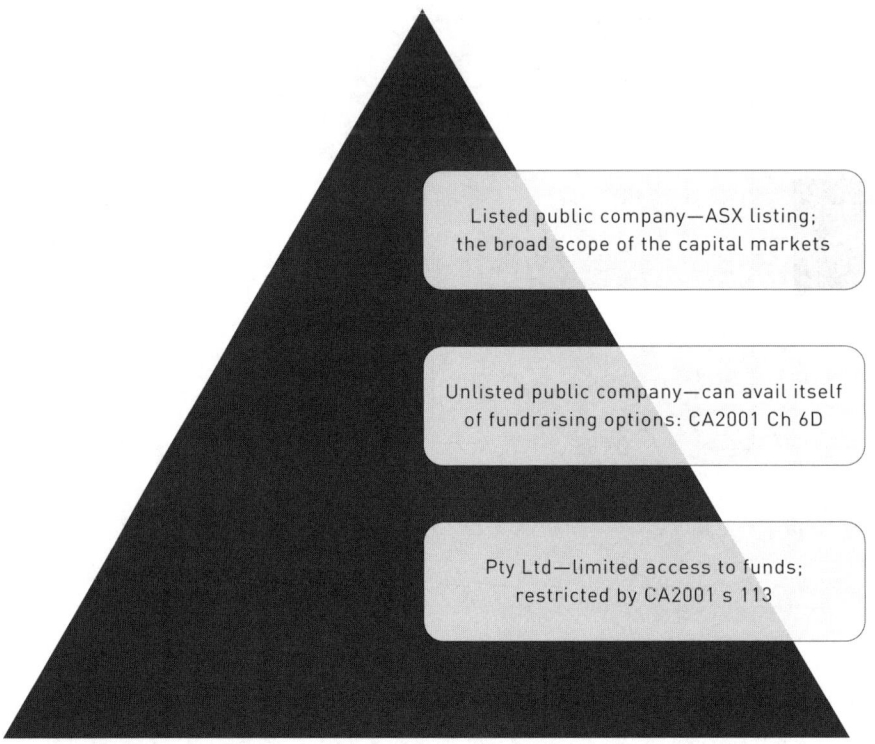

TABLE 12.1 The basic hierarchy between company types calls into play different provisions of the CA2001

Company type	Restrictions	Options
Pty Ltd	s 113 CA2001	
Public company	s 606 CA2001	s 608 s 610
Listed company	ASX Listing Rules	Ch 6D CA2001 ASX Listing Rules

The ASX is the site of buying and selling publicly listed securities. It is the modern equivalent of ancient markets catering for the sale and purchase of tangible goods and property. The ASX handles the buying and selling of intangible personal property, including shares and futures.

The historical developments giving rise to the current ASX can be set out as shown in Table 12.2.

TABLE 12.2 The historical development of the ASX

Year	Step	Notes
1773	London Stock Exchange	
1871	Australian Stock Market	Based in Sydney
1871–90	Other capital cities of Australia developed their own stock exchanges	
1980s	Mergers of Australian city-based stock exchanges	
1987	Australian Stock Exchange founded	
1996	ASX Ltd	Australian Stock Exchange became a company limited by shares (from a company limited by guarantee)
2006	Australian Securities Exchange established	Australian Stock Exchange merged with Sydney Futures Exchange CHESS (Clearing House Electronic Sub-register System) for the buying and selling of shares
2010	ASIC given responsibility for regulating securities markets	

How are companies valued?

There are several methods for valuing a company that may be relevant in a given case, including:

- multiple of cash
- multiple of profit
- multiple of earnings
- comparison to rivals, and
- market capitalisation, or stock market value.

'Market capitalisation' refers to the total dollar market value of a company's outstanding shares of stock. It is calculated as follows:

- by multiplying the total number of a company's outstanding shares
- by the current market price of one share.

As an example, a company with 10 million shares selling for $10 each would have a market cap of $100 million. The current and potential investment community uses this figure to determine a company's size, as opposed to using sales or total asset figures.

Using market capitalisation to show the size of a company is important because company size is a basic determinant of various characteristics in which lenders (and investors) are interested, including determination of risk.

There are thus several ways to value a company. It can be highly specialised and complex, and it will depend on the perspective of the stakeholder.

Activity 12.2
By reference to Table 12.1, make notes on the restrictions and options for the various company types.

12.3 RAISING SHARE CAPITAL FROM THE PUBLIC

A company may have plans to:
- grow and expand
- enter new contracts
- produce more products or services
- purchase new property
- enter major leasehold arrangements
- go into markets
- take on new staff, or
- take some new strategic direction not covered above.

It needs sufficient cash flow in order to do so. It may have the cash on its books, or it may need to raise funds and secure further capital.

The basic dichotomy for fundraising is shown in Fig 12.5.

CHAPTER 12 CORPORATE FINANCE I: RAISING SHARE CAPITAL

FIGURE 12.5 Fundraising: the divide between private and public companies and the limitations of s 113 of the CA2001

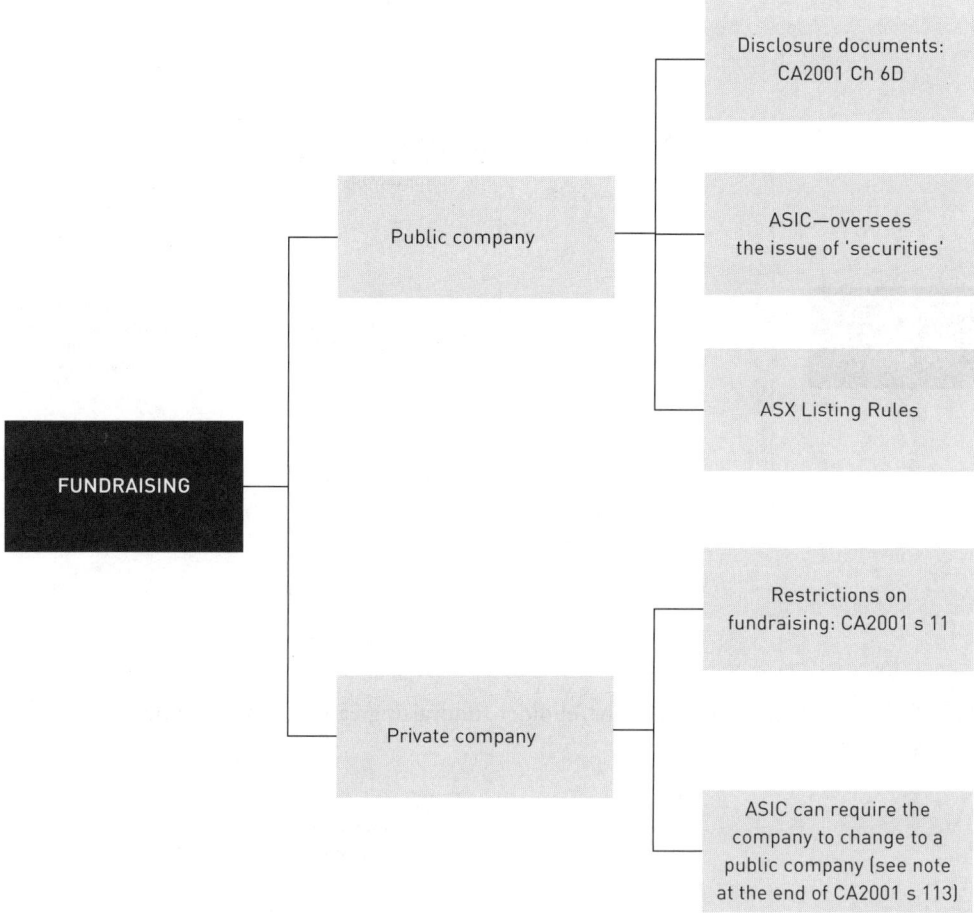

The note at the end of s 113 of the CA2001 ('Propriety companies') provides as follows:

Note: If a proprietary company contravenes this section, ASIC may require it to change to a public company (see section 165).

Section 113 is covered in the Textbook.

As we have noted, converting the value of a share in a Pty Ltd is paradoxically more complex than a readily tradeable share in a listed entity: see Fig 12.6.

FIGURE 12.6 Some of the issues relevant to investing in a Pty Ltd

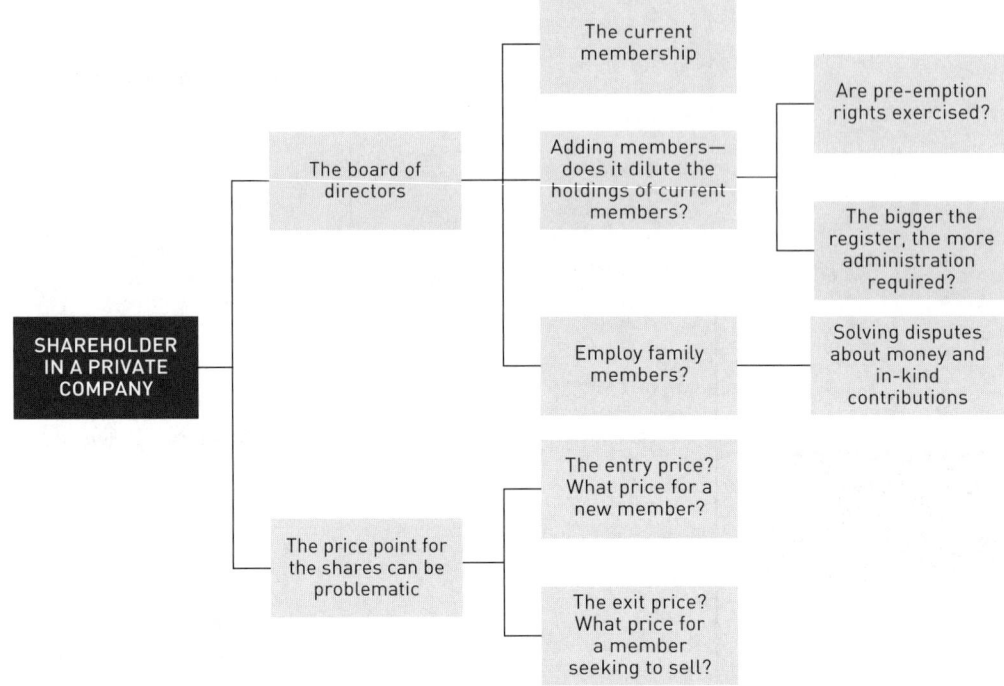

FIGURE 12.7 The restrictions on size and shareholder fundraising capacity imposed by s 113 of the CA2001

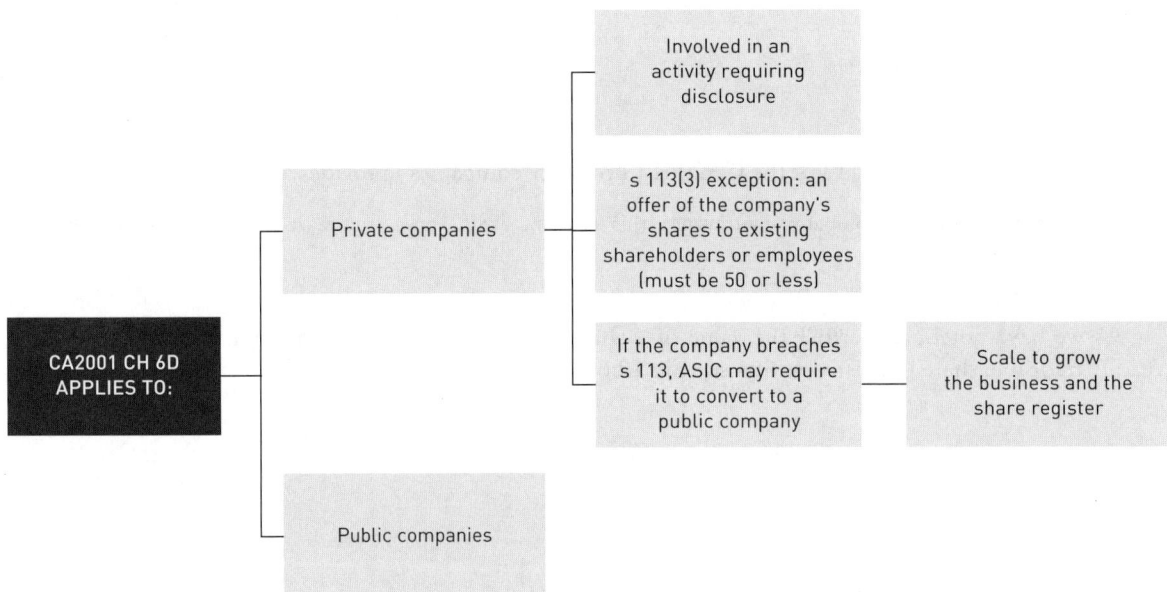

Activity 12.3
How are so-called 'sophisticated investors' treated under Ch 6 of the CA2001?

12.4 EMERGING METHODS OF RAISING SHARE CAPITAL

The fundraising by a company via Ch 6D of the CA2001 balances investor protection, and an efficient and credible capital market. Information has to be disclosed to the potential investors. It has to be clear, concise and effective.

The extent of disclosure depends on the type of disclosure document. There are four potential types of documentation required to be prepared by the company and, in turn, four features common to each, as shown in Fig 12.8.

FIGURE 12.8 Disclosure documents: the four issues common to each of the four options

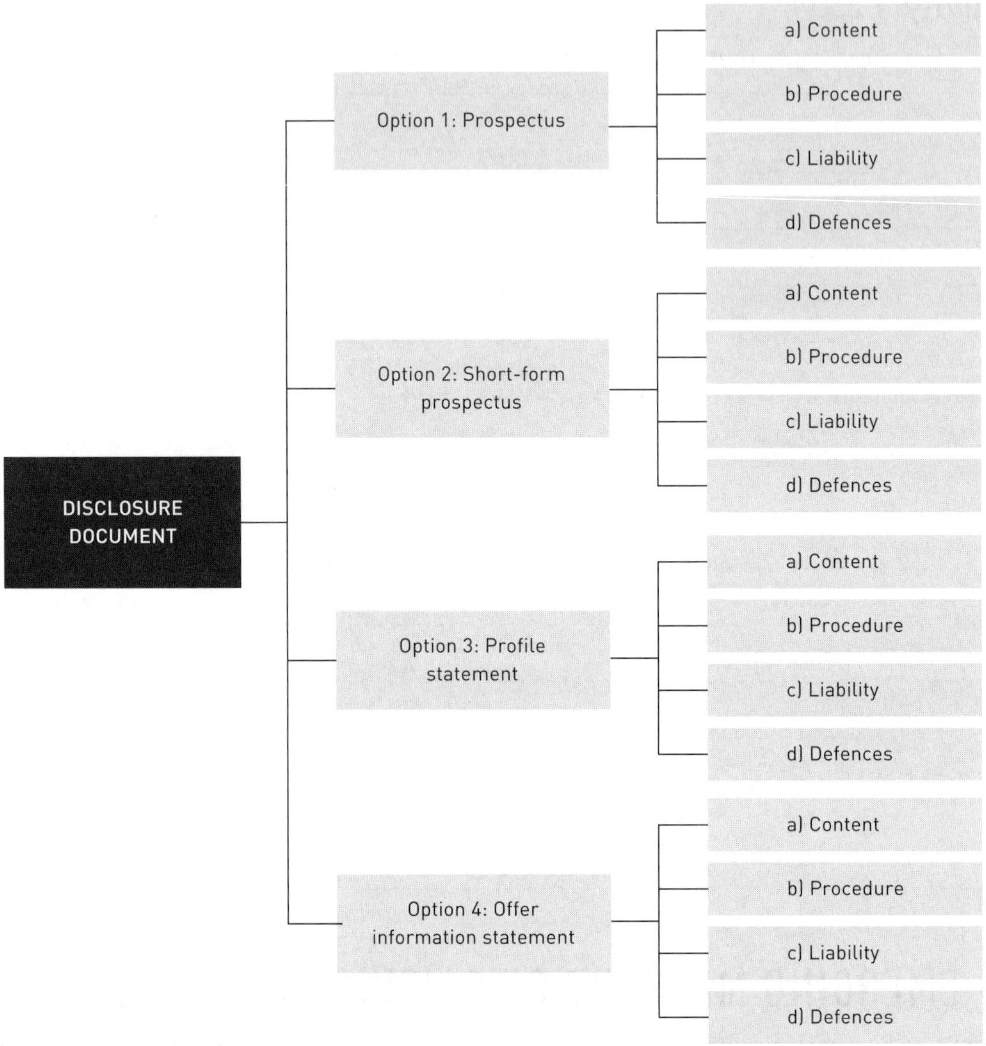

```
DISCLOSURE DOCUMENT
├── Option 1: Prospectus
│   ├── a) Content
│   ├── b) Procedure
│   ├── c) Liability
│   └── d) Defences
├── Option 2: Short-form prospectus
│   ├── a) Content
│   ├── b) Procedure
│   ├── c) Liability
│   └── d) Defences
├── Option 3: Profile statement
│   ├── a) Content
│   ├── b) Procedure
│   ├── c) Liability
│   └── d) Defences
└── Option 4: Offer information statement
    ├── a) Content
    ├── b) Procedure
    ├── c) Liability
    └── d) Defences
```

These matters can be set out in tabular format:

TABLE 12.3 The range of share capital-raising documentation

Type of disclosure document	Features and levels of complexity	Relevant provisions of the CA2001
1. Prospectus	The standard full disclosure document The most fulsome of the documentary types	Content: ss 710, 711, 713 Procedure: s 717 Liability: ss 728, 729 Defences: ss 731, 733

Type of disclosure document	Features and levels of complexity	Relevant provisions of the CA2001
2. Short-form prospectus	May be used for any offer. s 712 allows a prospectus to refer to material lodged with ASIC instead of setting it out. Investors are entitled to a copy of this material if they ask for it.	Content: s 712 Procedure: s 717 Liability: ss 728, 729 Defences: ss 732, 733
3. Profile statement	s 721 allows a brief profile statement to be sent out (with ASIC approval), but the prospectus must still be prepared and lodged with ASIC. Investors are entitled to a copy of the prospectus if they ask for it.	Content: s 714 Procedure: s 717 Liability: ss 728, 729 Defences: ss 732, 733
4. Offer information statement	s 709 allows an offer information statement to be used instead of a prospectus for an offer to issue securities if the amount to be raised is less than $10 million. The least fulsome of the documentary types.	Content: s 715 Procedure: s 717 Liability: ss 728, 729 Defences: ss 732, 733

Chapter 6D of the CA2001 covers fundraising by the company. It starts at s 700.

A preliminary point is to determine when disclosure is required by the offering company. It is when 'securities' are offered for sale:

- Section 706 of the CA2001 provides the general rule as to when securities are offered for sale.
- For the purpose of Ch 6D of the CA2001, 'securities' are defined in ss 9 and 92. Section 761A defines 'securities' for the purpose of Ch 7.
- 'Securities' include shares, debentures, options, and legal or equitable rights in relation to them.

Activity 12.4

Is a barrel of whisky a security over which ASIC has regulatory oversight?

In order to answer this question, go online and search 'Nant Whisky and ASIC', and variations on these search terms.

12.5 HYBRID SHARE CAPITAL/LOAN CAPITAL ARRANGEMENTS

The recent history of corporate law has seen new financial products. While the basic binary is between share capital and loan capital, there are also examples of hybrid forms of both share and loan capital. In the case of share capital, this hybridity refers principally to redeemable preference shares.

FIGURE 12.9 Hybrid forms of capital occupy the space between the two basic forms

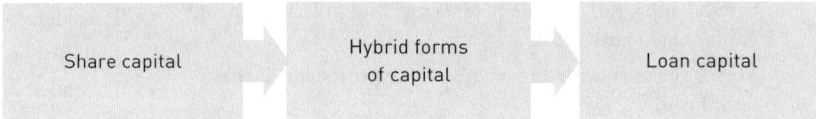

There are two examples of hybrid forms of capital that exhibit traits of both share and loan capital: see Fig 12.10.

FIGURE 12.10 Redeemable preference shares start as share capital with inherent loan capital capacity

Share capital: redeemable preference shares—entails a repurchase of the shares

Loan capital: convertible debentures—entails an option to convert the loan to share capital (see Ch 13)

Activity 12.5

Read the following and answer the question below.

IN THE NEWS: LISTED TECHNOLOGY UNICORNS

The corporations: Afterpay and Wisetech

The context: Afterpay and Wisetech are local 'unicorn' corporations. They are publicly listed technology companies; their shares are listed on the ASX. It was reported in late 2018 that in a volatile trading environment, each company shed more than $100 million in market capitalisation in a single day.

Question: As ASIC notes, share investments are inherently risky. What is the risk associated with 'unicorns', given their technology focus?

CORPORATIONS LAW: CONCEPTS, CASES AND CULTURE WORKBOOK

WORKBOOK CHAPTER 12 REVIEW

An illustrative summary of the key points

FIGURE 12.11   Raising share capital—some of the key issues

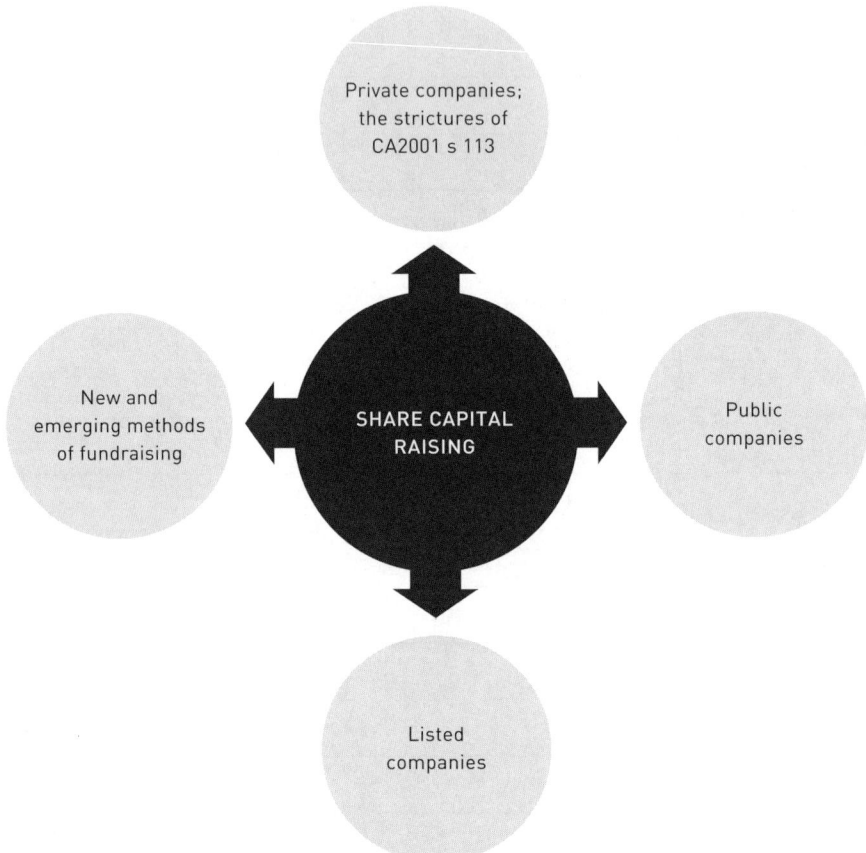

CHAPTER 12 REVISION ACTIVITIES

Consolidation of concepts, knowledge and content activities

TRUE OR FALSE?

1. Companies can only raise funds from members (existing and new).   True ☐ False ☐
2. A Pty Ltd with more than 50 members must become a public company.   True ☐ False ☐
3. Chapter 7 of the CA2001 deals with public disclosure documents as regards fundraising.   True ☐ False ☐

4. ASIC can be the main repository of a prospectus document. True ☐ False ☐
5. ASIC can be the main repository of a profile statement. True ☐ False ☐

FILL IN THE GAPS

1. The relevant provision of the CA2001 dealing with the need for a disclosure document is _____.

2. A profile statement must state the _____ in investing in the securities, as required by CA2001 section _____.

3. The defences for officer liability for a prospectus are set out in sections _____ and _____ of the CA2001.

4. The defences for director liability for a short-form prospectus are set out in sections _____ and _____ of the CA2001.

5. The content of an offer information statement is set out in section _____ of the CA2001.

6. The legal provisions regarding crowd-sourced funding are set out in Chapter _____ of the CA2001.

MULTIPLE CHOICE

1. An offer not requiring a disclosure document is covered by which section of the CA2001?
   A. 607
   B. 608
   C. 707
   D. 708

2. Offers exempt from the disclosure document regime involve what number of offers and what dollar amount within a 12-month period?
   A. 10 offers and $1 million
   B. 20 offers and $1 million
   C. 20 offers and $2 million
   D. 30 and $3 million

3. CSFs are dealt with under which Chapter of the CA2001?
   A. 6D.1A
   B. 6D.2A
   C. 6D.3A
   D. 6D.4A

4. The dollar amount of assets required for a company wishing to issue CSFs is:
   A. 10 million
   B. 20 million
   C. 5 million
   D. 25 million
5. Redeemable preference shares are best described as redeemable:
   A. At the shareholder's request
   B. At the company's request
   C. Given a prescribed event
   D. Any of the above

SHORT ANSWER QUESTIONS

1. What is a prospectus?

2. What is a short-form prospectus?

3. What is a profile statement?

4. What is an offer information statement?

5. What are redeemable preference shares?

6. What offers do not require disclosure documents?

Higher order thinking activities

Consider the following questions and provide detailed discussion and analysis.

PROBLEM A

Your firm acts for ABC Ltd, which is looking to raise funds from the public. The directors have some questions:

(a) Does Ch 6D of the CA2001 require complete accuracy of the disclosure document?

(b) What options do shareholders have if they are of the view, and ASIC confirms, that a disclosure document contravenes Ch 6D?

(c) If there is a problem with a disclosure document, can a company instead use television commercials to attract the public to invest?

PROBLEM B

The directors of ABC Ltd have a follow-up set of questions:

(d) If a company wants to organise another fundraising campaign to raise $1.5 million, does it still have to worry about Ch 6D?

(e) Can a director be held personally liable for any problem found to exist with the company's disclosure document?

(f) The directors of the company want to pay a high-profile person $1 million to travel to the east coast capital cities to personally hand out company brochures advertising the forthcoming company fundraising campaign. They want to target high net-worth individuals in strictly 'by invitation' events. What are the legal issues?

CHAPTER 13

CORPORATE FINANCE II: LOAN CAPITAL

Chapter synopsis and links to Textbook Chapter 13

This Workbook Chapter deals with five topics:

- 13.1 Loan capital: basic principles
- 13.2 Debentures and risk issues for lenders
- 13.3 Securing personal property and the *Personal Property and Securities Act 2009* (Cth)
- 13.4 Hybrid forms of loan capital/share capital: convertible debentures
- 13.5 Comparing loan capital with share capital.

Each of these topics is constructively aligned with, and linked to, the same topics in Chapter 13 of the Textbook.

Chapter executive summary

This Chapter examines the corporation's capacity to raise loan capital, and, in so doing:

- contrasts loan and share capital
- investigates the contractual and security elements of loan capital
- contrasts the securing of personal property under the *Personal Property and Securities Act 2009* (Cth) with the securing of other property of the company (e.g. real property by way of mortgage)
- compares the taxation and other facets of share and loan capital respectively.

CHAPTER DIAGRAMMATIC OVERVIEW

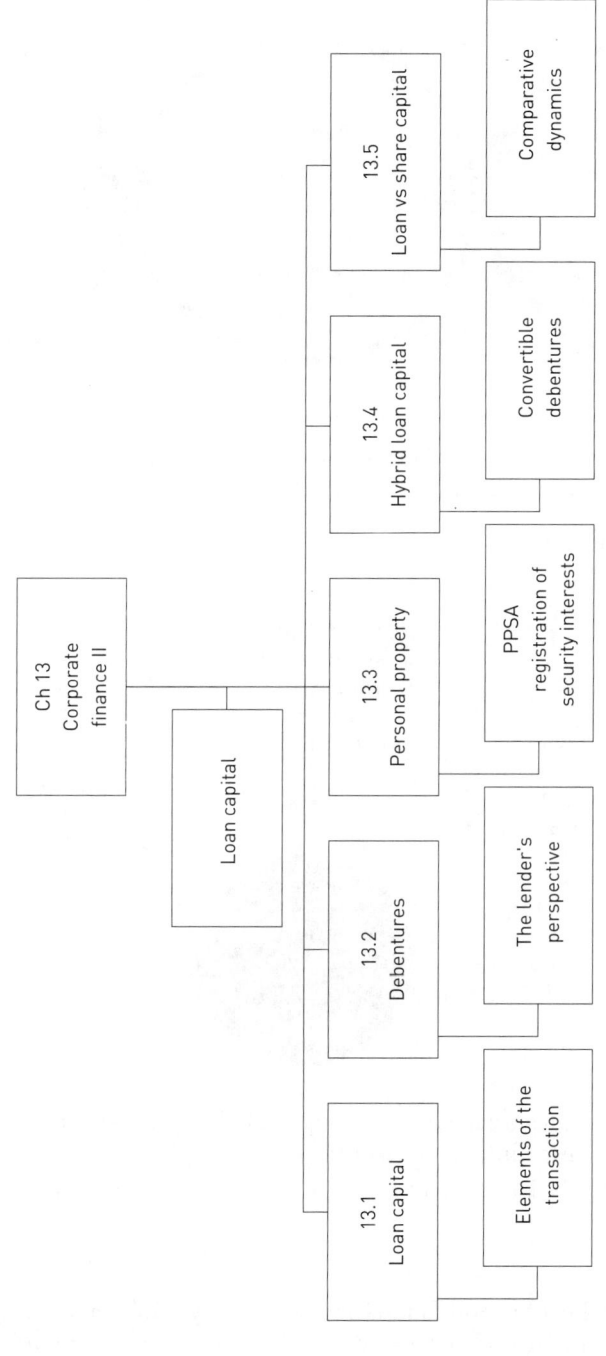

FIGURE 13.1 An overview of Chapter 13

13.1 LOAN CAPITAL: BASIC PRINCIPLES

FIGURE 13.2   The parties to a basic loan transaction involving the company as borrower

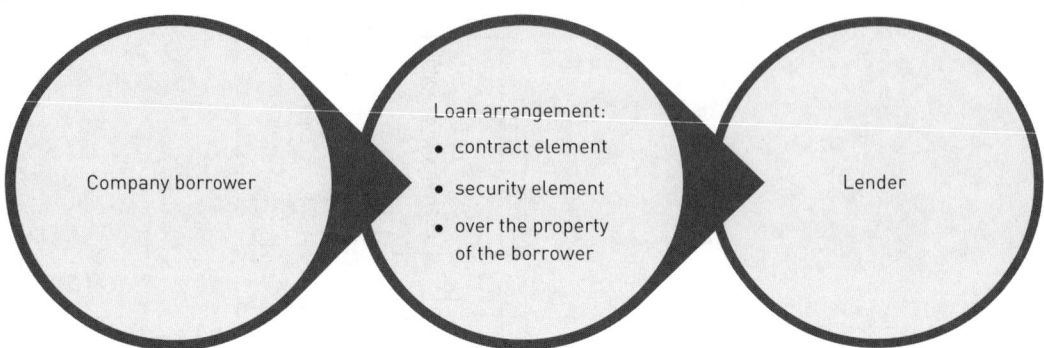

Debentures are covered in Ch 2L of the CA2001, which comprises ss 283AA–283L. Debentures, in essence, involve a contract to repay by the borrower to the lender. They may have an added security element. There are three types of debentures, as shown in Fig 13.3.

FIGURE 13.3   The three types of debentures

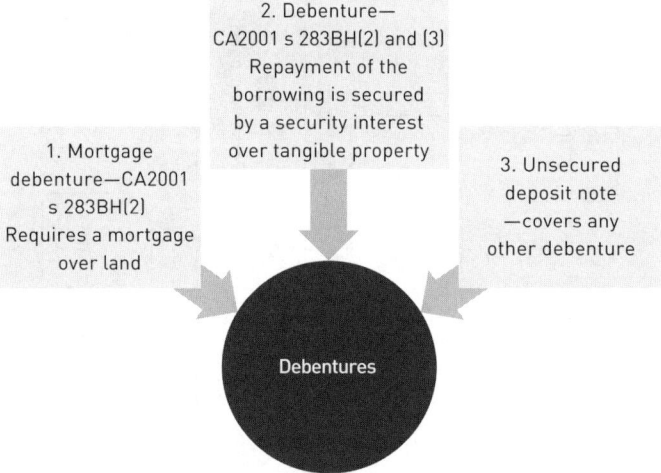

In relation to the second category referred to in Fig 13.3, the fundraising provisions of the CA2001 apply. A debenture comes within the definition of 'securities' as per s 92A.

As noted in Chapter 12, the basic potential choice of fundraising mechanisms for a company are:

- share capital, and
- loan capital.

There is also the possibility of hybrid fundraising, which may exhibit a mixture of characteristics of each. In respect of loan capital, the hybrid form of convertible debentures is discussed in Section 13.4 below. In terms of hybrid forms of share capital, this was discussed in terms of redeemable preference shares in Chapter 12, Section 12.5.

TABLE 13.1 The basic characteristics of loan capital compared with share capital

	Loan capital	Share capital
Alternative references or terms when referring to this type of capital:	Also referred to as debt capital	Also referred to as equity capital
The basis of the capital raising:	Borrowings by the company	The company issuing shares to raise share capital
The legal relationship with the company created by the capital raising:	Creates a debtor–creditor relationship The company is a debtor; the lender is a creditor The lender may be referred to as a debenture holder, lender or secured creditor, depending on the characteristics of the loan	X becomes a member/shareholder of the company
Rights against the company created by the capital raising:	The lender has contractual claims against the company	Proprietary rights in the shares are held by the shareholder (e.g. a right to vote)
Rights against property of the company:	The lender may also have security rights, which it can exercise against the company and its property	Shareholders do not own the property of the company (the company owns the property of the company)

Securities cannot be issued to the public by a company unless it complies with the disclosure document provisions in Ch 6D of the CA2001.

Activity 13.1

What is the role and function of a director's guarantee in terms of securing loans for Pty Ltd companies?

_____
_____
_____
_____
_____
_____
_____
_____

13.2 DEBENTURES AND RISK ISSUES FOR LENDERS

An overview of debentures issued by corporations is set out in Fig 13.4.

FIGURE 13.4   Debentures offered under Ch 6D of the CA2001

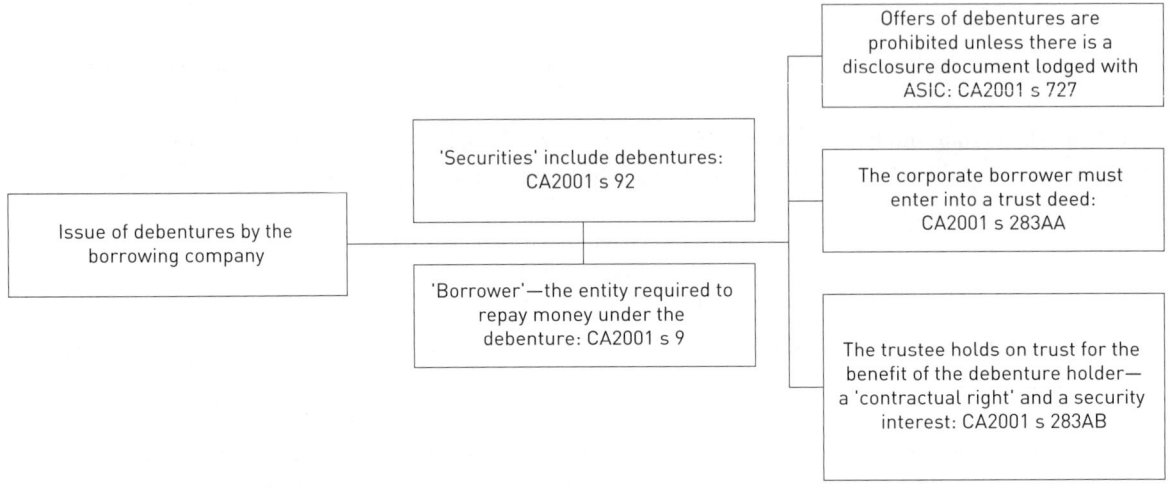

The duties of corporate borrowers under debentures are set out in the CA2001, summarised in Fig 13.5.

FIGURE 13.5   The duties relevant to the corporate borrower

Duties of corporate borrowers offering debentures under CA2001	s 283BB	Carry on business efficiently Provide financial records to the trustee Assist the trustee
	s 283BC	Notify ASIC of the name of the trustee
	s 283BD	Replace the trustee if necessary
	s 283BE	Keep the trustee informed about *Personal Property and Securities Act 2009* (Cth) 'security interests' it creates
	s 283BF	Provide the trustee and ASIC with regular reports
Note that under s 283BCA, ASIC maintains a publicly accessible register for debenture holders		

The duties relevant to a guarantor are set out in CA2001 Pt 2L.3.

The roles of the trustee and the guarantor can be depicted as shown in Fig 13.6. Note that:
- The borrowing company deals directly with the trustee.
- The trustee deals with a potentially large and diverse number of lenders.
- The lenders are given voice by the trustee.
- The guarantor provides 'insurance' for the lenders. If the borrower fails, the guarantor steps in.

FIGURE 13.6   The roles of trustee and guarantor; the trustee acts for and on behalf of the beneficiaries

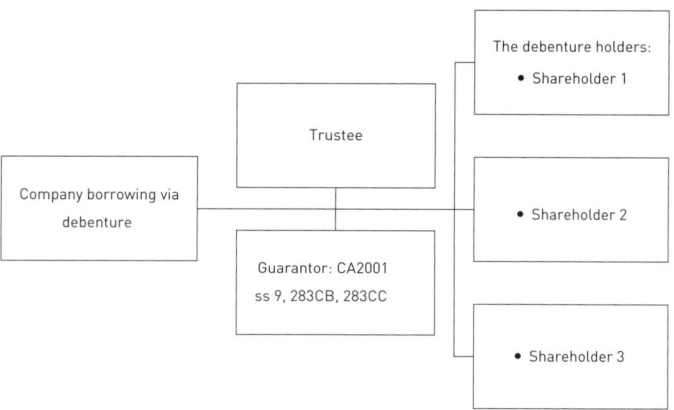

The trustee holds the rights of the debenture holders in trust under CA2001 s 283AB: see Fig 13.7.

FIGURE 13.7   The interlocking contractual and security rights

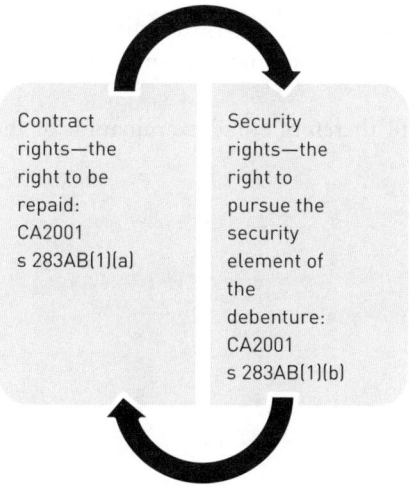

The duties of the borrower and guarantor body are set out in CA2001 ss 283BB–283CE. The debenture provided by the company has two protective mechanisms for the lenders:
- the appointment of a trustee acting on behalf of the collective interests of the lenders, and

- the appointment of a guarantor if the borrowing company defaults.

The CA2001 provides a framework and duties for guarantors, as set out in Fig 13.8.

FIGURE 13.8   Duties of the guarantor

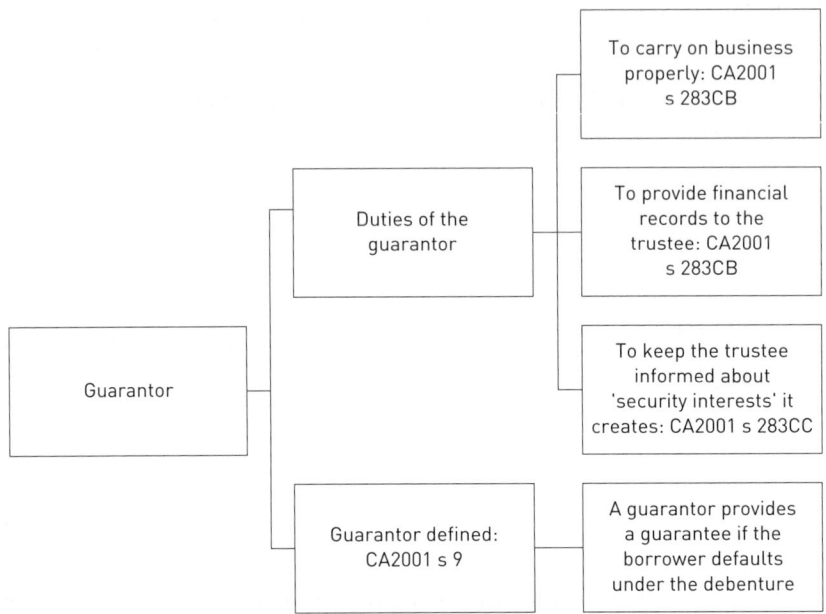

Risks for the lender under a mortgage debenture

The risk for the lender under a mortgage debenture is that the company's business fails and the assets of the corporation (and their forced sale) held under any relevant security instrument are not sufficient to repay the debt.

Securing debt by the lender will therefore entail examination of the company's assets. The assets of a company include:
- land (real property)
- fixtures and fittings
- contracts
- moneys owed
- capital
- cash at the bank
- work-in-progress
- debtors
- tangible assets
- intangible assets
- stock-in-trade
- intellectual property.

The orderly and advantageous debt recovery process for the lender is a crucial factor in assessing whether to lend finance (loan capital) to the company. The order of preference of creditors of a company on a winding-up proves the point that the characterisation of the creditor is vital to priority of the debt: see CA2001 s 556. This order applies to provable debts and claims, and is as follows:

- secured creditors
- unsecured creditors
- preferential debts:
  - company expenses of carrying on business
  - costs of the winding-up
  - liquidator's fees
  - employee entitlements—the company liquidator can initiate proceedings, and any amount recovered is regarded as a preferential debt owed to creditors
- other unsecured creditors (see the *pari passu* rule in CA2001 s 555—subject to judgments obtained etc, the creditors rank equally)
- the Commissioner of Taxation—a company's debts to the Commonwealth Government do not receive any special priority; this means that amounts in respect of unpaid income tax rank as unsecured debts and are payable only if there are sufficient funds left over after all preferential debts have been paid (but the directors may be liable to indemnify the Commissioner for losses where the liquidator obtains a s 588F order against the Commissioner to recover a voidable transaction)
- members/shareholders—these are entitled to share in the distribution of the surplus assets only after all the creditors have been paid in full, i.e. after:
  - secured debts to secured creditors
  - unsecured debts to unsecured creditors
  - deferred debts (the unsecured debts of members)
- only then may any surplus be distributed among the members.

These matters are also examined in Chapter 15.

Activity 13.2

What are the roles, rights and duties of the parties to a public debenture?

13.3 SECURING PERSONAL PROPERTY AND THE *PERSONAL PROPERTY AND SECURITIES ACT 2009* (CTH)

The scope of the *Personal Property and Securities Act 2009* (Cth) (PPSA) is provided in s 8—transactions involving 'security interests'.

FIGURE 13.9   A PPSA transaction and prioritisation process

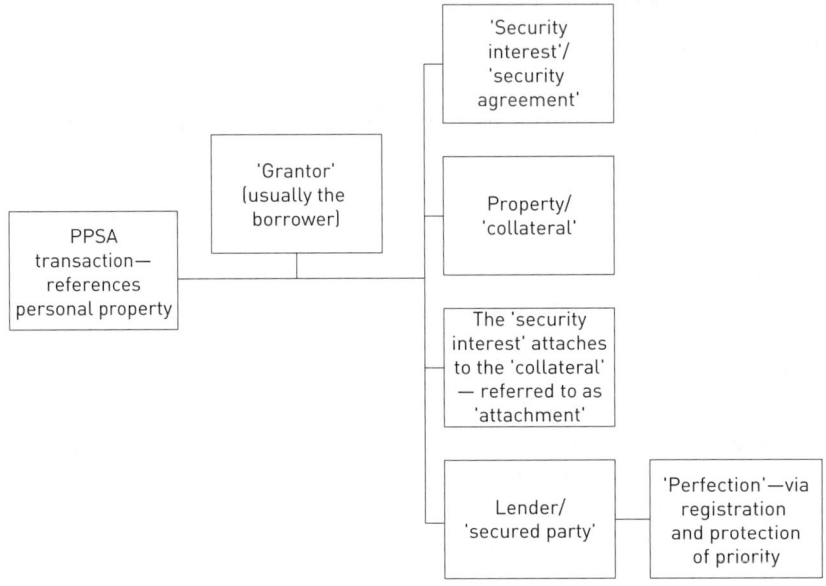

The Act operates by reference to several definitions in s 10: the Dictionary provision. These may link to the main operative provisions.

TABLE 13.2   The main PPSA provisions

Key PPSA terms from s 10	Operative provision in the PPSA

'attaches' has the meaning given by section 19.	**s 19: Enforceability of security interests against grantors—attachment**
	Attachment required for enforceability
	(1) A security interest is enforceable against a grantor in respect of particular collateral only if the security interest has attached to the collateral.
	Attachment rule
	(2) A security interest attaches to collateral when:
	    (a) the grantor has rights in the collateral, or the power to transfer rights in the collateral to the secured party; and
	    (b) either:
	        (i) value is given for the security interest; or
	        (ii) the grantor does an act by which the security interest arises.
	…

Key PPSA terms from s 10	Operative provision in the PPSA
'collateral': (a) means personal property to which a security interest is attached; and (b) in relation to a registration with respect to a security interest—includes personal property described by the registration (whether or not a security interest is attached to the property).	
'debtor' means: (a) a person who owes payment or performance of an obligation that is secured by a security interest in personal property (whether or not the person is also the grantor of the security interest); or (b) a transferee of, or successor to, an obligation mentioned in paragraph (a).	
'general law' means the principles and rules of the common law and equity.	

'grantor' means:
(a) a person who has the interest in the personal property to which a security interest is attached (whether or not the person owes payment or performance of an obligation secured by the security interest); or
(b) a person who receives goods under a commercial consignment; or
(c) a lessee under a PPS lease; or
(d) a transferor of an account or chattel paper; or
(e) a transferee of, or successor to, the interest of a person mentioned in paragraphs (a) to (d); or
(f) in relation to a registration with respect to a security interest:
  (i) a person registered in the registration as a grantor; or
  (ii) a person mentioned in paragraphs (a) to (e).	

'interest', in personal property, includes a right in the personal property.	s 12 [see below]

TABLE 13.2 The main PPSA provisions (continued)

Key PPSA terms from s 10	Operative provision in the PPSA

'perfected' has the meaning given by section 21.	**s 21: Perfection—main rule**
	(1) A security interest in particular collateral is perfected if:
	   (a) the security interest is temporarily perfected, or otherwise perfected, by force of this Act; or
	   (b) all of the following apply:
	      (i) the security interest is attached to the collateral;
	      (ii) the security interest is enforceable against a third party;
	      (iii) subsection (2) applies.
	(2) This subsection applies if:
	   (a) for any collateral, a registration is effective with respect to the collateral;
	…

'personal property' means property (including a licence) other than:
(a) land; or
(b) a right, entitlement or authority that is:
   (i) granted by or under a law of the Commonwealth, a State or a Territory; and
   (ii) declared by that law not to be personal property for the purposes of this Act.
Note: This Act does not apply to certain interests even if they are interests in personal property (see section 8).
	s 12 [see below]

'security interest' has the meaning given by section 12.	**s 12: Meaning of security interest** (1) A *security interest* means an interest in personal property provided for by a transaction that, in substance, secures payment or performance of an obligation (without regard to the form of the transaction or the identity of the person who has title to the property). …

Retention of title

The PPSA takes a functional approach to the retention of title issue. The property being the subject matter of the retention of title clause is classified as a 'security interest'. Given that the seller retains title in the goods/personal property until payment is complete, the parties to the transaction 'map' to the PPSA as follows:

- the seller adopts the function and role of the lender or 'secured party'
- the purchaser assumes the role of the borrower or 'grantor'.

FIGURE 13.10 A retention of title transaction 'mapped' to the PPSA framework transaction and prioritisation process

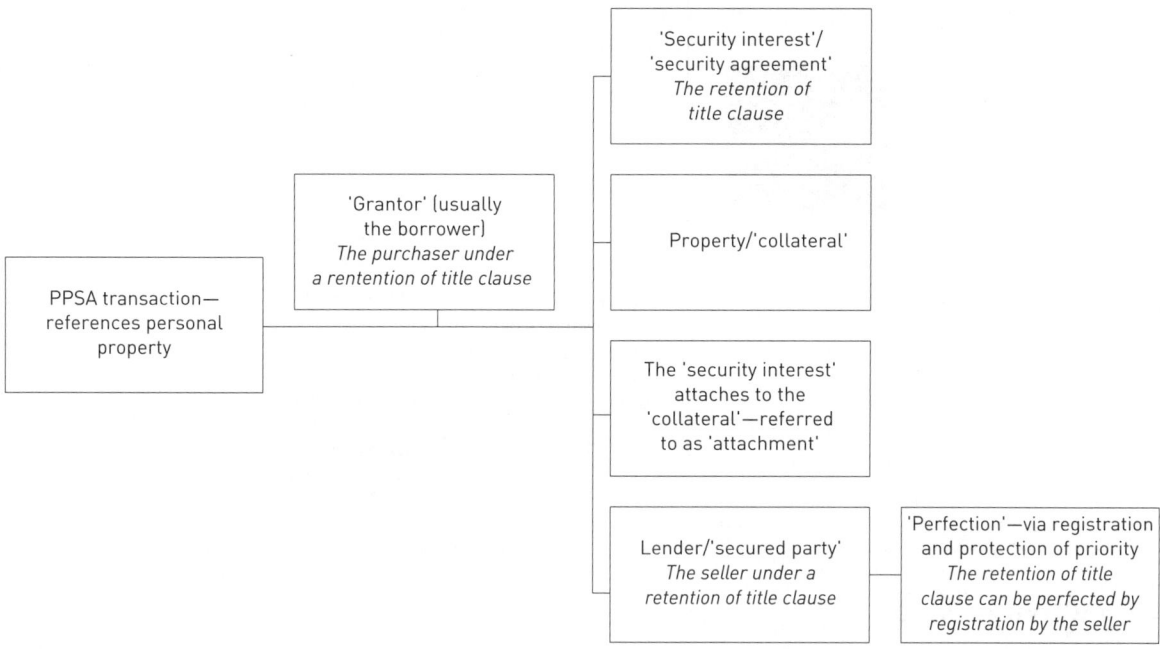

Invalidation of security interests

Division 2A of the CA2001 provides for circumstances in which the security interest can be invalidated. This usually occurs within the context of liquidation of the company. It involves a form of unfairness, or preferential treatment, as regards the security interest for which registration has been sought.

Issues relevant to the directors include those set out in Fig 13.11.

FIGURE 13.11 Intersection between the CA2001 and PPSA in terms of winding-up and directors' duties

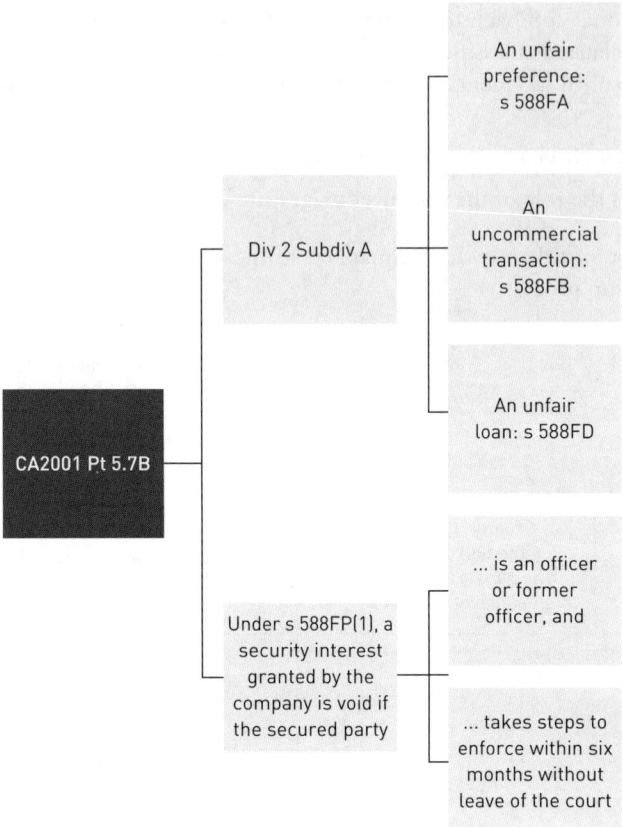

Activity 13.3

What are the main steps in a PPSA transaction?

_____
_____
_____
_____
_____
_____
_____

13.4 HYBRID FORMS OF LOAN CAPITAL/SHARE CAPITAL: CONVERTIBLE DEBENTURES

Convertible debentures give the shareholder/lender to the company the potential opportunity to convert the debenture into shares in the company: see Fig 13.12.

FIGURE 13.12   Convertible debentures: a hybrid financial instrument

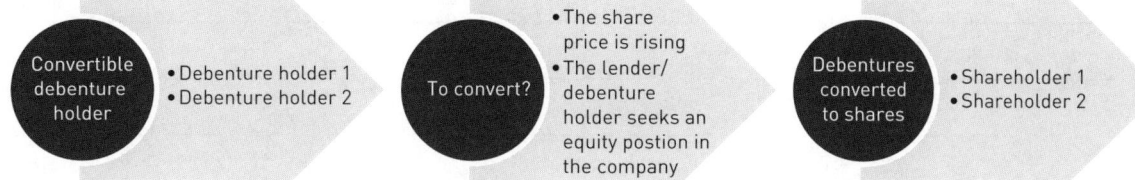

Examples of hybrid forms of capital

There are two examples of hybrid forms of capital that exhibit traits of both share and loan capital: redeemable preference shares and convertible debentures: see Fig 13.13.

FIGURE 13.13   Hybrids: elements of both loan and share capital

> **Activity 13.4**
>
> What are the main features of convertible debentures?

13.5 COMPARING LOAN WITH SHARE CAPITAL

In terms of raising funds to expand the business, a company, as a separate legal entity, has access to two broad options:
- share capital, and
- loan capital.

There are also the hybrid options of:
- redeemable preference shares, and
- convertible debentures.

The fact that there are two main options for companies provides them with numerous advantages:
- flexibility
- capacity for quick growth
- the ability to expand the size and scale of the share register
- potential access to capital markets
- potential access to institutional investors (such as superannuation funds) in addition to retail investors, and
- an inherent advantage over businesses such as partnerships and sole traders, which are not in themselves separate business entities.

FIGURE 13.14 The fundraising options for a company

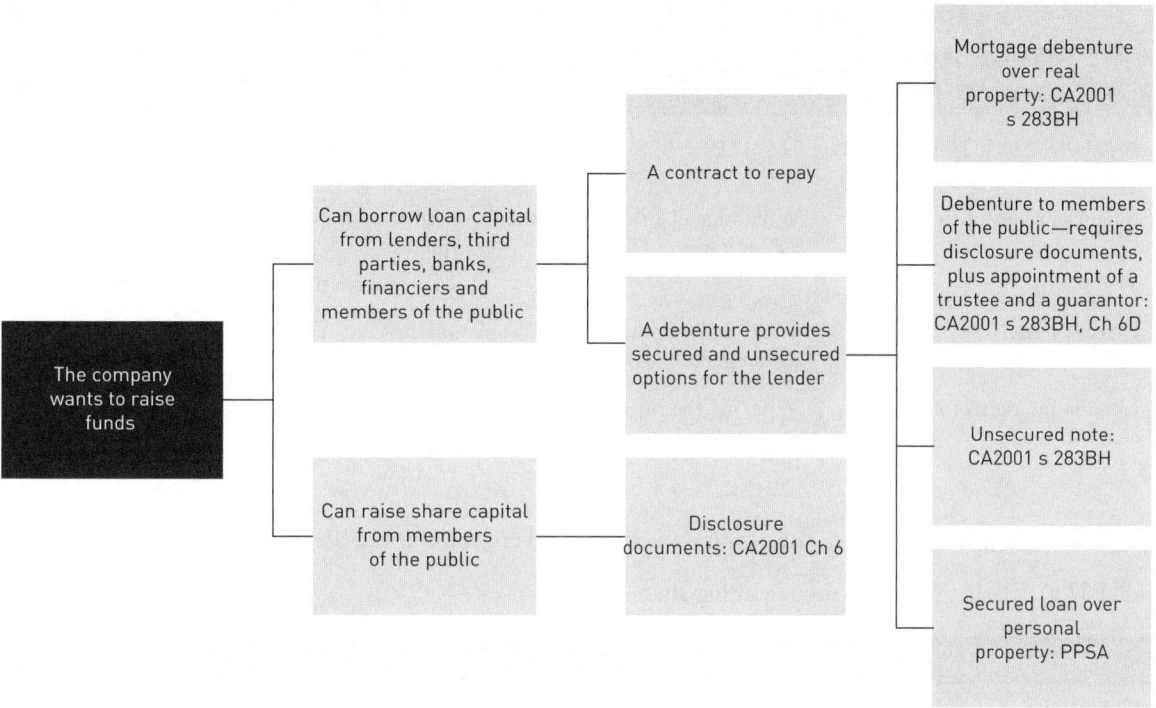

An analysis of the relative merits and legal issues as regards fundraising options depends on the particular perspective being examined in the contractual relationship; that is:
- the company as borrower, or
- the creditor/lender in their particular capacity as either:
  - a shareholder, or
  - a third party, such as a bank.

TABLE 13.3 Share capital from the creditor's viewpoint

	Particular questions	Share capital raising by the company and the provision of capital by the shareholders
Legal rights of the lender/creditor	What general rights does the capital provider have?	Becomes a shareholder
Financial rights of the creditor	What financial rights does the capital provider have?	Depends on the terms of the shares
Creditors' rights	What dollar return can the capital provider get?	Potentially, the shareholder may receive a dividend
Liquidation rights for the creditor	What are the rights of the creditor/lender on a liquidation?	Shareholders rank last after all other creditors

TABLE 13.4 Loan capital from the creditor's viewpoint

	Particular questions	Borrowing or loan capital being raised by the company and a lender providing capital to the company
Legal rights of the lender/creditor	What general rights does the lender have?	Becomes a creditor—may be secured
Financial rights of the creditor	What financial rights does the lender have?	Entitled to repayment of principal and interest May enforce the terms of the security
Creditors' rights	What dollar return can the lender get?	Interest
Liquidation rights for the creditor	What are the rights of the creditor/lender on a liquidation?	Paid well ahead of shareholders Secured creditors rank ahead of unsecured creditors

A secondary, but important, consideration is the tax effectiveness of the borrowing arrangement.

TABLE 13.5 Basic taxation issues regarding share capital

Legal rights and issues	Particulars	Share capital raising
Tax planning for the company in issuing shares to the shareholder	What tax entitlement does the company get?	Not tax deductible
Tax planning for the company in making any related payments on the loan	Dividends—are paid out of profits	Not tax deductible

RAISING FUNDS FROM THIRD PARTY LENDERS—SOME TAX ISSUES

TABLE 13.6 Basic taxation issues regarding loan capital

Legal rights and issues	Particulars	Borrowing or loan capital
Tax planning for the company for the expenses in setting up the loan for the company	What tax entitlement does the company get?	The expenses of setting up the loan are tax deductible
Tax planning for the company in making payments on the loan		Interest paid by the borrower is tax deductible

Activity 13.5

What are the tax implications of loan versus share capital?

WORKBOOK CHAPTER 13 REVIEW

An illustrative summary of the key points

FIGURE 13.15 An overview of the main issues regarding the raising of loan capital

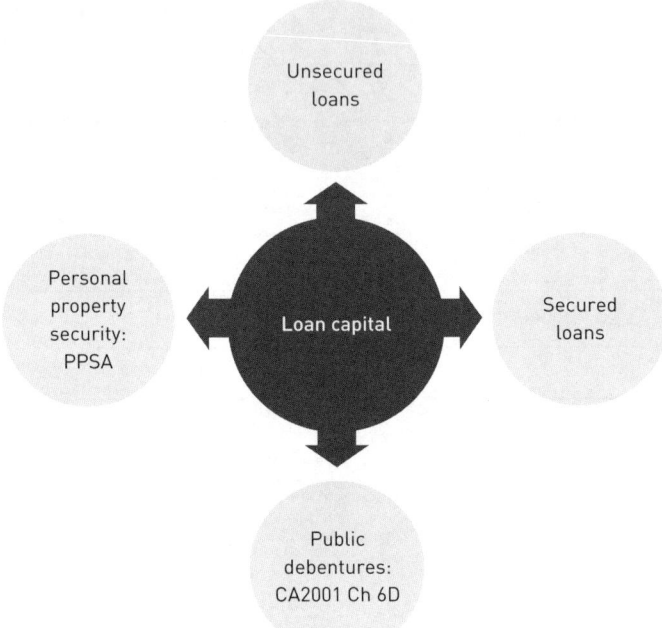

CHAPTER 13 REVISION ACTIVITIES

Consolidation of concepts, knowledge and content activities

TRUE OR FALSE QUESTIONS

1. A debenture is a form of loan arrangement. True ☐ False ☐
2. Car hire-purchase agreements are arranged differently in each state. True ☐ False ☐
3. The PPSA deals with land interests. True ☐ False ☐
4. Repayment of a debenture must be secured against property. True ☐ False ☐
5. The CA2001 is a code doing away with the need for consideration of general or common law as regards corporations. True ☐ False ☐

FILL IN THE GAPS

1. The PPSA operates by reference to perfecting _____ in relation to _____.

2. Section _____ of the PPSA deals with perfecting the security interest.

3. The term 'security interest' is defined by reference to sections _____ and _____ of the PPSA.

4. Disclosure documents are relevant to a company seeking to raise _____ from the public.

5. A debenture issued by a company raising funds from the public requires the appointment of a _____ and a _____.

6. The director's personal guarantee will likely arise with a _____ type of company.

MULTIPLE CHOICE

1. PPSA stands for:
   A. Private Property Shareholders Association
   B. Personal Protection Security Agency
   C. Personal Property Security Act
   D. Personal Property and Securities Act

2. The PPSA came into effect in which year?
   A. 2009
   B. 2010
   C. 2011
   D. 2012

3. By which section of the CA2001 will a liquidator seek to examine security interests entered into by the company?
   A. 188
   B. 588
   C. 288
   D. 488

4. Disclosure documents are covered by which Chapter of the CA2001?

    A. 2
    B. 4
    C. 6
    D. 8

5. An arrangement with a retention of title clause is principally dealt with under which Act?

    A. PPSA
    B. CA2001
    C. ASIC Act 2001
    D. Relevant state Partnership Act

SHORT ANSWER QUESTIONS

1. What is the role, purpose and context of a lender requiring a director's guarantee?

2. What is the perfection process under the PPSA?

3. How does a company raise funds? Outline the basic options.

4. What is the role of the trustee and guarantor with a debenture raising?

5. What is the background to the PPSA?

Higher order thinking activities

Consider the following questions and provide detailed discussion and analysis.

TOPIC A

A public company, ABC Ltd, wishes to raise debenture funds from the public. Provide an outline of what is involved.

TOPIC B

Re Maiden Civil (P&E) Pty Ltd (2013) deals with issues under the PPSA. Summarise the key events, issues and outcomes from the case.

CHAPTER 14

EXTERNAL ADMINISTRATION

Chapter synopsis and links to Textbook Chapter 14

This Workbook Chapter deals with six topics:

- 14.1 An overview of external administration
- 14.2 Solvency, external administration and directors' duties
- 14.3 Receivership
- 14.4 Voluntary administration
- 14.5 Deeds of company arrangement
- 14.6 Court-ordered schemes of arrangement.

Each of these topics is constructively aligned with, and linked to, the same topics in Chapter 14 of the Textbook.

Chapter executive summary

This Chapter examines the corporation in the context of financial difficulty:

- How is financial difficulty assessed and what is the legal concept of the going concern?
- What is the role of the board and the directors when this occurs?
- What is external administration and what are the various options designed to set the company back on a viable trading track?
- What is the interface between going concern, and the winding-up and eventual deregistration of the company?

CHAPTER DIAGRAMMATIC OVERVIEW

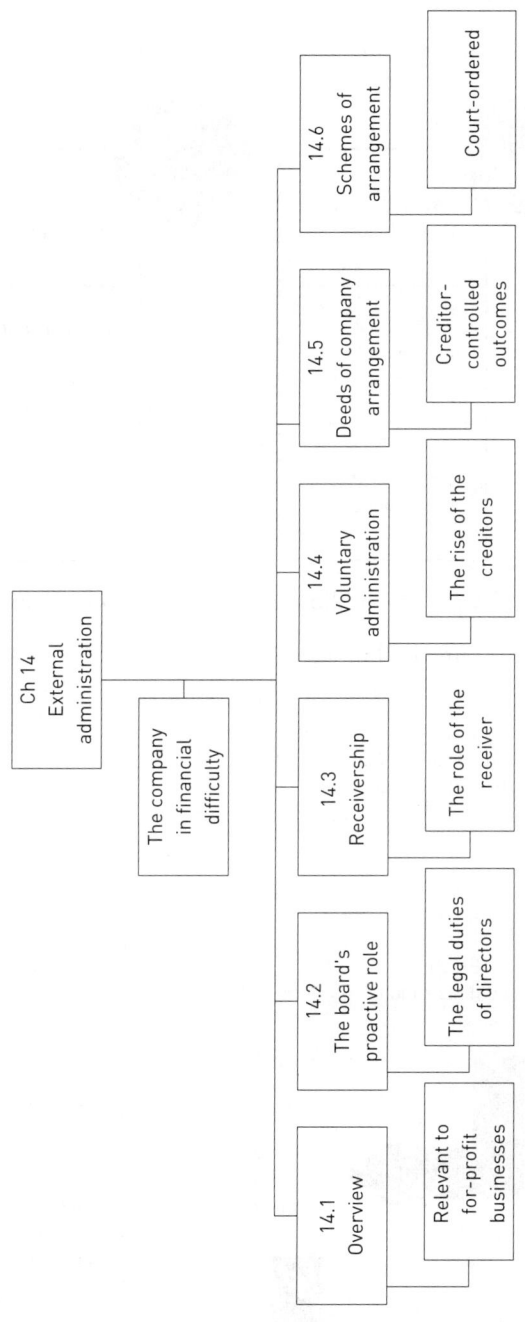

FIGURE 14.1 An overview of Chapter 14

14.1 AN OVERVIEW OF EXTERNAL ADMINISTRATION

External administration is dealt with in Ch 5.3 of the CA2001. The test of solvency or of being a going concern is a central consideration referred to in s 95A. The basic binary is set out in Fig 14.2.

FIGURE 14.2   The basic premise: can the company pay debts as they fall due?

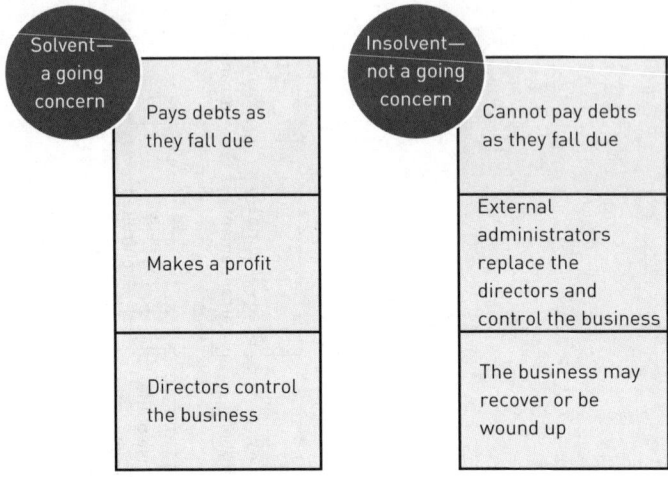

For a company, this can involve a series of 'slipping downs', as shown in Fig 14.3.

FIGURE 14.3   The consequences of financial problems

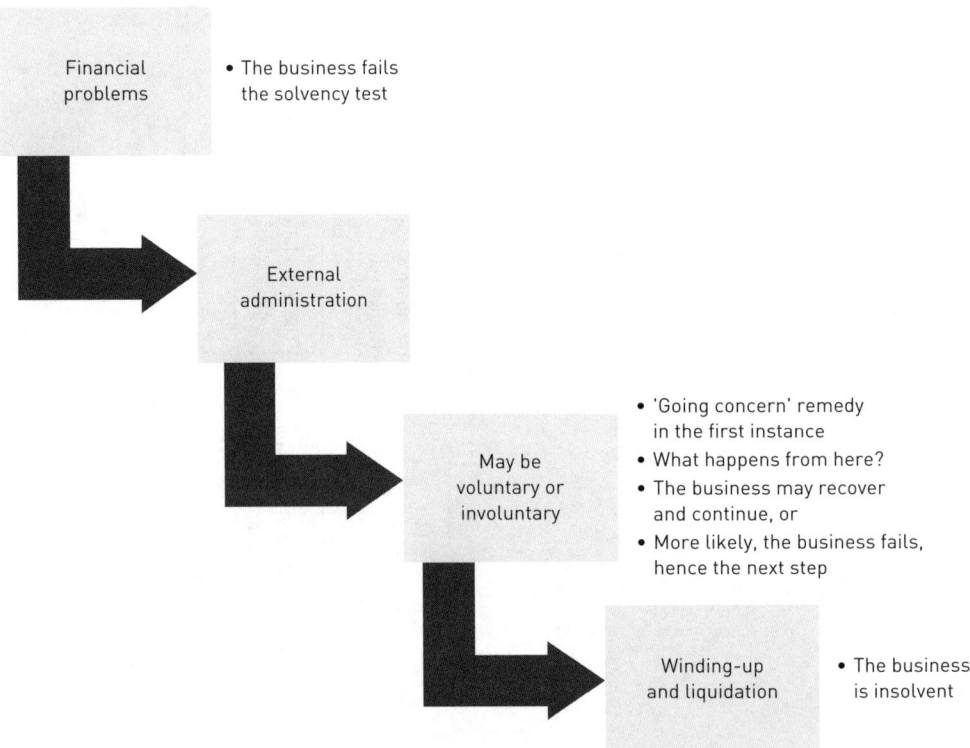

The company can go from operating at a profit to a perilous descent. This can happen slowly or due to a one-off calamity. The spiral of financial difficulty generally involves related steps, as shown in Fig 14.4.

FIGURE 14.4   The company descending into potential insolvency

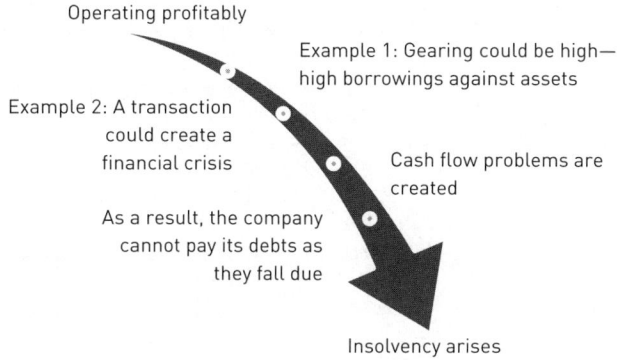

External administration is covered in Ch 5.3A of the CA2001.

FIGURE 14.5   An overview of external administration

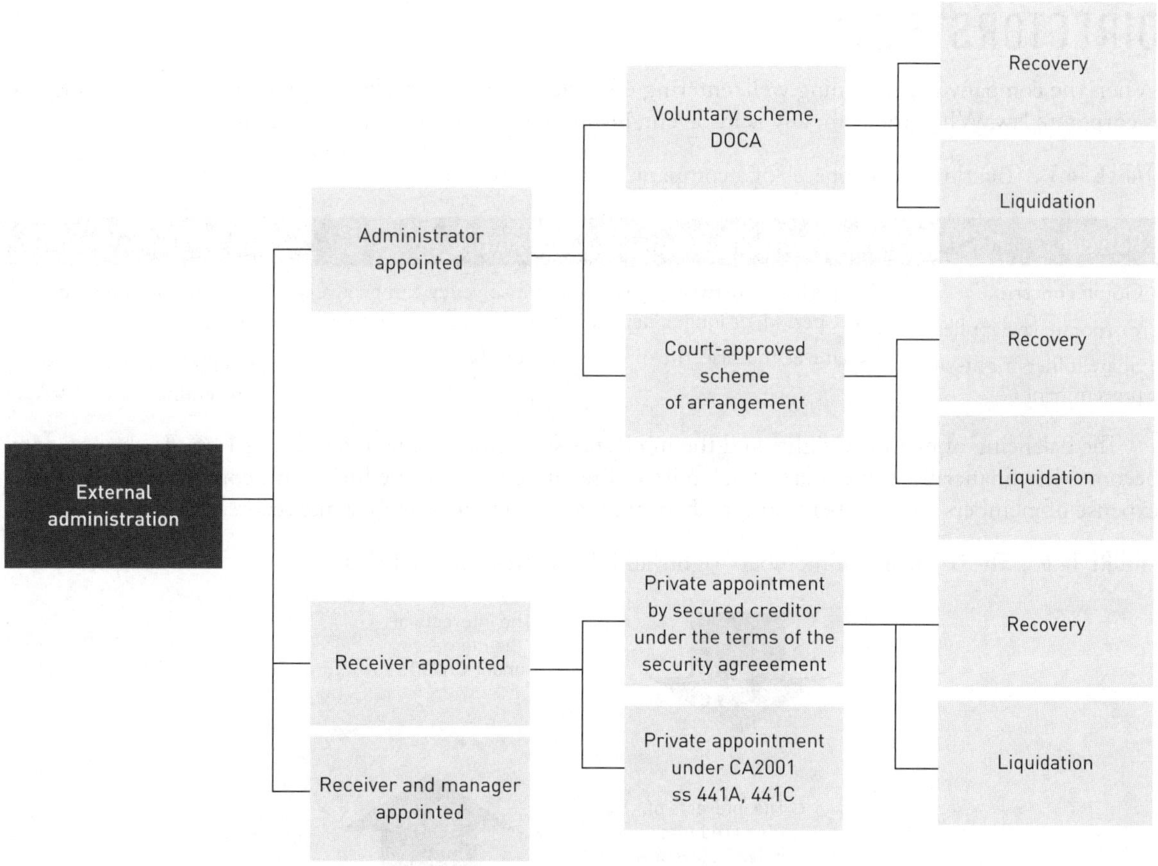

CORPORATIONS LAW: CONCEPTS, CASES AND CULTURE WORKBOOK

> **Activity 14.1**
>
> Review Figure 14.3. What are the main external administration options?

14.2 SOLVENCY, EXTERNAL ADMINISTRATION AND DIRECTORS' DUTIES

When the company is performing well, entering efficacious bargains, making a profit etc, the prevailing law is corporate law. When the company is insolvent, insolvency law becomes pre-eminent.

TABLE 14.1 The three basic phases of a company's financial health

Solvent	Uncertainty in terms of financial status	Insolvent
Going concern	The period in between solvency and insolvency can be a very short period, or longer, depending on the circumstances	External administration
Corporate law applies		Winding-up
Shareholders' rights are pre-eminent	Whatever the case, the directors need to be proactive	Creditors' interests are pre-eminent

The balancing of members' rights and the interests of creditors is illustrated in Fig 14.6. As the company becomes less financially viable there is an 'uplift' in the interests of the creditors. This comes effectively at the expense of members—remember that members rank last on a winding-up, while secured creditors rank first.

FIGURE 14.6 The balancing of members' rights and the interests of creditors

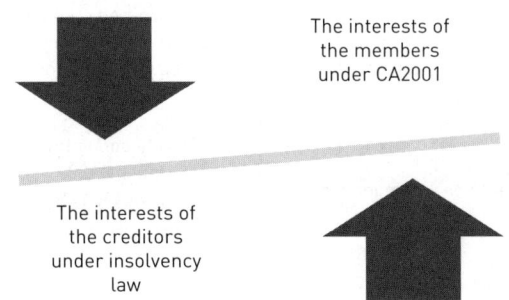

The rise and rise of the interests of creditors with a corporation in financial difficulty is shown in Fig 14.7.

FIGURE 14.7   Financial difficulty: the creditor ascendancy, and the descending nature of shareholdings

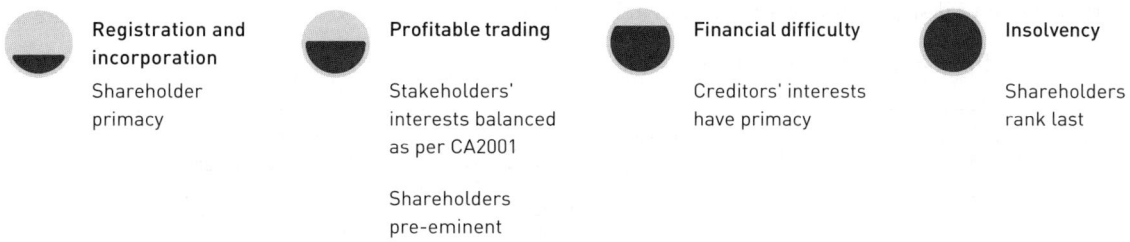

Registration and incorporation
Shareholder primacy

Profitable trading
Stakeholders' interests balanced as per CA2001

Shareholders pre-eminent

Financial difficulty
Creditors' interests have primacy

Insolvency
Shareholders rank last

The typical issues and events for a company in financial difficulty fall into a pattern, as shown in Fig 14.8. The creditors are centrally involved.

FIGURE 14.8   The creditors' role and interests rise in proportion to issues of financial instability, difficulty and onwards towards insolvency

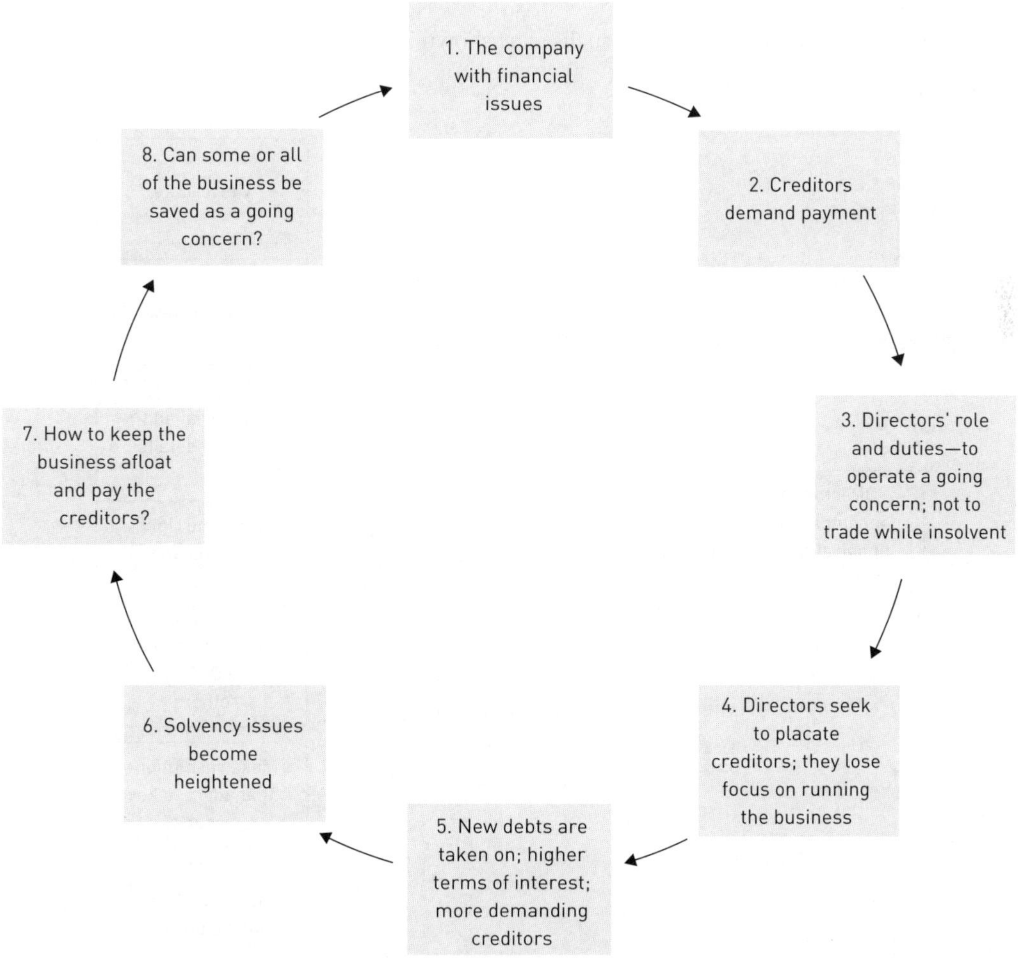

The directors owe duties to the current membership while the company is operating normally and trading solvently. This changes when the company's solvency is in doubt. The inflexion point means the rights of creditors subsume those of members. Insolvency law takes precedence over corporate law.

There are four distinct time phases, as shown in Fig 14.9.

FIGURE 14.9   The four distinct time phases of the company

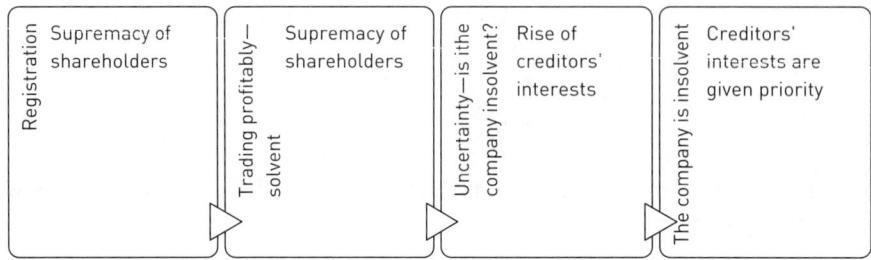

The directors of the company need to be proactive. They cannot sit back and do nothing. They are obliged to fulfil their full suite of duties under the CA2001. They are also subject to retrospective examination by the liquidator for their actions or inaction.

The types of proactive approach can be visualised as shown in Fig 14.10.

FIGURE 14.10   The active role of the directors

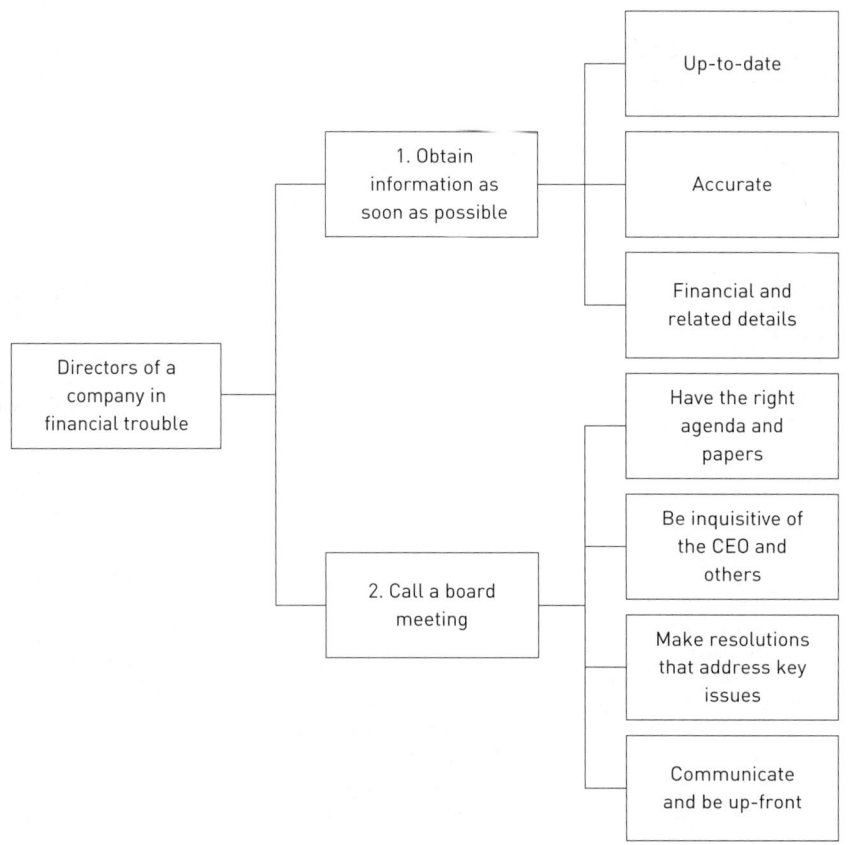

The directors are in breach of their duties if they allow the company to continue to trade while it is insolvent. In particular, CA2001 s 588G will apply, and will be applied retrospectively, as may be relevant. This is an example of piercing the corporate veil. The liquidator inquiries will focus on the elements in Fig 14.11.

FIGURE 14.11   The liquidator conducts a forensic examination of the company and the role of the directors, in particular

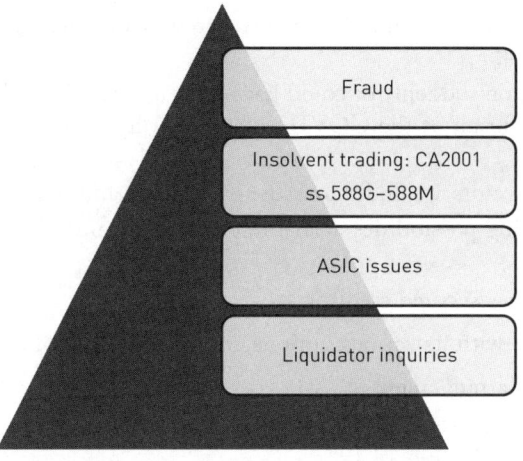

Activity 14.2

Outline the role of directors when a company is in financial difficulty.

_____
_____
_____
_____
_____
_____
_____
_____
_____
_____

14.3 RECEIVERSHIP

A company in financial difficulty, and more specifically the board of directors, faces the double challenge of simultaneously:

- conducting the business of the company, and
- dealing with the financial imperatives that will invariably involve creditors (one or several) agitating for repayment.

Financial difficulty begets further financial difficulty, and we can visualise this in terms of the downwards spiral, as shown in see Fig 14.4.

The issues may have come on suddenly or could have built up over time. For example, prior to going into voluntary administration as a result of the COVID-19 crisis, Virgin Australia, the airline, had not made a profit for some seven years.

Whatever the case, the directors are under pressure to perform and to meet their legal responsibilities.

There are three restructuring possibilities available to the company when it is in this phase of financial difficulty:

- receivership—controlled by a secured creditor
- voluntary administration—with its various options, including a deed of company arrangement (DOCA)
- a court-ordered scheme of arrangement.

Liquidation remains an ever-present option, depending on how matters transpire—note the two references to 'Does it need to be wound up?' in Fig 14.12.

FIGURE 14.12 The options when a company is in financial difficulty

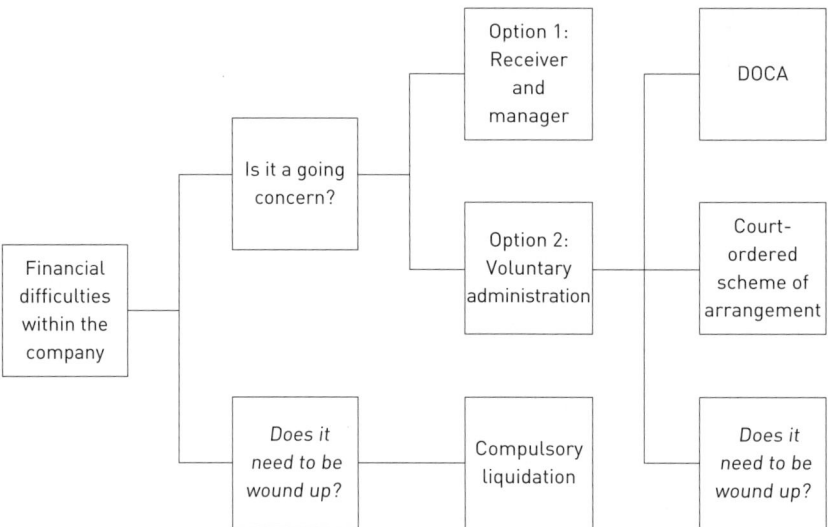

If, on the other hand, as noted above, the company's financial situation is serious and none of the restructuring options are viable, then the company may go into immediate liquidation without any intermediate steps: see Fig 14.13.

FIGURE 14.13   Is restructuring a viable option?

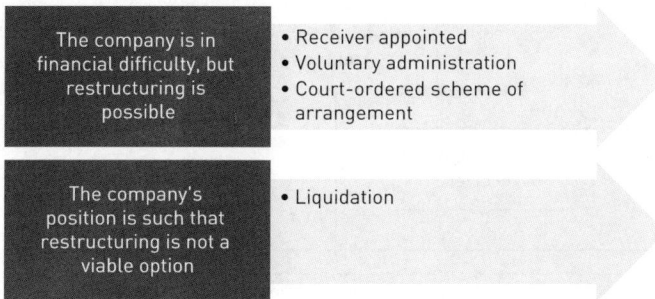

The flow-on consequences, intended and unintended, of the appointment of a receiver are serious and unpredictable in nature. The fate of the corporation is, in practical parlance, in jeopardy: see Fig 14.14, and note that the appointment and role of the receiver are specific to the particular secured creditor that is making the appointment under the terms of the loan and security.

FIGURE 14.14   The appointment and role of the receiver is specific to the particular secured creditor

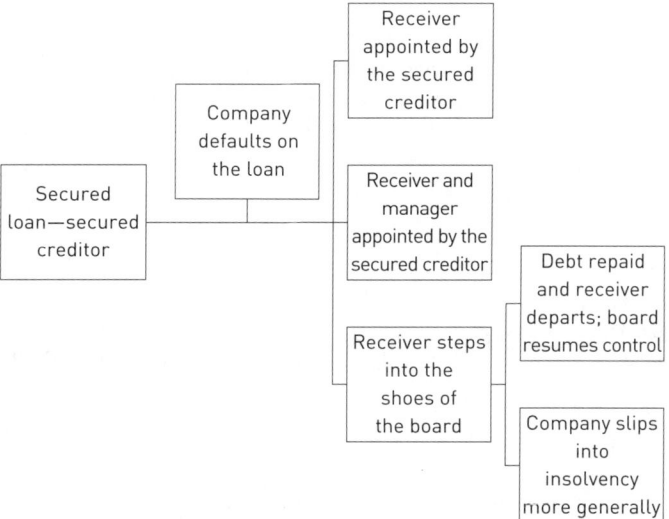

Receivership is, in theory at least, a going-concern remedy, although it is also somewhat confusingly referred to as 'insolvency procedure'. It is a question of time sequence; it may start as a going-concern process, but then become a winding-up procedure. The point is that the process is controlled by a particular party—the appointing secured creditor. This is the advantage of being a first-in-line secured creditor to the company.

FIGURE 14.15   An overview of the appointment of a receiver

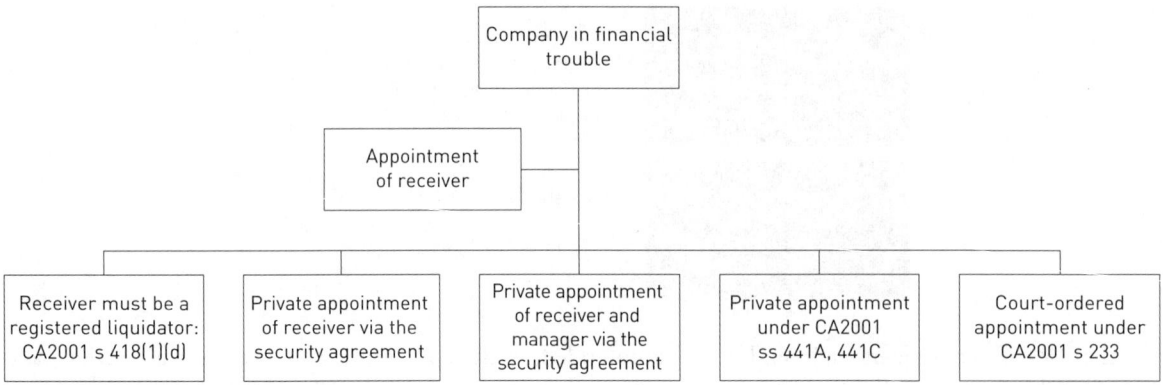

FIGURE 14.16   The process of appointing a receiver

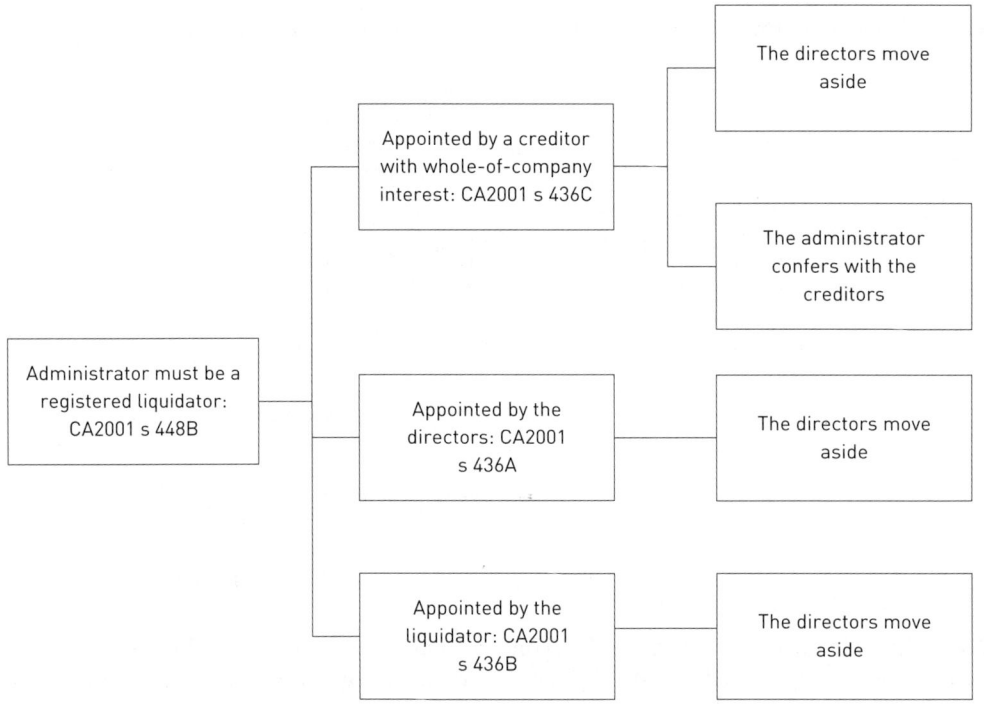

> **Activity 14.3**
>
> Outline the role of the receiver.

14.4 VOLUNTARY ADMINISTRATION

Voluntary administration is a measure that sits on the continuum of potential external administration processes between:

- the appointment of a receiver, and
- the appointment of a liquidator.

As such, it is a going-concern option, or at least it commences that way. Section 435A of the CA2001 sets out the aims and objectives of Pt 5.3A.

The history and development of voluntary administration in Australia includes some key events, as shown in Table 14.2. The aim was to establish a more creative approach to external administration and insolvency.

TABLE 14.2 Key events in the development of voluntary administration in Australia

Date	Step	Commentary
1988	*Harmer Report*	Recommended the introduction of voluntary administration

TABLE 14.2 Key events in the development of voluntary administration in Australia (continued)

Date	Step	Commentary
1993	Voluntary administration	

> ## Activity 14.4
> Complete Table 14.2.

There are three main stages to administration:

- the appointment process
- the first meeting and preliminary outcomes
- the second meeting and final outcomes.

Each of these is dealt with in turn below.

The administration process is set out in Pt 5.3A of the CA2001. The process is primarily aimed at devising a binding DOCA.

FIGURE 14.17 The appointment of the administrator

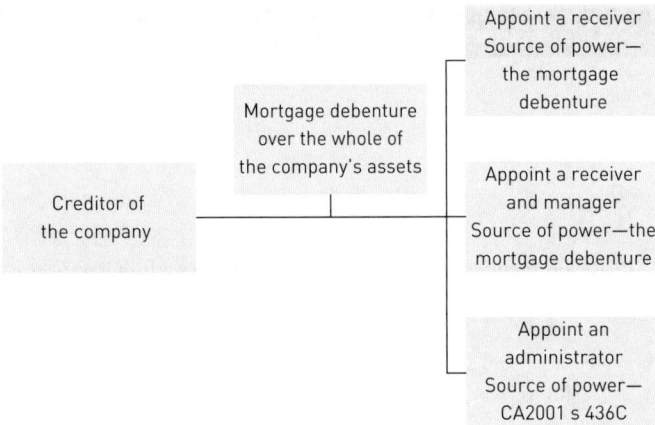

FIGURE 14.18 The first meeting process and preliminary outcomes

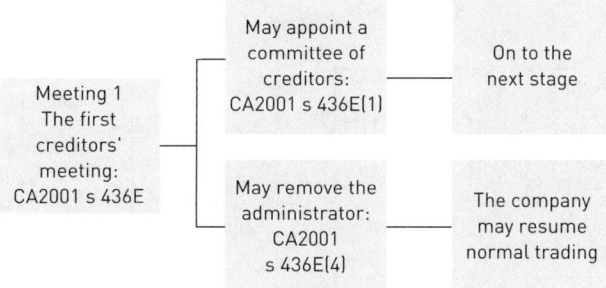

FIGURE 14.19 The second meeting process and final outcomes

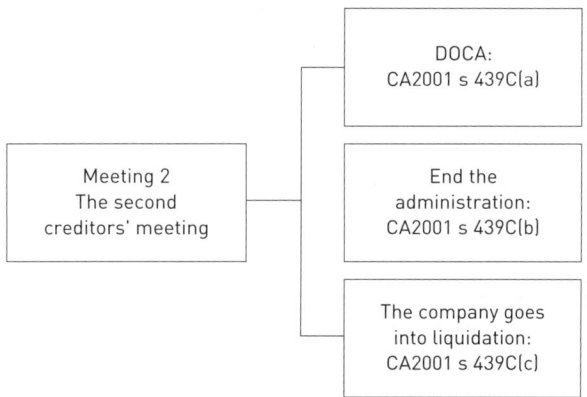

14.5 DEEDS OF COMPANY ARRANGEMENT

Appointment of the administrator

Appointment of the administrator is by:
- the directors
- a security holder covering all property of the company, or
- the liquidator.

TABLE 14.3 The potential outcomes after the appointment of the administrator

Meeting 1: The creditors' first meeting	Meeting 2: The creditors second meeting	Potential outcomes after Meeting 2
s 436E of the CA2001	s 439A of the CA2001	
The creditors may remove the administrator The creditors may appoint a committee of creditors	Decides the company's future	End the administration Enter a DOCA Liquidation

FIGURE 14.20   A composite overview of the DOCA process relevant to a DOCA

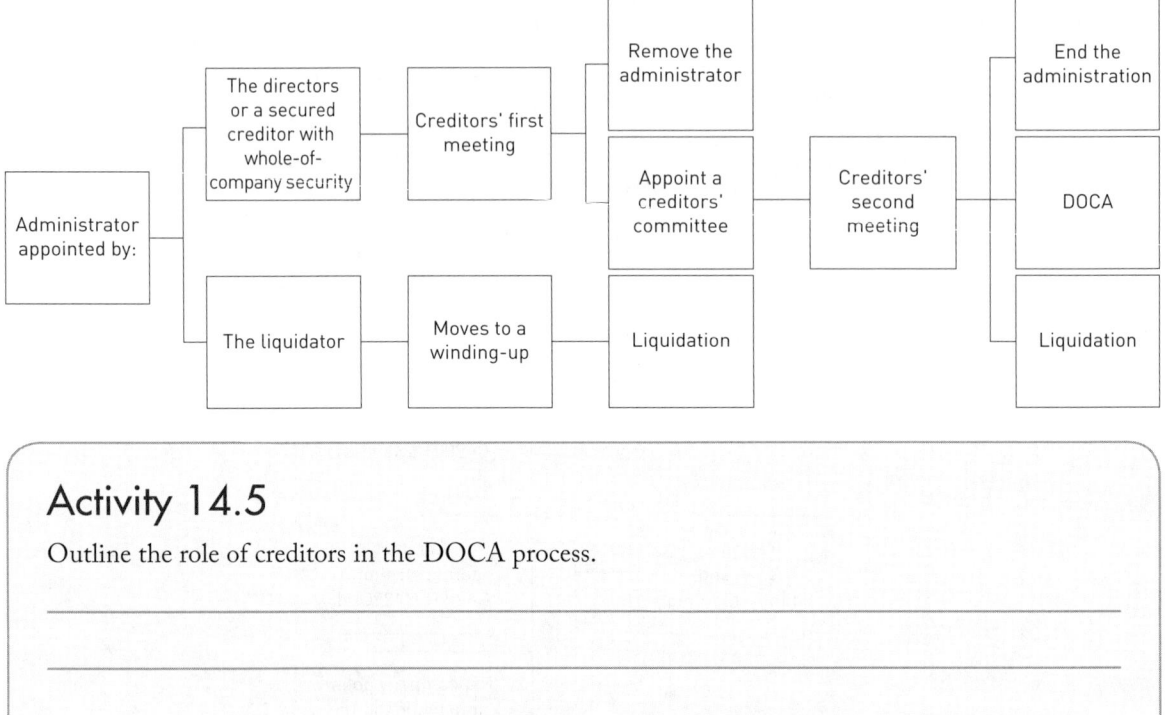

Activity 14.5

Outline the role of creditors in the DOCA process.

_____
_____
_____
_____
_____
_____
_____

14.6 COURT-ORDERED SCHEMES OF ARRANGEMENT

As noted in Chapter 11, court-ordered schemes of arrangement can be used in two contexts:
- as an alternative to takeovers, as discussed in Chapter 11, or
- as a form of potential external administration for a company in financial difficulty.

It is the second of these options we are discussing in this Chapter.

Court-ordered schemes of arrangement, by contrast to other forms of external administration, are slow, expensive and unpredictable. They involve several steps, two of which are court approvals:
- Step 1: the first court hearing—the preliminary proposal is put forward to the court
- Step 2: the creditors vote to affirm the proposal—it is still provisional, however, pending final court approval (see Step 3)

- Step 3: the second court hearing—the proposal may be approved by the court. The relevant test applied by the legislation is whether the proposed scheme is 'fair and equitable' as required by Pt 5.1 of the CA2001. The generality of this test makes the outcome unpredictable.

TABLE 14.4 The steps in a court-ordered scheme of arrangement

Step	Parties involved	What takes place

Litigation is, by its nature slow, expensive and unpredictable; it is a contest. Matters that get to court are always subject to two or more perspectives, each with their own merit—especially when seen from the viewpoint of the protagonist plaintiff or defendant. The merits of the claim are weighed against a host of factors. A court outcome always has a degree of uncertainty and unpredictability because of these factors, which include:

- the forum and the court
- the rights of appeal
- the precedents
- the legislative context
- the witnesses
- the case put by the other side
- the ability of counsel to optimise the argument
- the costs of proceeding with litigation (costs may or may not be recovered after the outcome)
- time, and
- the opportunity costs.

Activity 14.6

Complete Table 14.4.

WORKBOOK CHAPTER 14 REVIEW

An illustrative summary of the key points

FIGURE 14.21 The main options as regards external administration relevant to companies that are still potentially going concerns

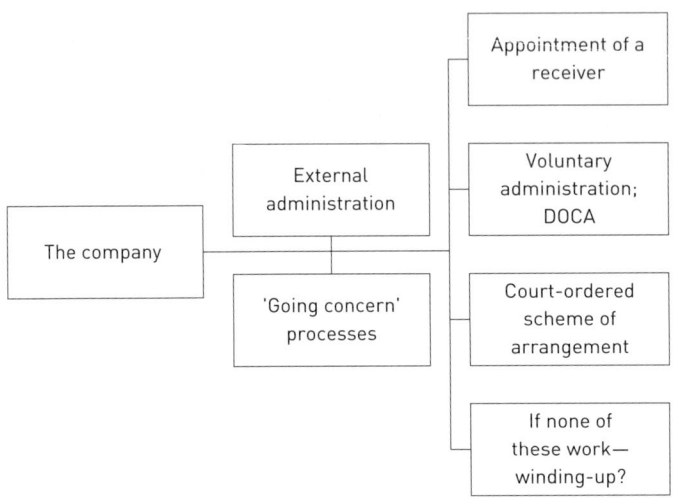

CHAPTER 14 REVISION ACTIVITIES

Consolidation of concepts, knowledge and content activities

TRUE OR FALSE QUESTIONS

1. Company solvency is an issue primarily the responsibility of the company's accountant.　　True ☐　False ☐

2. The company's solvency is a core responsibility of the directors.　　True ☐　False ☐

3. Once a receiver is appointed, the board can hand over their legal responsibilities to the receiver.　　True ☐　False ☐

4. A going-concern option includes the appointment of a liquidator.　　True ☐　False ☐

5. The CA2001 has specific provisions regarding director liability in relation to a company in danger of not paying its debts as they fall due.　　True ☐　False ☐

FILL IN THE GAPS

1. Companies in financial trouble may be subject to the provisions of the CA2001 known as _____

2. A person who cannot pay their debts may be subject _____

3. An insolvent company will be _____

4. Voluntary administration has a policy objective of corporate _____

5. A receiver selling an asset of the company is required to achieve the _____ _____ price under s 420A(a) of the CA2001.

6. The _____ of a going-concern company are prime stakeholders.

7. The _____ of an insolvent company assume a central place in the process.

MULTIPLE CHOICE

1. EA in relation to corporate law refers to:
   A. External affairs
   B. External administration
   C. External Australian audit
   D. External assistance

2. DOCA stands for:
   A. Deed of corporate affairs
   B. Deed of company arrangement
   C. Date of company arrangement
   D. Duty over company acts

3. The DOCA process requires, at a minimum, how many creditor meetings?
   A. 1
   B. 2
   C. 3
   D. 4

4. A creditor with a whole-of-company interest can appoint an administrator under the CA2001 by reference to:

   A. s 416C
   B. s 426C
   C. s 436C
   D. s 446C

5. The second creditors' meeting of a DOCA is primarily covered by the CA2001 under:

   A. s 419
   B. s 439
   C. s 449
   D. s 459

SHORT ANSWER QUESTIONS

1. What does a receiver do, and how are they appointed?

2. What distinguishes a 'managing controller' from other controllers?

3. What debts of a company in administration is the administrator personally liable to pay? How can the administrator be indemnified for these?

4. Who has the power to appoint an administrator?

5. How can an administrator avoid liability for payments under an arrangement entered into before the administration began, relating to the use of property owned by someone else (e.g. leased equipment)?

6. What are the three things that can happen when a voluntary administration ends?

Higher order thinking activities

Consider the following questions and provide detailed discussion and analysis.

TOPIC A

ABC Pty Ltd is going through severe cash-flow problems. What should the board do?

QUESTIONS

TOPIC B

Why are DOCAs popular?

CHAPTER 15

WINDING UP THE CORPORATION

Chapter synopsis and links to Textbook Chapter 15

This Workbook Chapter deals with five topics:

- 15.1 Overview of winding-up
- 15.2 Compulsory winding-up
- 15.3 Voluntary winding-up
- 15.4 The role of the liquidator
- 15.5 The role and responsibilities of the directors of a company in liquidation.

Each of these topics is constructively aligned with, and linked to, the same topics in Chapter 15 of the Textbook.

Chapter executive summary

This Chapter examines the winding-up of the corporation by reference to:
- the process of winding-up generally
- compulsory as opposed to voluntary winding-up
- the role and responsibility of the liquidator
- the legal position and duties of the directors to act in the best interests of the company, and
- the formal deregistration of the company and its removal from the ASIC register.

CHAPTER DIAGRAMMATIC OVERVIEW

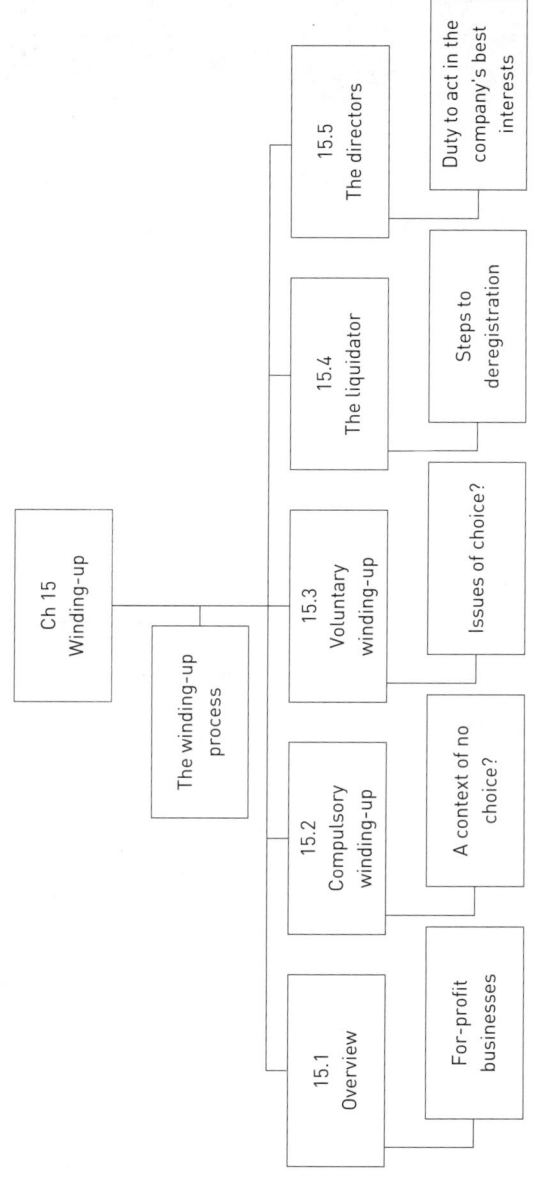

FIGURE 15.1   An overview of Chapter 15

15.1 OVERVIEW OF WINDING-UP

As has been noted, a company has four distinct phases to its existence, as shown in Fig 15.2.

FIGURE 15.2   The default linear track of a single company

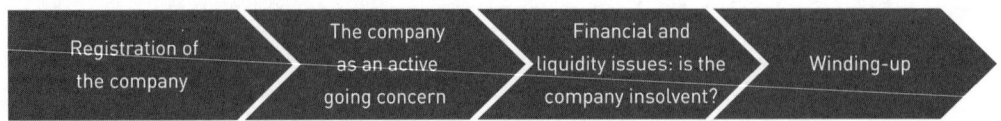

This straightforward linear model relevant to the company may, of course, be interrupted by other events, including 'intersections' (transactions and so forth, both intended/planned and unintended/forced) with other companies and legal entities: see Fig 15.3.

FIGURE 15.3   The potential events and intersections that may beset a single company are myriad in nature

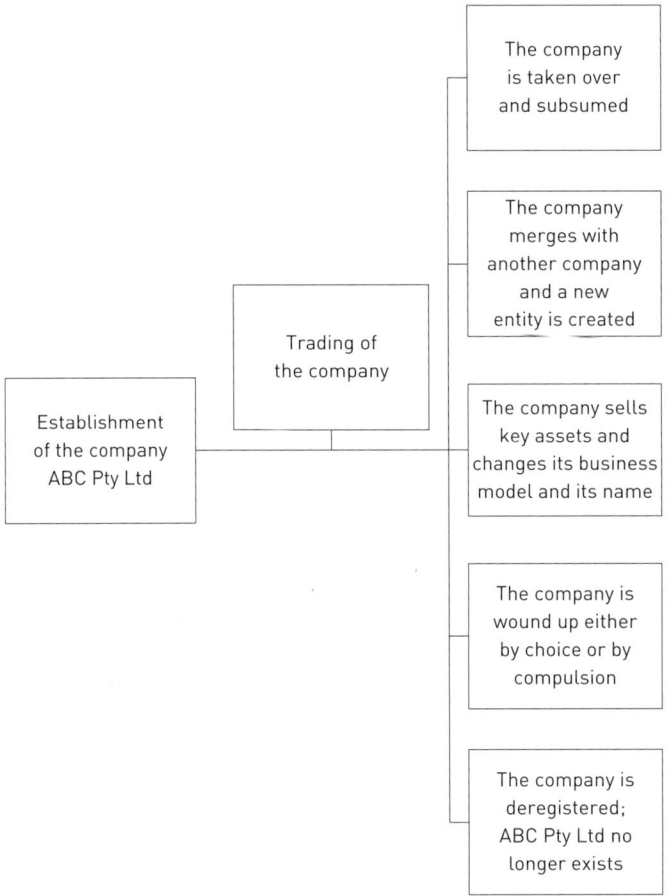

The winding-up phase of a company focuses on the third and fourth phases of Figure 15.1. These can be extrapolated upon as shown in Fig 15.4.

FIGURE 15.4   A company beset by serious (potentially existential) financial issues

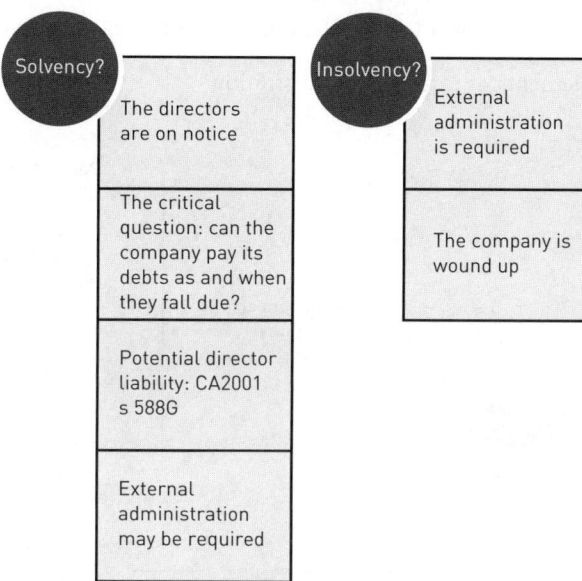

Naturally, a company may choose to wind up. This may be for several reasons, including lack of successors, lack of interest, change of business and so forth. There is, therefore, a bifurcation between choice and imposition: see Fig 15.5.

FIGURE 15.5   Winding-up: compulsory or voluntary

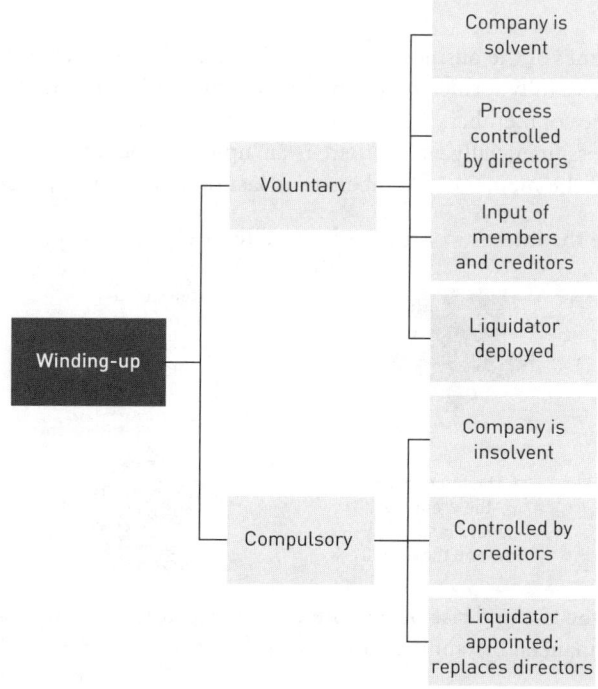

If a company is facing a compulsory winding-up, this means that any of the going-concern phases of external administration have either been deployed, or have not proven effective.

There are four distinct combinations of external administration aside from winding-up: see Fig 15.6.

FIGURE 15.6 The various elements of external administration

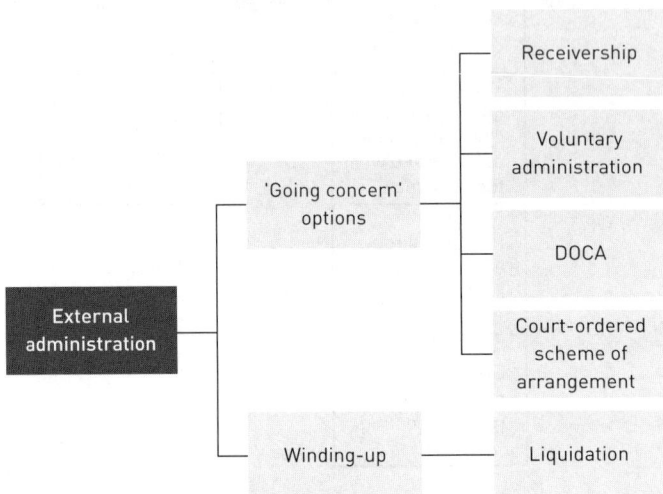

External administration highlights the role and capacities of the various stakeholders of and to the company. While the company has been a going concern, solvent, liquid, and able to pay its debts as they fall due, the shareholders/members have been the dominant stakeholders. They are classically 'insiders' who hold the directors to account—and, in so doing, reduce the agency gap that may exist between them and the directors, given the day-to-day insights and knowledge of the business that the directors possess. This is a case of 'information asymmetry'.

However, once the fortunes of the business turn, and a live question is whether the company is solvent, the interests of the creditors arrive fully formed on the potentially dramatic scene that may be about to unfold. At this point in time, the balance of members' rights and the interests of creditors effectively inverts: see Fig 15.7. As the company becomes less financially viable, there is an 'uplift 'in the interests of the creditors. This comes effectively at the expense of the members. Members rank last on a winding-up; secured creditors rank first.

FIGURE 15.7 The 'uplift' in the interests of the creditors, effectively at the expense of members

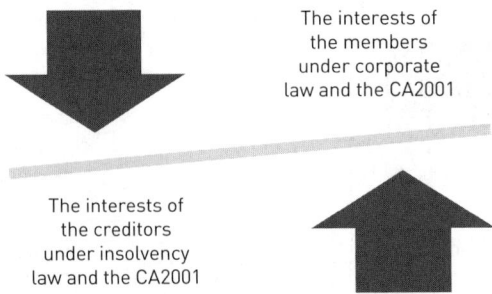

Figure 15.8 illustrates the rise and rise of the interests of creditors to a corporation in financial difficulty, in proportion to issues of financial instability, difficulty, and onwards towards insolvency.

FIGURE 15.8 The creditors' role and interests rise

The journey of a company into insolvency may be gradual or quick; in any event, it puts the directors in the spotlight: see Fig 15.9.

FIGURE 15.9 From solvency to insolvency

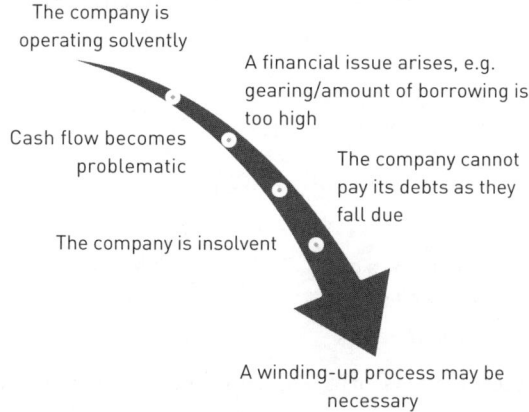

The shareholders and the creditors effectively invert their positions if the company slips into insolvency. Fig 15.10 illustrates that the directors owe duties to the current membership while the company is operating normally and trading solvently. This changes when the company's solvency is in doubt. The inflexion point means the rights of creditors subsume those of members. Insolvency law takes precedence over corporate law.

FIGURE 15.10 The four distinct time phases of the company

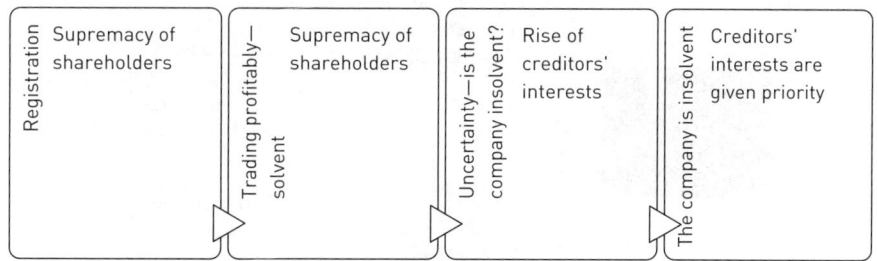

Members' contributions on a winding-up

Members' contributions on a winding-up are dealt with in CA2001 Pt 5.6 Div 2: 'Contributories'. They are informed for this purpose by the two types of member liability, as shown in Fig 15.11.

FIGURE 15.11   Liability of members

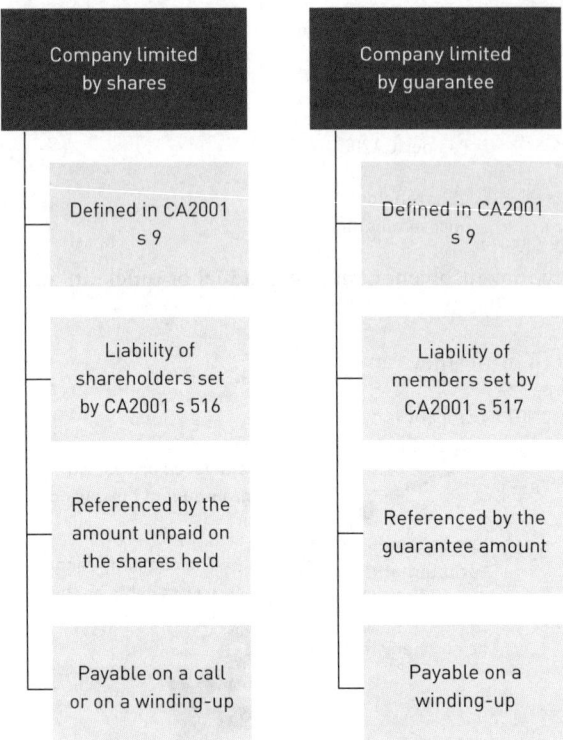

Note that the liability of the members of a company limited by guarantee is limited to the event of winding-up: see Fig 15.12.

FIGURE 15.12   Contributories: the members of companies limited by shares and by guarantee respectively

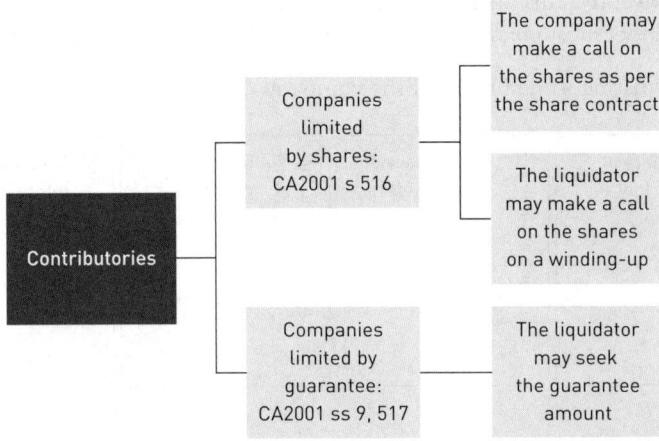

The liability of shareholders is therefore limited.

By contrast, there is no theoretical limit to the gains to be made by the shareholder: see Fig 15.13.

FIGURE 15.13   The distinction between limited liability for a shareholder and potentially unlimited gains

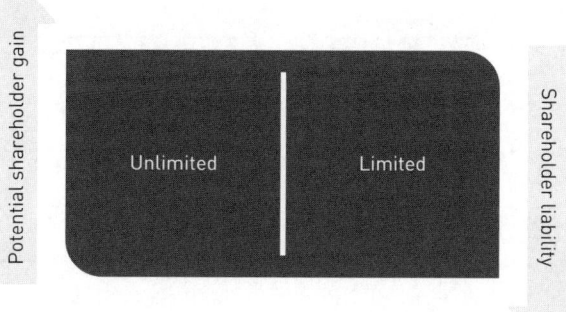

The potential gains for a shareholder are influenced by several factors: see Fig 15.14.

FIGURE 15.14   Factors leading to an increase in the value of a member's shareholding

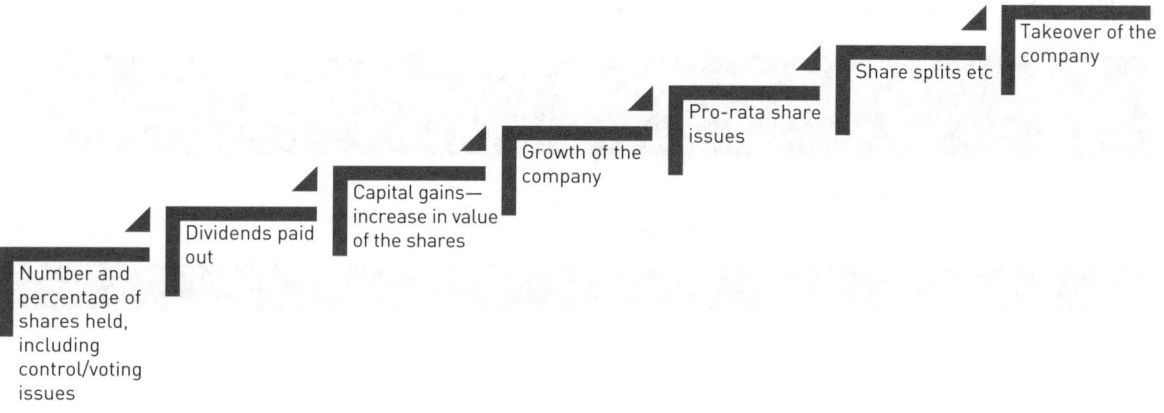

Activity 15.1

Critically review the concept of limited liability of shareholders.

_____
_____
_____
_____
_____

15.2 COMPULSORY WINDING-UP

The winding-up process means the company is no longer a 'going concern'. It can be illustrated as shown in Fig 15.15.

FIGURE 15.15   The phases of a company facing a compulsory winding-up

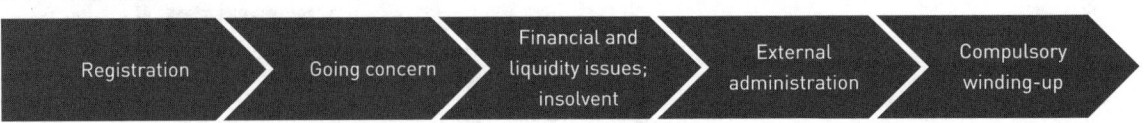

TABLE 15.1   The process of compulsory winding-up

Steps	What is involved	Notes

Steps	What is involved	Notes

> **Activity 15.2**
> Fill in Table 15.1.

15.3 VOLUNTARY WINDING-UP

Voluntary winding-up may be initiated and overseen by the members, or by the creditors.

A members' voluntary winding-up may be effected for several reasons; it may be done on the basis that the company no longer has a purpose (that is, it has done what it set out to do), or because there is no succession plan (for example, with a family business such as a farm or agri-business). The company is solvent; hence this is a choice by the members.

The relevant steps are set out in Table 15.2.

TABLE 15.2 The process of a voluntary winding-up initiated by the members

CA2001	What is involved	Notes
s 495	Power to the members: The members may voluntarily wind up the company	

TABLE 15.2 The process of a voluntary winding-up initiated by the members (continued)

CA2001	What is involved	Notes
s 494	Directors' declaration: If the company is solvent, the directors must declare the company to be solvent	
s 491	Special resolution: The members must pass a special resolution to wind up the company	
s 491	Lodgment with ASIC: The special resolution must be lodged by the company with ASIC within 7 days	
s 491(2)	Publication in the Gazette: Notice must be published in the Government Gazette within 28 days	

TABLE 15.3 The steps involved in a creditors' winding-up

CA2001	What is involved	Notes
s 497	The directors' opinion: The company cannot pay its debts	
	Meeting of creditors: Called by the directors	
	Notice of the creditors' meeting: In the prescribed form	
	Advertisements: To be placed in accordance with CA2001	

CORPORATIONS LAW: CONCEPTS, CASES AND CULTURE WORKBOOK

TABLE 15.3 The steps involved in a creditors' winding-up (continued)

CA2001	What is involved	Notes
	Directors' statement provided at the meeting: A full statement of the company's affairs	
s 497	Appointment of the liquidator:	
	Replacement choice of liquidator:	

Activity 15.3

Complete Tables 15.2 and 15.3.

15.5 THE ROLE AND RESPONSIBILITIES OF THE DIRECTORS OF A COMPANY IN LIQUIDATION

The role of the directors is important in each phase of the company's business. The usual directors' duties of:
- competence (s 180 of the CA2001), and
- honesty (ss 181–184 of the CA2001)

apply throughout.

Additional responsibilities and potential legal liabilities arise for the directors if the company gets into financial difficulty: see Fig 15.16.

FIGURE 15.16 Potential director liabilities arising as a result of external administration

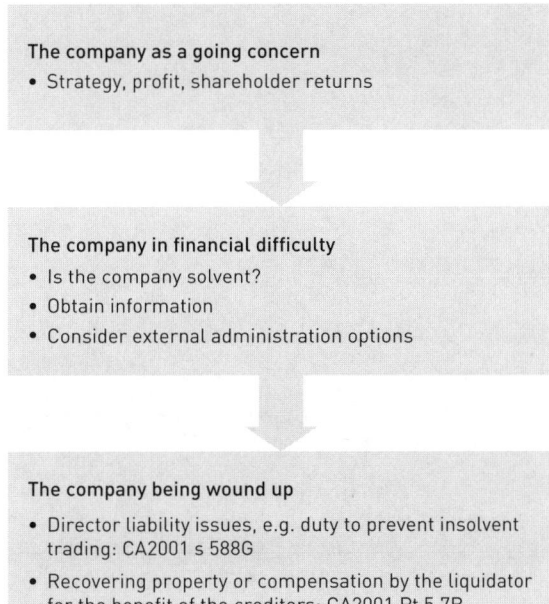

15.4 THE ROLE OF THE LIQUIDATOR

TABLE 15.4 The role of the liquidator

Steps	What is involved	Notes

Activity 15.4
Fill in Table 15.4.

WORKBOOK CHAPTER 15 REVIEW

An illustrative summary of the key points

FIGURE 15.17   An overview of the winding-up of the company leading to deregistration

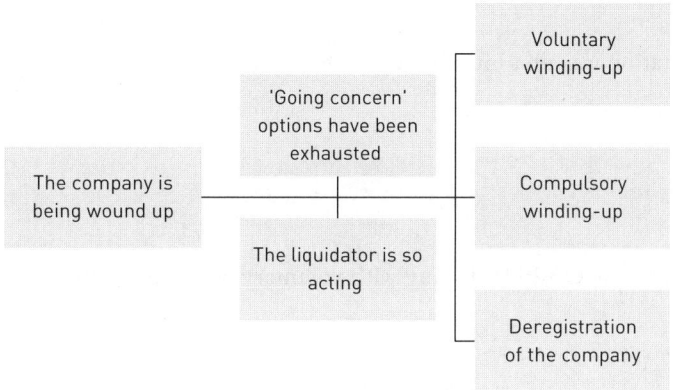

CHAPTER 15 REVISION ACTIVITIES

Consolidation of concepts, knowledge and content activities

TRUE OR FALSE?

1. Determining the solvency of the company is principally a matter for the directors.   True ☐ False ☐
2. Directors can be personally liable for the insolvent trading of the company.   True ☐ False ☐
3. Receivership is a going-concern remedy.   True ☐ False ☐
4. Shareholders are paid ahead of employees on a winding-up.   True ☐ False ☐
5. The liquidator can seek any outstanding amounts payable on a member's shares.   True ☐ False ☐

FILL IN THE GAPS

1. The relevant part of the CA2001 dealing with compulsory winding-up is _____
2. Schemes of court-ordered arrangement are _____ because of the uncertainties of the court process.
3. Winding-ups may be either _____ or compulsory.
4. Secured creditors rank _____ on a winding-up.

5. The tax debts of a company on a winding-up are considered to be part of the collective of _____ creditors.

6. The members are entitled to any surplus after _____ the other creditors have been paid _____.

MULTIPLE CHOICE

1. Voluntary administration was first introduced in which year?

    A. 1982

    B. 1992

    C. 2002

    D. 2012

2. The main provisions of the CA2001 dealing with voluntary winding-up are:

    A. ss 426 and 427

    B. ss 426A and 427A

    C. ss 439 and 446

    D. ss 439A and 446A

3. A liquidation prioritises the interests of:

    A. Promoters

    B. Directors

    C. Creditors

    D. Members

4. Deregistration for a company is confirmed by:

    A. The creditors

    B. ASIC

    C. The liquidator

    D. The directors

5. Which of the following is not a going-concern remedy?

    A. Winding-up

    B. Receivership

    C. Voluntary administration

    D. DOCA

SHORT ANSWER QUESTIONS

1. How are share transfers affected by a winding-up of a corporation?

2. Who must have the leave of the court before applying for an order that an insolvent company be wound up?

Higher order thinking activities

Consider the following question and provide detailed discussion and analysis.

TOPIC A

What defences are available against a liquidator seeking to recover voidable transactions?

CHAPTER 16

CORPORATIONS AND THE CULTURAL CONTEXT

Chapter synopsis and links to Textbook Chapter 16

This Workbook Chapter deals with four topics:

- 16.1 A case study in corporate culture
- 16.2 Corporate law theory
- 16.3 Corporate social responsibility in the 21st century
- 16.4 A brief review of the unit of study: Company Law.

Each of these topics is constructively aligned with, and linked to, the same topics in Chapter 16 of the Textbook.

Chapter executive summary

This chapter examines corporate culture and corporate social responsibility (CSR) by way of a case study. CSR is one of the theories of the corporation, along with others such as shareholder primacy and the concession theory of the firm.

The Chapter concludes with an overview of the previous chapters.

CHAPTER 16 CORPORATIONS AND THE CULTURAL CONTEXT

CHAPTER DIAGRAMMATIC OVERVIEW

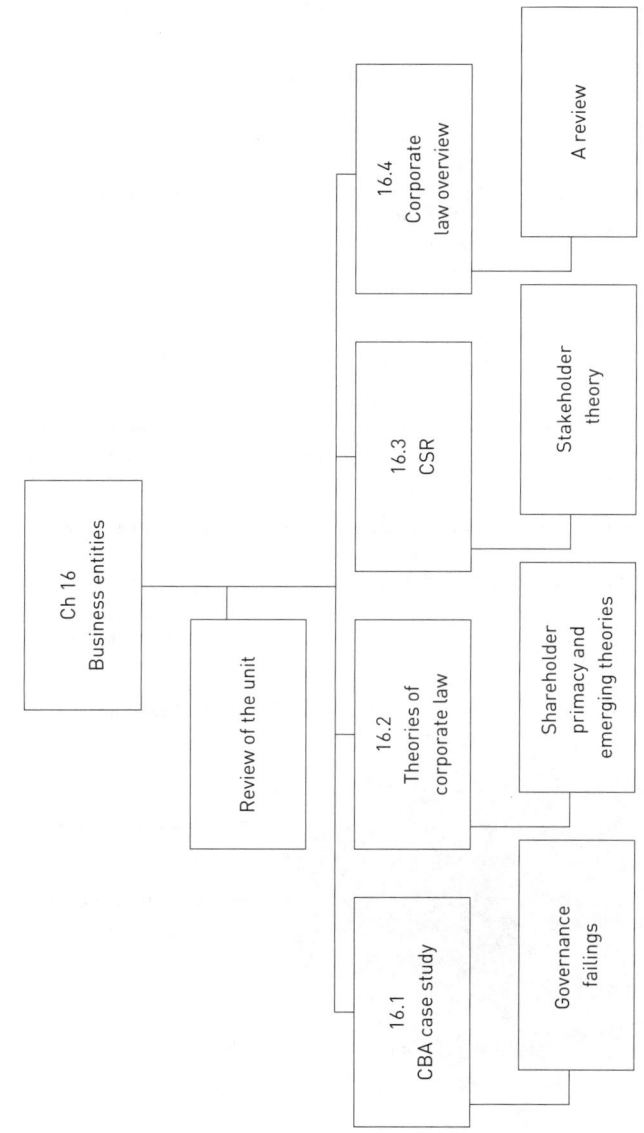

FIGURE 16.1 An overview of Chapter 16

16.1 A CASE STUDY IN CORPORATE CULTURE

Identifying the elements of corporate culture is becoming increasingly important. Culture links to other key corporate strata, as shown in Fig 16.2.

FIGURE 16.2   The context of corporate culture—the emerging third element of the corporation?

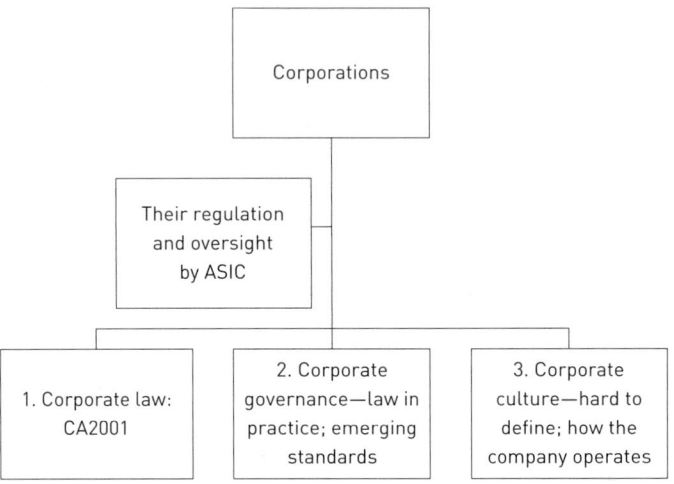

Alternatively, culture can be visualised as an element of the corporation's oversight, as shown in Fig 16.3.

FIGURE 16.3   Culture and law—the related elements

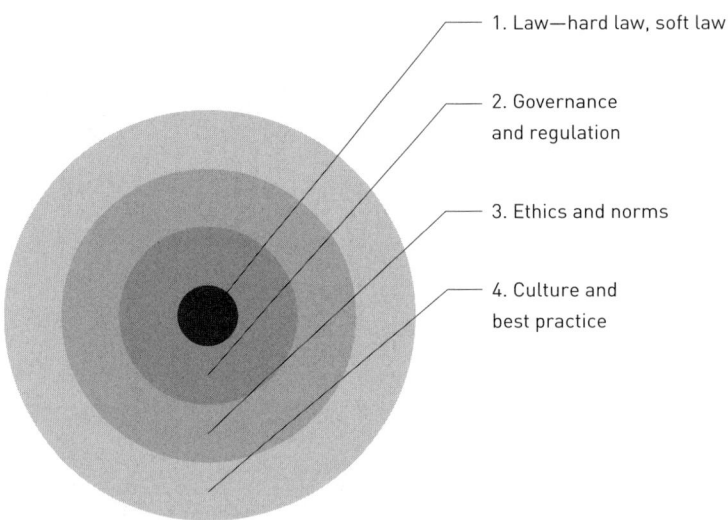

Governance and its cultural reference point

Look at Figs 16.4 and 16.5. The elements shown in bold text in these diagrams are crucial to the Commonwealth Bank of Australia (CBA), which is the focus of the case study in the Textbook.

FIGURE 16.4 The elements of the various models of culture within a firm

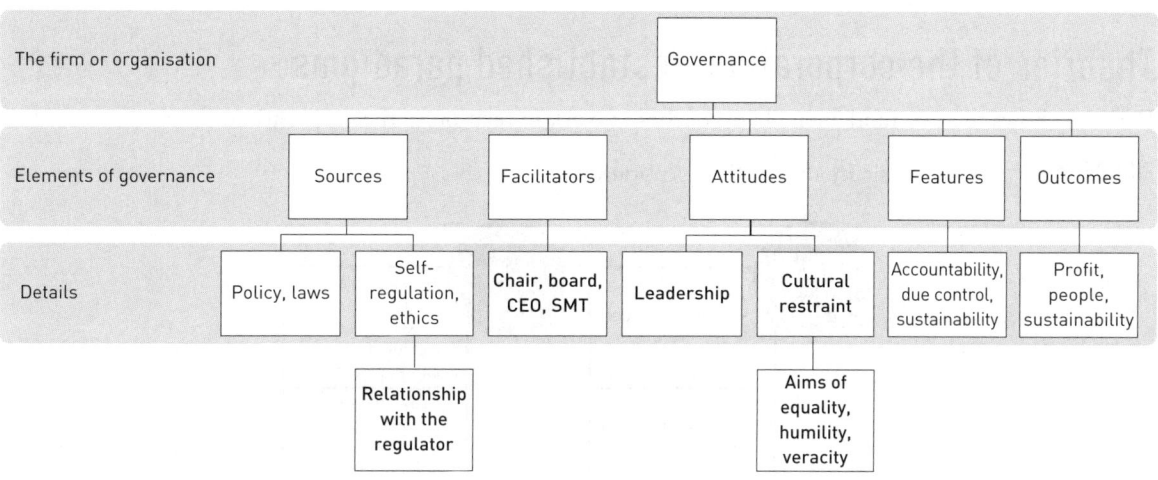

FIGURE 16.5 Potential models of culture within a firm and related practices/outcomes

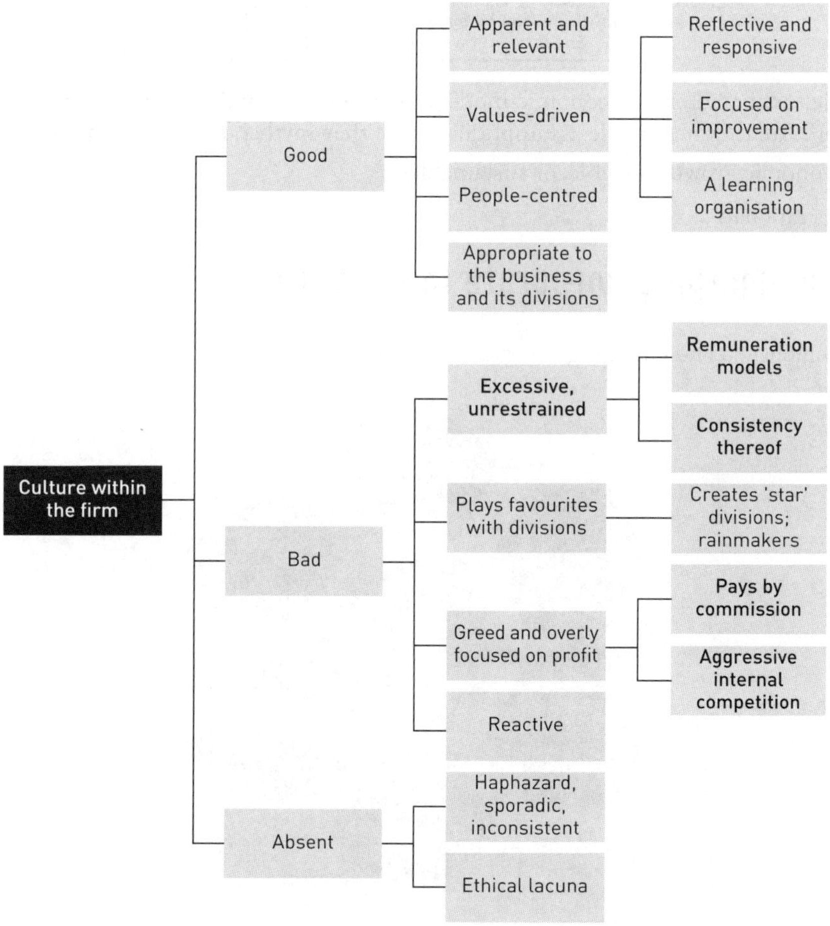

16.2 CORPORATE LAW THEORY

Theories of the corporation—established paradigms

Fig 16.6 shows the two fundamental approaches at work in relation to the corporation.

FIGURE 16.6 The two basic models of the corporation

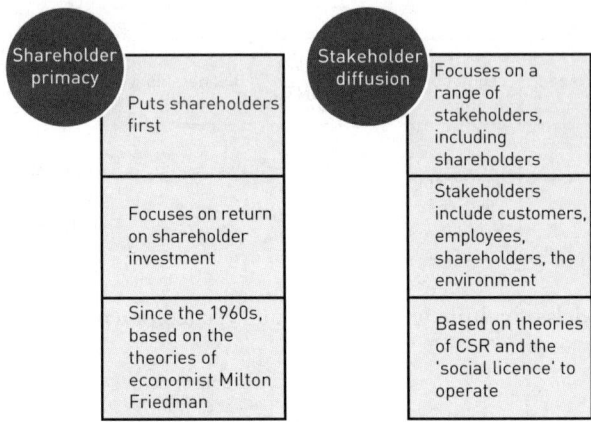

These theories are based on an economic model of continued growth and wealth building, based on the 'rational investor'. Are they reasonable assumptions, or are they myths? Two questions are key:

- Is endless economic growth possible, or sustainable?
- Are investors rational?

Current and emerging corporate law theories

FIGURE 16.7 Established and emerging theories of corporate law

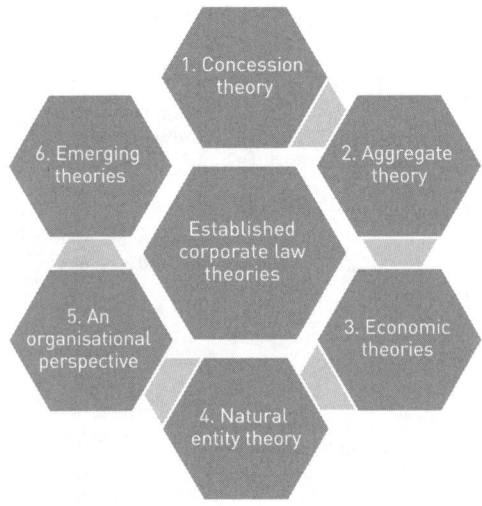

These emerging paradigms shown in Fig 16.7 are variously based on:
- sustainable practice
- a circular economy
- a balancing of stakeholder interests, and
- the theories of behavioural economics and psychology. A leading exponent of this area of research is the Nobel Prize-winning economist, Daniel Kahneman.

Behavioural economics pre-supposes that:
- investors are not always rational; in fact, often they are irrational, and
- the post-Second World War model of continued growth and expansion is not a possibility. There was a 'golden period' of economic growth from 1950 to 1970. This is unusual, however, and almost unprecedented, according to economic research. Since the Global Financial Crisis (GFC) there has been very slow growth, despite historically low interest rates; and wage stagnation may, in fact, be the new normal. Others argue that the GFC is being replaced by the CCC (Climate Change Conflict, or Climate Change Crisis). This requires a new circular and sustainable economy.

FIGURE 16.8   Emerging models of the company

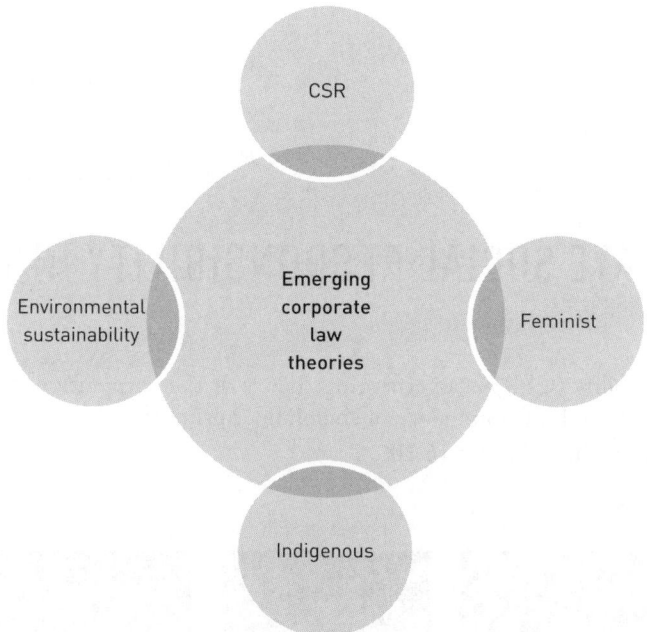

---

1   See Thomas Piketty, *Capital in the Twenty First Century*, Harvard University Press, 2014.

The main actors in the corporate law sector include and interplay between private and state actors:

FIGURE 16.9 The main actors in the corporate sector

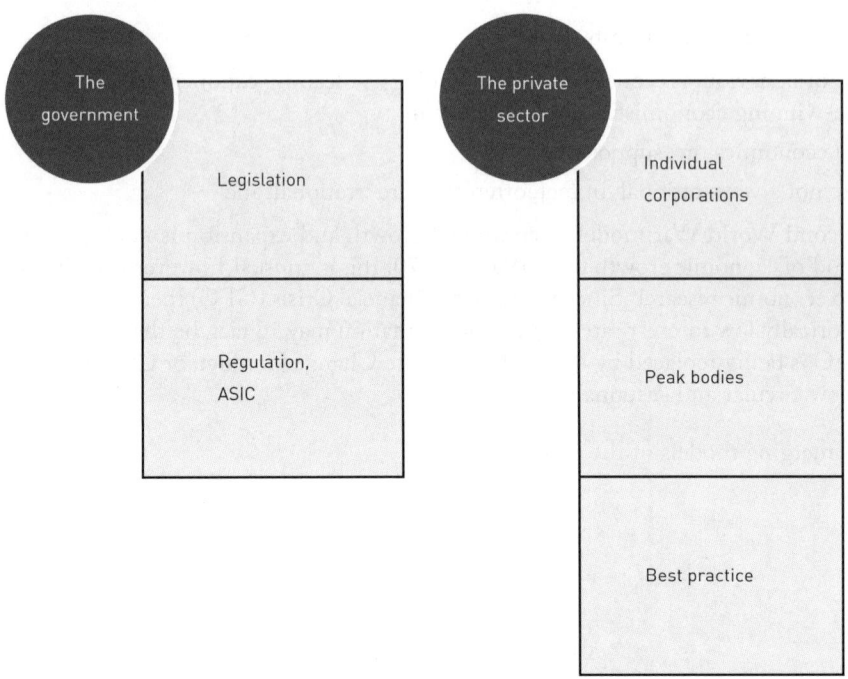

16.3 CORPORATE SOCIAL RESPONSIBILITY IN THE 21ST CENTURY

Corporate social responsibility (CSR) is an emerging theory of the corporation. Its impact in Australia is constrained by the CA2001 and the dominance of shareholder primacy.

CSR is multi-faceted, as shown in Fig 16.10.

FIGURE 16.10 The facets of CSR

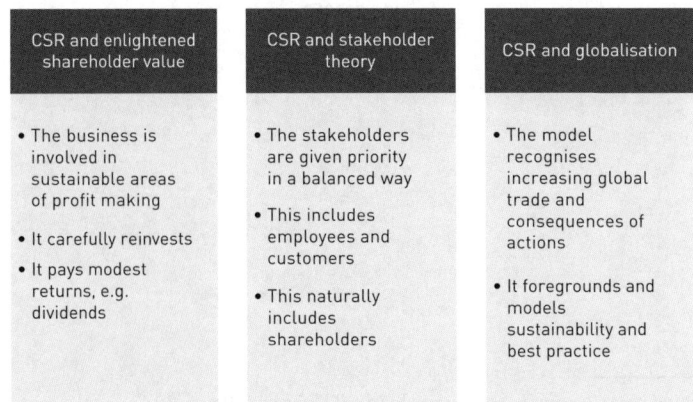

Figure 16.11 offers a comparison of CSR and shareholder primacy:

FIGURE 16.11   CSR and the potential multiple focuses of the company

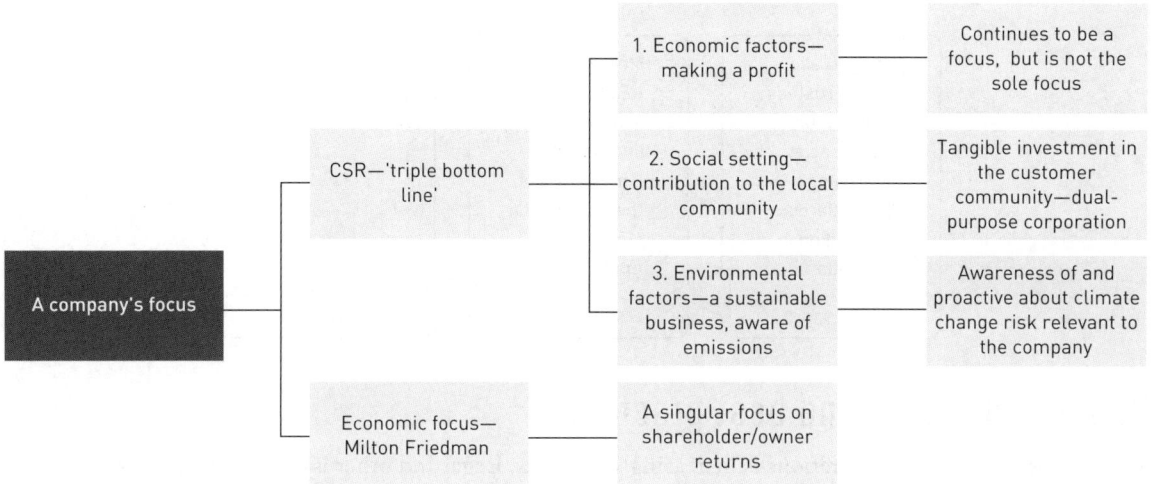

CSR theories of the corporation will be increasingly important in the context of superannuation and long-run investment decisions by the trustee: see Fig 16.12.

FIGURE 16.12   CSR and links to superannuation funds

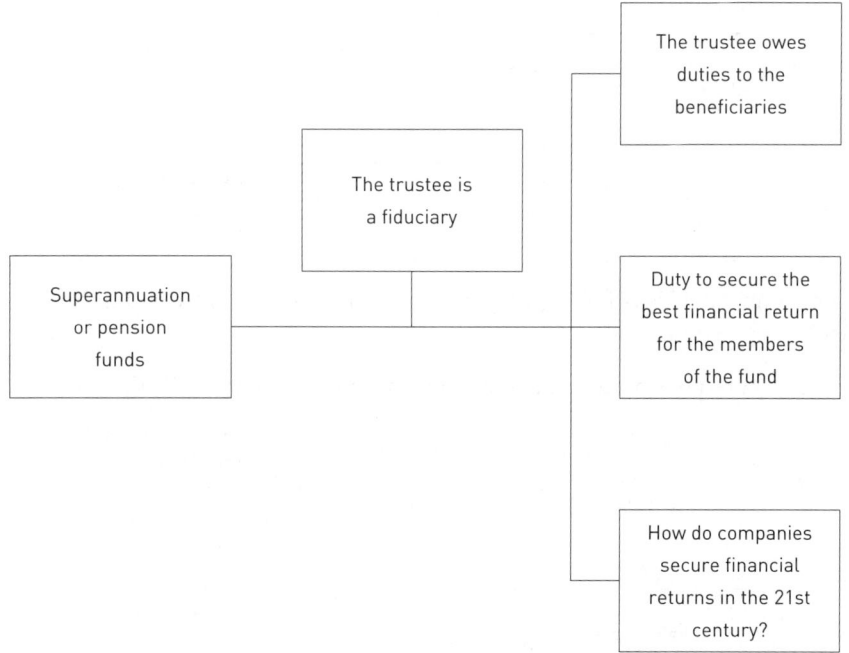

The evolving nature of trustee liability can be illustrated as shown in Fig 16.13.

FIGURE 16.13   Pension fund litigation involves, by necessity, long-term fund management decision making by the trustee

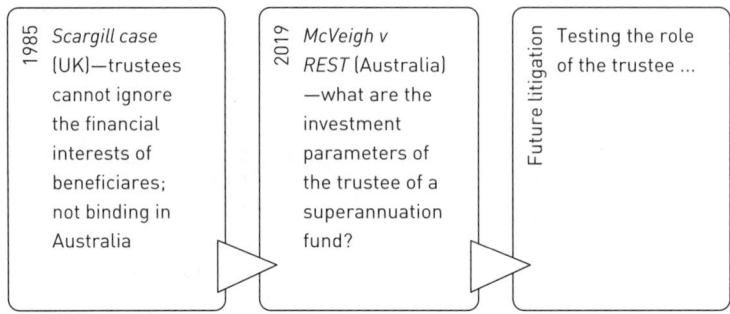

Law, regulations, and best practice

The risk assessment for corporations is increasingly complex. Legal and other issues form part of this matrix: see Fig 16.14.

FIGURE 16.14   The range of actors and issues driving the behaviour of corporations

Additional environmental risks for big corporations such as BHP and Rio Tinto can be visualised as shown in Fig 16.15.

FIGURE 16.15   The extra responsibilities of a multinational company such as BHP

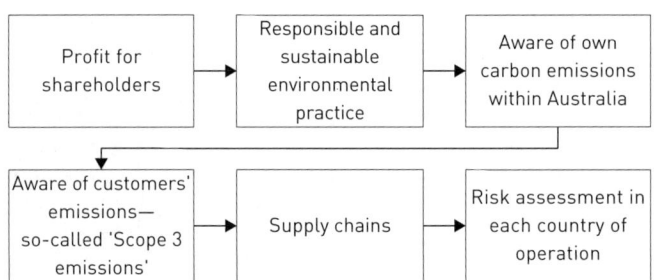

16.4 A BRIEF REVIEW OF THE UNIT OF STUDY: COMPANY LAW

The book has adopted a modular approach. This is because the topics naturally bracket or group themselves in pairs, and, in the case of shares and shareholdings, in triplicate. This is indicated in Fig 16.16.

FIGURE 16.16 *Corporations Law: Concepts, Cases and Culture* comprises eight modules

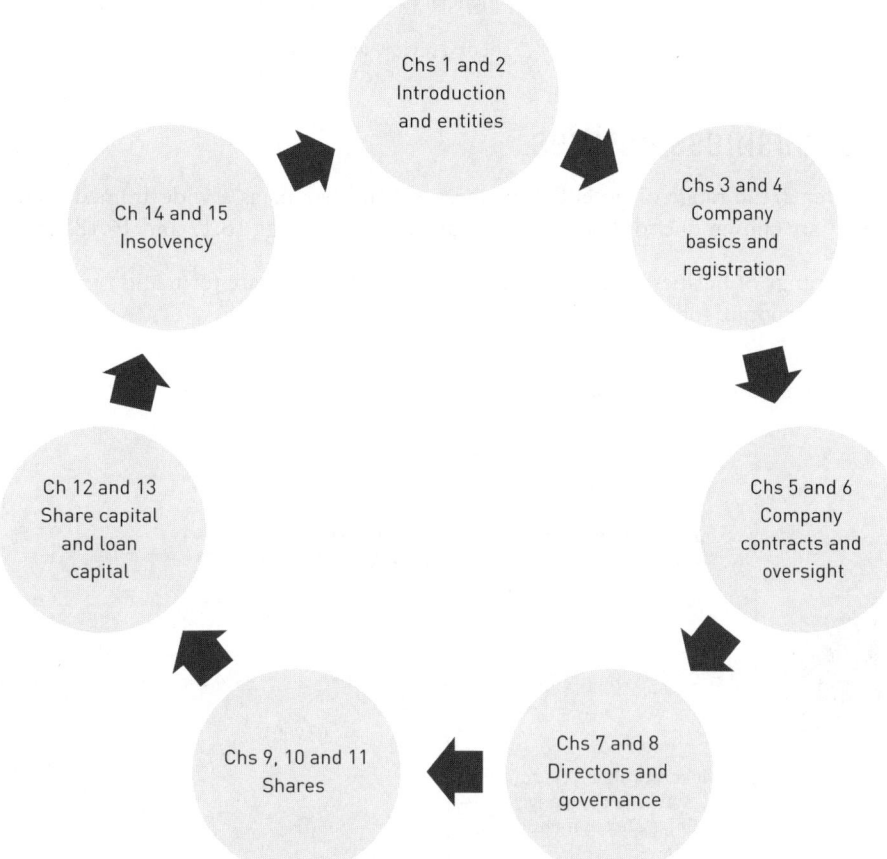

These modules can also be represented in tabular form, as set out below:

TABLE 16.1 An overview of the unit, taking a modular approach

Module	Chapters	Overview
1	1 and 2	Fundamentals History Choice of business entity and context
2	3 and 4	Company establishment, registration and rules
3	5 and 6	Company contracts and regulation
4	7 and 8	Directors

CORPORATIONS LAW: CONCEPTS, CASES AND CULTURE WORKBOOK

TABLE 16.1 An overview of the unit, taking a modular approach (continued)

Module	Chapters	Overview
5	9, 10 and 11	Shares, members and share capital
6	12 and 13	Corporate finance—forms of capital raising
7	14 and 15	Financial issues—from solvency to winding-up
8	16 and 17	Theory, review and reflection

The range of business entities

As noted in Chapter 2, the range of potential business entities begins as a wide-framed search. Invariably, Pty Ltd companies are chosen due to their practical advantages: see Figs 16.17 and 16.18.

FIGURE 16.17 The range of business entities divides between the corporate form and the non-corporate form

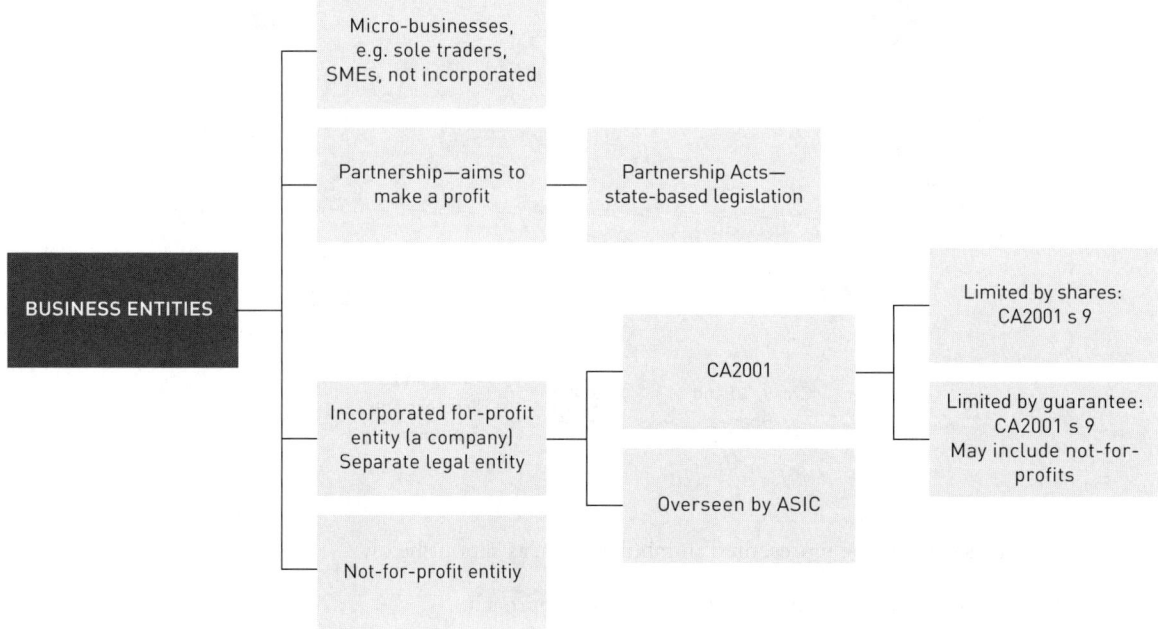

CHAPTER 16 CORPORATIONS AND THE CULTURAL CONTEXT

FIGURE 16.18 An overview of business entities

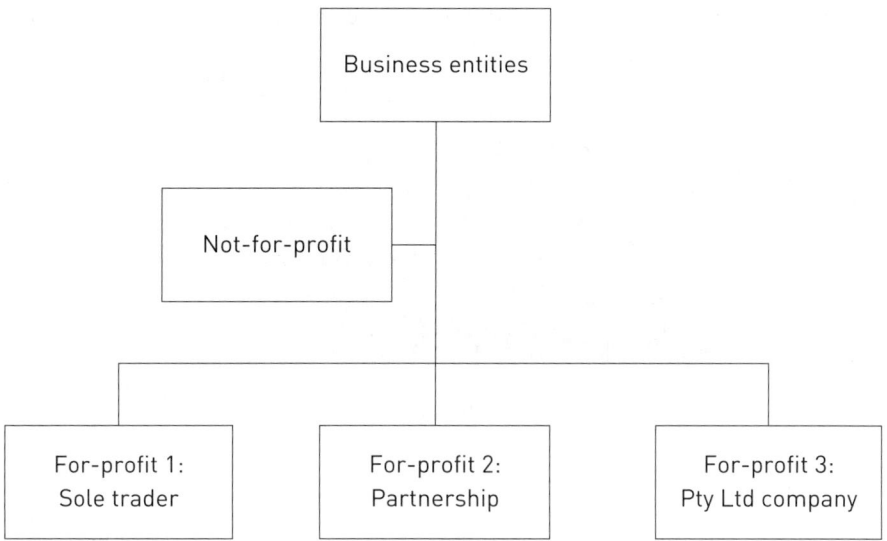

The range of organisational frames can be illustrated as shown in Fig 16.19.

FIGURE 16.19 Business entities by reference to profit and aims

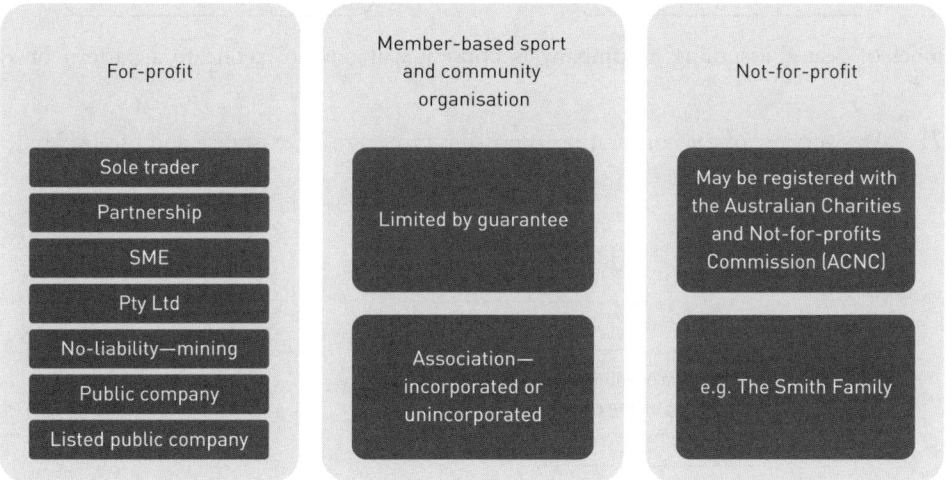

An alternative way of casting the distinctions is shown in Fig 16.20.

FIGURE 16.20   The range of business entities via form/structure and aims (profit or community)

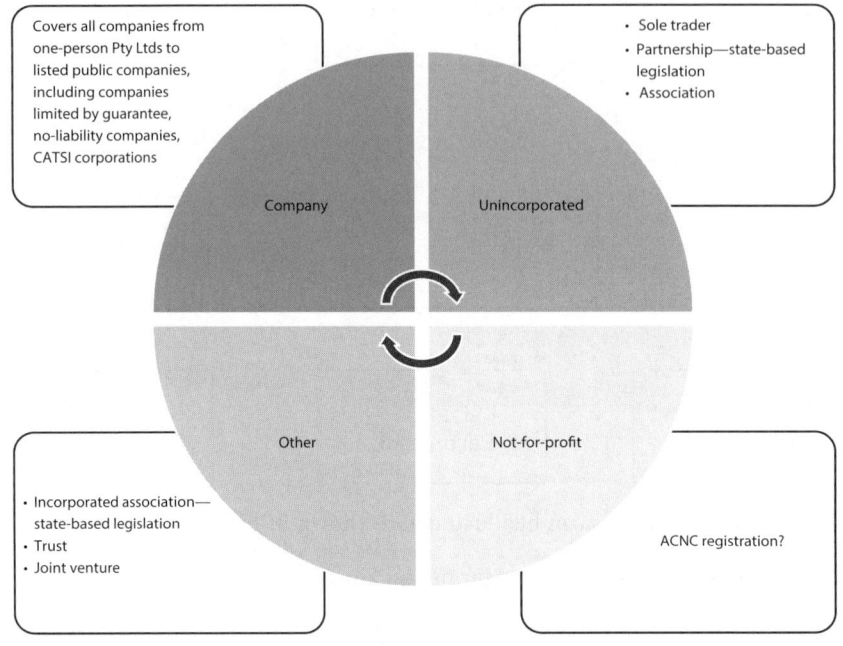

The funnel of issues, assuming a company is chosen, will tend to replicate a pattern or system: see Fig 16.21.

FIGURE 16.21   An overview of the corporation and issues typical to its existence and life-cycle

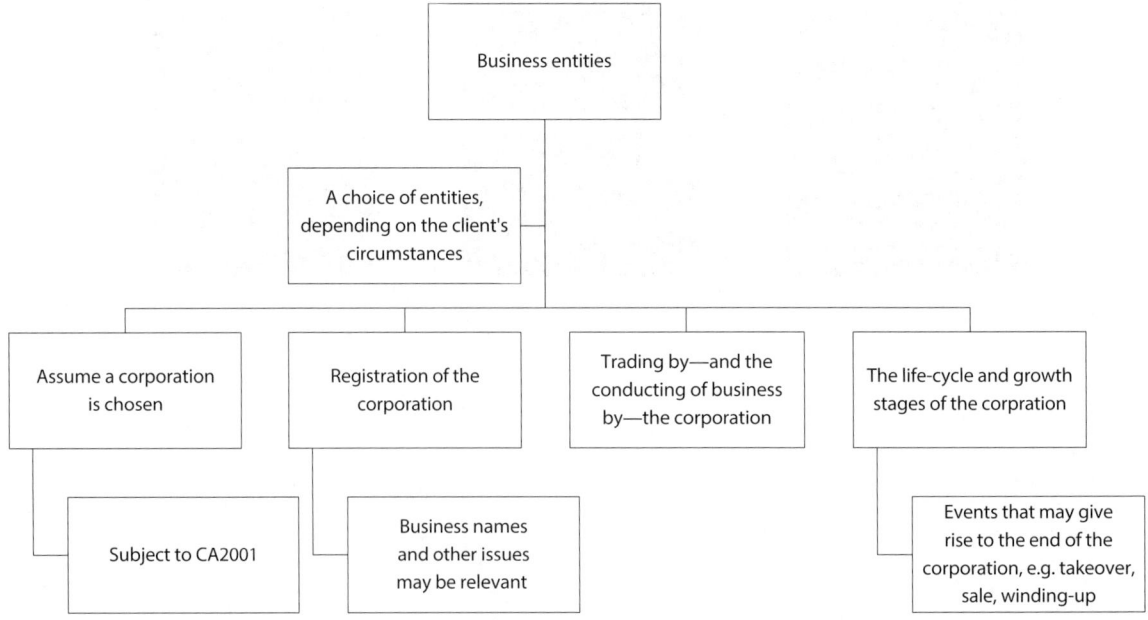

For-profit companies are essentially the same in terms of features. They are characterised by 'homogeneity' (sameness). The differences lie in terms of scale.

By contrast, not-for-profit (NFP) entities are characterised by 'heterogeneity' (difference), with a range of differences in terms of size and scale, structure, focus etc: see Fig 16.22.

FIGURE 16.22 The relatively wide range of NFPs

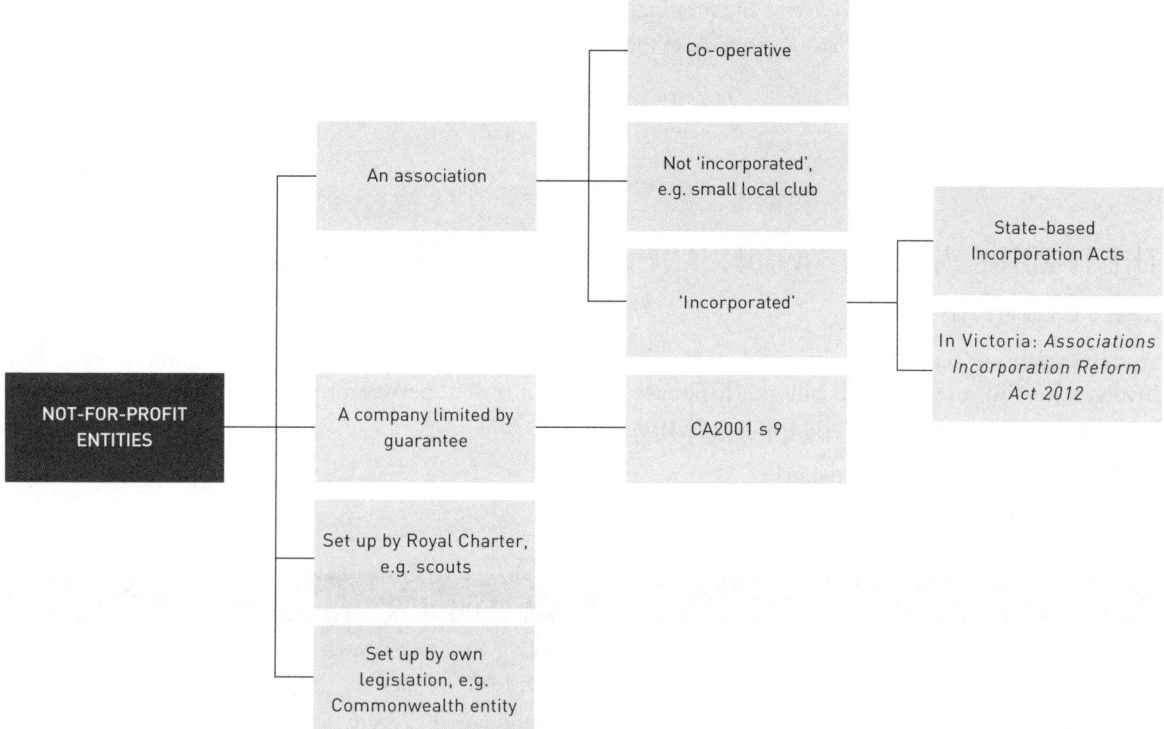

Elements of the timeline of a corporation

The timeline for setting up a business, if a corporation is chosen, involves the following components:

TABLE 16.2 The main time phases of a corporation

Pre-incorporation	Incorporation	The company is actively trading	The end game and deregistration
Range of potential entities For-profit entities Not-for-profit entities Choice of business entity Promoter— fiduciary Pre-incorporation contracts	Separate legal entity status Process lodgment with ASIC Share register Shares and members' rights Ratification of pre-incorporation contracts	See Table 16.3	Could be taken over Could merge with another entity Could experience financial difficulty 'Going concern'—administration Winding-up—liquidation

TABLE 16.2 The main time phases of a corporation (continued)

Pre-incorporation	Incorporation	The company is actively trading	The end game and deregistration
	Ongoing lodgments with ASIC Decisions and meetings Pierce the corporate veil		Liquidators' appointment Voidable transactions (in the previous 12 months) Preferences Insolvent trading Deregistration—the company no longer exists, as confirmed by ASIC

THE TRADING PHASE OF A COMPANY: COMPARING SMALL AND LARGE COMPANIES

As referred to in Table 16.2, the main phase for most companies will be their active trading period. This involves growing a profitable business. This phase can be contrasted between two broad types of companies:

- small- and medium-sized enterprises (SMEs), and
- larger public or listed companies.

TABLE 16.3 The additional layer of legal issues for larger companies

All companies	Larger companies only
Directors as fiduciaries and agents Directors' duties: • Act in best interests of the company • Competence • Honesty • Good faith • To disclose personal interests Transactions: company bound in contracts with third parties Membership Meetings Finances: • Members—share capital • Lenders—loan capital	Listing on the stock exchange ASX Listing Rules Continuous disclosure Market misconduct Takeovers ASIC policy dimensions Corporate governance and CSR

Liability issues in hybrid companies and firms

Unlimited companies and partnerships share the same feature—potential unlimited exposure to a member or partner respectively in the case of corporate or partnership debt.

FIGURE 16.23 The common feature of potential unlimited liability relevant to unlimited companies and partnerships

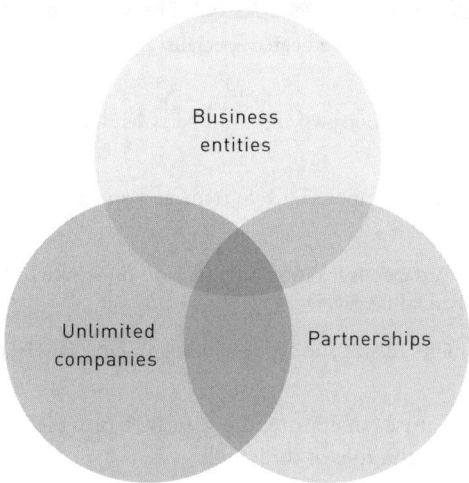

Companies: the advantages afforded to them as a form of business entity

Companies have been afforded a range of at least 15 distinct advantages over other potential business entities:

TABLE 16.4 The advantages for companies over other potential business entities

	Corporate advantage
1.	Can range from one member to many members; there is effectively no upper limit for a public company
2.	Are separate legal entities from Day 1 of their registration/incorporation
3.	Have the legal capacities of an adult individual without legal impairment
4.	Are provided with potential perpetual succession—they can theoretically outlive the current owners many times over
5.	Provide their owner/member/shareholders with limited liability (referenced to the amount unpaid on shares)
6.	Provide mechanisms for financial returns to members through dividend income and the capital appreciation of shares
7.	Provide mechanisms such that the shares can be transferred
8.	Have their official start date as per the certificate of registration
9.	Are given the imprimatur of state approval, or a 'licence to operate', as per the registration process (this forms the basis of the concession theory of the corporation, discussed in Chapter 16)
10.	Have automatic national reach under the CA2001

TABLE 16.4 The advantages for companies over other potential business entities (continued)

	Corporate advantage
11.	Enjoy the benefits of a dedicated specialist national regulator, ASIC, paid for by the Commonwealth
12.	Have the ability to borrow from third party lenders and the potential ability to raise share capital from members
13.	Have national geographic reach to trade and operate under uniform rules within the whole of Australia
14.	Have an advantageous taxation rate; the corporate rate of tax is less than the higher rates of tax for individual taxpayers
15.	Enjoy flexibility of size and type including micro-, family, public and listed companies

Given that corporations are creatures of statute, the CA2001 provides guidance on most of the material aspects of the corporation, including the role of directors:

TABLE 16.5 Directors—an overview of the main aspects of the role with the CA2001

Topic	CA2001 provisions	Notes
Definition of 'directors'	s 9 • appointed or not • shadow and de facto • executive vs non-executive	
Definition of 'officers'	s 9	
Powers	s 179	Includes general law/case law
Relevant replaceable rules	ss 198A–198D (ss 135 and 141)	
Roles	Agent of the company (as principal) Fiduciary to the company Employee of the company?	Typically deal with third parties on behalf of the company
Duties owed to whom?		Owed to the company—the members as a whole: *Percival v Wright* (1902)
Can directors owe a duty to a particular member?		Possibly, depends on facts and circumstances: see e.g. *Glavanics v Brunninghausen* (1996)
Negligence/competence	s 180 Defence in s 180(2) (business judgment rule)	See *ASIC v Healey* (2011)
Honesty/fiduciary	ss 181–183: civil obligations s 184: criminal offences	

CHAPTER 16 CORPORATIONS AND THE CULTURAL CONTEXT

Topic	CA2001 provisions	Notes
Disclosure	s 191 Voting/attendance: • s 194: Pty Ltd • s 195: public company	
Solvency	s 588G s 254T	Legislative removal of the corporate veil
Appointment and qualifications	s 201	Need to be 18
Removal	s 203	By a majority vote of directors
Banned or disqualified from being a director	s 206	ASIC has power to disqualify

Legal methodologies

We can discern several strands of legal method, ranging from those most relevant to law students to those most relevant to judges.

FIGURE 16.24   There are at least four discernible strands to the legal methodology paradigm

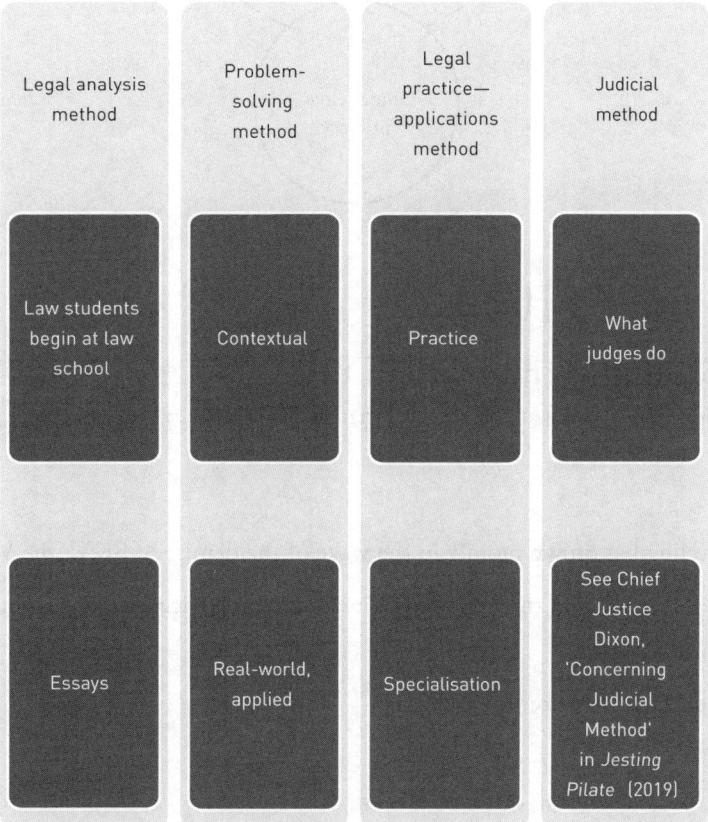

WORKBOOK CHAPTER 16 REVIEW

An illustrative summary of the key points

FIGURE 16.25   The evolving context of the corporation

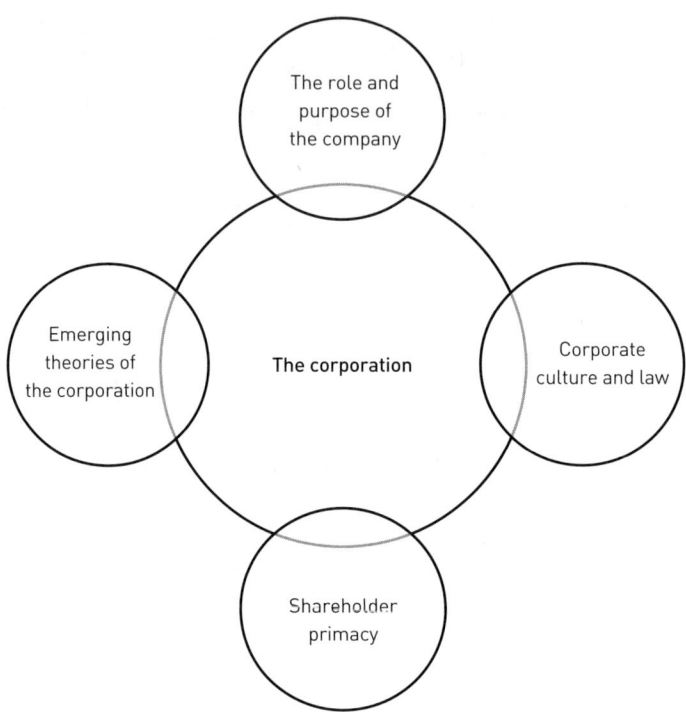

FOLLOW-UP CASE STUDIES

FOLLOW-UP CASE STUDY 1: HOMESMART RECYCLING

Refer to the foundational case study at the end of Chapter 5.

FURTHER FACTS

1. HomeSmart Recycling has grown rapidly in the wake of the demise of SKM, the Victorian recycler.
2. Jacqui has left the company, and the remaining directors want advice on a non-competition clause that they would like Jacqui to sign.
3. HomeSmart is seeking a listing on the ASX.

REQUIRED

The directors of HomeSmart would like a memorandum of advice as regards the issues above.

The memorandum is written by you in your capacity as a legal trainee, and addressed to your supervisor Jo Delaney, Lawyer.

It should contain comprehensive advice on the legal and related matters pertinent to the issues referred to above.

NOTES

This intermediate assignment covers the following Chapters:
- Chapter 8 (directors' duties)
- Chapter 7 (corporate governance principles)
- Chapter 12 (initial public offerings, public disclosure documents).

You will need to conduct research on:
- what happened to SKM, and why
- what is required to list a company on the ASX.

To: (recipient)
From: (trainee)
Subject matter/heading:
Feel free to use subheadings and navigation guides for the reader

FOLLOW-UP CASE STUDY 2: FINE ART FACTORY

Refer to the foundational case study at the end of Chapter 5.

FURTHER FACTS:

1. Fine Art Factory is a bespoke business, and has been successful in its niche market segment, but has struggled with traditional sources of finance.

2. Fine Art Factory has loyal customers, and seeks crowd-sourced funds (CSFs). It wants to have people own percentage shares in physical assets, such as paintings and sculptures.

3. Fine Art Factory's former managing director, Glen, has left the business. He is belatedly claiming 30 per cent of the profits, even though he was on a salary and not paid commission.

REQUIRED

The directors of Fine Art Factory would like a memorandum of advice as regards the issues above.

The memorandum is written by you in your capacity as a legal trainee, and addressed to your supervisor Jo Delaney, Lawyer.

It should contain comprehensive advice on the legal and related matters pertinent to the issues referred to above.

NOTES

This intermediate assignment covers the following Chapters:
- Chapter 7 (regarding the claims of the managing director)
- Chapter 8 (the role of the directors in dealing with a fellow director)
- Chapter 9 (shares)
- Chapter 12 (CSF).

You will need to conduct research on:
- What is a security? Is art capable of being a security?

To: (recipient)
From: (trainee)
Subject matter/heading:
Feel free to use subheadings and navigation guides for the reader

FOLLOW-UP CASE STUDY 3: SEAFOOD BOUNTY CAFÉ
Refer to the foundational case study at the end of Chapter 5.

FURTHER FACTS

1. Seafood Bounty Café has converted from a Pty Ltd to a public company.
2. Seafood Bounty Café has borrowed heavily on a debenture and brought in new management.
3. Seafood Bounty Café is under pressure financially, and is then hit by a scandal—it is reported to be underpaying its staff.

REQUIRED

The directors of Seafood Bounty Café would like a memorandum of advice as regards the following issues:

- What is involved if Seafood Bounty Café goes into voluntary administration?
- What is involved if Seafood Bounty Café then goes into compulsory liquidation?
- Are the directors personally liable for the debts of the company?

The memorandum is written by you in your capacity as a legal trainee, and addressed to your supervisor Jo Delaney, Lawyer.

It should contain comprehensive advice on the legal and related matters pertinent to the issues referred to above.

NOTES

This intermediate assignment covers the following Chapters:

- Chapter 8 (directors' duties and potential legal exposure)
- Chapter 13 (debentures and receivership)
- Chapter 14 ('going concern' questions and the role of the board)
- Chapter 15 (winding-up).

You will need to conduct research on:

- the two well-known restaurant chains, Rockpool (Neil Perry) and George Calombaris' restaurants.

To: (recipient)
From: (trainee)
Subject matter/heading:
Feel free to use subheadings and navigation guides for the reader

CHAPTER 17

LEGAL SKILLS AND LAW IN THE 21ST CENTURY

Chapter synopsis and links to Textbook Chapter 17

This Workbook Chapter deals with four topics:

- 17.1 An overview of legal skills
- 17.2 Developing a toolkit for legal analysis
- 17.3 Law, career planning and life-long learning
- 17.4 Law in the 21st century.

Each of these topics is constructively aligned with, and linked to, the same topics in Chapter 17 of the Textbook.

Chapter executive summary

This Chapter examines some of the key issues facing the law in the 21st century:

- the toolkit of legal skills that are pervasive in the ways of legal thinking and analysis
- the evolution and adaptability of legal careers in the evolving economic paradigm; this includes the rapidly emerging nature of what a sustainable economy and society look like, and
- the evolving nature of law in the increasingly complex social and economic environment.

CHAPTER DIAGRAMMATIC OVERVIEW

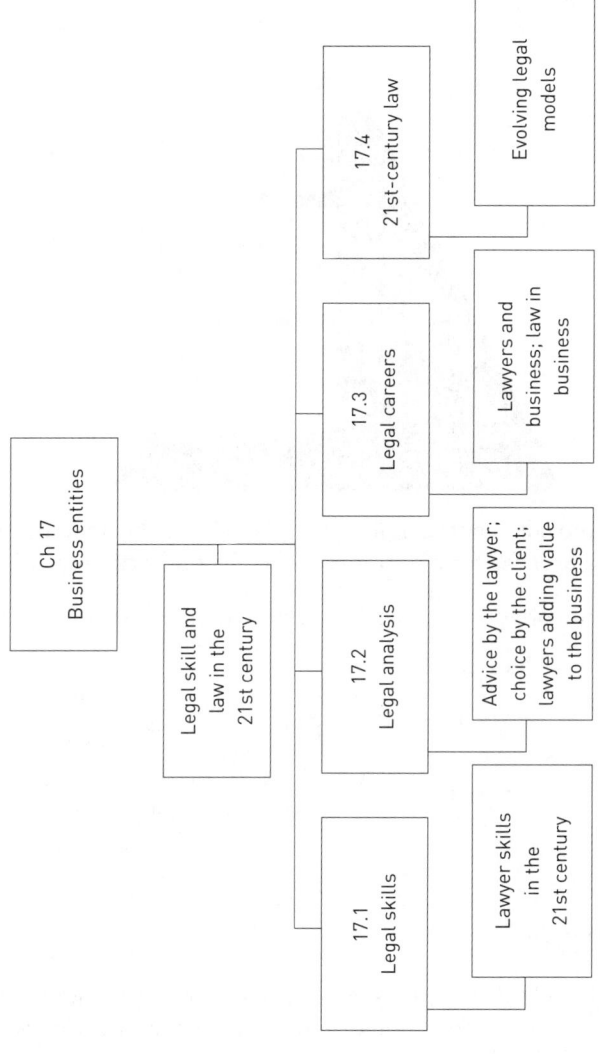

FIGURE 17.1 An overview of Chapter 17

17.1 AN OVERVIEW OF LEGAL SKILLS

There is a 'hierarchy of veracity' in law, which invariably places documents/writing ahead of oral matters/testimony: see Fig 17.2. Several important consequences flow from this hierarchy. For example, items that have been confirmed between the parties in writing are generally pre-eminent, at least initially, as a form of evidence in court. This will depend on other relevant facts and circumstances particular to the case, but this implicit assumption applies at the outset.

FIGURE 17.2 The 'hierarchy of veracity'

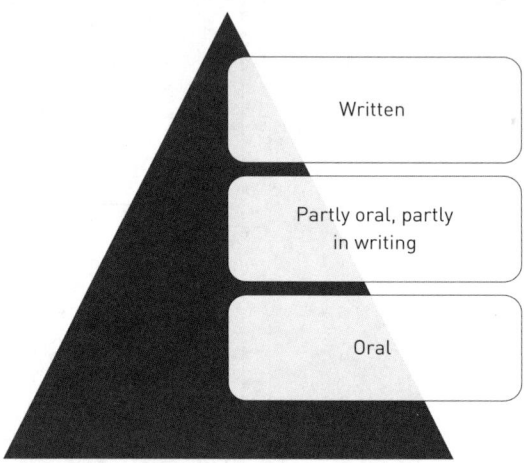

Form versus substance provides another point of legal analysis. The underlying character or substance of a matter is usually preferred over the form or titles assumed by the parties: see Fig 17.3.

FIGURE 17.3 Substance is important in the legal characterisation of issues

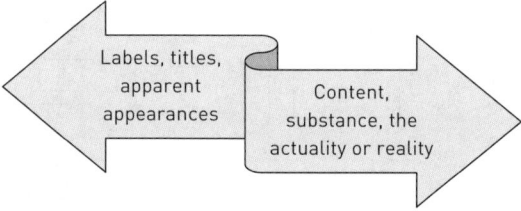

Hohfeld's correlatives

US legal scholar Wesley Hohfeld devised a system of pairs of concepts. There were two forms—first, those concepts that were opposite to one another; and second, those concepts that were relational, forming two component parts of a legal relationship.

FIGURE 17.4 The so-called 'jural opposites' developed by Wesley Hohfeld

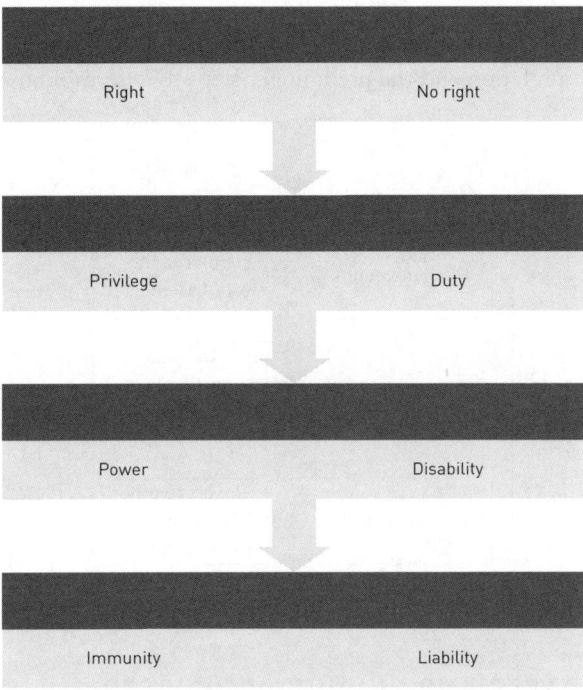

FIGURE 17.5 The so-called 'jural correlatives', also systematised by Wesley Hohfeld

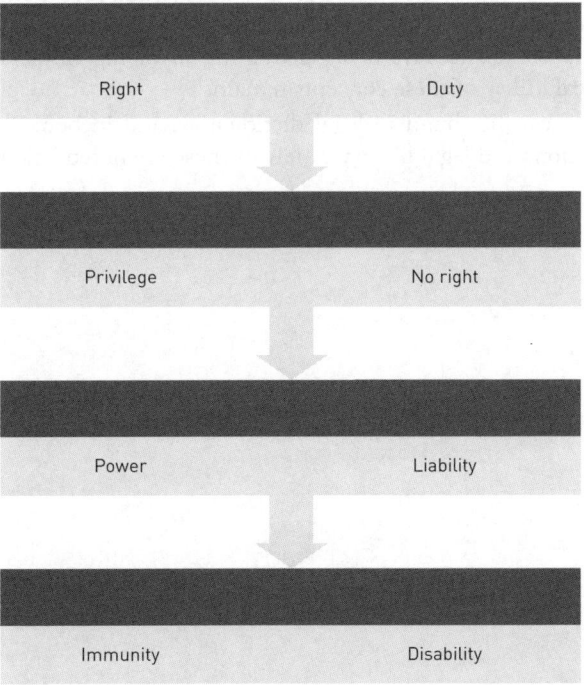

Statutory interpretation

The preliminary steps to determining the meaning of a statutory provision can be visualised as shown in Fig 17.6.

FIGURE 17.6   Statutory interpretation and the preliminary steps to determining meaning

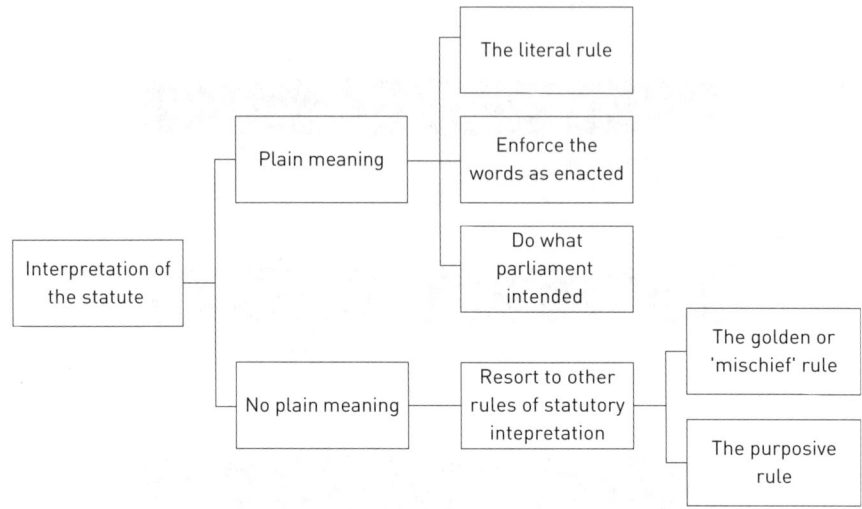

SOME KEY LEGAL PHRASES AND GUIDING PRINCIPLES

Latin is an originary language of law in England, given the symbiotic influence of ecclesiastical and religious orders. The law in English is only five centuries old or thereabouts, and rose alongside the printing press and improved literacy. Latin precepts and maxims, therefore, have been important in the development of English and, by extension, Australian law. The days of legal training involving immersion in Latin maxims have disappeared, but the practical utility of these concepts remains.

Maxims and expressions can be found in legal dictionaries, and in books on topics such as statutory interpretation, legal foundations and legal history. A few of these are noted below:

- *ad idem*
- *contra proferentum*
- *ejusdem generis*
- *moot*
- *noscitur a sociis*
- *obiter dictum*
- *primus inter pares*
- *pro bono*
- *quid pro quo*
- *ratio decidendi*
- *stare decisis*
- *sui juris*
- *sui generis.*

LEGAL WRITING AND PINPOINT REFERENCING

Legal communication is generally exacting. Just as the matters raised in a courtroom are not free-flowing discussions or conversations, but means of communication conducted by reference to carefully proscribed and comprehensive rules of evidence, so too is any piece of legal communication—commencing with written work typically completed as part of legal studies. These include:

- essays (typically up to 2,000 words) and Honours dissertations (typically up to 10,000 words)
- contextual advice items, such as file notes, memoranda to clients, and letters to clients (generally on non-litigious matters)
- contextual litigious matters, such as advices, draft pleadings and so forth, including those forming part of moots.

These three broad categories of written communication be visualised as shown in Fig 17.7.

FIGURE 17.7   The typical range of legal writing by law students

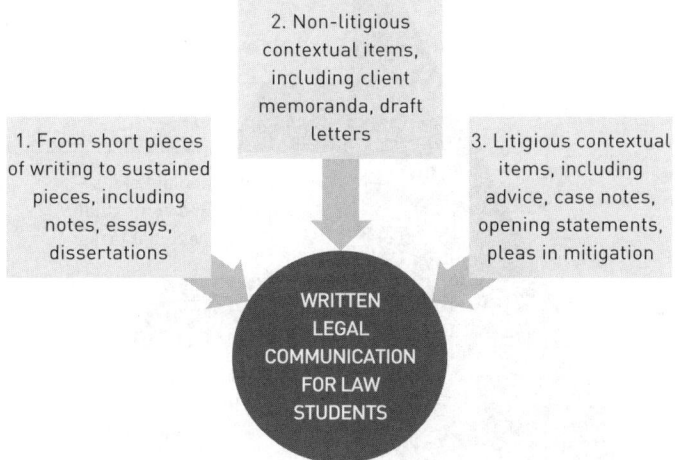

Each piece of writing can be broken down into its component elements or parts as follows:

TABLE 17.1   The common elements of different types of legal writing

Item	Parameters
Legal issues	Identify the core and ancillary issues
Answer and generic source	What is the broad answer?
Pinpoint references	What are the particular sources of law giving rise to the broad answer?
Academic approach, e.g. essay, dissertation	What is the context and purpose of the writing?
Legal/professional practice, e.g. legal transactions, litigious events	What are the current issues? What are the evolving issues?
Notes and guidance	What matters require follow-up?

17.2 DEVELOPING A TOOLKIT FOR LEGAL ANALYSIS

We could argue that the nature of law is inherently 'hierarchical' or ordered. There are numerous instances of this phenomenon. For example:

- the court system, with appellate or apex courts sitting at the top of the process
- the use and application of binding precedent
- sources of law and the supremacy of statute.

It is no coincidence, therefore, that the development of legal skills aligns with this approach. In very broad terms, we can identify three types of skills within the legal context: see Fig 17.8.

FIGURE 17.8 The hierarchy of legal skills

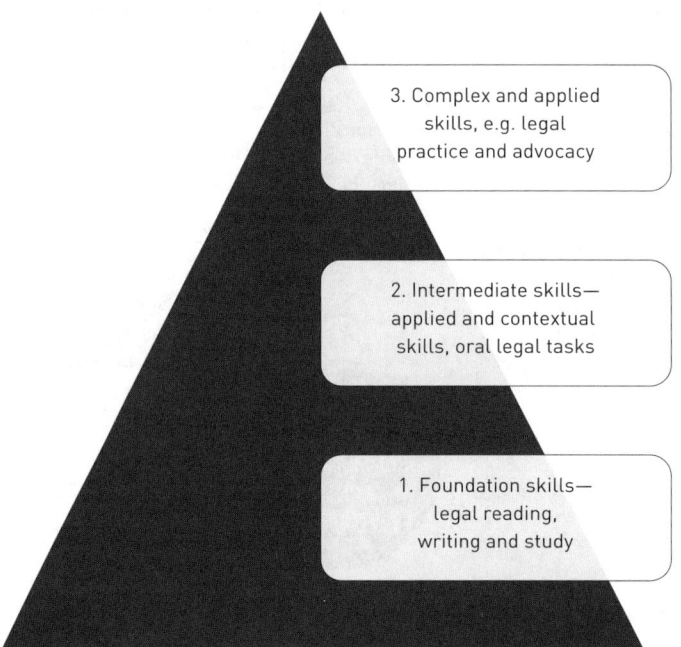

Legal study is typically followed by legal careers with certain elements. These can be described by way of a timeline:

TABLE 17.2 Law studies and post studies—a basic overview of the development of legal skills

	Law student	Practical Legal Training	First-year practice	Admission	Specialisation—work as a solicitor in private or public settings	The Bar
Key skills development relevant to this part of the timeline:	Introduction to the law	Practice-ready skills	Practice and learning on the job	A public officer of the court	Solicitor—full range of relevant applied and contextual skills	Advocacy

17.3 LAW, CAREER PLANNING AND LIFE-LONG LEARNING

There are many books and much advice on career planning.

In law, the basic binary between the solicitor and barrister is still relevant, and provides an interesting dynamic for those graduates seeking to use their legal degree within the ambit of the legal profession.

The oft-quoted figure is that about 50 per cent of law graduates go into legal careers, and 50 per cent into a diverse range of other career destinations: see Fig 17.9.

FIGURE 17.9   The broad range of potential career destinations for law graduates

Specialisation and transferable skills

Legal careers involve building a suite of skills. Transferability of skills and life-long learning are inherent to these tasks. The various skill and learning acquisition points can be set out as follows:

- LLB
- Honours
- Masters
- PhD
- Practical Legal Training
- in-law firm training
- admission to the legal profession
- specialisation in a particular area of legal practice; further qualifications
- law firms—solicitor, associate, partner, consultant
- a wide range of career options, including public (e.g. government, legal aid, community legal service) and private dimensions (in-house)
- the Bar

- the Senior Bar
- judiciary
- appellate judiciary.

SO-CALLED 'HARD' AND 'SOFT' SKILLS

The phases above are inextricably linked in terms of skills, both 'hard' and 'soft'.

Hard skills are traditionally around content and knowledge. Soft skills are perhaps more amorphous, but just as critical. There is an increasing literature on soft skills, which in the legal context include:

- listening
- empathy
- communication
- understanding the client's viewpoint
- persuasion.

TIME MANAGEMENT

Time management is another vital legal skill:

- Brevity, or concision, is generally a uniting factor in each of the career facets in corporate and commercial law.
- Brevity goes variously to relevance, costs for the client, and focus on the task at hand (these skills may well vary for other legal tasks or areas of the law).
- Time management skills are essential to the professional, whether a person has:
  - oversight of several non-litigious files, or
  - management of many litigious files.
- There will be deadlines to meet. Such deadlines emanate from several sources, including:
  - the client
  - the court, and
  - third parties, such as ASIC.

Again, there are numerous articles and books on the topic of time management.

Lawyers need to meet a double set of co-ordinates:

- first, to deliver a service that meets the client's interests and the legal standard, subject to the point below, and
- second, and fundamentally, to always uphold their duties as public officers of the court.

A system of effective time management is inevitably part of this dual responsibility.

Professional time management can be seen on a day-to-day basis. It requires a good diary system. As such, it distinguishes between three types of matters: see Fig 17.10.

FIGURE 17.10 The three types of day-to-day time management

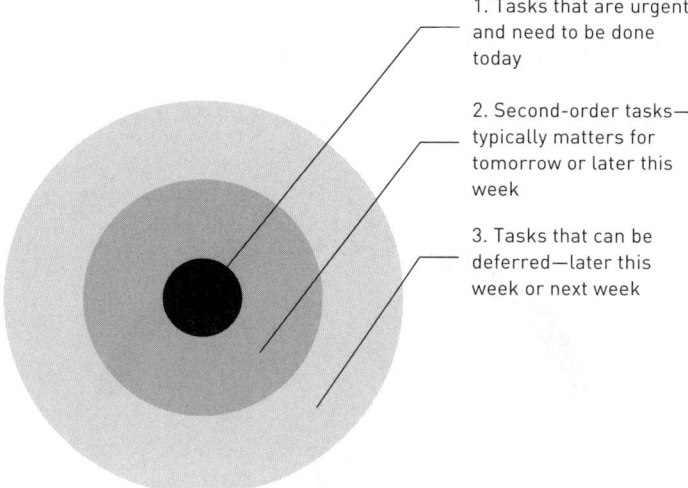

1. Tasks that are urgent and need to be done today
2. Second-order tasks—typically matters for tomorrow or later this week
3. Tasks that can be deferred—later this week or next week

17.4 LAW IN THE 21ST CENTURY

Emerging issues: technology, corporations and the law

There are many books and articles on the future of the legal profession. They contain numerous predictions about the future of lawyering. What we can observe with some certainty is that the context for legal services is changing rapidly: see Fig 17.11.

FIGURE 17.11 Law and emerging issues

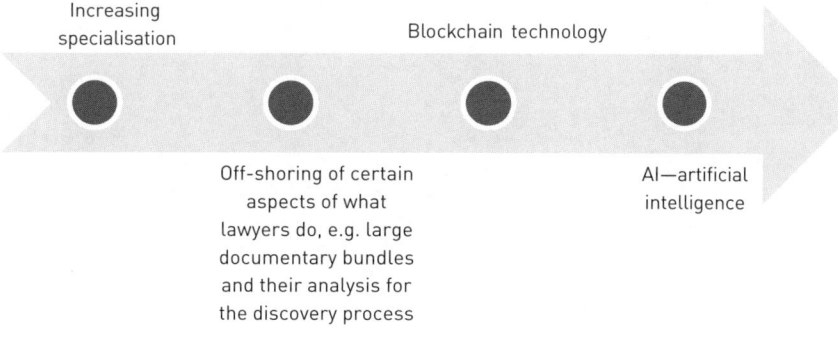

Increasing specialisation

Off-shoring of certain aspects of what lawyers do, e.g. large documentary bundles and their analysis for the discovery process

Blockchain technology

AI—artificial intelligence

WORKBOOK CHAPTER 17 REVIEW

An illustrative summary of the key points

FIGURE 17.12 This diagram contextualises corporate law and the role of the lawyer in the 21st century

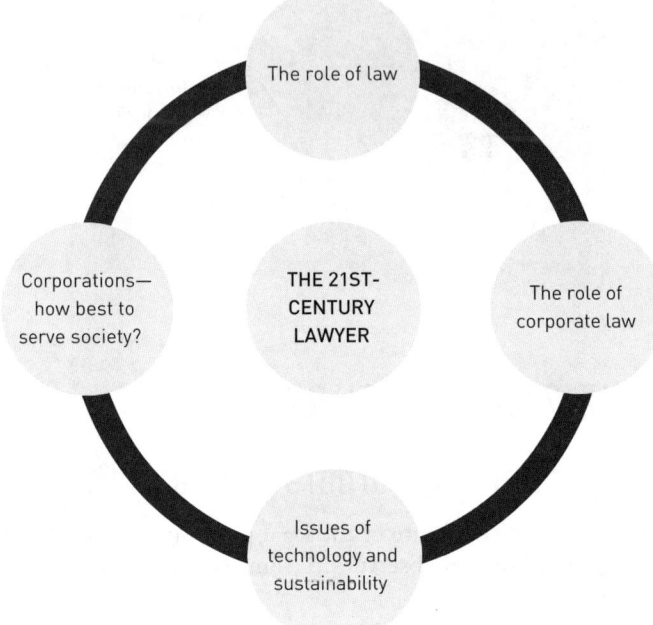

CHAPTER 18

REVISION ACTIVITY ANSWERS

CHAPTER 1 REVISION ACTIVITY ANSWERS

TRUE OR FALSE?

1. **False.** There can be one-person companies
2. **False.** Pty Ltd companies need only one director
3. **False.** Section 51(xx) does not give the Commonwealth power over corporations
4. **True.** The Act is at the gift of the co-operative scheme with state and territory approval
5. **False.** The general law is still important, particularly as it elucidates the meaning of provisions in the CA2001

FILL IN THE GAPS

1. s 51(xx)
2. 1909
3. *Huddart, Parker v Moorehead*
4. literal
5. purposive
6. 1958

MULTIPLE CHOICE

Q1 a	Australian Securities and Investments Commission
Q2 b	The states could not confer state jurisdiction on Commonwealth courts
Q3 b	The Commonwealth did not have the power to provide for the incorporation of companies
Q4 d	For the Commonwealth to seek the cooperation of the states and to establish the Corporations Law scheme
Q5 c	Council of Australian Governments

SHORT ANSWER QUESTIONS

1. **What is the difference between a company and a corporation?**

   Company—is effectively the same as a corporation. It is a separate legal entity registered with ASIC (the Australian Securities and Investments Commission); note the Priestley 11 unit used the title 'Company Law' in 1992; by 2001 the term 'corporation' had become more common, hence the name of the Commonwealth Act.

   Corporation—is effectively the same as a company, and the terms are co-extensive. However, s 57A(1)(a) of the CA2001 provides that 'Subject to this section, in this Act, *corporation* includes: (a) a company', so for the purposes of the CA2001, the term 'corporation' is the broader of the two.

2. **What does s 51 of the Australian Constitution provide for?**

   Enumerated powers conferring specific power on the Federal Parliament.

3. **What does s 51(xx) specifically address?**

   Section 51(xx) addresses 'foreign corporations, and trading or financial corporations formed within the limits of the Commonwealth'.

4. **What effect did the High Court's narrow interpretation of s 51(xx) have on the powers of the Commonwealth in relation to making laws in respect of corporations?**

   The High Court's narrow interpretation had the effect of denying the Commonwealth the power to make laws with regard to companies. The Commonwealth had only limited jurisdiction to make laws with respect to companies—this was historically a state matter.

   From the 1960s, the Commonwealth and the states sought to enter into various agreements, aiming to achieve greater uniformity in company regulation.

5. **What effect did the *Uniform Companies Act 1961* (Cth) have?**

   The *Uniform Companies Act 1961* (Cth) aimed to achieve uniform legislation throughout the country, and was largely successful. This uniformity was shortlived, however. This was because, over time, some states adopted amendments to the Act while others did not, leading to differences between the jurisdictions.

6. **What was the High Court's position as regards the corporations law power in the Australian Constitution as enunciated in *New South Wales v Commonwealth* ('*Incorporation case*') (1990)?**

   In the *Incorporation case*, the High Court held that the Commonwealth did not have power under s 51(xx) to pass laws regarding the incorporation of trading and financial corporations. Therefore, the Commonwealth did not have the power to take over corporate regulation.

7. **What important decision/agreement occurred in the year 2000 between the states and the Northern Territory regarding corporations law in Australia?**

   In order to resolve the constitutional crisis, the states and the Northern Territory came to an agreement in principle to the substance of the Corporations Law scheme. The states and the Northern Territory also agreed to refer to the Commonwealth the powers to carry out the scheme.

Higher order thinking activities

TOPIC A

THE HISTORY OF AUSTRALIAN CORPORATIONS LAW HAS BEEN LARGELY FOCUSED ON ISSUES OF CONSTITUTIONAL POWER. DISCUSS.

Relevant points include the following:

- Section 51(xx) of the Constitution does not provide a power for the Commonwealth to oversee the regulation of companies formed after 1901.

- The arrangements put in place to deal with this gap were subject to successful High Court challenge until the end of the 20th century.

- Only when the states, territories and the Commonwealth provided series of interlocking statutes, which commenced in 2001 with the CA2001, did the arrangement have constitutional validity.

- Challenges on the basis of constitutional invalidity commenced with *Huddart Parker* in 1909 and went right up until *Wakim's case* in 1999.

- There is a case to be made that the first century of the Australian Commonwealth, from 1901 to 2001, was therefore as much about the constitutional arrangements for companies as it was about commercial and regulatory oversight.

TOPIC B

DOES CORPORATIONS LAW NECESSARILY HAVE TO CHOOSE BETWEEN THE INTERESTS OF SHAREHOLDERS, CUSTOMERS AND EMPLOYEES? DISCUSS.

This discussion can concentrate on models of the corporation and of corporate law.

Shareholder primacy focuses largely on shareholder returns. In this model, the interests of shareholders are paramount.

Stakeholder models can more readily incorporate a wider array of interested parties, including employees and customers.

These are both theoretical models on a continuum. In reality, a nation's corporations law may demonstrate aspects of each model.

In Australia, for example, corporate law is characterised as largely based on the Anglo-American model of shareholder primacy. However, there are clear examples in the CA2001 that give particular rights to employees; see, for example, Pt 5.8A ('Employment entitlements') of Ch 5 ('External administration'). Indeed, a search of the sections and provision headings of the CA2001 shows that the term 'employee' is specified 27 times.

Further, we can see that systems change over time; for example, the UK *Companies Act 2006* specifically provides in s 172 that directors must take into account a range of factors and stakeholders, including employees and customers.

We can conclude that national systems differ, and that they change over time. Furthermore, they can accommodate taking into account several stakeholders. This is an evolving area of corporate law and governance.

CHAPTER 2 REVISION ACTIVITY ANSWERS

TRUE OR FALSE?

1. **False.** Unlike the company, the partnership is not a separate legal entity
2. **True.** The term 'business' is a wide, generic term
3. **True.** See the relevant state or territory Partnership Act
4. **False.** Partnerships can exist informally, and without writing
5. **False.** The business owner and the business are the same legal entity
6. **False.** The CA2001 refers to the general law as a relevant and legitimate source of locating and interpreting corporate law

FILL IN THE GAPS

1. a profit
2. three; two
3. joint ventures
4. 400
5. notice to the other partners
6. the UK *Partnership Act 1890*

MULTIPLE CHOICE

Q1 c	Joint and several
Q2 d	Not transferable
Q3 a	Limited by guarantee
Q4 b	Limited
Q5 b	An association
Q6 d	Number over 2 million and make up 50 per cent of the workforce

SHORT ANSWER QUESTIONS

1. **What is a business organisation?**

   'A business organisation is an individual or group of people who collaborate to achieve certain commercial goals' (scribd.com).

2. **What are the main forms of business other than a compamy?**

   The main forms of business other than a company are sole trader, partnership, trust, unincorporated not-for-profit association, and unincorporated joint venture.

3. **What is a sole trader?**

    A sole trader business structure is a person trading as the individual legally responsible for all aspects of the business. This includes any debts and losses, which can't be shared with others. This is the simplest, and relatively inexpensive business structure you can choose when starting a business in Australia. As a sole trader, you'll generally make all the decisions about starting and running your business, although you can employ people to help you.

    Department of Industry, Innovation and Science

4. **What is a partnership?**

    A partnership is a business structure that involves a number of people who carry on a business together. You may choose a partnership over a sole trader structure for example, if you'll be jointly running the business with another person or a number of people (up to 20). There are two types of partnerships—general and limited.

    www.jrcorporate.com.au

    Partnerships are governed by the Partnership Act in the relevant state or territory.

5. **How is a partnership established?**

    Answers may include the following:

    - A partnerhip is fairly easy and cost-effective to set up. The partnership needs to have a separate Tax File Number (TFN), and must file a tax return with the ATO (even though it is not a separate legal entity). The partners pay tax on their individual shares of the income. The purpose of the partnership return is to enable the ATO to correlate the amount of tax owed by individuals to the gross amount specified in the partnership return.
    - If you are carrying on an enterprise, you can apply for an Australian Business Number (ABN), but this is not compulsory.
    - It is not a separate entity—like a sole trader, you and your business partners are usually each personally liable for the debts of the business.
    - You usually have shared control and management of the business with your partners. Note that these matters should be specified in a partnership agreement; if not, they will be determined by reference to the relevant Partnership Act of the state or territory in which the firm is established.
    - Each partner is responsible for their own superannuation arrangements—you are not an employee of the partnership.
    - You must be registered for GST if the annual income turnover is $75,000 or more.

6. **What is a trust and how does it operate?**

    A trust is a private legal arrangement where the ownership of someone's assets (which might include property, shares or cash) is transferred to someone else (usually, in practice, not just one person, but a small group of people or a trust company) to look after and use to benefit a third person (or group of people).

    Types of trusts include: express; constructive; resulting; charitable; and cy-pres.

7. **What are the main types of corporation chosen to conduct a business seeking to make a profit?**

    A Pty Ltd; a public company; and a publicly listed company.

ANSWERS

Higher order thinking activities

TOPIC A

WHAT LIABILITY ATTACHES TO A PARTNERSHIP?

In a general partnership:

> all partners are equally responsible for the management of the business, and each has unlimited liability for the debts and obligations it may incur.
>
> *www.business.vic.gov.au*

In a limited partnership:

> the liability of one or more partners for the debts and obligations of the business is limited. A limited partnership consists of one or more general partners (whose liability is unlimited) and one or more limited partners (whose liability is limited in proportion to their investment). There is no maximum number of limited partners.
>
> *www.business.vic.gov.au*

TOPIC B

HOW IS PROPERTY—BOTH PERSONAL AND REAL—TREATED IN PARTNERSHIPS?

> Whether the property of a partner becomes partnership property depends on the agreement of the parties. Failing any clear agreement between the parties, the acts and intention of the parties will ultimately determine whether property owned by a partner becomes partnership property.
>
> … Generally, all assets brought into the partnership or which are afterwards acquired on account of the partnership will be partnership property. This proposition is stated in, for example, *Partnership Act 1958* (Vic) s 24.
>
> *www.butlers.com.au*

TOPIC C

HOW DO YOU TERMINATE/DISSOLVE A PARTNERSHIP IN VICTORIA?

Under Pt 2 Div 4 of the *Partnership Act 1958* (Vic) ('Dissolution of partnership') sets out the ways in which a partnership can be dissolved. These include:

- the partnership term as stated in the formal partnership agreement expires
- one partner gives written notice to the other partners to exit the partnership
- one or more partners can no longer legally own a business
- a court issues a court order to dissolve the business
- a partner becomes bankrupt
- one of the partners dies
- the business is bankrupt or insolvent.

www.business.gov.au

If the partnership is a limited partnership, there are three ways in which it can end:

1. It can be changed from a limited partnership to a partnership in which all partners have an equal share in the management and liabilities. A limited partnership will end if it has no limited partners. All the partners must agree to the change from a limited partnership.

2. It can be dissolved:

    Subject to the terms of the partnership agreement, there are certain restrictions when dissolving a limited partnership.

    A limited partner cannot dissolve a limited partnership by issuing a notice on their own. The general partner(s)—or the other limited partner(s)—cannot dissolve a limited partnership on the basis that the limited partner:

    - has allowed their share of the partnership property to be used as collateral (charged for) debts outside of the partnership
    - has died
    - has become bankrupt
    - has retired
    - is a body corporate and has become dissolved.

    www.business.vic.gov.au

3. It can be wound up.

    You must notify Consumer Affairs Victoria (CAV), using the required form, within seven days of the limited partnership ending.

TOPIC D

PROVIDE AN ANALYSIS OF THE MAIN DIFFERENCES BETWEEN ASSOCIATIONS—INCORPORATED AND UNINCORPORATED.

Your answer should include the following points:

Unincorporated

- Liability—unlimited personal liability
- Ownership—owned by the individuals
- Accountability—none, unless it is a charity
- Costs—minimal

Incorporated

- Liability—limited personal liability
- Ownership—owned by the organisation
- Accountability—shareholders, stakeholders and regulators
- Costs—set-up, regulatory and ongoing

CHAPTER 3 REVISION ACTIVITIES

TRUE OR FALSE?

1. **True.**
2. **False.** No-liability companies are available in the mining sector
3. **False.** It can be one member who bears unlimited liability
4. **False.**
5. **True.**

FILL IN THE GAPS

1. one
2. 18
3. 50 (as per s 45A of the CA2001)
4. 112
5. cannot be registered as a company
6. 5 (see s 293(1)(a) of the CA2001)

MULTIPLE CHOICE

Q1 d	Is referenced by the amount unpaid on their shares
Q2 b	A public company limited by guarantee
Q3 d	Be at least 18 years of age
Q4 d	1 year
Q5 d	3 directors and 1 secretary

SHORT ANSWER QUESTIONS

1. **What is the difference between a company limited by shares and a company limited by guarantee?**

   A company limited by shares is 'a company formed on the principle of having the liability of its members limited to the amount (if any) unpaid on the shares respectively held by them': CA2001 s 9.

   Around 99 per cent of all companies registered in Australia are companies limited by shares.

   A company limited by guarantee is 'a company formed on the principle of having the liability of its members limited to the respective amounts that the members undertake to contribute to the property of the company if it is wound up': CA2001 s 9.

2. **What does 'no liability' mean in relation to a corporation?**

   A no-liability company is prohibited from engaging in activities that are outside its mining purposes objectives.

According to the Corporations Act, a company may be registered as a no-liability company only if the following three requirements are met:

- the company has a share capital
- the constitution of the company clearly states that its sole purpose is mining, and
- the company does not have a contractual right to recover calls made on its shares from a shareholder who fails to pay them.

www.studocu.com

3. **What is an unlimited company?**

   An unlimited company is 'a company whose members have no limit placed on their liability': CA2001 s 9.

4. **Can a company, once registered, change to a different type or form of company?**

   Part 2B.7 of the CA2001—comprising ss 162–167AA—sets out the requirements with regard to changing a company to a different type or form. This is possible in most instances. It requires a special resolution under s 162, and compliance with s 163.

5. **What is the separate legal entity status of a one-person company?**

   - A company is a separate legal entity even if a single person owns all its shares.
   - A one-person company is a separate entity from its controller, who may also be its sole employee.
   - The shareholder of a one-person company does not have a legal or equitable interest in the company's property.

6. **What is the separate legal entity status of a company within a corporate group?**

   Companies in a group are treated as separate legal entities.

7. **To whom do the directors of a company that is part of a corporate group owe their duties?**

   Directors of Company A, which is a part of a corporate group, owe their duties to Company A. They cannot act in the best interests of the group and disregard the interests of Company A's shareholders and creditors.

Higher order thinking activities

TOPIC A

EXPLAIN THE VEIL OF INCORPORATION CONCEPT, ITS EFFECTS, AND HOW IT MAY BE LIFTED.

What is the 'veil of incorporation' and what is its effect?

The 'corporate veil', which comes into existence once the company is created, can be thought of as a barrier separating the company—and confirming its separateness—from the founders, directors, members, employees and so on. Registration or incorporation of the company is therefore both potentially:

- a protective mechanism, and
- an enabling structure.

   For further discussion, see www.youtube.com/watch?v=UZnN11318M4/.

ANSWERS

Can this corporate veil be lifted?

Oscar Shub, in his presentation 'Separate Corporate Body, Piercing the Corporate Veil' in July 2005 said:

> The case law in Australia has demonstrated that the courts are generally reluctant to lift the corporate veil.[1] Yet, the limits of an occasional decision of a court to lift the corporate veil is not concluded. It is, therefore, difficult to predict the situations in which the courts will pierce the corporate veil, and there seems to be a tendency to 'reinvent the wheel' each time it is argued.[2]
>
> Australian courts have approached veil-piercing cases in an ad hoc manner with underlying policy considerations in mind. As Rogers AJA confirmed in *Briggs v James Hardie & Co Pty Ltd*:
>
>> The threshold problem arises from the fact that there is no common, unifying principle, which underlies the occasional decision of courts to pierce the corporate veil. Although an ad hoc explanation may be offered by a court which so decides, there is no principled approach to be derived from the authorities ...[3]
>
> When deciding to disregard the separate legal personality principle Jenkinson J, in *Dennis Wilcox Pty Ltd v Federal Commissioner of Taxation*,[4] stated that a court should do so,
>
>> ... only if [they] can see that there is, in fact or in law, a partnership between companies in a group, or that there is a mere sham or façade in which that company is playing a role, or that the creation or use of the company was designed to enable legal or fiduciary obligations to be evaded or a fraud to be perpetrated.[5]
>
> Jenkinson J's summation, while not exhaustive, does include some indicators where Australian courts have been willing to pierce the corporate veil.

For further discussion, see www.youtube.com/watch?v=N97ifFaxjt0/.

TOPIC B

WHAT ARE THE REGISTRATION PROCESSES FOR A COMPANY, INCLUDING THE STEPS BEFORE AND AFTER INCORPORATION?

The registration procedures associated with registering a corporation

The procedure of registering a company is set out in CA2001 s 117. The application must state various matters, including:

- the name and address of each person who consents to become a member, director or secretary: s 117(2)(c)–(f)
- 'the address of the company's proposed registered office': s 117(2)(g)
- 'for a public company—the proposed opening hours of its registered office (if they are not the standard opening hours)': s 117(2)(h)
- 'the address of the company's proposed principal place of business (if it is not the address of the proposed registered office)': s 117(2)(j).

Section 117(3) states that '[i]f the company is to be a public company and is to have a constitution on registration, a copy of the constitution must be lodged with the application.'

---

1   *Hadoplane Pty Ltd v Edward Rushton Pty Ltd* [1996] 1 Qd R 156 at 160.
2   D Noakes, 'Reform to the Law of Corporate Groups in Australia to Protect Employees' (2000) 34 *University of British Columbia Law Review* 239 at 259.
3   *Briggs v James Hardie & Co Pty Ltd* (1989) 16 NSWLR 549 at 567.
4   *Dennis Wilcox Pty Limited v Federal Commissioner of Taxation* (1988) 79 ALR 267.
5   *Dennis Wilcox Pty Limited v Federal Commissioner of Taxation* (1988) 79 ALR 267 at 272.

A new company may choose to be governed by the replacement rules, its constitution, or a combination of both.

The post-registration requirements

- Section 168 of the CA2001 states that a company must set up and maintain a register of members, a register of option holders (together with copies of options documents) and a register of debenture holders (if applicable). A company must allow anyone to inspect its registers.
- All companies must keep minute books. These record resolutions of meetings of the members and directors.
- A company, once registered, has the power to issue shares. A share certificate must be lodged within two months after a share has been alotted.
- Where a director or secretary is appointed after registration, the company must lodge a notice with ASIC containing the person's details within 28 days. Similarly, ASIC must be notified within 28 days when a person ceases to be a director or secretary.
- A company must prepare written financial reports.
- A company's directors must appoint an auditor within one month after its registration: ss 327A–327I.
- A company 'must display its name prominently at every place at which the company carries on business and that is open to the public': s 144.
- The company's name and either its ACN or its ABN must appear on every public document.
- A company must appoint a 'public officer' within three months of starting to carry out business.

ANSWERS

CHAPTER 4 REVISION ACTIVITIES

TRUE OR FALSE?

1. **False.** They may choose to do so, but they do not have to do so
2. **False.** They only apply if the company chooses to adopt some or all of them: see s 134 of the CA2001
3. **False.** It requires a special resolution (75 per cent of the votes cast): s 136(1)(b) of the CA2001
4. **True.** Confirmed by s 140 of the CA2001
5. **False.** See s 135 of the CA2001

FILL IN THE GAPS

1. s 141
2. company (see CA2001 s 140)
3. ASIC; s 136(5)
4. director
5. judicial activism; rights
6. 1961

MULTIPLE CHOICE

Q1 c	Is largely abolished by s 125 of the CA2001
Q2 d	Confirmed by s 124 of the CA2001
Q3 d	A Memorandum and Articles of Association
Q4 d	A minimum of one director
Q5 c	75 per cent of votes
Q6 d	Within 14 days

SHORT ANSWER QUESTIONS

1. **Do all of the replaceable rules need to be included in a corporation's constitution?**

   You need to include the replaceable rules in so far as the constitution—if any—has not accounted for the provisions contained in them.

2. **What does s 141 of the CA2001 provide?**

   A table of the replaceable rules.

3. **What purpose do the replaceable rules fulfil?**

   Replaceable rules are found in the CA 2001 and govern a company's internal administration and management. They provide a set of default rules for the company to use and adapt to suit their purposes.

Companies to which replaceable rules apply are set out in s 135. (Section 135 does not apply to a single-director company.)

4. **Are replaceable rules used 'across the board' for all types of corporations?**

    Most replaceable rules apply to both public and proprietary companies. However, according to s 135 of the CA2001, some replaceable rules apply only to proprietary companies.

    A mandatory rule applies despite anything to the contrary in the public company's constitution.

Higher order thinking activities

TOPIC A

PROVIDE A MEMORANDUM SETTING OUT THE SITUATION PRE-1998 AND POST-1998 CONCERNING A COMPANY'S CONSTITUTION.

Your answer should take the form of a memorandum; for example:

To: Partner

From: Trainee

Draft

Re: Corporate constitutions

Thanks for your note regarding this matter.

I enclose a draft explanatory note/paper regarding the matter intended for the firm's website. The intended audience is a business-type client.

I divide companies into two date periods, post-July 1998 and pre-July 1998. I will deal with them in that order.

I have also assumed we are dealing with Pty Ltd companies.

Your answer should include the following points:

Post-July 1998 companies

These corporations are subject to the CA2001.

CA2001 s 134 relevantly provides as follows:

> A company's internal management may be governed by provisions of this Act that apply to the company as replaceable rules, by a constitution or by a combination of both.

CA2001 s 136(1) relevantly provides that a company adopts a constitution:

(a) on registration—if each person specified in the application for the company's registration as a person who consents to become a member agrees in writing to the terms of a constitution before the application is lodged; or

(b) after registration—if the company passes a special resolution adopting a constitution or a court order is made under section 233 that requires the company to adopt the constitution.

CA2001 s 135(1)(a) sets out the companies to which replaceable rules apply:

(i) each company that is or was registered after 1 July 1998; and

(ii) any company registered before 1 July 1998 that repeals or repealed its constitution after that day.

Pre-July 1998 companies

The context pre-July 1998 was the Memorandum of Association, the Articles of Association and the doctrine of *ultra vires*.

The *ultra vires* doctrine has been effectively removed by s 125 of the CA2001.

Section 135(1) provides that the replaceable rules apply to 'any company registered before 1 July 1998 that repeals or repealed its constitution after that day'.

Section 135(3) provides that:

> A failure to comply with the replaceable rules as they apply to a company is not of itself a contravention of this Act (so the provisions about criminal liability, civil liability and injunctions do not apply).

TOPIC B

WHAT IS THE CONTRACTUAL EFFECT OF A COMPANY'S CONSTITUTION UNDER THE CA2001 AND WHAT IS THE RELEVANCE OF THE REPLACEABLE RULES?

A company's constitution and any replaceable rules have contractual effect under s 140 of the CA2001.

A company's constitution and any applicable replaceable rules have effect as a contract between:

- the company and each member
- one member and each other member, and
- the company and each director and the company secretary.

Regarding members: only those provisions in a constitution or replaceable rules that confer rights on members *in their capacity as members* are enforceable as a contract. That is, provisions in a constitution that give members rights in some other capacity than that of a member do not have contractual effect.

Regarding directors: it is quite common for directors to enter into separate contracts of service (employment contracts) that are independent of the company's constitution (if any) and applicable rules.

CHAPTER 5 REVISION ACTIVITIES

TRUE OR FALSE?

1. **True.** See s 9 of the CA2001
2. **False.** They can enter pre-incorporation contracts that are later ratified
3. **True.**
4. **False.** Only if the third party is acting in good faith: s 128(4) of the CA2001
5. **False.** An ordinary resolution is required

FILL IN THE GAPS

1. s 129
2. vicariously; employment
3. a separate legal entity
4. contract
5. an officer; constitution

MULTIPLE CHOICE

Q1 d	Adopted and replaced by s 129 of the CA2001
Q2 b	Fiduciaries to the company
Q3 d	All of the above
Q4 b	Section 128 of the CA2001
Q5 a	The company

SHORT ANSWER QUESTIONS

1. **Who is an officer of the company?**

    Section 9 of the CA2001 defines the term 'officer' to include:

    - a director or secretary
    - a person:
        (i) 'who makes, or participates in making, decisions that affect the whole, or a substantial part, of the business of the corporation'
        (ii) 'who has the capacity to affect significantly the corporation's financial standing', or
        (iii) 'in accordance with whose instructions or wishes the directors of the corporation are accustomed to act', or
    - a receiver, administrator, liquidator, or a trustee administering a compromise or arrangement.

2. **Is a senior executive of a company an officer?**

   Given the definition in s 9 of the CA2001, a senior executive would likely include the chief operating officer, the chief financial officer and others whose roles cover the whole of the organisation, or a substantial part of the organisation.

3. **What is the legal significance of being an officer of the company?**

   There are three main potential legal parameters relevant to officers:
   - the liabilities under the CA2001 and other relevant statutes
   - the application of relevant general law principles that underpin and inform the CA2001, including potential fiduciary duties, and
   - access to professional insurance, usually referred to as 'D&O', or directors' and officers' insurance.

4. **Can individuals contract on behalf of the company?**

   An individual acting with the company's express or implied authority may contract on its behalf. This is likely to be a director, an officer or a senior manager.

   It will depend on several variables:
   - the type and size of the company
   - the type and size of the contract
   - the role of the person.

5. **How are documents executeed for and on behalf of companies?**

   A company can make a contract directly by executing a document.

   A company with a common seal executes a document by affixing its common seal to a document, which is witnessed by the appropriate officers. Company constitutions often set out provisions regarding the use of the company seal.

   A company can execute a document without a seal if the appropriate officers sign it.

   A sole director may witness the fixing of the seal of a proprietary company that has only one director, who is also the sole secretary. This can also be actioned without the use of a seal.

Higher order thinking activities

TOPIC A

A CLIENT, DANNI, HAS BEEN OFFERED THE ROLE OF 'SENIOR MANAGER AND HEAD OF MARKETING' IN A PUBLIC COMPANY. SHE WANTS TO KNOW WHAT HER LIABILITIES WOULD BE UNDER THE CA2001, GIVEN THESE PROPOSED ROLES.

Your answer should refer to the following definitions in s 9 of the CA2001:
- *officer*
- *senior manager.*

As 'senior manager and head of marketing', Danni prima facie appears to meet the definition of senior manager in the CA2001 (in accordance with her title), and being head of marketing would likely mean that she is an officer under s 9, in that her role will involve her making decisions that affect 'the whole, or a substantial part, of the business of the corporation'.

The High Court of Australia has recently dealt with the scope of the 'officer' concept: see *ASIC v King* (2020).

If Danni is an officer, her liabilities are set out in Ch 2D of the CA2001, in particular ss 180–184. They are similar to the liabilities of directors.

TOPIC B

DISCUSS HOW (A) ORGANIC THEORY AND (B) VICARIOUS LIABILITY IMPACT UPON THE PRINCIPLE THAT THE COMPANY IS A SEPARATE LEGAL ENTITY.

(a) Organic theory

The actions of the 'organs' of a company are the actions of the company itself, and their (the officers') state of mind is the state of mind of the company.

Organic theory is a legal fiction that allows the company to be identified with the individuals/officers who control it. The officers are equated with being the controlling mind of the company.

(b) Vicarious liability

Torts

If a company has employees, and those employees are negligent, causing loss to a third party, then the company is vicariously liable. This pre-supposes two common law pre-conditions:

- first, that there is an employment contract, rather than a self-employment arrangement or a situation characterised as that of independent contractor status, and
- second, that the act complained of was carried out within the course and scope of the employment.

However, these traditional common law limitations are subject to being overridden by statute. For example, they have been adapted and broadened in the case of a corporate employer by ss 128 and 129 of the CA2001. The vicarious liability of the company is sheeted home even where the employee has clearly acted outside the scope of their employment, such as where they have been fraudulent (see s 128(3)).

Criminal liability

It is generally only under statute that a company may be found guilty of vicarious criminal liability, with the wording and intentions of the statute relevant as to whether or not vicarious criminal liability may be imposed on a company.

CHAPTER 6 ACTIVITY ANSWERS

TRUE OR FALSE?

1. **True.** Under the shareholder primacy principles and practice
2. **True.** As part of co-determination
3. **False.** It is funded by the Commonwealth Government
4. **False.** The Banking Royal Commission criticised their use; it preferred the use of formal litigation practices by ASIC
5. **True.** Social, economic and environmental factors all feature

FILL IN THE GAPS

1. 5
2. 10
3. lost; judgment
4. Full Federal Court; High Court
5. disclosure

MULTIPLE CHOICE

Q1 c	Australian Securities and Investments Commission
Q2 d	Australian Prudential Regulation Authority
Q3 c	Australian Securities Exchange
Q4 d	Australian Competition and Consumer Commission
Q5 a	Critical of ASIC

SHORT ANSWER QUESTIONS

1. **Why are shareholders important stakeholders?**

   Shareholders are essentially the owners of a corporation. The power of a shareholder varies as per the volume and type of shares owned.

2. **What is meant by the phrase 'triple bottom line'?**

   Analysis of a company's performance can be expanded beyond simple financial matrices of profit and shareholder returns. The company can be measured in additional ways, including its environmental and social impact.

   'Triple bottom line' (TBL) reporting is one example of how a company can demonstrate that it is committed to more than simply profits. It focuses on three key areas: social, environmental and financial.

3. **What does CAMAC refer to?**

   The Corporations and Markets Advisory Committee (CAMAC) was established in 1989 under the *Australian Securities and Investments Commission Act 2001* to provide advice and recommendations to the Minister about matters relating to corporations and financial services law, administration and practice.

   As part of the 2014–15 Budget, the Government announced its decision to cease the operation of CAMAC and its legal committee. CAMAC was abolished by Schedule 7 of the *Statute Update (Smaller Government) Act 2018*, which commenced on 21 February 2018.

   https://treasury.gov.au/publication/p2018-t319861

4. **What is the Takeovers Panel and what is its function?**

   The Takeovers Panel is a specialist federally funded agency charged with overseeing corporate takeovers and related company transactions. It is the main forum for resolving disputes that relate to takeovers, having replaced the courts in this regard; and its members are government-appointed.

   The Takeovers Panel was set up by s 171 of the ASIC Act, and Pt 6.10 Div 2 of the CA2001 gives it broad powers.

5. **What is the scope and purpose of the ASX Listing Rules?**

   The Listing Rules are produced by the ASX (Australian Securities Exchange). They govern all aspects of the listing of securities of the public companies listed on the main exchange. The Listing Rules are in addition to any legal requirements, such as under the CA2001. In terms of corporate governance, the Listing Rules are an additional form of regulation and compliance for public companies that have chosen listing. The purpose of the rules seeks to strike a balance between:

   - market nimbleness for companies operating within a competitive environment, and
   - investor protection for members of the public and others investing in such securities.

   For further information, see www.asx.com.au/regulation/rules/asx-listing-rules.htm/.

Higher order thinking activities

TOPIC A

WHAT IS THE FUNCTION, PURPOSE AND SCOPE OF ASIC, AND WHAT CHALLENGES DOES IT FACE IN THE NEXT FIVE YEARS?

The function, purpose and scope of ASIC is to:

- maintain, facilitate and improve the performance of the financial system and entities in it
- promote confident and informed participation by investors and consumers in the financial system
- administer the law effectively and with minimal procedural requirements
- receive, process and store, efficiently and quickly, information [it] receive[s]
- make information about companies and other bodies available to the public as soon as practicable
- take whatever action [it] can, and which is necessary, to enforce and give effect to the law.

https://asic.gov.au

The challenges faced by ASIC in the next five years will be concerned with its regulatory function; in particular, how does it best spend its necessarily limited budget and resources to oversee more than

2 million companies. In the wake of the Banking Royal Commission, the focus will be on how it litigates against companies so as to enforce the rules.

For further information, see Michael Legg and Stephen Speirs, 'Why Not Litigate? The Royal Commission, ASIC and the Future of the Enforcement Pyramid' (2019) 47 ABLR *244.*

TOPIC B

WHAT IS THE FUNCTION AND PURPOSE OF THE ASX?

- The ASX is the largest stock exchange in Australia. It is where investors trade shares and derivative products.
- As a market operator, the ASX 'is required to ensure that each of its licensed markets is fair, orderly and transparent' (asx.com.au).
- The ASX produces the Listing Rules, which govern all aspects of the listing of securities, including obligations in relation to continuous disclosure. Continuous disclosure obligations require a company to make timely, accurate public disclosure to the market, so that people can be fully informed about investment decisions.

CHAPTER 7 ACTIVITY ANSWERS

TRUE OR FALSE?

1. **False.** Two of the three are required to reside in Australia
2. **False.** They do not have to appoint a company secretary
3. **False.** They may hold shares, but it is not compulsory
4. **True.** A board meeting requires a chair
5. **False.** It depends on the constitution and replaceable rules: see s 248G of the CA2001

FILL IN THE GAPS

1. 9
2. first; *pares*
3. *Daniel v Anderson*
4. 1984; fiduciary duties
5. alternate

MULTIPLE CHOICE

Q1 d	Is judged by the same standard as other directors
Q2 c	Be 18 years of age
Q3 c	Based on the 'if not, why not' principle
Q4 a	The only employee of the board
Q5 b	1992 (UK *Cadbury Report*)

SHORT ANSWER QUESTIONS

1. **How are directors appointed?**
    - A single director/shareholder of a proprietary company may appoint another director by recording the appointment and signing the record.
    - If it is a proprietary company, the appointment of a director by the other directors must be confirmed by resolution of the shareholders within two months after the appointment is made.
    - If it is a public company, the appointment by the directors must be confirmed by the members at the company's next annual general meeting.
    - Subsequent appointments of directors may be made by a shareholders' resolution passed in a general meeting.
    - A casual vacancy occurs if a director dies, resigns, or is otherwise unable to continue to act as a director.

2. **What is a shadow director?**

   A shadow director is a person not formally appointed as a director but on whose instructions or wishes a company's board members are accustomed to act.

3. **What is a de facto director?**

   A de facto director is someone who has not been formally appointed to the role of director, but who acts in that capacity.

4. **What is the role of the chair?**

   The chair is a director of the relevant company and, as such, bound by the duties and relevant matters set out in the CA2001. The chair is an officer of the company. The chair is required to chair the board meetings; that is, to oversee the business of the meeting. The chair is referred to as the 'first among equals' (*primus inter pares*) in terms of their role as both a director and convenor of the meeting. There is surprisingly little formal direction for the role provided in the CA2001. There are some relevant replaceable rules referred to in s 141 of the CA2001.

   For further information, see AD Clarke, 'The Lacuna in Corporate Law: The Role of the Company Chair' (2018) 33 Australian Journal of Corporate Law *125.*

5. **What are the key features of the relationship between the CEO and the chair?**

   The CEO is the senior employee of the company and the appointee of the board. The board, as led by the chair, sets the terms of the CEO's tenure, and the succession plan relevant to the CEO. The board oversees strategy as relevantly developed by the CEO and others. The working relationship between the chair and CEO is therefore pivotal to the success of the company.

   For further information, see AD Clarke, 'Corporate Law and Enhancing Leadership: A Missed Opportunity?' (2018) 19 SCULR *25.*

6. **Can directors be disqualified from acting?**

   There are a number of provisions under which a person may be disqualified from managing corporations.

   Disqualification serves three main purposes:
   - to protect a company's shareholders against further abuse
   - to punish an offender, and
   - to generally deter improper behaviour from others.

   Automatic termination of directorships occurs when a director is:
   - convicted of certain criminal offences, or
   - an undischarged bankrupt.

   Disqualification by court order may occur in the case of:
   - contravention of a civil penalty provision (applications for disqualifications can only be made by ASIC)
   - failed companies—within the last seven years, if the person has been an officer of two or more failed companies and the court is satisfied that the manner in which the corporation was managed was responsible for it failing, or
   - repeated contraventions of the CA2001.

Section 206F of the CA2001 gives ASIC the power to disqualify a person from managing corporations for up to five years. In order to exercise that power, ASIC must give the person a 'show cause' notice requiring the person to demonstrate why they should not be disqualified and an opportunity to be heard on the question.

Higher order thinking activities

TOPIC A

WHAT IS THE SCOPE OF THE TERM 'DIRECTOR'?

The term 'director' encompasses managing directors, chair-directors, executive directors and non-executive directors.

An executive director is a member of the board who has management responsibilities. A non-executive director is a member of the board without responsibilities for daily management or operations.

Also note the following:

- *Alternate directors:* an 'alternate director' is appointed as a substitute for an existing director for a specified time, where the existing director is unable to attend board meetings or otherwise exercise their powers as a director.

- *De facto director:* a 'de facto director' is someone who has not been formally appointed to the role of director, but who acts in that capacity.

- *Independent director:* 'an "independent director" can be broadly defined as a non-executive director who is not a member of management and who is free from any business or other relationship that could materially interfere … with the independent exercise of that director's judgment' (http://aicd.companydirectors.com.au).

- *Shadow director:* 'a "shadow director" is a person not formally appointed as a director but on whose instructions or wishes a company's Board members are accustomed to act' (http://aicd.companydirectors.com.au).

TOPIC B

WHAT IS THE ROLE AND FUNCTION OF THE BOARD?

- The essential functions of the board are to provide strategic guidance for the company and effective oversight of management.

- One of the most important functions of the board is appointing and (if necessary) removing the CEO.

- The replaceable rule in s 198A of the CA2001 states that the business of a company is to be managed by, or under the direction of, its directors.

- Shareholders cannot, therefore, generally override the directors and involve themselves in the management of their company.

- The theory is that the board's wide powers of management result in the separation of management and ownership. That is, the interests of management may diverge from the interests of the shareholders. However, in smaller companies there may be directors with substantial shareholdings, so the interests and roles overlap.

CHAPTER 8 ACTIVITY ANSWERS

TRUE OR FALSE?

1. **False.** The general law (case law) remains important
2. **False.** There is no requirement for these attributes
3. **True.** They are essentially treated the same
4. **False.** It is only irrational decisions that would not be afforded protection: see CA2001 s 180(2)
5. **False.** There is little reference to either role

FILL IN THE GAPS

1. 189; competence and reliability
2. 190; reasonable grounds; capable
3. must
4. attend; vote
5. the prior approval of its shareholders under ss 207–230 of the CA2001

MULTIPLE CHOICE

Q1 a	CA2001
Q2 d	Case law
Q3 d	The directors owe their duties to the company
Q4 b	5 per cent (as per s 202B of the CA2001)
Q5 d	The categories of commercial fiduciaries are not closed

SHORT ANSWER QUESTIONS

1. **What are considerations relevant to the directors paying a dividend to members?**

   The company needs to be solvent and able to pay the dividend as per the requirements of s 254T of the CA2001. The dividend cannot put the company into insolvency. If it did, it would trigger s 588G.

2. **Do directors owe duties to particular shareholders?**

   The general position is that the directors owe their duties to the company, or the shareholders in general, not to a particular shareholder. This is established by *Percival v Wright* (1901). There may be exceptions; such as when a director is in negotiation with a particular shareholder to, for instance, buy their shares. This can give rise to a duty owed by the director to the particular shareholder, depending on the facts and circumstances, as per *Glavanics v Brunninghausen* (1999).

3. **Do the directors have exclusive rights to bring actions for and on behalf of the company?**

   The usual situation is that the directors have carriage of the company's main business decisions, including whether to pursue legal action in the name of the company. The company has all the powers of a natural person, as per s 124 of the CA2001. The members may pursue an action in the company's name if the company has refused to take action, and the member has received the leave of the court. This is potentially available under the process outlined in ss 236 and 237 of the CA2001.

4. **Do directors have a duty to disclose personal profits that arise from their position?**

   Directors do have a fiduciary duty to disclose personal profits that arise from their position. It is a strict disclosure—see CA2001 s 191—applicable to all directors. It goes to the heart of the fiduciary duty of utmost good faith or *uberrimae fidae*.

5. **What does s 182 of the CA2001 provide for/address?**

   Officers and employees must not improperly use their position: CA2001 s 182.

   Officers contravene s 182 if improper use is made of their office in order to gain advantage for themselves or to cause detriment to another.

   This is a civil obligation primarily, but may be pursued as a criminal matter under s 184 if there is recklessness or actual dishonesty, e.g. a pattern of repeat behaviour, actual concealment etc.

Higher order thinking activities

TOPIC A

WHAT ASSUMPTIONS CAN A THIRD PARTY MAKE WHEN DEALING WITH A COMPANY?

A person is entitled to make a number of assumptions regarding regularity when dealing with a company: see CA2001 ss 28 and 29. These assumptions, to a certain extent, codify the rule in *Turquand's case* (1856). They include:

- 'A person may assume that the company's constitution (if any), and any provisions of this Act that apply to the company as replaceable rules, have been complied with': s 129(1).
- 'A person may assume that anyone who appears, from information provided by the company that is available to the public from ASIC, to be a director or a company secretary … has been duly appointed … [and] has authority to exercise the powers and perform the duties customarily exercised or performed by a director or company secretary of a similar company': s 129(2).
- 'A person may assume that anyone who is held out by the company to be an officer or agent … has been duly appointed … [and] has the authority to exercise the powers and perform the duties customarily exercised or performed by that kind of officer or agent of a similar company': s 129(3). Such a 'holding out' must come from a person who has actual authority.
- 'A person may assume that the officers and agents of the company properly perform their duties to the company': s 129(4).
- 'A person may assume that a company can execute a document either with or without affixing a seal to the document. It is sufficient if the document appears on its face to have been signed, or the company seal witnessed, by the required officers': s 129(5), (6).
- 'A person may assume that an officer or agent of the company who has authority to issue a document … on its behalf also has authority to warrant that the document is genuine…': s 129(7).

ANSWERS

TOPIC B

EDDY, A DIRECTOR OF COMPANY ABC PTY LTD, OWNS THE COMMERCIAL PROPERTY THAT ABC IS KEEN TO PURCHASE. EDDY WANTS TO ACHIEVE TOP PRICE. ADVISE EDDY.
HOW WOULD YOUR ANSWER DIFFER IF THE COMPANY WERE PUBLIC?

In your answer, you should aim for an analytical legal approach, dealing with the transactional and related commercial analysis.

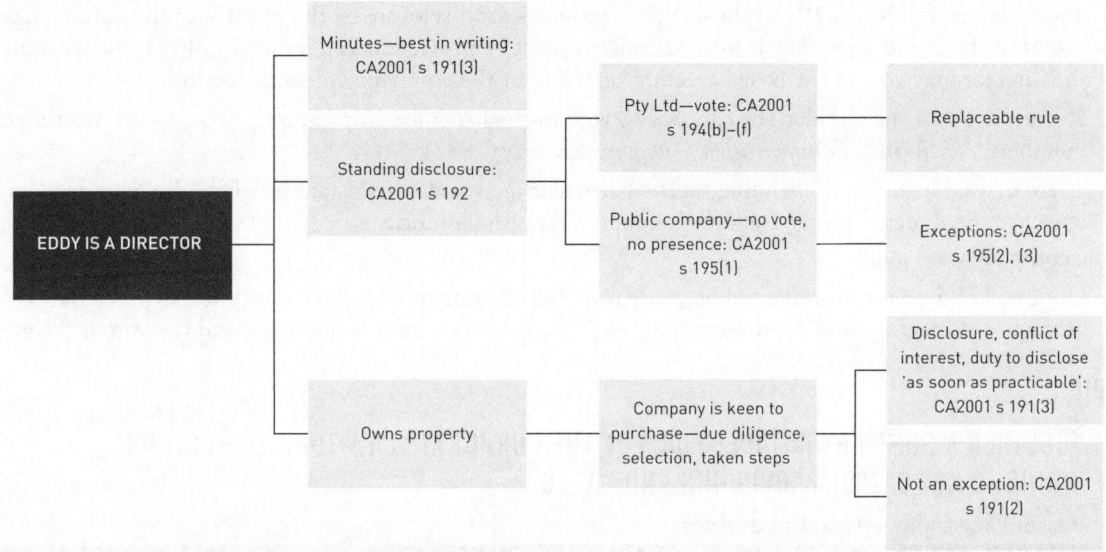

Principles regarding conflicts of interest for directors

1. Eddy is a director of ABC Pty Ltd, a proprietary limited company.
2. As such, she is in a fiduciary position in relation to the company, as per *Hospital Products Ltd v United States Surgical Corporation* (1984).
3. As such, she needs to act in the best interests of the company, and observe the 'no conflict, no profit' set of rules relevant to fiduciaries. As fiduciaries, directors need to avoid undisclosed conflicts of interest.
4. She needs to put the best interests of the company (to pay the lowest price possible for the commercial property) ahead of her own personal interests (to obtain the highest price possible for the commercial property).
5. As owner (presumably sole owner), she has a personal interest in that she owns the commercial property.
6. She therefore has a clear conflict of interest.
7. The conflict has to be of a contractual nature as per *Baker v Palm Bay Island Resort Pty Ltd* (1970), as evidenced by the fact that the company is 'keen' to purchase the commercial property.
8. Hence, this conflict of interest for Eddy needs to be declared and disclosed to the company and board.

Steps to be taken

9. Eddy must disclose the details of her personal interest, and obtain the company's fully informed consent.
10. The best form of evidence for these matters—so as to provide current clarity and to avoid later dispute—would be in writing.

Statute

11. Directors' duties, including conflicts of interest, are covered in general by ss 181–183 of the CA2001.
12. Section 181: three elements—a director needs to act in good faith, in the best interests of the company, and for a proper purpose.
13. Sections 182 and 183 relate to improper use of a director's position and improper use of information.
14. Eddy must (usually) refrain from voting at the directors' meeting—this requires checking of the constitution of ABC.
15. The replaceable rule in s 194 of the CA2001 provides for disclosure by the director of the nature and extent of the interest, i.e. fully informed consent must be provided. As a result, s 194(c) provides that the director may vote at the board meeting on whether the company enters the contract.
16. If Eddy is also a shareholder, she can *usually* vote in their membership capacity at a general meeting of members: *North-West Transportation Company v Beatty* (1887).
17. There may be instances, depending on the particular facts and circumstances, where the members may object to the director voting, e.g. oppression, fraud on the minority.

If the company were public

18. Under s 195(1), a director of a public company who has a material interest must declare it, cannot vote at the board meeting, and must leave the meeting while the matter is discussed and the vote is taken.

TOPIC C

PUT TOGETHER A SUMMARY IN TABLE FORM OF THE CORPORATE LAW TOPIC 'DIRECTORS', REFERRING TO KEY CA2001 PROVISIONS AND CASES.

Statutes and key topics relevant to directors

Topic	CA2001 provisions	Notes
Definition of 'directors'	s 9 • appointed or not • shadow and de facto • executive vs non-executive	
Definition of 'officers'	s 9	
Powers	s 179	Includes general law/case law
Relevant replaceable rules	s 198A–198D (ss 135 and 141)	
Roles	Agent of the company (as principal) Fiduciary to the company Employee of the company?	The directors typically deal with third parties on behalf of the company
Duties owed to whom?		Owed to the company—the members as a whole: *Percival v Wright* (1902)

Topic	CA2001 provisions	Notes
Can directors owe a duty to a particular member?		Possibly, depends on facts and circumstances: see e.g. *Glavanics v Brunninghausen* (1996)
Negligence/competence	s 180 Defence in s 180(2) (business judgment rule)	See *ASIC v Healey* (2011)
Honesty/fiduciary	ss 181–183: civil obligations s 184: criminal offences	
Disclosure	s 191 Voting/attendance: • s 194: Pty Ltd • s 195: public company	
Solvency	s 588G s 254T	Legislative removal of the corporate veil
Appointment and qualifications	s 201	Need to be 18 years old
Domicile requirements	s 201A	A public company must have three directors One must reside in Australia. A sole director of a Pty Ltd must reside in Australia
Removal	s 203	By a majority vote of directors
Banned from being a director	s 206	ASIC has the power to disqualify a director: *ASIC v Vizard* (2005)

TOPIC D

DIRECTORS ARE CENTRAL TO CORPORATE LAW. DISCUSS.

Directors' duties and responsibilities go to the heart of the fiduciary concept. They are one of the core commercial fiduciary relationships, along with partners, agents and others. Fiduciary duties are necessarily relational; they are owed by X to Y. In the case of directors, they are owed to the company.

Solicitors are fiduciaries in relation to their clients, and public officers in relation to the courts. The asymmetric information, knowledge and expertise they possess give rise to a relationship with a fiduciary layer of responsibility. Solicitors are taken to have a professional qualification, together with knowledge and skills their clients do not possess.

With companies, there is the so-called 'agency gap' in which directors operate and owe their duties to the company; and through the entity, to the shareholders. There is, therefore, a quite natural doubly reinforced fit that makes directors' duties a core part of the Priestley 11 coverage of corporate law.

There are several potential areas to examine to a greater or lesser extent (depending on the particular context):

- the definition of 'director' in s 9 of the CA2001, and its scope and application to the facts provided—this might involve determining whether there is a shadow or de facto director; it may also involve looking at the definition of 'officer' in s 9
- the fiduciary nature of the role of directors, and the relevant considerations—this may also involve determining whether the role of a promoter is relevant
- the negligence law as provided by s 180(1) of the CA2001 and the general law (see s 9 and Ch 2D)
- the business judgment rule defence for directors provided by s 180(2) of the CA2001
- the honesty provisions, which are encapsulated in the CA2001 ss 181–183 (civil matters) and 184 (criminal matters)
- the disclosure provisions, which are encapsulated in the CA2001 ss 191–194; for public companies, the restrictions set out in s 195 apply.

Note that problem-based factual scenarios in this area will variously involve facts based on:
- *determining disclosures*
- *identifying oversights, mistakes and possible negligence (ASIC v Healey (2011))*
- *identifying instances of dishonesty, being misleading, withholding information, or being dishonest.*

The facts will give rise to relevant relationships; these anchor the duty owed by X to Y. There may be multiple parties and multiple relationships to consider. Consider each of them on their merits.

The sources of law will be:
- *the CA2001—the headline statute; a primary source of law*
- *general law—case law, including common law and equity; a primary source of law, but one that gives way to statute*
- *other sources—secondary sources, including textbooks and journal articles.*

The approach may well implicitly involve a problem-solving methodology such as the following:
- *issue—what are the relevant and prescient issues; what issues are pressing to the client, and what are the legal risks of which the client needs to be aware?*
- *research*
- *argument*
- *conclusion—use temperate or guarded language; you may not have all the facts, and facts that are withheld, not provided or overlooked may well change the nature of the advice. Hence, use phrases such as: 'Based on the information to date it would appear that …'*

The methodology provides a flexible framework, not a rigid approach. Taking an adaptable and principles-based approach is the key to meeting the requirements of the task in a timely, efficient and legally propitious manner.

The actions/inactions of the directors may variously affect:
- *the fate and value of the company*
- *other directors*
- *shareholders*
- *creditors.*

ANSWERS

AN OUTLINE OF ISSUES REGARDING DIRECTORS

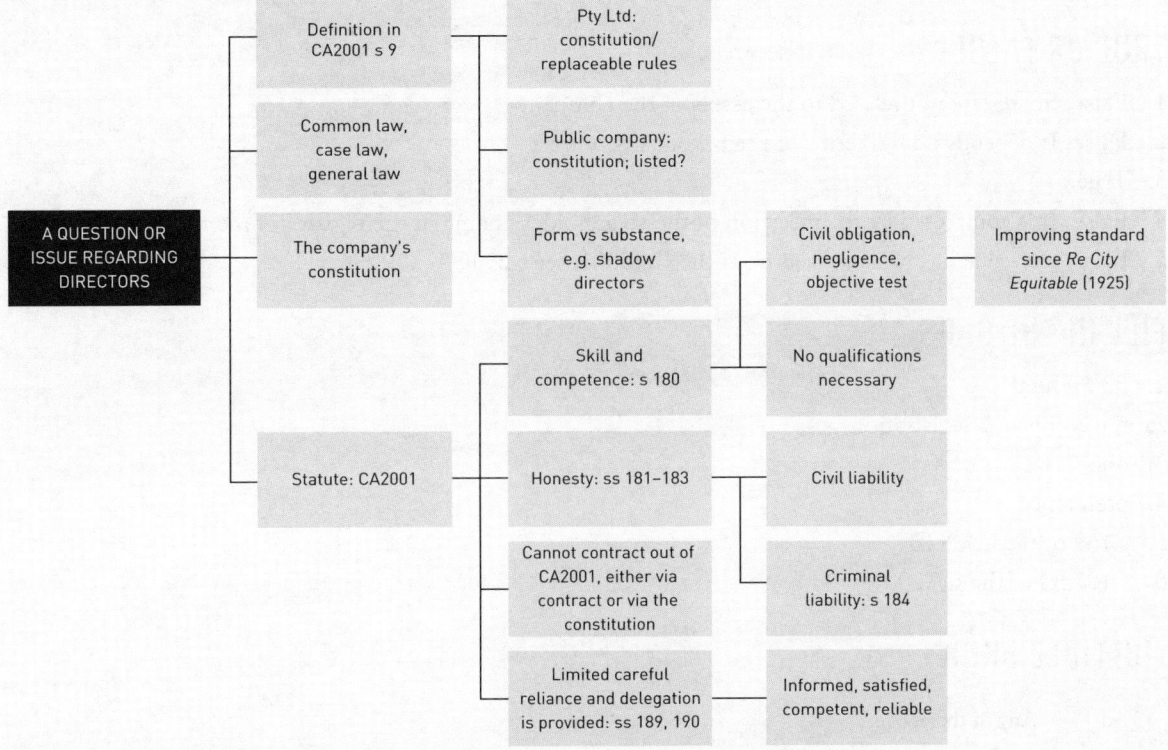

CHAPTER 9 ACTIVITY ANSWERS

TRUE OR FALSE?

1. **False.** Shares are not related to the assets of the company
2. **False.** It depends on the terms of the particular contract
3. **True.**
4. **False.** It is completed by the insertion of the shareholder's name in the register of members
5. **False.** Par value has been excised from the CA2001: see s 254C

FILL IN THE GAPS

1. first refusal
2. the company's registration
3. one
4. preference
5. s 169 of the CA2001
6. s 1072G of the CA2001

MULTIPLE CHOICE

Q1 d	Any of the above
Q2 c	A Pty Ltd
Q3 c	The right to be consulted
Q4 d	All three of the above
Q5 a	$5,000

SHORT ANSWER QUESTIONS

1. **What are shares?**

   A share is a unit of company ownership—an intangible chose in action. Each share represents a portion of the total ownership of a company. Ownership of shares in a company makes the shareholder a member of the company, who is usually entitled to receive a share of its profits (dividends) and to receive a share of its remaining assets upon its dissolution. Key provisions under the CA2001 include:
   - s 1070A(3): property and contract rules apply
   - s 253C: the right to vote at general meetings (see also s 252G, regarding notice)
   - s 254W: dividends
   - s 231: shareholders.

ANSWERS

2. **How do you become a member of a corporation?**

    Section 231 of the CA2001 provides that a person is a member of a company if they:

    (a) are a member of the company on its registration; or
    (b) agree to become a member of the company after its registration and their name is entered on the register of members; or
    (c) become a member of the company under section 167 (membership arising from conversion of a company from one limited by guarantee to one limited by shares).

    See also Ch 2B.1 ('Basic features of a company') and s 169 ('Register of members').

3. **How do you cease to be a member?**

    You cease to be a member:
    - by selling all your shares by transfer
    - by selling all your shares back to the company
    - where all your shares are cancelled following a selective reduction of capital under CA2001 ss 256B and 256C
    - where all your shares are transferred involuntarily via a scheme of arrangement or compulsory acquisition
    - where the company is deregistered by ASIC
    - following death or bankruptcy, and
    - following forfeiture of the shares for non-payment of calls.

4. **Are details of members recorded/registered? What is recorded and where?**

    Yes. All companies must keep a register of their members containing prescribed information: CA2001 ss 168 ('Registers to be maintained') and 169 ('Register of members').

    Section 175 ('Correction of registers') allows for amendments.

5. **What are stapled securities?**

    Stapled securities are created when two or more different securities are legally bound together so that they can't be sold separately. Many types of securities can be stapled together. For example, many property trusts have their units stapled to the shares of companies with which they are closely associated.

    Although the stapled security must be dealt with as a whole, the individual securities that are stapled are treated separately for tax purposes.

    https://ato.gov.au

6. **What is CHESS?**

    CHESS stands for Clearing House Electronic Sub-register System. It is the electronic settlement and transfer system operated by the ASX.

7. **What are 'redeemable preference shares'?**

    Redeemable preference shares:
    - are defined in s 9 of the CA2001
    - were previously referred to as 'convertible preference shares'
    - are a type of share—a hybrid form of equity capital, also exhibiting features of loan capital.

Note that:
- certain shares may be redeemed (effectively bought back from the shareholder) by a body corporate
- the shares being redeemed must be fully paid shares, and the company must redeem the shares out of accrued profits (so as not to prejudice the rights of creditors or other members): see s 254A(3).

Higher order thinking activities

TOPIC A

HOW ARE SHARES TRANSFERRED, AND WHAT ARE THE POWERS OF THE DIRECTORS TO PREVENT TRANSFERS?

For listed companies, shares may be transferable without restrictions, subject to takover provisions: see CA2001 Ch 8; ASX Listing Rules.

For Pty Ltds, the transfer of shares is subject to the constitution, which may impose restrictions.

If a Pty Ltd company has not adopted a constitution, the following replaceable rules apply:
- ss 1072A, 1072B, 1072D: transmission of shares on death, bankruptcy or mental incapacity
- s 1072F: registration of transfers
- s 1072G: additional discretion for directors of proprietary companies to refuse to register a transfer of shares.

See also s 1070A.

Can directors restrict/limit the transfer of shares?

For listed companies: in most contexts the answer is no.

Pty Ltds, via the constitution, can impose a first right of refusal. The restriction on the transfer of shares contained in the company's constitution must be clear and unambiguous.

The replaceable rules in ss 1072F–1072G also provide restrictions.

The case of *Smith v Forster* (1942) sets out a good faith test for the directors.

TOPIC B

WHAT RESPONSIBILITIES ATTACH TO SUBSTANTIAL SHAREHOLDERS?

'Substantial holding' is defined in CA2001 s 9. It is a 'relevant interest' that comprises at least five per cent of the voting shares.

In the takeover context, CA2001 Pt 6C.1 ('Substantial holding information') (primarily ss 671B and 671C) covers:

> … the requirements and obligations on Substantial Shareholders of companies listed on stock exchanges in Australia, including those incorporated in foreign countries. But the requirements do not extend to any other company, even if an Australian company listed on a foreign stock exchange or unlisted disclosing entities, although some may consider that similar information should be lodged with ASIC under the 'continuous disclosure' obligations of unlisted disclosing entities so that 'the market' is adequately informed.

> *https://companysecretary.com.au*

CHAPTER 10 ACTIVITY ANSWERS

TRUE OR FALSE?

1. **False.** Only if the constitution requires it
2. **True.** See CA2001 s 249G
3. **True.** See CA2001 s 250N
4. **False.** Only if there is 'substantial injustice': see s 1322 of the CA2001
5. **True.** That is, 50 per cent plus one vote
6. **False.** It is s 236 of the CA2001

FILL IN THE GAPS

1. independent valuation
2. pre-emption rights
3. overturned
4. 232
5. *Gambotto v WCP Ltd*

MULTIPLE CHOICE

Q1 b	50 per cent plus one vote
Q2 d	21 (as per CA2001 s 249H)
Q3 b	75 per cent
Q4 b	A substitute shareholder (see CA2001 ss 249X and 250D)
Q5 a	5 per cent (see CA2001 s 249F)

SHORT ANSWER QUESTIONS

1. **How are company resolutions passed?**

    Ordinary resolutions are passed by a simple majority vote (50 per cent plus one vote—it needs to be a numerical majority of votes, e.g. 51 votes out 100, 101 out of 200, and so on).

    Special resolutions are passed by at least a 75 per cent majority vote.
    See CA2001 ss 248B and 249B.

2. **What does 'quorum' mean in relation to a company meeting?**

    A quorum is the minimum required number of people to be present, and who can vote (as opposed to being present as observers, guests, etc).

That is, a quorum is the minimum number of:
- directors necessary for a valid resolution to be passed at a directors' meeting.
- members necessary for a valid resolution to be passed at a members' meeting.

3. **Can irregularities invalidate the meeting?**

   No, not necessarily, unless the court deems the irregularity has caused or may cause 'substantial injustice' that may not be remedied by order of the court: see s 1322 of the CA2001.

4. **What is the rule in *Foss v Harbottle* (1843) and what is its status?**

   The rule in *Foss v Harbottle* is a common law principle that provides that individual members have no cause of action in law for any wrongs done to the corporation, and that if an action is to be brought in respect of such losses, it must be brought either by the corporation itself (through the management—the proper plaintiff rule) or by way of a derivative action.

5. **What was the significance of the decision in *Jordan v Avram* (1997) as regards irregularities?**

   The case examined s 1322 of the CA2001. This allows for the court to overlook procedural irregularities in respect of the company's affairs.

   The case is useful in that it set the limits of this corrective power of the courts. The issue for deliberation was the fact that a notice of meeting had not been sent to members for a meeting to amend the constitution. Could the Court correct this? The Court found that this was a matter involving 'substantial injustice' being caused to the members. As such, it was not something that the Court could remedy.

   Although 'procedural irregularity' is given a relatively wide meaning, it does not extend to, for example:
   - a failure to give notice to half the members of a proposal to amend the company's constitution, and
   - a resolution to amend the constitution without the knowledge of those members.

   The court cannot validate such egregious oversight of statutory procedures set out in the CA2001. The amendment power under s 1322 is thereby limited.

Higher order thinking activities

TOPIC A

WHAT ARE THE PERSONAL RIGHTS OF MEMBERS AND HOW ARE THEY PROTECTED UNDER STATUTE?

Both the general law and statute provide for personal rights of members (rights *qua* members). These rights include:
- the right to challenge the majority (members), e.g. in relation to a fraud on the minority (see below)
- voting rights
- the right to sue directors (e.g. for breach of fiduciary duties), and
- the right to challenge the modification of internal rules.

The constitution of the company may also be relevant.

Fraud on the minority refers to an improper exercise of (voting or other) power by the majority of members of a company:
- It is an abuse of power (as compared with the concept of 'deceit', which is narrower).
- It is, as such, a broad concept.

- It could include evidence of a failure to cast votes for the benefit of the company as a whole. A resolution passed upon such voting is voidable.

The following sections of the CA2001 are relevant to protecting the personal rights of members:

   i.   s 247A: the right to inspect the company's books
   ii. s 175: the right to apply to court for an order to correct a company register
   iii. s 246D: the right to challenge decisions by the majority that affect members' special rights
   iv. s 1324: the right to seek an injunction against a breach of the CA2001
   v.   Pt 2F.1: the right to seek a remedy for oppression (e.g. under s 232; see *Gambotto's case* (1995))
   vi. s 461(1): the right to apply for a winding-up order
   vii. s 233(1)(e): the right to apply to court for an order that the company purchase a member's shares.

Under s 1322, the court has a broad power to fix procedural irregularities.

TOPIC B

A, B AND C HAVE BEEN IN A PTY LTD FOR SEVERAL YEARS. A AND B WANT C OUT OF THE COMPANY. THEY ISSUE FURTHER SHARES ON THE CONDITION THAT THEY ARE FULLY PAID, KNOWING C IS SHORT OF FINANCE. WHAT ARE C'S OPTIONS?

Section 232 of the CA2001 provides a member the right to seek relief from oppression if:

(a) the conduct of a company's affairs; or

(b) an actual or proposed act or omission by or on behalf of a company; or

(c) a resolution, or a proposed resolution, of members or a class of members of a company;

is either:

(d) contrary to the interests of the members as a whole; or

(e) oppressive to, unfairly prejudicial to, or unfairly discriminatory against, a member or members whether in that capacity or in any other capacity.

A member may apply for such an order. C's options include:

- an injunction: s 1324(1)
- winding-up: s 461.

CHAPTER 11 REVISION ACTIVITIES

TRUE OR FALSE?

1. **False.** The rule has been superseded by the CA2001
2. **False.** It protects creditors
3. **True.**
4. **False.** See CA2001 s 124
5. **True.** See CA2001 s 46

FILL IN THE GAPS

1. voting
2. 260A
3. 6
4. strict legalism
5. judicial creativity/judicial activism
6. Eggleston; public

MULTIPLE CHOICE

Q1 d	Creditors
Q2 c	The Takeovers Panel
Q3 c	20 per cent (see s 606 of the CA2001)
Q4 a	An alternative to a takeover
Q5 d	The law often does not reflect commercial reality

SHORT ANSWER QUESTIONS

1. **What is share capital?**

   Share capital is the aggregate or composite amount of the capital invested by all of the company's shareholders in the company. Companies have an inherent power to issue shares. The issue of shares to members, and the members' capacity to transfer those shares, are fundamental features of the corporation.

   The issue of shares is covered by CA2001 ss 254A–254Y.

2. **What do shareholders receive for their contribution of share capital?**

   In return for their contribution of share capital, shareholders receive a percentage of the ownership and control of the company. They may also receive income.

3. **What is a reduction of share capital?**

   Capital reduction is the process of decreasing a company's shareholder equity through share cancellations and share repurchases, also known as share buybacks.

   www.investopedia.com

4. **Why would a company seek to reduce share capital?**

   The reduction of capital is done by companies for numerous reasons, including increasing shareholder value and producing a more efficient capital structure.

   www.investopedia.com

5. **What is the rule in *Trevor v Whitworth* (1887)?**

   At common law, the rule in *Trevor v Whitworth* (1887) states that a company is generally prohibited from reducing its issued share capital because this may prejudice the rights of creditors.

   Therefore, a company can only deal with its share capital as expressly permitted by the CA2001, e.g. ss 257A–257J provide a statutory process providing for the reduction of a company's share capital.

6. **What tests must a proposed reduction of capital meet, and for whose benefit?**
   - A reduction of capital must be 'fair and reasonable to the company's shareholders as a whole'; it must 'not materially prejudice the company's ability to pay its creditors' and it must be 'approved by shareholders under section 256C': CA2001 s 256B(1).
   - Sections 258A–258F of the CA2001 cover 'Other share capital reductions'.
   - The case of *Re CSR Ltd* (2010) involved a proposed corporate scheme of arrangement and a demerger. A preliminary reduction of capital necessitated examining whether the interests of creditors were prejudiced by the proposal. At first instance in the Federal Court, Stone J found the proposed reduction of capital offended principles of 'commercial morality'. The matter was appealed to the Full Court of the Federal Court, where this finding was overturned. The Full Court found that the test to be used was not an abstract one, but rather whether there was a material risk of prejudice.

   For more information, see Louise Floyd, '"Commercial Morality" as a Legal Concept: The Full Federal Court Decision in Re CSR Ltd' *(2010) 28(6)* Company and Securities Law Journal *411.*

7. **What is an indirect self-acquisition?**

   Indirect self-acquisition occurs where shares (or units of shares) in a company are issued or transferred to an entity it controls.

   The *Corporations Act* voids such an issue or transfer of shares (or units of shares) unless certain exceptions apply: s 259C.

   ASIC has the power to exempt a company from these provisions: s 259C(2). This exemption can be subject to conditions.

   https://asic.gov.au

Higher order thinking activities

TOPIC A

WHAT TYPES OF BUY-BACKS DOES THE CA2001 PROVIDE FOR?

The CA2001 provides for the following types of buy-backs:
- equal access buy-backs: s 257C
- selective buy-backs: s 257D.

The general procedure is set out in s 257B.

The following definitions are contained in s 9:
- on-market buy-backs
- employee share scheme buy-backs, and
- minimum holding buy-backs.

Equal access buy-backs

> The most straightforward form of share buy-back is an equal access buy-back. All ordinary shareholders are offered a reasonable opportunity to consider the offer, which is to buy back the same percentage of their ordinary shares. An equal access scheme can include only marginal differences between offers, relating to, for example, differing accrued dividend entitlements or the calculation of odd lots.
>
> *https://asic.gov.au*

Equal access buy-backs are covered by CA2001 s 257B.

Selective buy-backs

> In broad terms, a selective buy-back is one in which identical offers are not made to every shareholder, for example, if offers are made to only some of the shareholders in the company. The scheme must first be approved by all shareholders, or by a special resolution (requiring a 75% majority) of the members in which no vote is cast by selling shareholders or their associates. Selling shareholders may not vote in favour of a special resolution to approve a selective buy-back.
>
> *https://asic.gov.au*

Selective buy-backs are covered by CA2001 s 257D.

Other types of buy-backs

> An **employee share scheme buy-back** involves the buy-back of shares held by employees or salaried directors under an employee share scheme. Similar to the equal access buy-back, this requires an ordinary resolution of shareholders if it is over the 10/12 limit. There are less onerous company obligations for these buy-backs.
>
> *https://legalvision.com.au*

TOPIC B

PROVIDE A CASE ANALYSIS OF *ELKINGTON V COSTAEXCHANGE LTD* (2011).

The relevant legal context

Under s 256B(1) of the CA2001, a company can only reduce its share capital if the reduction is 'fair and reasonable to the company's shareholders as a whole'. A special resolution is needed.

ANSWERS

The facts

The plaintiff was a minority shareholder of CostaExchange Ltd (Costa). Costa sought to selectively reduce its share capital by cancelling the shares held by minority shareholders.

A special resolution was passed, which approved the reduction, and the plaintiff sought an injunction to prevent the reduction from going ahead.

The decision

The Victorian Supreme Court held that the proposed reduction was 'fair and reasonable'. In reaching this conclusion, the Court considered the particular facts and circumstances of the case, including that:
- an independent expert had valued the shares, and
- over 80 per cent of the shareholders had approved the resolution.

While the value of the shares was a factor to be taken into consideration, it was not conclusive.

CHAPTER 12 REVISION ACTIVITIES

TRUE OR FALSE?

1. **False.** They can also raise loan capital
2. **True.** See s 113 of the CA2001
3. **False.** It is Ch 6D
4. **False.** The company is the main repository
5. **False.** The company is the main repository

FILL IN THE GAPS

1. s 706
2. risks; 714(2))
3. 731; 733
4. 732; 733
5. 715
6. 6D.3A

MULTIPLE CHOICE

Q1 d	708
Q2 c	20 offers and $2 million (a small-scale offering as per CA2001 s 708)
Q3 c	6D.3A
Q4 d	25 million (see s 738H of the CA2001)
Q5 d	Any of the above (see s 254A(3)C of the CA2001)

SHORT ANSWER QUESTIONS

1. **What is a prospectus?**
    - The prospectus is the standard, full disclosure document.
    - The content of the prospectus is set out in ss 710, 711 and 713 of the CA2001.
    - The procedure relevant to the prospectus is set out in s 717 of the CA2001.
    - The liability of the issuing company and its officers is set out in ss 728 and 729 of the CA2001.
    - Defences to issues of liability that may be available to the issuing company and its officers are set out in ss 731 and 733 of the CA2001.

2. **What is a short-form prospectus?**
   - Essentially, the short-form prospectus may be used for any offer.
   - Section 712 of the CA2001 allows a prospectus to refer to material lodged with ASIC, instead of it being set out within each document. This centralises the process.
   - Investors are entitled to a copy of this material from the company, if they make a request.
   - The contents requirements for a short-form prospectus are set out in s 712 of the CA2001.
   - The procedure is set out in s 717 of the CA2001.
   - Liability issues are covered in ss 728 and 729 of the CA2001.
   - Defences are covered in ss 732 and 733 of the CA2001.

3. **What is a profile statement?**
   - Section 721 of the CA2001 allows a brief profile statement to be sent out by the company (with ASIC approval).
   - The prospectus must still be prepared and lodged with ASIC, as is the case with a short-form prospectus.
   - Similarly, investors are entitled to a copy of the prospectus, if they ask for it.
   - The content is set out in s 714 of the CA2001.
   - The procedure is set out in s 717 of the CA2001.
   - Liability issues are covered in ss 728 and 729 of the CA2001.
   - Defences are covered in ss 732 and 733 of the CA2001.

4. **What is an offer information statement?**

   Section 709 of the CA2001 allows an offer information statement to be used instead of a prospectus for an offer to issue securities, if the amount to be raised by the company is less than $10 million. The following provisions of the CA2001 apply:
   - content: s 715
   - procedure: s 717
   - liability: ss 728, 729
   - defences: ss 732, 733.

5. **What are redeemable preference shares?**

   The issue by the company of redeemable preference shares is a type of capital raising that combines elements of both share capital and loan capital, and is covered by CA2001 ss 124 and 254A. These shares start out as share capital, but become a form of loan capital, given that the company may have to repay shareholders, in due course, for the redemption and cancellation of the shares. The ATO treats them as loan arrangements.

6. **What offers do not require disclosure documents?**

   CA2001 s 708 sets out the four main types of exempt offers:
   i. small-scale offerings—i.e. up to 20 investors investing a total of no more than $2 million in a 12-month period
   ii. offers to sophisticated investors—offers involving subscribing at least $500,000 are 'sophisticated'; also a person who has net assets of $2.5 million or a gross annual income of at least $250,000 is

'sophisticated'; offers made through licensed dealers to persons they believe to be sophisticated are excluded

iii. offers to professional investors—including Australian financial services (AFS) licensees acting on their own behalf, trustees of super funds and people with more than $10 million to invest; an AFS licence is required in order to be able to conduct a financial services business under Ch 7 of the CA2001

iv. offers to the company's executive officers and their families: see s 708(12) of the CA2001.

Higher order thinking activities

PROBLEM A

YOUR FIRM ACTS FOR ABC LTD, WHICH IS LOOKING TO RAISE FUNDS FROM THE PUBLIC. THE DIRECTORS HAVE SOME QUESTIONS:

(a) Does Ch 6D of the CA2001 require complete accuracy of the disclosure document?

(b) What options do shareholders have if they are of the view, and ASIC confirms, that a disclosure document contravenes Ch 6D?

(c) If there is a problem with a disclosure document, can a company instead use television commercials to attract the public to invest?

Answers

(a) *Points to address:*
- Section 710 of the CA2001: a disclosure document needs to contain sufficient information for investors and their advisers to make an informed decision of the matters listed in s 710—including the rights and liabilities attached to the securities, and the financial position and performance of the company.
- Section 711: specific disclosures need to be included in a prospectus, e.g. the terms and conditions of the offer, the consent of the directors, details of any personal interest of directors and others involved in the offer in the last two years, and the expiry date of the offer (no later than 13 months after the date of the prospectus).
- The prospectus must also comply with:
  - s 715A (the requirement for the disclosure document to be clear, concise and effective)
  - s 728 (regarding misleading or deceptive statements, or omissions in a disclosure statement).

(b) *Points to address:*
- Under s 729, the stakeholders have the right to claim for loss or damage resulting from a disclosure document that is in contravention of Ch 6D due to being misleading or deceptive, or containing a material omission (see also s 728).
- Section 729 includes a list of persons/entities to whom a stakeholder can turn for recovery—this is mainly the company and its directors, but can also extend to law firms, accounting firms and individuals within those firms generally if they were involved in the contravention, or consented to a particular statement being included in the prospectus that is misleading or deceptive or contains a material omission, etc.
- Another option is s 737, which is the right of investors to withdraw and return the shares; however, this option is only open for up to one month after the issue of the shares.

- ASIC has powers in relation to stop orders under s 739, which apply when the company's disclosure document is misleading or deceptive, contains omissions, or is not clear, concise and effective etc.
- Another option may be for the company to lodge a supplementary or replacement prospectus under s 719. This can occur if there is new information, or if there is an omission in the original prospectus.
- Of the above, ss 729 and 737 would appear to be the most useful.

(c) *Points to address:*
- Section 706: an offer of securities for issue needs disclosure under Ch 6D.
- Section 727: it is an offence to offer securities without a disclosure document.
- Section 734 contains a prohibition on advertising before or after a fundraising where a disclosure document is required, unless the advertisement is designed to refer readers/listeners/viewers to the disclosure document and the application form therein.
- It is useful to note that, under s 708, the share offer may not require a prospectus if it is just directed at sophisticated investors (s 708(8)), experienced investors (s 708(10) or professional investors (s 708(11)).

PROBLEM B

THE DIRECTORS OF ABC LTD HAVE A FOLLOW-UP SET OF QUESTIONS:

(d) If a company wants to organise another fundraising campaign to raise $1.5 million, does it still have to worry about Ch 6D?

(e) Can a director be held personally liable for any problem found to exist with the company's disclosure document?

(f) The directors of the company want to pay a high-profile person $1 million to travel to the east coast capital cities to personally hand out company brochures advertising the forthcoming company fundraising campaign. They want to target high net-worth individuals in strictly 'by invitation' events. What are the legal issues?

Answers

(d) *Points to address:*

Section 708 raises the issue of whether this is a 'small-scale offering' pursuant to the CA2001. The issue here is of timing—the exemption from disclosure where there is a small-scale offering applies where a company raises less than $2 million in a '12 month period', and also requires that the amount be raised through essentially personal offers where there is some sort of existing relationship between the company and the potential investor: see s 708(1)–(4).

The key issues are whether this new round of fundraising is being proposed within 12 months from the time of the large fundraising campaign, as well as whether it is a 'personal offer' pursuant to the Act.

(e) *Points to address:*

If it is found that statements and representations in the company's disclosure document are misleading or deceptive or contain omissions (contrary to s 728), then a director could be liable under s 729(1) for 'any contravention of section 728(1) in relation to the disclosure document'.

Section 728(3) provides that it is in fact a criminal offence if a misleading or deceptive statement or omission is 'materially adverse from the point of view of the investor'.

If s 729 is an issue for the directors on the facts, they would need to avail themselves of a defence under ss 731–733.

The main defence in s 731 is that the misleading/deceptive statement or omission occurred despite the director having made reasonable inquiries and believing on reasonable grounds that there is no misleading or deceptive statement or omission. This is the so-called 'due diligence' defence.

Section 732 applies where a director believes that the prospectus does not contain any misleading or deceptive statements (s 732(1)) or omissions (s 732(2)).

Other defences are in s 733—these are the general defences, including reasonable reliance on information provided by someone else and withdrawal of consent in relation to a statement given for the prospectus etc.

(f) *Points to address:*

The main issue is that this could constitute 'securities hawking' under s 736— unsolicited inducement of someone in person or by telephone to buy securities. Note, however, that it is not a contravention of s 736 if the 'sophisticated investor' exception in s 708(8), the 'experienced investor' exception in s 708(10) or the 'professional investor' exception in 708(11) applies: s 736(2). These exceptions could indeed apply in this case given that the directors did expressly state that the intention was to target high net-worth individuals in strictly 'by invitation' events.

CHAPTER 13 REVISION ACTIVITIES

TRUE OR FALSE?

1. **True.**
2. **False.** The PPSA provides a national scheme
3. **False.** It deals with personal property
4. **False.** It may be secured against property
5. **False.** The general law informs the CA2001

FILL IN THE GAPS

1. security interests; personal property
2. 21
3. 10; 12
4. loan capital and share capital
5. trustee; guarantor
6. start-up Pty Ltd

MULTIPLE CHOICE

Q1 d	Personal Property and Securities Act
Q2 d	2012
Q3 b	588
Q4 c	6
Q5 a	PPSA

SHORT ANSWER QUESTIONS

1. What is the role, purpose and context of a lender requiring a director's guarantee?

   This is typically done for small or start-up companies with few assets and little trading history. A potential lender will seek security for the repayment of loans. A debt incurred by a company as a separate entity is feasible, given the company is a separate legal entity. The practicality is that the lender will additionally seek a guarantee or indemnity involving the personal assets of the director(s). Once the company is established with assets and a profitable trading record, this should no longer be necessary.

2. **What is the perfection process under the PPSA?**

   This can be illustrated as shown in this diagram.

   THE PERFECTION PROCESS UNDER THE PPSA

   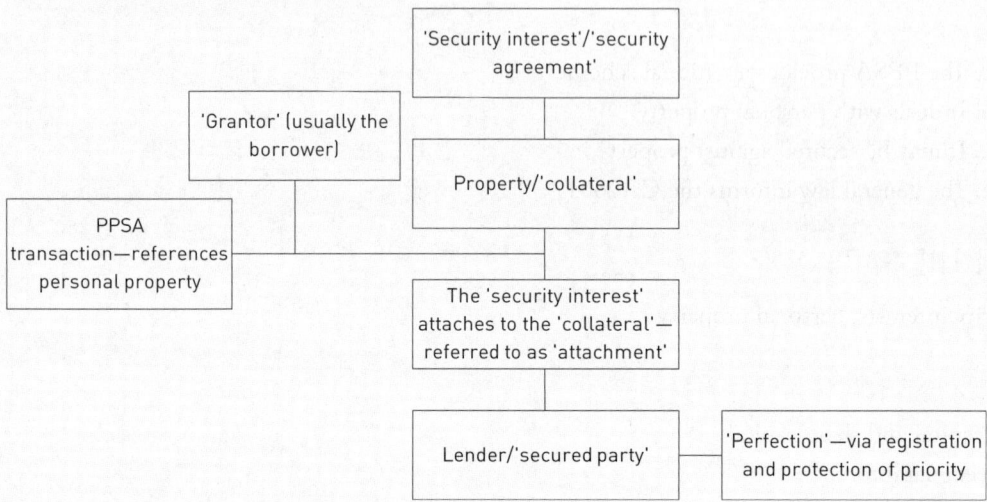

3. **How does a company raise funds? Outline the basic options.**
   - A company, as a separate legal entity, has the capacity to raise funds.
   - The basic types are loan capital and share capital.
   - The CA2001 provides process and protection when the company seeks to raise funds from members of the public.
   - This can be by way of share issue or debenture issue.
   - More recently, online and crowd-sourced funding (CSF) mechanisms have become available under the CA2001.
   - In basic terms, disclosure documentation needs to be prepared by the company setting out accurately and in sufficient detail the terms upon which an investor may invest, and the nature and scope of the investment. The rules as to disclosure are set out in Ch 6D of the CA2001.

4. **What is the role of the trustee and guarantor with a debenture raising?**

   The company may raise funds from the public if it complies with the CA2001.

   If the company raises debentures from the public, it is essentially borrowing funds from people. This could, depending on the circumstances, be many thousands of individuals. In order to protect the lender/members of the public, there is interposed between the company on the one hand, and the myriad lenders on the other, a trustee who holds the company to account as borrower. The trustee acts for and on behalf of the multiple lenders. The trustee is able to exercise the guarantee on their behalf in the event of default by the company.

5. **What is the background to the PPSA?**
   - The PPSA is a national scheme that replaced the previous piecemeal state-by-state arrangements. It sought to harmonise the law on a national basis.
   - While the PPSA is a 2009 Act, it came into effect in January 2012.

- It provides oversight of personal property security by means of a national register.
- As a model national law, it adapts concepts variously from the USA, Canada and New Zealand.

For further information, see Anthony Duggan and David Brown, Australian Personal Property Securities Law, *LexisNexis, 2012.*

Higher order thinking activities

TOPIC A

A PUBLIC COMPANY, ABC LTD, WISHES TO RAISE DEBENTURE FUNDS FROM THE PUBLIC. PROVIDE AN OUTLINE OF WHAT IS INVOLVED.

A company, as a separate legal entity, has the capacity to raise funds, including issuing debentures: see s 124(1)(b) of the CA2001.

Issues to the public are governed by Ch 6D: 'Fundraising'.

If a public company wishes to raise debenture funds from the public, the company needs to comply with Ch 2L ('Debentures'), comprising ss 283AA–283I. In particular, a trustee must be appointed in accordance with s 283AA to act for and on behalf of the lenders/members of the public. A guarantor is also required to guarantee the performance of the borrowing company under s 283CA.

TOPIC B

RE MAIDEN CIVIL (P&E) PTY LTD (2013) DEALS WITH ISSUES UNDER THE PPSA. SUMMARISE THE KEY EVENTS, ISSUES AND OUTCOMES FROM THE CASE.

Facts

2010

- Queensland Excavation Services (QES) purchased three caterpillar vehicles.
- QES leased them to Maiden Civil under a verbal lease.
- The lease could have been registered on the Northern Territory Register of Interests in Motor Vehicles—a pre-PPSA register of assets—but it was not so registered.
- Maiden Civil used the caterpillars for its business and made periodic lease payments.

2012

- Maiden Civil borrowed funds from Fast Financial Solutions Pty Ltd (Fast).
- Fast took security over all Maiden Civil's property, including the caterpillars.
- Fast registered its security interests in Maiden Civil's property on the PPS Register.
- Maiden Civil defaulted on the loans. Fast appointed receivers, who took possession of the caterpillars.

Legal issues

Was QES's interest as lessor of the caterpillars superior to Fast's security interest?

Held

- QES had a security interest under the PPSA.
- The lease of the caterpillars was a 'PPS lease' under s 13(1) of the PPSA.
- It was therefore a security interest under s 12(1) of the PPSA.
- QES did not register or perfect it.

- Fast had a security interest in the caterpillars by virtue of its financing agreement.
- Under s 21 of the PPSA, Fast's security interest was perfected because it was registered.
- Under s 55(3) of the PPSA, Fast's perfected security had priority over QES's unperfected security interest in the caterpillars.
- The receivers were entitled to retain possession of the caterpillars, sell them, and repay the loan to Fast.

CHAPTER 14 REVISION ACTIVITIES

TRUE OR FALSE?

1. **False.**
2. **True.**
3. **False.** The board's duties remain in place
4. **False.** A liquidator is part of the winding-up process
5. **True.** The CA2001 contains insolvency provisions, particularly s 588

FILL IN THE GAPS

1. external administration
2. bankruptcy
3. wound up
4. rescue
5. market
6. members
7. creditors

MULTIPLE CHOICE

Q1 b	External administration
Q2 b	Deed of company arrangement
Q3 b	2
Q4 c	s 436C
Q5 b	s 439

SHORT ANSWER QUESTIONS

1. **What does a receiver do, and how are they appointed?**

    A receiver receives the proceeds of sale, collects the debts etc, and oversees the realisation/sale of the secured assets.

    A receiver is appointed:
    - by the creditors, under the loan security interest/instrument that creates the security, or
    - by the court.

    See CA2001 Pt 5.2.

2. **What distinguishes a 'managing controller' from other controllers?**

    A 'controller' is defined in s 9 of the CA2001. A controller has the power to manage the company. They are an officer of the company, and are appointed to enforce a security interest or as a receiver.

A 'managing controller' is also defined in s 9. A managing controller is a receiver and manager, and has more stringent reporting requirements than a controller. Section 434G(b) governs the situation where there are two or more managing controllers.

A managing controller:
- has the power to carry on business: s 420C
- has 30 days to prepare a report about the corporation's affairs: s 421A(1) (a controller has two months)
- must lodge an annual report as required by ss 422A–422D.

3. **What debts of a company in administration is the administrator personally liable to pay? How can the administrator be indemnified for these?**
   - Administration is covered by Ch 5.3A Div 9.
   - The administrator has personal liability under s 443A(1) of the CA2001 for the debts of the company in its usual business.
   - Indemnity is provided out of the company's property under s 443D. The right of indemnity has priority over other debts of the company under s 443E.
   - To secure the right of indemnity, the administrator has a lien (a right to hold property as a form of security obligation) in respect of the company's property: s 443F.

4. **Who has the power to appoint an administrator?**
   An administrator may be appointed by:
   - the directors under s 588H(5) and (6) of the CA2001
   - the liquidator or provisional liquidator under s 436A–436C, or
   - a creditor with a security interest under the terms of the relevant document.

5. **How can an administrator avoid liability for payments under an arrangement entered into before the administration began, relating to the use of property owned by someone else (e.g. leased equipment)?**
   The administrator can, within five business days:
   - cease to use property, and
   - serve notice on the owner of the property under ss 443A and 443B(3)–(5) of the CA2001.

6. **What are the three things that can happen when a voluntary administration ends?**
   Under Pt 5.5 of the CA2001, the three things that can happen are:
   - a deed of company arrangement (DOCA)
   - winding-up of the company
   - control reverts to the directors.

Higher order thinking activities

TOPIC A

ABC PTY LTD IS GOING THROUGH SEVERE CASH-FLOW PROBLEMS. WHAT SHOULD THE BOARD DO?

The board is the 'brains trust' of the corporation. It needs, as a collective, to be vigilant and to pay attention to the business and its stability. A crucial part of this role is to monitor financial risk and to ensure systems are fit for purpose. Directors are responsible in law for the proper oversight of the corporation. As *ASIC v Healey* (2011) confirms, this is both a collective and individual responsibility.

There are three financial states the corporation may find itself in:

- The corporation is solvent—it is profitable, business is sound, and it is a viable operation.
- The corporation is insolvent—it is not able to pay its debts as they fall due, it is not able to make a profit, and it is falling behind in repayments. Its total debts may outweigh its total value.
- The corporation is 'in the vicinity of insolvency'. This is a more difficult period to ascertain. It is, however, incumbent on the directors to take a careful and conservative approach to the issue of solvency, rather than a reckless or careless attitude. If there is a valid question of solvency, then the directors are on notice and must act. To do otherwise risks breaching their core duties concerning financial prudence and responsibility as set out in the CA2001, particularly ss 180(1) and 588.

The board cannot ignore what is going on. It needs information and it needs to act. Directors are potentially individually liable.

TOPIC B

WHY ARE DOCAS POPULAR?

The popularity of DOCAs lies in their commercial and legal flexibility. The chances are that if the company goes into liquidation, any payout for many of the creditors will be zero, or just a few cents for each dollar owed. This means that many creditors may have lost their whole investment in the company. Seen in this way, DOCAs may buy time and flexibility for the company, in return for the creditors emerging in a better position than would otherwise be the case.

In particular, DOCAs may:

- provide the possibility of the parties, including the creditors, agreeing to flexible terms, and seeking the highest possible return of cents in the dollar
- more flexibly meet the needs and circumstances of the company, and of the various creditors
- allow for extra time for the company to pay its debts
- allow for the continued operation of the business
- allow for creditors/directors to keep the business trading rather than going into liquidation
- encourage compromises and quicker settlements of debt, e.g. a creditor may prefer the certainty of a smaller percentage return in a shorter time period, than the possibility of a greater return over a longer time period, and
- facilitate commercially attuned transactions, such as an orderly sale of certain assets over an agreed time period.

The DOCA, once established, confirmed and signed, acts as a fully enforceable legal document (as the term 'deed' connotes historically at common law). It 'locks in' an orderly process binding to, and relevant for, all creditors and others bound by the document. It focuses on an orderly restructure of the company and its viability as a going concern, and provides the significant social and economic benefits extant to the company—central to which is the employment of potentially many people.

CHAPTER 15 REVISION ACTIVITIES

TRUE OR FALSE?

1. **True.**
2. **True.** See CA2001 s 588G
3. **True.**
4. **False.** Shareholders are paid last
5. **True.**

FILL IN THE GAPS

1. Part 5.4
2. very rarely used
3. voluntary
4. first
5. unsecured
6. all; in full

MULTIPLE CHOICE

Q1 b	1992
Q2 d	ss 439A and 446A
Q3 c	Creditors
Q4 b	ASIC
Q5 a	Winding-up

SHORT ANSWER QUESTIONS

1. **How are share transfers affected by a winding-up of a corporation?**

    Generally, '[a] transfer of shares in a company that is made after the commencement of the winding up by the Court is void …': CA2001 s 468A(1).

    Where the winding-up is voluntary, a transfer of shares that is made after the passing of the resolution to wind up the company is void, unless it is approved by the liquidator or the court: s 493A(1).

2. **Who must have the leave of the court before applying for an order that an insolvent company be wound up?**

   Under CA2001 ss 459P and 459Q, any of the following stakeholders must seek leave from the court to apply to wind up the company:
   - a contingent or prospective creditor
   - a member as a 'contributory' under s 9 of the CA2001
   - a director, or
   - ASIC.

Higher order thinking activities

TOPIC A

WHAT DEFENCES ARE AVAILABLE AGAINST A LIQUIDATOR SEEKING TO RECOVER VOIDABLE TRANSACTIONS?

A court may not make an order under CA2001 s 588FF with regard to a voidable transaction if it is proved by the relevant party that:
- there was good faith, and
- there were no reasonable grounds to suspect insolvency, and
- certain commercial issues are satisfied:
  - that no benefit was received because of the transaction: s 588FG(1), or
  - that valuable consideration was given: s 588FG(2).

Section 588FA(3) provides for commercial transactions to be exempted from being voidable transactions in certain circumstances; for example, if there is a 'running account'—an established and continuing business relationship between the company and the third party.